READINGS ON SOCIAL STUDIES
IN SECONDARY EDUCATION

READINGS ON

SECONDARY

Edited by

SOCIAL STUDIES
IN
EDUCATION

JONATHON C. McLENDON
Professor of Social Studies Education, The University of Georgia

THE MACMILLAN COMPANY · NEW YORK
COLLIER-MACMILLAN LIMITED · LONDON

© Copyright, Jonathon C. McLendon, 1966

First Printing

Library of Congress catalog card number: 66-20821

THE MACMILLAN COMPANY, New York
COLLIER-MACMILLAN CANADA, LTD., Toronto, Ontario

PRINTED IN THE UNITED STATES OF AMERICA

PREFACE

BOTH *fundamental and immediate reasons underlie this volume of readings specifically devoted to the evolving program of secondary school social studies. These reasons relate to such qualities of a publication as its up-to-dateness, authoritativeness and breadth of viewpoints represented, emphases in contents, and organization of selections.*

Human entry into outer space elicited an immediate intensification of technological development and scientific thought. Fuller contemplation has by now facilitated recognition that the even more crucial, as well as the most persistent, problems which civilization faces are social in nature. Many leaders in public affairs, as well as in education, have increasingly recognized the urgent and the essential need to improve instruction and learning about society. Proposals, studies, experiments, and even some new programs have begun to appear. Fundamental elements and characteristics of secondary social studies are up for review and potential replacement.

It is highly important that the still valuable and appropriate features of secondary social studies be retained as schools also test and adopt desirable new practices. The emerging program, not yet precisely clear, will contain elements of both the old and the new. To identify and analyze these elements is a dominant purpose of this volume. It is aimed to aid teachers in interrelating these same elements as, in the final analysis, only teachers can actually give effect to such relationships in their teaching.

The authors of the selections herein include many outstanding leaders in the field. Of course, a single volume cannot contain contributions from all who have done significant writing. The number of such individuals has grown greatly as the social studies have regained major attention, a noteworthy group of social scientists have increased their participation, organized improvement efforts have expanded, and professional and public interest in the field has heightened.

A chief purpose of this book is to challenge, stimulate, and provide food for thought and such action as the reader may select or infer. It does not aim to persuade readers toward a particularized approach to the social studies. No identifiable school of thought predominates. The editor has attempted to incorporate a range of viewpoints and varying aspects of secondary social studies. These include the old and the new, curriculum and methods, social sciences and their secondary school counterparts, junior and senior high school levels, fundamentals and current trends, objectives and means, resources and procedures.

The aspects of secondary social studies dealt with include both basic and current elements in the field. The book opens with a consideration of the democratic and other cultural features of American society that underlie needed recognition of the objectives that the field should serve. Academic underpinning of the social studies derives from the social sciences. These are dealt with collectively, by each discipline significantly represented in the secondary social studies curriculum, and with specific attention to the major multidisciplinary or interdisciplinary elements in that curriculum. Methods of teaching and learning are considered in relation to both teachers and students, the organization and activities of study, newly emphasized techniques and approaches, and the appraisal of students' learning. The chief types of learning resources dealt with are reading and programed materials, audiovisual aids, classroom equipment, and local resources. A concluding section takes a forward look at the emerging nature of the social studies through the identification of outstanding current needs, experiments, and improvement efforts.

The organization of this book parallels that of major textbooks and references on secondary social studies. It may thus serve as a complement to such a book in senior college or graduate courses in social studies curriculum and methods. Where a readings approach is preferred, the volume will provide a handy collection of basic and current materials. They introduce the newcomer to the field and refresh the experienced teacher with recent ideas and interpretations. Those who prefer another organization of the selections will find the index a useful guide to the volume's contents in any sequence desired. Readers seeking facts and ideas on particular aspects of secondary social studies will find the book useful for reference purposes.

Special features of the volume should prove helpful to teachers and supervisory personnel in social studies. The recent availability of federal matching funds for the purchase of instructional material is stimulating schools' acquisition of resources that are needed in almost every classroom. Unfortunately, the success of social studies has been widely handicapped by the limited availability to students of sound sources of social information in a variety of appropriate forms. Recommendations for consideration in selecting quality resources appear in the listings in the Appendix. These citations consist primarily of recently produced materials, thus complementing the sizable bibliographies in Chapters 5, 6, 12, 13, and 15 of Social Studies in Secondary Education.*

* Macmillan, 1965.

Additional features are intended to serve especially the large number of school systems that are contemplating or involved in curriculum revision in secondary social studies. Among these features are the recurrent attention, throughout the volume, to current proposals for improving each aspect of the curriculum, the extended attention to current developments in Part Six, and the Special Bibliography of professional materials that will aid teachers, individually and cooperatively, to improve the field. Curriculum planning groups may find worthwhile guidance also in the "Questions to Aid in Curriculum Improvement Efforts in Social Studies" in Social Studies in Secondary Education. Also, the list following the Preface shows the selections of this book of readings organized in relation to the chapters in Social Studies in Secondary Education.

Appropriate acknowledgments for the stimulation and ideas that have resulted in this volume are due numerous individuals and groups. I am grateful for the acquaintances I have had the good fortune to make among leaders in social studies. Their lasting devotion, frequent courage, professional zeal, exemplary teaching, and challenging thoughts have stimulated not only admiration but also a desire to share such contacts with a wider group of teachers. Thus many, though not all, of these leaders are represented here in excerpts from their writings. Gratitude for permission to use these selections is expressed to the appropriate source at the beginning of each selection. Special appreciation is hereby expressed to the National Council for the Social Studies for allowing, with authors' approval, reproduction of significant extracts from several of its publications. In addition, thanks are due The Macmillan Company for patience, editorial advice and assistance, and help in other regards. And the editor is much indebted to cooperative librarians at the University of Denver, University of Houston, and the University of Miami as well as Florida Atlantic University.

J. C. McL.

THE SELECTIONS
Organized to Parallel
Social Studies in Secondary Education

The following list is for the convenience of readers using *Social Studies in Secondary Education* (Macmillan, 1965). The chapter titles of that book are listed below in *italic type,* and the entries below each chapter title list the pertinent selections from this book of readings.

CONTENTS

PART THREE
MULTIDISCIPLINARY ELEMENTS IN THE
SOCIAL STUDIES   129

APPENDIX
SPECIAL BIBLIOGRAPHIES OF RECENT INSTRUCTIONAL MATERIALS

PART ONE
UNDERGIRDING THE SOCIAL STUDIES

In a democratic society the social studies strive to serve special and difficult functions. The entire school inherits a responsibility to uphold the society that supports it. That part of the school program which teaches students about society seeks to infuse in the upcoming generation the basic principles of democracy. Are those who teach social studies sufficiently committed to democratic principles to fulfill this function? Can democratic values be imparted without particularist dogma or doctrine? Can the school effectively influence toward democracy the values of adolescents who otherwise find in American culture much of materialism, corruption, waste, selfishness, greed, ethnocentrism, double standards, and clearly antidemocratic practices?

The demands of a dynamic culture require schools to aid in improving it. Contemporary and emerging social changes, many of them technologically based, call upon the social studies to reflect the ever more rapidly shifting needs of society. Even the fundamental principles of democracy must vary in application in order to serve adequately in a viable society. Can the social studies furnish substantial background for understanding the basic nature of society while also developing the social skills and sensitivity needed by prospective citizens and leaders of the twenty-first century?

In the ever-pressing rush of daily activities, the teacher can too easily lose perspective on underlying reasons for the social studies and a vision of their ultimate utility. It is, therefore, in the spirit of placing the social studies in their social and educational setting that this volume begins with a group of pertinent readings.

Meanwhile a distinctively adolescent subculture shows evidence of expanding and becoming even more separated from American adult society. Teachers have frequent need to apply psychology and have studied the subject as part of their professional training. Social studies teachers, at least, may need to give increasing attention to the sociology

1

of adolescence. Should the social studies attempt to develop adolescents' understanding of their subculture? Should the curriculum and methodology of social studies be more fully adapted to teenagers' cultural characteristics and their relations to adult society?

The formulation of objectives for social studies has generally fallen into a pattern characterized by profusion, vagueness, and grandiosity, frequently to the point of meaninglessness. The time may be near for a reappraisal and redefinition of the role of the social studies in school and society. What are the fundamental contributions that the social studies should seek to make? Can consensus be secured regarding objectives that are realistic and worthy, significantly attainable, and directly relatable to society and the social sciences?

The selections in this Part discuss these and related issues, offer analyses of varying viewpoints, and suggest directions that the social studies should or may take in relation to these underlying social elements.

1

Democracy as the Touchstone

THE REALITIES OF DEMOCRATIC CITIZENSHIP TODAY

Helen McCracken Carpenter

Though the bases of democracy may remain changeless, clearly their applications must change to fit varying conditions. In this selection appears a thoughtful review of outstanding historical and contemporary influences on the idea of democratic citizenship in American life. Certainly the dominant con- temporary elements of social change call for reconsideration and revitalization of approaches to the education of emerging citizens. This critical need consti- tutes a challenge to schools and society generally and to the social studies espe- cially.

THE REALITIES OF DEMOCRATIC CITIZENSHIP TODAY

BOTH the needs and the conditions for the functioning of citizens in our democracy derive from the characteristics of American life. What are the implications for responsible citizenship in the current trends . . . —the rapid rate of increase and spread of peoples, the mushrooming advances in science and technology, the strivings for security, status, and the good life—and in others . . . such as increased leisure, international interdependence, the complex of urbanization, the extension of commerce and industry, and the accretion of bureaucratic government? Before proceeding to an examination of these relationships, it is necessary to consider democracy and citizenship as conceived by Americans.

The Virility of the American Ideal of Democracy

Although the nature of political democracy (or a "free society" as it is often called lately) and the attributes of democratic citizenship are necessarily related, the concept of one has attracted the attenion of articulate Americans

FROM *Skill Development in Social Studies*, Helen McCracken Carpenter, ed., Washington, D.C.: National Council for the Social Studies, 1963, pp. 7–13. Used by permission. Dr. Carpenter is a professor of history at Trenton State College, New Jersey.

more than has the meaning of the other. When allowance is made for the fact that wording varies with the time, many expressions reveal surprising agreement in viewpoint on the bases, purposes, and functioning of democracy. The simple statement of the Pilgrims in the Mayflower Compact embodies most of the characteristics of political democracy as conceived over subsequent years. Jefferson, shaping the ideas of the Enlightenment into the Declaration of Independence, penned what has remained the classic expression of the philosophy of political democracy. Here are laid down the principles that constitute the essence of the American ideal: government by consent which implies participation of citizens in the process of government; the maintenance of civil and political rights or liberties; and the supreme importance of the individual.

Utterances of modern-day Americans attest the continuing virility of these tenets. Franklin Roosevelt made them the heart of his famous "four freedoms" speech. Senator Estes Kefauver in the opening line of the 1951 NCSS Yearbook writes, "By political democracy I mean a form of government based upon the consent of the governed in which the will of the majority of qualified citizens rules." (1) And again, Henry M. Wriston affirms the ideal with an emphasis reflecting a concern of the 'sixties, "The acid test of successful democratic government is the degree of effective liberty it makes available to the individual." (2) The various aspects of the classic ideal have been interpreted according to the needs and insights of different eras but the tenets have remained the criteria for the examination of our society.

The Changing View of Democratic Citizenship

Americans have not addressed themselves with equal vigor to consideration of the qualities of democratic citizenship. The expressions which have been made tend to be minutely analytical of behavioral characteristics rather than broadly philosophical. Some of this accrues, perhaps, from the nature of citizenship. Fundamentally, citizenship is the means of denoting the legal status of an individual and hence signifies membership in a political society. It implies the reciprocal obligations of allegiance owed by the individual and of protection assumed by the government.

Interpretations of even this elemental concept of citizenship have varied. What constitutes evidence of allegiance, for example, has been subject to differing opinions. In the days when loyalty oaths were not as generally demanded as they are today by government at all levels, most citizens born in the United States had no occasion to attest their fidelity by repeating the official oath of allegiance required of naturalized citizens. One accepted manner of expressing loyalty to the country was through the salute to the flag and the repeating of the pledge of allegiance. These acts became almost standard practice in classrooms across the nation until the right of parents to forbid their children to participate in the observance for religious reasons created a legal controversy. The Supreme Court at first upheld boards in excluding from public schools children who did not comply. Later, however, the Court declared invalid a West Virginia statute requiring the salute on penalty of expulsion. As the matter now stands, a schoolchild may or may not salute the flag depending on his conscience or that of his parents. Such observance is not today considered evidence of the allegiance of a citizen, young or old.

The connotations of citizenship beyond the narrow legal sense have always been and continue to be yet more nebulous. The broad meaning of citizenship is constantly subject not only to shifting judicial and legislative interpretations but to changing popular ones as well.

Americans for decades, even centuries, thought of the rights and responsibilities of citizenship primarily in terms of activities related to political functions. The right to be represented in government, to hold public office, to vote for men and measures of one's own choosing were considered inherent characteristics of democracy. The history of this country from its very beginning is studded with incidents in which some of these rights were an issue. In 1619 the Virginia Company deemed it wise to grant the Jamestown colonists a share in government and established what proved to be the first legislative assembly in America. The men of Watertown in 1634 sent a strong protest to Boston because a small minority in the latter center insisted on controlling all the Puritan settlements roundabout. A number of decades later Nathaniel Bacon, in an abortive rebellion, symbolized the determination of the small Virginia farmers to secure a voice in the decisions of government. A century afterward the back-countrymen of North Carolina broke into open conflict with their fellow citizens of the coastal plain in a drive to administer their own affairs. To protect the rights of Englishmen, conceived chiefly as political, thirteen colonies dared to assert their independence and fight for freedom from a powerful European nation.

And so the story of the struggle to achieve the hallmarks of citizenship might be traced through the pages of America's history. First it was a struggle to secure full political citizenship for some men, then for all men and finally for women. This early interpretation of citizenship as related chiefly to political functions rested on basic civil rights. Although a complete enumeration of the civil rights of a citizen at any time in the nation's history would be impossible, the first ten amendments to the United States Constitution have been considered a fundamental statement of these classic civil liberties.

Concurrently with the development of the idea of citizenship in terms of political rights and civil liberties went the concept of civic duties. In a government in which sovereignty resides in the people, it has been assumed that rights must be accompanied by responsibilities for those enjoying them. Thus a good citizen, as first understood, was a person who considered the privilege of voting a serious matter and cast his ballot thoughtfully; who deserved the right to equal protection of the laws by obeying the laws; who earned the precious freedoms of speech, press, and religion by not abusing them nor interfering with the enjoyment of these rights by others; who merited the protection of the government against evildoers at home and aggressors from abroad by paying taxes and giving service, if necessary, to police and military forces; who warranted the benefit of the processes of justice by his willingness to assist in law enforcement and jury duty. The criteria of democratic citizenship still include all of the obligations just mentioned. Today, however, the concept of what constitutes a good citizen in a democracy has so broadened that these characteristics alone are insufficient.

The widening view of democratic citizenship evident by the middle decades of the twentieth century has resulted from a variety of factors, some of which are interrelated. By the turn of the century America had changed from an agricultural to an industrial nation. This fact together with the advance of technology made possible a life of greater physical comfort for many Americans but one attended by increasing social and economic tensions. In addition, the status and responsibilities of Americans have been affected in the last forty years by the steady rise of this nation to a position of world leadership. The same decades have been marked likewise by a growing consciousness of human relations and of the need to focus on them in school and in society. Although full political democracy has not yet been attained in fact for all citizens, gradually the horizon of Americans has widened enough to make clear that the goals of democracy must be social and economic as well as political.

From the combined effect of all these forces an expanded concept of democratic citizenship has emerged. The need for the individual to assume greater responsibility in political citizenship is acknowledged. Progress toward realization of the latent social and economic phases of citizenship can be discerned. Definitions of the effective citizen today often include those qualities desirable in the personal relationships of daily living. At all points there is recognition of the importance of action if a democratic citizen is to be effective.

Perhaps the most representative characterization of a good democratic citizen, among analytical statements, still is that prepared for the Armed Forces Information and Education Division, Department of Defense, by the National Council for the Social Studies in consultation with 300 leaders in practically every field of American life. (3) The scope of the recent National Council Yearbook, *Citizenship and a Free Society*, indicates acceptance of a comprehensive view of democratic citizenship. Various chapters treat the needs of citizens for economic effectiveness, responsible individualism, successful intergroup relations, and world consciousness, as well as for political participation. (4)

The Paradoxes of Theory and Reality

It is now time to put the parts of our discussion together and to examine the impact of social realities in the 'sixties on the functioning of democratic citizenship today. From such considerations flow the imperatives for skill development in social studies.

The classic concepts prevailing in our society derive chiefly, as has been indicated, from the era of the Enlightenment which was a far different world from ours. The strength of democracy was predicated on government by consent of an informed, interested, active citizenry. The chief justification for the establishment and expansion of public education has been, and still is, the provision of a means for equipping citizens with the knowledge, attitudes, and skills necessary to the maintenance of democratic government. The theory still holds; it is the concept of the functioning of the theory which needs revision.

Wherever the citizen turns today he is confronted with the need to cope with bigness. The rapidity of change has, by this decade, accelerated and compounded aspects of this phenomenon which has been present in our society since the advent of industrialization. Bigness is evident in our rapidly sprawling communities, our mushrooming schools, our *super*markets, and our many-storied hospitals. Evidence of the same trend is to be found also in organizations with which the individual is associated. Many groups, such as service clubs, labor unions, religious societies, educational associations, cultural groups, and sports organizations are now international in scope and structure. The same element of bigness is to be found in government today as it reaches out, more and more at all levels, to serve the multiplying needs of citizens. In an era of big business, government has become the biggest business of all. A component of bigness is the pervading presence in all of these facets of a citizen's life of the effect of automation—usually silent, sometimes remote, but frequently threatening both status and security and always dwarfing the stature of human achievement.

The implications of these factors for responsible citizenship are worthy of consideration. Bigness brings impersonality and robs some people of a sense of individual identity with constructive effort. There is the tendency to depreciate individual worth and to lose faith in the efficacy of social action. Robert M. MacIver identifies this development as one of the perils of democracy. He refers to it as the danger of personal anomy in which citizens with a sense of frustration, losing sight of social values and ethical goals, turn instead to the pursuit of personal objectives of wealth or power to the detriment of the common good. (5)

What of the great majority of Americans who do not lose their perspective on the obligations of citizenship? For the citizen with a strong sense of purpose and the will to act responsibly, the current situation presents obstacles as well. Bigness implies complexity which, coupled with multiplicity and rapidity of change, makes necessary the services of the expert. The magnitude and ramifications of the issues of government—political, economic, and social; national, international, and interplanetary—require the combined talents of experts from many fields. No one citizen can be expected to know enough to determine public policy today, even in matters of local concern. Furthermore, the direct involvement at the core of the governmental process can be the experience of only a relative few. Most Americans must depend on the decisions and abilities of experts in the various areas of mass communication for any information about the course of events in which he, as Mr. Citizen, is theoretically an active participant. In an age with better distribution of news than ever before, there exists the paradox of knowing more which amounts, against the sum total of knowledge, actually to knowing less. As Dr. Kennamer points out, the world of the individual citizen is not shrinking today; instead it is getting larger and larger.

MacIver sees in this growing specialization of function another peril to democracy. With the tendency and necessity to focus on less and less in the process of earning a living, there is the possibility that Americans may lose a view of the whole. He fears the rise of competition among specialized groups and the diverting of the loyalty of individuals from the general welfare to the special interest. MacIver labels this "the peril of group anarchy." (6)

How can the functioning of democratic citizenship be reconciled with the realities of government and society today? This is the supreme challenge of the social studies teacher.

(1) "The Vitality in Political Democracy." *Education for Democratic Citizenship*, Twenty-Second Yearbook. Washington, D.C.: National Council for the Social Studies, a department of the National Education Association, 1952, p. 1.

(2) Commission on National Goals. *Goals for Americans*. p. 48.

(3) "Characteristics of the Good Democratic Citizen." *Education for Democratic Citizenship*. Twenty-Second Yearbook. Washington, D.C.: National Council for the Social Studies, a department of the National Education Association, 1952. pp. 154–160. See also NEA *Journal*, 39:612–14; November 1950.

(4) Patterson, Franklin, editor. *Citizenship and a Free Society: Education for the Future*. Thirtieth Yearbook. Washington, D.C.: National Council for the Social Studies, a department of the National Education Association, 1960. 292 pp.

(5) MacIver, Robert M. *The Ramparts We Guard*. New York: The Macmillan Co., 1950. 152 pp. Chapter 10, "Descent to Anomy."

(6) MacIver. *The Ramparts We Guard*. Chapter 9, "The Peril of Group Anarchy."

DEMOCRACY IN THE CLASSROOM
—THE BROAD VIEW

John F. Ohles

What are the implications of democratic principles for school practices? To what extent should the social studies assume responsibility for the teaching of democracy? In what ways should learning of democracy involve other fields of the curriculum, the school administration, and indeed agencies beyond the school? How do and should schoolteachers and administrators complement each other in contributing to the development of citizens for a democratic society? The writer explores the relative roles of teachers and administrators in fostering democracy in the schools. Omitted here is much of his original analysis of desirable democratic functions for school administrators.

Perhaps it is implicit that the social studies alone can no more assume full responsibility for teaching democracy than English teachers alone can succeed in fully developing student's usage of their native language. But the role of the social studies is both central and essential to upholding democracy.

E DUCATIONAL literature abounds with discussions concerning democracy in the classroom—and well it might, for a major educational task is cultivation of the democratic ideal.

But the popularity of the subject may also suggest difficulties in reaching this worthwhile objective, frequent frustrations in furthering these aims, a gnawing conscience telling us that we are dissatisfied and still searching for answers. And yet, a glance at the literature suggests that the task ought not to be too difficult if we but follow the many tales of success detailed by enthusiastic colleagues. Combining a myriad of gimmicks and projects should satisfy our needs—but it doesn't.

What's the flaw in this process? It's primarily centered in the error of seeking simple answers for complex problems, in making general assumptions on the basis of isolated experiences, in reading into our "research" the things we would like to find.

Unfortunately, the complex personal and social relationships implicit in a practicing democracy are not resolved alone by mock elections, student councils, elimination of hand-raising, adoption of the core curriculum, or textbooks and courses in "problems in democracy." If the problem were this simple it would have been solved long ago; our literature would not be concerned with democracy in the classroom.

FROM The Social Studies, 53:144–147, April, 1962. Used by permission. Dr. Ohles is a professor of education at State Teachers College, Cortland, New York.

After all, democracy is a way of life, not a collection of symbols—as we frequently remind Khrushchev, Castro, Trujillo, and others.

If the simple answer, the short view, is not the solution, we might better profit with a concern for the broad view, a recognition of the complexities involved. Our discussions must rise above the level of a solitary experience, a parliamentary structure, a curricular innovation. We ought, instead, speak of the basic means of democratizing our school *life*, of nourishing those healthy relationships—broad tolerance of ideas, traditions, and actions; mutual acceptance of oneself, each other, the group; willingness to speak, listen, lead and follow; recognition of the need for rights, and duties—which serve to create a self-governing society.

The ordering of this structure of a school community cannot be accomplished by compiling a checklist of scattered do-it-yourself projects. If this is to be a way of life rather than an assignment for Tuesday of next week, we must concern ourselves with the essentials that make up a democratic school unit.

To make a logical start, we cannot presume to speak of a democratic school society under an autocratic school administration. Let it not be ignored that the tenor of a school, the feeling tone in corridors or before blackboards is set on the highest administrative level.

Lest we stray down a common tangent, a distinction might well be made between governing and administering democracy. The former concerns a representative legal structure and constitutional protections, responsibilities, and prerogatives as well as a philosophical premise and a routinized regard for human values, a reciprocal respect among the citizenry.

Administrative democracy need have slight regard for structure, legal forms, or a written guarantee of rights and processes. It is, instead, anchored to a philosophy, practiced as well as expressed, and greased by a mutual respect toward and among each member of the particular organization. The basic requisite for democratic administration is built about principles of human dynamics rather than the science of politics. In contrast to a political democracy, representative bodies are not necessary, as a matter of fact frequently are used to legitimatize the most autocratic regimes. Committees, councils, and the like may, of course, be useful—may, in some instances make possible an operational democracy; their existence alone, however, guarantees little.

In essence, if the administrator is to be an effective leader, he must be a practitioner of the art of group dynamics, a student of personnel relations, a devotee of the cooperative approach toward the resolution of mutual problems. The success of his primary endeavors has little to do with bookkeeping procedures, building programs, public relations, bus schedules, or merit pay schedules. The success of instruction for adult living in a modern democracy has a great deal to do with human relationships as structured by school administration.

It is not surprising that the same principles of human interaction are as appropriate to the classroom as to larger school units. Without doubt, the classroom situation is more complex than the administrative, as it involves constant interaction with groups of twenty-five to forty pupils of differing backgrounds, values, abilities, emotional and psychological needs, and levels of maturity. But it is here that, in the final analysis, democratic procedures must operate with effectiveness.

The individual teacher must win the respect of her pupils to realize the greatest success in the learning process as well as to establish a democratic atmosphere. Like the administrator, the teacher must accept each individual; unlike the administrator, she must demonstrate a great deal of flexibility to meet the wide range of social, intellectual, emotional, and behavioral extremes. A constant effort is called for to handle situations fairly, with assurance and a sense of humor. Of great importance is the competence of the teacher in the appropriate academic areas of instruction.

Again, a paramount requisite is the ability of the teacher to play her role as an adult, a guide in instruction, arbiter of disputes, discussion leader, chief initiator and primary enforcer of reasonable classroom standards. That unfortunate creature, who attempts to achieve teaching success by surrendering the adult role for one akin to that of the pupils in the mistaken idea that such is the key to schoolroom togetherness, is, most certainly, the most tragic of teaching's misfits.

Corollary to the teacher's role-playing is the expectation that the pupils will accept and play their role as learners with a myriad of needs to be met, but not detailed with responsibility for classroom procedures or outcomes. Holding youngsters to their role suggests avoiding the imposition on them of a teacher's responsibilities, but does not imply that they cannot be partners in planning, consultants in evaluation, proponents for change in procedures, or critics in matters of a specific or general concern.

Of course, the skill with which a teacher measures the developmental level of a class determines the appropriateness of her expectations of them. Most frequently the error lies in underestimating the ability and maturity of youngsters. Most difficult to assess are the early adolescents, who hover between child and adult levels of maturity (and who frequently use this ambivalence to further their own immediate aims). There is, of course, no suggestion that errors in judgment cannot occur, but they must be relatively infrequent if a satisfactory relationship is to endure.

Essential to the development of an operating democracy is the establishment of standards of work, limits of behavior. This classroom alternative to a governing democracy's complex legal and constitutional framework can well be informal, relatively flexible, and easily changed. It also requires acceptance by all concerned whether or not it has been cooperatively evolved. Actually, the promulgation of these standards and limits by the adult responsible for the on-going process can well be accepted by youngsters when shown to be in line with practices pupils adjudge to be "reasonable and proper."

Now we have been proceeding on the supposition that democratic procedures must be accepted by every individual concerned—and that, of course, is the ideal. Realistically, it can approach that ideal in a school organization where administrators select their subordinates and have a voice in their continuance in the organization. Public schools, to the contrary, have little or no control over the unselected masses enrolled in their classes and must tolerate an occasional maverick who disavows the value system of the majority. It would be tragic, indeed, if a small minority deprived the average classroom of its democratic heritage. A democratic classroom, as its community counterpart, may have to forcibly restrain its recalcitrants, but the method it uses ought to find acceptance or approval by the group.

This, then, is the way to a democratic school society; a means worthy of our time and effort; an ever more necessary educational experience in an era when modern democracy faces a power and philosophy unmatched in its religious fervor since the tides of republicanism reached a high water mark scarcely more than one hundred years ago. It is more than form, goes beyond contrived systems of representation, supersedes written expressions of philosophy; it is, indeed, a way of life in the classroom.

And strangely enough, after we have commenced the development of a democratic environment in the school we will find that our emerging needs require the founding of representative councils, an abundance of committees, means of fostering joint discussion, joint decision, joint planning, and joint action. Functions and institutions growing out of democratic processes have a genuine value for the transmission of a hard-won and bloodily preserved heritage of self-government.

2

Changing Society

THE AMERICAN HIGH SCHOOL —TODAY AND TOMORROW

Franklin Patterson

Both the present and the emerging future are characterized by vast, complex, and increasingly rapid technological and social changes. Each year seems to outstrip the statistical record of civilization's status of the preceding year. These changes involve material progress but often include or encourage social disorganization, disruption, and even disintegration. In a very real sense, society seems faced with ever greater social problems. What can and should the mass of citizens do in the face of such far-reaching and overwhelming complexity? How can the secondary school most appropriately react to social changes and best prepare prospective citizens for meaningful roles in such a world? In his book, from which this selection is taken, the writer considers these interrelated problems and offers suggestions that have particular applicability to the social studies.

DIMENSIONS OF THE FUTURE

A PRODUCTIVE view of the American high school today includes an assessment of the responsibilities that free citizens will carry in tomorrow's world. These responsibilities will be great, complex, and changing. They will demand many levels of insight, judgment, and civic ability on the part of all our people.

The problems of civilization in the next several decades will be so difficult that broad-scale citizen responsibility for their solution may seem increasingly impractical. Yet it is in keeping the fullest measure of such responsibility alive that the spirit of a free society resides. How to do so, when it is temptingly easier to leave more and more of our civic, social, and economic problems to specialists, will be a unique challenge.

REPRINTED WITH PERMISSION FROM *High Schools for a Free Society* by Franklin Patterson. Copyright © 1960 by The Tufts Civic Education Center. Dr. Patterson is professor of civic education and director of the Lincoln Filene Center, Tufts University.

The responsibilities of citizenship for which the American high school must now prepare youth are being defined by certain major developments that characterize the present and will shape the future. These developments, of massive importance, and impact, include:

1. An ongoing scientific and technological revolution.
2. A contracting world of complex international relations.
3. A world-wide population growth of unprecedented proportions.
4. The penetrating influence of public policy on all phases of life.
5. Changing economic structures and patterns.
6. The emergence of the behavioral sciences.
7. Conflicts in values and ethics. (1)

Such developments bring tremendous new alternatives and remarkable opportunities into human life. At the same time, they create conditions and problems that involve new responsibilities for the citizen.

The revolutionary development of science and technology lies at the heart of most of the other developments. Endowed with the apparently infinite potentials of science and applied technology, we are somewhat in the position of the sorcerer's apprentice. We have gotten, or are getting, more power than we bargained for. Suddenly, we have on our hands an embarrassment of riches that threatens to swamp us.

For example, we asked for: *And we have gotten:*

Swifter travel, more abundantly supplied

Average individual yearly travel that has increased from 350 miles in 1916 to over 3,500 miles this year; motor vehicles (some 70 million in the United States); world-wide jet-plane travel at the speed of sound; roads that are congested to virtual strangulation; airlanes and airports crowded to the danger point; air in our cities polluted by smog; railroads in serious trouble; enormous rising costs for construction of rapidly obsolescent super-highways, super-airports; expensive—and promising—efforts to achieve rocket travel into space. What will the future bring?

Better communication

Over 60,000,000 telephones, 208,000,000 radios, 60,000,000 television sets, 40,000,000 phonographs in the United States alone; motion pictures and theaters; a vast mass-entertainment industry; instantaneous direct links with virtually all parts of the world; a world in which peoples have suddenly been placed in face-to-face contact across yet unresolved age-old barriers of nationality, race, religion, politics, and general culture. What will the future bring?

More governmental services

A gigantic growth of technical, financial, educational, and other governmental services along with an almost comparable growth of governmental controls and the penetration of public policy into private lives; a national debt that has grown from 2½ billion to nearly 300 billion in a century; federal appropriations that have averaged over 70 billion per year for the last decade; 2½ million civil employees in the federal service; great increases in the costs of local, county, and state government; taxes that spiral steadily upward. What will the future bring?

More production

By far the most productive economy in the world, with the highest standard of living; the greatest abundance and variety of material possessions; industry and business that are more and more automatized, that depend increasingly on complex, large organization; agriculture which is also highly mechanized and large-scale, with small producers disappearing; giant labor organizations with paid staffs, millions of members, and large treasuries and other funds; a towering structure of consumer credit; new varieties of markets; surpluses; advertising; and restless, continual economic change. What will the future bring?

The pleasures of urban life

Technology and industry concentrated in great metropolitan regions; two thirds of our giant population living in 168 of these urban areas; development of suburbs; slums and urban blight in the central cities; delinquent youth; traffic problems; problems of housing, commuter traffic, regional forms of government; development of special authorities; costly and dramatic projects for renewal and redesign of central cities; the melding of people with diverse standards, values, religions, politics, race. What will the future bring?

These are only a few of the multitude of changes and developments which are proceeding in our way of life, and which are thrown into high gear by the revolution in science and technology. Their story, and the story of many other developments, is available in detail in governmental reports, in the press, in scholarly studies, and in countless other analyses. The central thread in all these accounts, however, is the same. We are living in a time of almost incredible change, of immense opportunity, and of new responsibilities and challenges. The swift river of our age is overturning and undermining things that stand in its way. New channels, new energy, new areas are being opened up for us to make the most of as best we can.

DILEMMAS OF FREEDOM

This new age affords opportunities for individual development—for what Norbert Wiener calls the human use of human beings—beyond anything we have dreamed. These are only opportunities, however, not guarantees. Achieving abundance without drudgery leaves men free to be their worst or their best. What men make of these opportunities for living freer lives in the future will depend in great part on the way the new dilemmas of freedom are resolved. These dilemmas and others like them constitute broad, developing challenges of citizenship today and tomorrow:

How can men be self-reliant, actively independent, individual citizens in a civilization dominated by large organizations?

> That is, how can responsible individualism survive in the midst of big government, big business, big labor, big cities? How can the individual citizen continue to count in political, economic, and social affairs as the institutions of our society grow larger and more highly organized?

How can men achieve a clear, coherent picture of their world on which to base judgments and support policies as citizens, when there is so much to know and the world in every way becomes more complex?

> That is, how can ordinary citizens obtain and comprehend enough relevant information about political, social, and economic matters to make reliable decisions when everything in our age is rapidly becoming bigger, more complex, more specialized, and more highly technical? How can the citizen know enough to know what is right?

How can men have stable, constructive political, social, and economic values in an era of such vast change and frequent contradiction?

> That is, how can citizens identify worthy values and grasp first principles of government, economy, and society when there is so much change and when so many values are in conflict?

How can free citizens confront the drive of communism for control of the world without, in the process, diminishing or abandoning the political and economic bases of their own freedom?

That is, how can a free society reply to communism effectively without finally converting itself into a competing totalitarianism? How can both pusillanimous default and the abdication of democratic traditions be avoided in facing such an adversary?

Dilemmas such as these suggest responsibilities that individuals will face as citizens of our nation in the foreseeable future. These responsibilities will involve the safeguarding and wise use of a number of crucial institutions and patterns, such as the suffrage and individual participation in politics, in the midst of great growth and change. These responsibilities are likely also to require citizens to rebuild certain older institutions and invent new ones, such as new responsible forms of government for great metropolitan regions, in order to keep the indispensable elements of a free society alive.

THE HIGH SCHOOL AND THE FUTURE

The American high school is the last formal education that many of our citizens receive. For those who end their education at the secondary level, as well as for those who go on, the high school should be an important source of more mature civic information, insight, and competence.

Speculations about the present and future of our society underline the critical importance of the second historic goal of secondary education. Citizenship never could be taken safely for granted; it has been a proper concern of American education since the founding of our Republic. But for today and tomorrow there is no concern of our schools that is more crucial.

It is mistaken to infer from present world developments that the challenges our society faces can be met primarily by increasing our schools' output of scientists, mathematicians, linguists, and technicians. The true tests that lie ahead certainly will demand increasingly large forces of qualified manpower to staff the technical, scientific, political, economic, and social developments that we can foresee. And it is certainly a fundamental task of the American high school to help individuals develop and prepare themselves as the professionals and competent workers who will make up these manpower forces.

But the future will demand of us much more than simply improved quality and output in professional and vocational training. The true tests ahead will require a universally higher level of responsible, intelligent citizenship to deal with the revolutionary changes that science and technology bring about. It is a most critical task of the American high school today and tomorrow to prepare citizens who understand and value the basic ideas of freedom, who

are literate in political, economic, and social affairs, and who are ready
and able to participate effectively in the civic life of a free nation.

(1) See "Curriculum Planning in American
Schools: The Social Studies." A Draft
Report from the Commission on the
Social Studies of the National Council
for the Social Studies. Washington,
D.C.: The National Council, Novem-
ber, 1958. Mimeographed. 23 p.

THE SOCIAL STUDIES AND
THE EMERGING ERA

Richard E. Gross

*Education in general and the social
studies in particular may assume revised
and new responsibilities as the social
world continues to change. What are
the implications of contemporary social
change for the social studies? The
writer of this selection calls attention to
some of the dramatic modifications
underway in society. He then suggests
three types of changes in the social
studies curriculum that may emerge
from the shifting characteristics of modern civilization. Although the reader
may interpret differently the signs of
our times, the writer's suggestions constitute stimulating illustrations of the
principle that the social studies can and
should reflect the society the schools
serve.*

A WORLD IN FLUX

BY ANY measure the world that produced our times is gone. On sweeping international scale a new age emerges. In many places this new era
rises from its chrysalis in dangerous but understandable haste; it is taking
wing without caution and without the tried safeguards of social metamor-
phosis. The forces responsible for this onrush into tomorrow and the masses
involved can be held back only with explosive results. Like the insect that
has but a twenty-four-hour period to complete its life cycle, peoples who have
been downtrodden and underprivileged display an insatiable drive to attain

FROM *Social Studies Curriculum Improvement*, Bulletin 36, Raymond Muessig, ed.,
Washington, D.C.: National Council for the Social Studies, 1965. Used by permission.
Dr. Gross is a professor of education at Stanford University.

all now. In the rapidly changing crucible of human affairs they portray a seemingly instinctive realization that their day will be short. In fact, for all of us, a most different and assuredly strange future lies immediately ahead. How shall we prepare for such a morrow when we recognize that within a generation entire established patterns of living may well be ripped asunder? What kind of a program of social education is imperative for an era in which the day of the father is indeed ancient history to his offspring?

Most children entering school this year should live approximately half of their lives in the twenty-first century; but the Buck Rogers elements of that one-time far-off period now impinge upon us daily. For children and youth in school, education should be the threshold for an adventure into this unknown. In this fact lies one of the major hopes of society, as education promises the knowledge and competencies for meeting the future. This has always been true even though the story of education down through the centuries is largely a dreary tale of hard-headed and heavy-handed arrangements evolved piecemeal to instill the young with the beliefs, understandings, and performance characteristics deemed essential by backward-looking adults of a conservative, ruling minority. Educational progress has been distressingly slow. Often, when changes become imperative, they appear as a patchwork of adjustments rather than as any sort of an insightful preparation aimed at creating individuals who may play effective roles in building a purposefully improved social order.

World civilization has, however, been able to stumble ahead. In spite of factors tending toward the status quo or even retrogression, snail-like progress has been made from generation to generation. Key inventions frequently "made" by mistake have been communicated largely by chance. Exceptions are isolated, as when Napoleon, anxious for improved military field rations, offered a rich prize for food preservation, thus leading directly to modern canning. Fresh social ideas have had even more difficult birth and nurturing. While new processes and products have often had to overcome seemingly impossible inertia, there has been outright opposition from both entrenched leaders and the populace who might ultimately benefit from these new idea and arrangements in the social and institutional realm. Since schools have existed primarily for inculcation and maintenance functions, it is easy to perceive why program alterations are difficult and how the schools lag perennially behind the demands of their time.

In the United States there were over 50,000 patents granted last year and the Patent Office is being increasingly engulfed in a backlog of applications, now almost four years behind, that reflect the geometric progression of inventions. Each new creation, whether a result of burgeoning basic research or of applied product development, can lead to a host of related elements. Thus, as a pebble thrown into a pond, both material creations and mental ideals ripple outward till they reach millions throughout the globe.

Today the ramifications of international cultural exchange bring all the more striking challenges not only because of the sheer number of mounting accretions but also because of the revolution in rapid communication between peoples and nations. With Telstar satellites we can achieve instantaneous visual reporting of events halfway around the world. Orbital, telephone, and postal arrangements are contemplated for the near future. Other new developments in communication include the production of machines for simultaneous translation and oral typewriters operating directly from dictation. Yet we are just in the opening stages of an electronic advance that includes innumerable automatic devices, such as district-wide, computerized Federal Reserve banking forms; transistorized, nation-wide income tax records; and instantaneous, international hotel reservations. Immediately ahead are machines that have not only built-in memories but the capacity to analyze and predict.

Developments in transportation are equally demanding of new conceptions of social relations. We now confidently approach the moon. Dramatic as space exploration is, it is but symbolic of the more immediate alterations in human affairs that must come when men can whip across the oceans from continent to continent in several hours. Breakfast in Paris and supper in San Francisco is now a regular occurrence, and by 1970 we are promised jets that will cross the Atlantic in less than three hours. There are surely implications in the fact that an airplane can now cross the English Channel in three minutes. Revealing of the tendency of educated men to live primarily in terms of past orientations are the recent discussions in the British press and debates that have even echoed in the House of Commons as mossbacks chant the dangers of an underchannel tunnel to the Continent!

In many ways the image of the future is not clear. But who can remain calm, certain, and complacent when just beyond are the promises and threats of inexpensive distillation of the seas into fresh water, of abundant solar energy, or of synthetic drugs that control the mind, let alone limit or promote the production of male semen or ovulation in the female?

Problems abound that cry out for study, explanation, and control. Issues surround us that, even if we cannot resolve them in our day, demand thorough understanding. However, mere understanding seems to become more difficult each year as problems become increasingly many-sided and as answers for one person, group, nation, or situation may not fit another. Both youth and adults must come to know how to live with the continuing crises and alterations that mark our onrushing times. The school has a special responsibility, in concert with the home, the church, and other agencies of socialization, to help the young perceive how this complex present has come to be and what is sound and valuable out of past human experience. At the same time education must strive to instill both the skills and attitudes that enhance the human potential for improvement, that wonderful spirit toward progress, so the best hopes of men may still be attained.

THE SOCIAL STUDIES AND THE EMERGING ERA

In the brilliant flashes of achievement and the deep shadows of trial and tribulation that characterize our times are there not significant implications for the social studies? Indicative of the need for rethinking school programs is the fact that this barely familiar present now disappears so soon. It must be abundantly evident that the technological and scientific advances attained or impending from the labor-saving aspects of automation to the laboratory creation of photosynthesis insure tremendous accompanying social implications. No matter where the horizons of the social sciences have existed, they can only promise to expand and to become further interrelated among themselves and with the other disciplines involved in the enlarging field of human knowledge. Certainly this is the time for realistic stock-taking in the social studies. Where are we overloaded with outmoded facts and outlooks which need to be drastically pruned and reshaped? Where should we add new emphases and topics? Where have we taken on so much that some of it must be eliminated or shared? Where can we cooperate with other fields of the school program or with out-of-school agencies in our desire to blaze new trails? How shall we retain essential learnings, but organize to impart them most effectively?

We have reviewed a few of the forces and conditions that call for curricular revision. They affect many aspects of education from the preparation of personnel to the tools we use. Consider, for example, the disparity between the facts and methods that were once deemed fundamental and those that are now essential in modern teacher training. Implications also exist for the content of undergraduate courses in social science and reach to the practices of administrators in appointing and assigning teachers for high school social studies courses. School programs are also clearly in need of updated subject matter. Elementary social studies programs often reveal an inheritance of a supposedly child-centered emphasis based upon outmoded adult conceptions that in many ways seem set in the pleasant, bland, middle-class American communities of thirty years ago. At the high school level a program dominates whose outlines were forged by an N.E.A. commission in 1916. Some local and state programs recently promulgated are closer to the recommendations of the Committee of Ten of 1893 for the social studies curriculum than to any other prototype!

Meanwhile, textbooks, the heart of American social studies courses, continue to grow in size and cost. Some, with their color picture inserts and distracting makeup and page arrangements, even make it difficult to read for an idea! Some still attempt to cover enough of everything to satisfy every possible adoption committee. This results in an appearance, as colorful as seed catalogs, of names, dates, places, and events. In view of their importance in both the formation and implementation stages of curricular development, radical alterations in the typical textbook would provide a major breakthrough in curriculum change.

In spite of the superficiality of some textbooks which fail to explain essential content in sufficient depth, American textbook publishers do deserve credit for curricular stabilization across the nation. With the tradition of local control and the freedom for individual schools and teachers, surprising unanimity exists. Three major forces have tended to bring some uniformity and concurrence between programs in different states. In the first instance, textbook companies have tended to produce volumes that imitate one another and frequently there is an amazing similarity between social studies texts published by different concerns. Our teachers have long been text-oriented (this may reflect our perennial shortage of adequately trained mentors, as well as the unfortunate habit of too many principals to encourage anyone to try teaching social studies) and thus many similarities exist in patterns of scope and sequence at state and local levels. This is a boon to the countless children among the fifty million Americans who change their residence each year.

A second factor in national curricular agreement is the tendency of curriculum groups to build upon or to modify (at best) courses of study and syllabi guides developed in other states and districts. Frequently these have been organized in terms of the traditional textual approach and content of a favored book, so once again more unity exists than an observer from outside the country who has heard of the variety of local programs in fifty sovereign states would believe possible.

Third, both textbooks and course guides tend to repeat that which is familiar and that in which instructors find security; they reflect fairly common college entrance requirements, as well as the lectures and traditional content of the university courses to which the teachers and the curriculum makers have been exposed. These factors explain the vicious circle of lags, broken most frequently by incongruities appearing as the result of the devastating power used by some state legislatures to establish curriculum by fiat.

The most evident example of the combination that results from the hangover of tradition, from the reticence of teachers and publishers, and from the influences of pressure groups and legislative action is the recurring, duplicative cycle of United States history found typically at grades five, eight, and eleven. With the growth of junior and community colleges, well-meaning boards of education and legislators are now perpetrating a four-cycle American history on public school students. It is the writer's conclusion that the repetition of these courses in the social studies, particularly the maintenance of the eighth-grade offering which is a carryover from a period when most children ended their school experience there, is the single greatest bottleneck in the evolution of a timely and comprehensive program that gives necessary attention to contributions from all of the social sciences, as well as to other parts of the world.

3

The Culture of Adolescents

SWEET LAND OF LIBERTY

H. H. Remmers and R. D. Franklin

Adolescent attitudes toward democracy are necessarily of concern to the social studies teacher. Probably it is too easy to mistake teenagers' lip service to democratic values, and especially to symbols of democracy, for sincere devotion to fundamental democratic principles. Willingness to examine carefully acquired data, however, forces a more realistic recognition. Adolescent commitment to the basic principles in the American Bill of Rights is, at best, partial, contradictory, and frequently lacking. The actual status of teenagers' outlook toward democracy should stimulate social studies teachers to renewed efforts toward helping students develop a reasoned comprehension and an appreciation of fundamental American liberties.

P OSSIBLY because applications of the First Amendment of the United States Constitution are "controversial," they are not well taught by the agencies primarily responsible—the home and the school—for the meaning of this amendment is rejected by many who will shortly be voting citizens, i.e., teenagers. A very reasonable inference is that this general proposition holds for the adult population, too, as will appear below.

Beginning early in the McCarthy era (1951) the Purdue Opinion Panel in its regular operations has at various times polled a nationally representative sample of .high school students regarding their attitudes toward relevant current applications of the Bill of Rights. The results have not been reassuring.

Before presenting them, however, in view of fairly widespread suspicions of polls and their results, perhaps a bit of legitimatizing of such results is in order.

Predictions of election outcomes based on pre-election polls constitute the most convincing evidence of the validity of adult poll results. Here the Purdue poll, based on representative samples of 2,000 to 3,000 individuals,

FROM *Phi Delta Kappan*, 44:22–27, October, 1962. Used by permission. For many years, until recently, Dr. Remmers directed the Purdue Opinion Panel on which Dr. Franklin has been a staff member.

have come off at least as well as the Gallup, Roper, and other polls. We have asked, at about mid-October, "If the coming election were being held today and you could vote in it, for whom would you vote?" Our results predicted the winners and the popular vote with less than 1 per cent error. Our pre-election polls of 1952 and 1956 were similarly accurate. Apparently, youngsters faithfully reflect their parents' political orientation. Further evidence of close correspondence between many parents' and children's attitudes has been presented elsewhere. (1)

Abridgment of the freedom of the press is by no means abhorrent to many if not most of our young citizens. In fact, it is less so now than it was ten years ago, as these figures show in response to the statement: "Newspapers and magazines should be allowed to print anything they want except military secrets."

	1951	1960
Agree	45%	29%
Disagree	41%	51%
Undecided	14%	19%
No response	0	1%

The above is clearly a very general statement of the meaning of "freedom of the press." When the issue is made more specific, only 11 per cent vote for no limitation on "the sale and distribution of 'objectionable' printed matter." "Objectionable" was defined as material that many or most people consider "sexy, profane, obscene, immoral, filthy, etc." Since instructions were to "Mark as many as you wish," the percentages add to more than 100. Obviously, in the eyes of the teenager the Federal Government is much more trustworthy in defining and limiting what is objectionable than are parents. Fears of federal thought-control through censorship are evidently not very salient.

The occasions or reasons teenagers list for limiting or prohibiting printed matter, movies, and the like come as no surprise since the advent of Freud. Frequency of choice:

Sex-perversion, sexual promiscuity, pornography, etc.	63%
Irreligion—profanity, atheism, etc.	43%
Political—un-Americanism, radicalism, etc	35%
Violence—assault, sadism, gore, etc.	28%
They shouldn't be limited or prohibited for any reason	15%

It seems clear that controversy concerning issues of censorship will continue and that freedom of the press is not likely to be the absolute that a strict construction of the First Amendment language appears to make it. The psychological mechanism of projection ("It won't influence me, but think of all those with less character!") will continue to ensure such controversy. As the late Heywood Broun once observed, "To the pure all things are rotten." Thus Anthony Comstock, responsible for most of the federal statutes on use of the mail for obscene purposes, was active shortly after the turn of the century in attempting to obtain federal legislation to prohibit the exposure to view of unclothed wooden manikins used in store window displays.

Further specific probing of attitudes toward freedom of the press yields no comfort to those who would protect this right guaranteed in the First Amendment. The typical teenager believes that "police and other groups" should have the power to impose censorship as shown in the following item:

"Police and other groups have sometimes banned or censored certain books and movies in their cities. Should they or should they not have power to do this?"

	1951	1960
Should	60%	60%
Should not	27%	24%
Uncertain	13%	15%
No response	0	4%

Obviously, there has been no significant change with respect to this issue over the ten-year period from 1951 to 1960.

A series of poll items asked two or more times over the ten-year period show that the right to trial by jury, protection against arrest without formal charge, and protection against search without a warrant are reasonably safe. . . .

It is not reassuring that while in 1951 only one in four (26 per cent) would forego the right of search without a warrant, ten years later one of every three (33 per cent) would yield this right.

The attitude toward the rights of foreigners in this country, in the light of constitutional guarantees, has clearly deteriorated over the ten-year period. Xenophobia appears to be significantly on the increase, with 54 per cent in 1951 and only 42 per cent in 1960 willing to allow "the same basic freedom that citizens have" to foreigners.

The right of private property is in no danger, as shown by the disagreement with the proposition that the government should have the right to dispossess persons without due legal process. . . .

. . . . nor shall be compelled in any criminal case to be witness against himself . . .

—from Article V, Bill of Rights

Physical and psychological torture via the "third degree" is significantly less favored in 1960 than in 1951, but the proportions who would condone this practice—from more than a third in 1958 (37 per cent) to more than a half in 1951 (58 per cent)—constitute cause for serious concern. Doubtless the revulsion against "McCarthyism" accounts for the very significant change in the attitude concerning refusal to testify against oneself; while less than half (47 per cent) disagreed in 1951 with the proposition that such individuals should "either be made to talk or severely punished," in 1960 (61 per cent), disagreed.

No state shall make or enforce any law which shall abridge the privileges or immunities of citizens of the United States; nor shall any state deprive any person of life, liberty, or property without due process of law; nor deny to any person within its jurisdiction the equal protection of the law.
        —from Article XIV, Amendments to the Constitution

A series of items aimed at exploring attitudes relevant to protection of the rights of minorities. . . .

Nationally, we are rather clearly in favor of desegregation of schools, as shown by the fact that approximately two-thirds, over a five-year period, "agree" or "probably agree" that "pupils of all races and nationalities should attend school together everywhere in this country." However, to no one's surprise, we find large regional differences in the East, 90 per cent; Midwest, 78 per cent; West, 85 per cent; and South, 29 per cent. Laws against marriage between persons of different races again show regional difference: East, 39 per cent; Midwest, 44 per cent; West, 33 per cent; and South, 67 per cent.

Protection of a person suspected of being a Communist in his right to a job is fairly staunchly supported. Presumably, these teenagers would not approve of blacklists for what in a recent unhappy period of our history came to be labeled "Fifth Amendment Communists," particularly by the late junior senator from Wisconsin, Joseph McCarthy.

Segregation in housing—perhaps an even more basic problem than segregation in education—is definitely disapproved by a majority and shows little change over time. The same holds for attitudes toward a proposed fair employment practices law.

In summary, teenagers—and inferentially the adult population back of them—accept the Bill of Rights with respect to religious freedom, trial by jury, and the rights of property. Refusal to testify against oneself has lost much of its odium over a decade beginning in 1951.

On the debit side of the ledger are attitudes toward the constitutionally guaranteed rights of foreigners and of minorities generally. The world's image of the world minority in skin color (only about one-fourth of the population is white) needs much improvement. Supreme Court Justice William O. Douglas has phrased it succinctly:

We cannot glorify Little Rock, anti-Semitism, supremacy of the police, downgrading of education at home, and at the same time be strong abroad. We are the same people in Guinea as we are in Boston. We cannot be leaders of people abroad unless we honor at home the democratic ideal in race relations, in labor relations, in community development.

(1) H. H. Remmers, Chapter 4, "Early Socialization," in *American Political*   *Behavior.* Burdick and Brodbeck (editors). Glencoe, Ill.: Free Press, 1959.

TEEN-AGERS AND THEIR CROWD

James S. Coleman

Has adult society's increasingly higher valuation of schooling during the past couple of decades been matched by a change in the adolescent's outlook? Not so, according to the survey made by this writer. His findings indicate some of the difficulties and challenges to be faced if adolescents are to develop the rational background and skills that effective citizenship demands more and more. Although the writer's data derive from early in the sputnik era, it would be indiscriminate to assume that overwhelming advances have been made since that time.

MUCH of what young people learn they learn from one another. Parents recognize this when they are concerned about their child "getting in with the wrong crowd." During adolescence youngsters begin to look to each other rather than to adults for support and leadership. Their "crowd" becomes enormously important. Its ways are their ways, its values theirs. These constitute what has been called the "adolescent subculture," which is, as parents and teachers are well aware, a powerful device to motivate young people and channel their energies.

One of the most important elements in secondary education, then, is the kind of adolescent subculture that develops in a high school. What activities does it reward? On what basis does it admit some students to the select inner circle and consign others to the outer fringes? What activities does it see as childish? Achievement or destructiveness? What qualities does it hold to be admirable? Conscientiousness or "living it up?"

FROM *PTA Magazine*, 56:4–7, March, 1962. Used by permission. Dr. Coleman is professor of psychology and director of the Institute of Social Relations, Johns Hopkins University.

The values of the adolescent community in one school may be far different from those in another. And the values of adolescent communities in one society may propel young people into productive, creative futures, while in another they may lead them into dead ends, wasted years, or poor adjustment to adult life. But adult communities and societies can do something about these matters, for it is they who determine the patterns of adolescent activities.

These concerns prompted me a few years ago to undertake research on American high schools and the adolescent communities that grow up in them. I studied ten schools (nine public, one Catholic) in the Midwest. In size they ranged from a hundred students to two thousand; in the parents' economic background, from predominantly working class to predominantly business executive and professional. Their locations included farm, town, city, and suburb. This range makes it possible not only to see the inner workings of the adolescent community but also to get some idea of what makes it what it is.

SURMISES AND SURPRISES

Some of my findings are common knowledge, but others were unexpected and surprising indeed. Yet when they are put together, they suggest basic defects in our educational system.

It is common knowledge that admission to a good college is getting more difficult each year. This led me to expect that students would become increasingly interested in their work throughout the four years in high school.

I found precisely the opposite. Following the same students from fall to spring, I found a slight decrease in the value they placed on scholastic brilliance and an increase in their esteem for popularity, athletics, and extracurricular activities. And comparing the values held by freshmen, sophomores, juniors, and seniors, I found the same trend over the four years of school.

This is not to say that seniors were less concerned than freshmen with getting into the right college and with keeping their grades up. But for most of the students the concern came rather late, about the middle of the senior year. And when it did come, it was a concern with getting "good grades for college," not an interest in learning itself or in being considered a brilliant student by their classmates. Throughout the four years basic interest in learning consistently declined.

I had supposed also that the leading crowd (which usually has a slightly higher economic background and includes more college-bound boys and girls than the student body as a whole) would be most interested in presenting a scholastically bright image, in being seen as the top in academic achievement. This was so only in rare instances. Instead, the leading cliques wanted to be seen as the socially dominant crowd or the one that controlled important extracurricular activities (among the girls) or the one composed of conquering athletic heroes (among the boys).

The young people most attracted to scholastic brilliance were quiet, conforming, unsophisticated boys and girls, who remained unnoticed and often unhappy in the background of the adolescent community. Their chief characteristic was that they seemed less grown-up than the others, more nearly children, still listening to their parents' desires.

For two reasons I had expected that an expressed interest in learning and a desire to be seen as a brilliant student would be greatest in the suburban school whose students were children of business executives, physicians, and lawyers. First, a far higher proportion of the parents of these students had attended college and, second, a far higher proportion of the students planned to go to college. But in their expressions of interest in learning and brilliance, the suburban school's students rated seventh among the ten schools. This finding, coupled with the previous one, meant that the leading crowds in the suburban high school rated brilliance lower than did either the leading crowd or the student body in any of the ten schools.

In comparing schools, I had expected that interest in learning would be higher in the more urban or cosmopolitan communities. But this was not so. It is true that among the student body as a whole there was about as much concern for scholastic achievement in the urban schools as in the rural ones. But when we look at the kind of leaders the adolescent community thrusts up and respects, we see something different.

In the smaller, more rural schools the leaders were less likely to question the value placed on scholarship by their parents and teachers and more likely to hold it in high esteem. Besides being more amenable to their parents' desires, they were less socially sophisticated, less sure of themselves than were the leaders among the urban and suburban adolescents.

The attitudes of boys toward bright or studious girls are a sensitive indicator of the status of scholastic effort in a school. In which schools did boys want to date girls who got good grades, and in which schools were such girls neglected or even shunned? Here too the results brought a sharp surprise.

It was not in the chiefly working-class or farm schools that the bright, studious girl was neglected, but in the upper-middle-class urban and suburban ones. Further investigation of this curious fact showed its source. Urban middle-class boys were interested in the "activities" girl, the one who spent her energies on extracurricular and social affairs. They looked upon the studious girl as a child, still conforming to her parents' demands. They were interested in girls who, like themselves, showed their independence by engaging in activities not imposed by parents or teachers.

All these findings gave me a picture of adolescent communities quite different from what I had expected. I had casually accepted the view that as people become better educated, schools better equipped, and teachers better trained, students will be more and more interested in learning. It was a shock to discover otherwise.

The picture includes two especially important features, with disturbing implications for high schools. The first is the rapidly increasing independence of adolescents and their unwillingness to be passively obedient to adults.

This independence is evident in the increasing separateness of adolescents from their family and in the family's inability to impose discipline. The growth of separateness, sophistication, and self-assurance is greatest among surburban, upper-middle-class youth. Indeed, it could be argued that the middle-class suburban home is worse than useless as a place for teenagers to live. They exploit it but receive little psychological support from it. They flout its discipline but are bound to it by a kind of indentured servitude. Their parents have little need for them and little to offer them.

Of course, like all generalizations, this one may be violently reversed in any individual case. There are still strong, tightly knit families in modern society, even in the upper middle classes, where the family is nearest collapse. But extraordinary circumstances or extraordinary people account for these strong families; they are less and less an outcome of everyday living.

Teenagers' sophistication and independence could, under the right circumstances, mean greater ability to accept responsibility for serious intellectual effort. But the second important feature in the adolescent subculture indicates the opposite, and also suggests the reason: Teenagers associate scholastic achievement with adult domination, studiousness with obedience to adult demands. They distinguish sharply between achievement in schoolwork and achievement in areas they regard as more nearly their own—athletics and extracurricular activities. To be sure, a few extracurricular activities, such as the school newspaper, reinforce educational goals, but many—cheer leading, for instance—do not.

ADOLESCENT VALUES VERSUS SCHOOL GOALS

Taken together, these two features of teenage life suggest certain difficulties confronting our high schools. Unless something changes, the adolescent community will turn more and more against the scholastic preparation that is so important to the future of many of its members. This prediction flies in the face of current confidence that our schools are bound to improve as we put more money into them and as more students go on to college.

What can we do? It seems unlikely that the increasing worldliness and independence of adolescents will be reversed, and there is some question whether a reversal would be desirable. What seems more easily changed is the association of scholastic achievement with adult dictation. What produces this association?

For one thing, scholastic activities have little voluntary quality in them. A student does not "go out" for English or math as he does for the football team or the school newspaper. He simply carries out adult-imposed assignments.

For another thing, scholastic achievement is principally rewarded by grades, and the grading system has some unfortunate consequences. It metes out as many psychological punishments as rewards. Whether or not a teacher grades explicitly on a curve, grades are measures of comparative achievement. They are meaningful only compared to grades of others in the same school.

An A rewards a student and encourages his effort; a D punishes him and discourages effort. In some scientific circles this is known as a zero-sum game— that is, some lose as much as others gain. But note that some school activities are not zero-sum games, so far as the school itself is concerned. In a basketball game with another school the whole school wins or loses together, or in an all-school work project the student body succeeds or fails as a unit.

In response to the grading system the adolescent community develops ways to hold down effort. And this is a reasonable response. Since as many lose as win, why not keep the whole level down? In factories the person who breaks the norm is called a "rate buster." In schools his title is similar and no more complimentary: "Curve raiser" or the like.

Also, since grades are dispensed on a single standard despite students' differing abilities, the grading system provides no real inducement for a bright student to go "all out" in his work and pursue his interests intensely. There are rewards only up to the grade he aspires to, and whether his goal is an A or a gentleman's C, he may not be challenged. In contrast, some activities, such as athletic games, scientific investigations, or business enterprises, provide increasing rewards for increasing effort. Consequently they call forth special energies and provide the special satisfaction that goes with high achievement.

Finally, scholastic activities provide almost no opportunity for the adolescent to be responsible, to exercise authority, or even to see himself and be seen by his fellows as a man. In contrast, a whole range of nonscholastic activities do provide this opportunity—smoking, drinking, driving a car, being nonchalant toward adult authority, quarterbacking a football team, acting as a boys' club or boy scout leader, raising an animal for a 4-H show. In a few schools there are opportunities for responsibility and autonomy in scholastic activities—in heading the debate squad if debating is a vigorous school pursuit, or in editing the school paper if the editor is given some freedom. But the opportunities are few.

These, then, are the factors that lead teenagers to associate scholastic achievement with adult dictation. But none of them is intrinsic to scholastic pursuits. Brilliant strategy and tactics occur in politics and business as well as athletics, and business and politics are central to the academic study of economics and political science. Scientific research is a perfect example of a *non* zero-sum game, for there is a continuing gain in knowledge to everyone's benefit.

STRATEGY FOR SCHOLARSHIP

What could capture the energies of adolescents and pull them toward educational goals? It is clear that some of the basic assumptions of education must be reexamined. Why, for example, should there be such an involuntary, passive quality in high school studies? Real scholarship is active and exciting. But by fixing a standard, rather than providing rewards for greater and greater accomplishment, there is no opportunity for passionate action, but only for passive acquiescence. The adolescent has abundant energy, but he will not spend it on his studies unless there is a possibility for positive action.

And why must scholastic activity be so individualistic? The athlete, the businessman, the researcher has the support and understanding of his associates, who exult with him in his successes, commiserate in his failures. But the high school student who devotes himself to his work has no alternative but to appear coldly selfish. His accomplishments help no one, while his failures may ease the pressure on others.

What can we do to change the situation? Because the problem lies in the structure of education itself and in the resulting values of the adolescent community, there is not much one teacher or parent can do. But for the school there are possibilities.

Certain well-known activities, like debating, . . . tournaments, and similar interscholastic contests, can be promoted, not as part of prescribed classwork but on a voluntary basis. They are not passive nor do they necessitate selfishness. Work projects that permit responsible creative activity and at the same time require scholastic skills are another possibility. These projects can induce the fascinated devotion on which learning depends, and are wholly without the punishment that low grades inflict on slower students.

To give an obvious example, for urban children there has never been any activity comparable with 4-H clubs for farm children. As a consequence, city youth miss this opportunity for autonomy and responsibility.

As a single practical step to help bring about needed changes, I would recommend incorporating tournaments, games, and projects into a scholastic fair, rather like current science fairs. The competition, however, would be between schools, with students representing their school just as athletes do. The fair would include a wide range of games of scholastic strategy, as well as contests in music, drama, sports, and poetry; and projects in science, business, homemaking, and industrial arts. If my analysis is right, such a fair, entered into wholeheartedly by the schools of an area, could mobilize and direct the energies of adolescents to a degree unimagined by adults.

A scholastic fair, however, touches merely the fringes of the basic problem in secondary education. Far more important is a clear understanding of this problem. For the problem implies that there are fundamental defects in our very conception of teaching and learning in the classroom.

4

Objectives for Social Studies

VALUES AND BEHAVIOR AS SOCIAL STUDIES GOALS

John S. Gibson

Teachers have tended to regard learning primarily in terms of knowledge, understanding, and skill. Probably such learning is most attainable; clearly it constitutes the most ascertainable. Often, however, teachers are tempted to consider the importance of developing student's "attitudinal" and behaviorial learning. It is difficult to resist the hope that social studies will contribute effectively to prospective citizens' social values, beliefs, appreciations, and actual conduct. It may also be naïve to presume that subject matter analyzing social behavior is likely to affect significantly the learner's attitudes and conduct. The writer of this selection considers some of the problems, issues, and viewpoints regarding such hoped-for outcomes of instruction.

To value some tangible thing or intangible belief is to give it special importance and a high place in one's hierarchy of human wants and needs. Educators have debated for ages the extent to which they should stress in the educational process those standards and convictions which they feel should be conveyed to the student, internalized, and manifested in the student's overt behavior. We are still arguing about the role of values in education today, especially in the scoial disciplines.

Plato believed firmly that the state had the obligation and even the mission to inculcate values into students and to shield students from those beliefs and influences which were considered harmful to the goals of the state. Since that time, dominant societal institutions such as the state and church have pounded their value structures into the minds of students through the educational process. *The New England Primer* of early colonial days in America is an excellent case in point. The advent of progressive education almost three hundred years later, however, launched a trend toward letting students come to their own conclusions about societal values; and many feel today that this

FROM *New Frontiers in the Social Studies,* by John S. Gibson, Medford, Mass.: Lincoln Filene Center, Tufts University, 1965, pp. 8–15. Used by permission and revised in part for its appearance here. Dr. Gibson is on the staff of the Lincoln Filene Center.

trend should continue. On the other hand, no educational system in the United States has really been as "value free" as some people like to think.

Some educators feel that emphasizing values in the social studies is engaging in a very controversial and even dangerous process of seeking to mold student attitudes and consequent overt behavior. Others say that values are much too elusive, that teachers are not always well equipped to convey them to students, and that in the last analysis, it is up to the student to determine for himself what really is of importance in social, political, and economic life. But if one agrees that desired patterns of civic behavior constitute an important goal for the social studies, then social, political, and economic values can hardly be excluded from the curriculum.

The process of socialization, or the individual's absorbing the patterns and teachings of his society as he matures, includes the acquisition of social, political, economic, and moral values. Family, church, school, government, economic, and recreational institutions, and the society at large serve as the agents of socialization. In this process of forming attitudes and values, the school is becoming an increasingly powerful force, and its impact upon the development of young minds is bound to expand with time. Can it be argued, then, that the school has no role in identifying and incorporating into the curriculum values which are vital to a free society at home and abroad? Can one honestly contend that the school should refuse to serve as an agent of socialization in the area of values and leave this task to the society at large?

Certainly this is a delicate issue, and there are many interpretations one can place on the statement that the school has definite responsibilities in helping young people to develop values necessary for the preservation and strengthening of a free society. But clearly we are not talking about indoctrination. We are largely concerned with educators helping students to identify desirable values from the substance of the social studies and to develop priorities of social, political, and economic values which will advance the cause of responsible civic behavior. Some of these values might include the following: the dignity of the individual, the long evolution and functioning of democracy as a way of life and governing, the richness imparted to any society by cultural diversity, an understanding of and respect for those who are different in terms of appearance, race, creed, or national origin, a free and open market in the exchange of goods and services, a positive acceptance of obligation and loyalty to one's nation and then to the peaceful interdependence of nations, and education itself as a powerful vehicle in the pursuit of human and social happiness. There are many other important values, but certainly these rank high in the scale of values which the social studies can and should convey to our students.

Values are not taught per se but emerge from the content of the social studies, from the basic understandings we can derive from these disciplines, and from the skills which enable students to gain knowledge and put it into motion. Sound pedagogy calls for values to be inductively advanced in the educational process and for a constant reassessment of the role and functioning of values in the curriculum. Finally, all of us could benefit greatly from more evaluation and research in the area of values and a continuing dialogue between advocates and opponents of the inclusion of values in the social studies teaching and learning process.

BEHAVIOR

Franklin Patterson has written that "knowledge and values become really meaningful only to the extent that they are effectively used in individual and social life." Those who would argue that education must stop at "knowledge" or "skills" artificially sever from the process of education its ultimate purpose. Huxley pointed out that "the great end of life is not knowledge, but action." Alfred North Whitehead added this.

Pedants sneer at an education which is useful. But if education is not useful, what is it? Is it a talent to be hidden away in a napkin? . . . Knowledge isn't just having the dignity that goes with possession. It all depends on who has knowledge and what he does with it.

The knowledge, understandings, skills, and values which can be derived from the content of the social studies may be directed toward many behavioral goals; however, two seen to be of paramount importance. The first is behavior by the young person which seeks to mobilize all the capacities he has so as to realize his inborn and acquired potentialities. The second is behavior which exercises those duties and responsibilities of democratic citizenship which must accompany the rights and privileges one receives in a free and open society. Self-fulfillment and responsible citizenship are prime behavioral goals for the social studies, and, in a larger sense, for education itself.

The goal of self-realization is an understanding by the student of self-potential and a desire to maximize his capacities and talents in such a way as to try to fulfill this potential. This key goal includes striving toward that personal happiness which accompanies the assurance that one is doing the best one can. As Aristotle put it, "the state of happiness is the exercise of all a man's vital powers along lines of excellence." A positive self-concept, a sense of confidence in self, personal motivation, and an essential inner-happiness are all components of this goal.

The goal of responsible citizenship may be placed within the context of a challenge from James Conant. He has called "for stressing in education that type of behavior on which a free society depends." What, then, are those types of behaviors which we would wish the graduating high school student to be committed toward so that his behavior as an adult would help to sustain and strengthen a free society? Certainly four can be identified.

1. A reverence for the law, and behavior which covertly and overtly conforms to public policy, democratically made.
2. Participation in the shaping of public policy.
3. Acquiring the knowledge that is necessary for effective participation in the governing process of the democratic society.
4. Responsibility to family and society in terms of that overt behavior which recognizes and accepts equal rights and opportunities for all in a society marked by diversity.

These behavioral goals for responsible democratic citizenship obviously are closely interrelated with each other. Conformity to public policy does not mean blind and uncritical subservience, and it most assuredly requires effective participation in the shaping of policy. But participation, in turn, necessitates enlightenment, and all depend upon genuine democratic behavior in a racially and culturally diverse society.

A statement by John Gardner magnificently unites these two goals.

. . . a society such as ours, dedicated to the worth of the individual, committed to the nurture of free, rational, and responsible men and women, has special reasons for valuing education. Our deepest convictions impel us to foster individual fulfillment. We wish each one to achieve the promise that is in him. We wish each one to be worthy of a free society, and capable of strengthening a free society. Education is essential not only to individual fulfillment but to the vitality of our national life. The vigor of our free institutions depends upon educated men and women at every level of society. And at this moment in history, free institutions are on trial. (1)

. . . There will always be a gap between the ideals and the realities of citizenship in a democracy, but certainly in our behavior, we can strive toward the ideal. As educators, we can promote the same objective for our students. There will be differences on what constitutes positive and responsible social, political, and economic behavior. Nevertheless, some of these desirable behavior patterns might include in the *social* realm behavioral respect for the rights of others despite difference from self; the enactment of patterns of cooperation with others; deference and obedience to one's superiors and respect for one's subordinates; selflessness when feasible and self-assertion where desirable and necessary; and a demonstration of confidence in the future. Desirable *political* behavior might include striving toward civic enlightenment; participation in the governing process in an effective and responsible manner in such areas as voting, working for and contributing to political parties, and contending for or holding public office. To the extent that the individual and members of society regulate themselves in a manner compatible with the well-being and the security of the society, the force of public policy need not intervene in the private lives of the governed. Thus self- and societal regulation constitute a vital segment of desirable citizenship behavior.

Economic behavior which should gain approval would include regulation of one's economic life to an appreciable degree so that someone else need not intervene to any great extent. The personal economic responsibility for self and family is a behavioral pattern that is often ignored in much of the social studies work in American schools. Working at one's job with a conviction of its importance and of its contribution to the well-being of society, the budgeting of one's time and money, saving a portion of one's income for future needs, and using one's wealth to assist others to progress toward higher stages of well-being are all, hopefully, economic behavioral patterns which can receive approbation. In brief, then, knowledge, understandings, skills, and values, if effectively communicated to the student through pedagogy, materials, and curriculum, and other means, can do much to promote those positive and responsible patterns of citizenship behavior without which an open and free society cannot long survive. . . .

The reader is strongly encouraged to turn to the works of Franklin Patterson and others who identify the goals of the social studies with the ideals of citizenship behavior. Patterson's studies include the following: *Citizenship and a Free Society: Education for the Future* (ed.) (Washington, D.C.: Thirtieth Yearbook of the National Council for the Social Studies, 1960) (see, especially, Jean D. Grambs's chapter entitled "The Challenge to the Social Studies," p. 273); *The Adolescent Citizen* (ed.) (Glencoe, Illinois: The Free Press, 1960); and *High Schools for a Free Society* (Glencoe, Illinois: The Free Press, 1960). Neal Gross prepared a scholarly and critical paper entitled *Memorandum on Citizenship Education in American Secondary Schools* (Cambridge: Graduate School of Education, Harvard University, 1960, mimeograph). The outstanding citizenship education study developed by the Detroit Public Schools and Wayne University merits wide acclaim, especially Meier, Cleary, and Davis's *A Curriculum for Citizenship* (Detroit: Wayne University Press, 1952) and Stanley E. Diamond's *Schools and the Development of Good Citizens* (Detroit: Wayne University Press, 1953), the final report of that study. Among the more classic works on civic education is that by John Mahoney cited above and Howard Wilson's *Education for Citizenship* (New York: The McGraw-Hill Book Company, 1938). The Citizenship Education Committee of the National Council for the Social Studies, chaired by Natalie J. Ward, devotes considerable energies to the problems of civic education, as does the Citizenship Committee of the National Education Association. The Robert Taft Institute (420 Lexington Avenue, New York, New York) is professionally concerned with problems and studies in civic education. Finally, a valuable contribution to the cause of civic education may be found in *Education for Citizenship*, prepared under the supervision of the Commissioners of Education of the Nine Northeastern States in 1952. A new edition of this monograph will be published by the Lincoln Filene Center in 1965.

A major, nationwide research and development program in civic education was launched in 1964 with support from the Danforth Foundation in St. Louis. The Council on Civic Education was established by the National Council for the Social Studies, the Survey Research Center of the University of Michigan, the University of California (Los Angeles), and the Lincoln Filene Center of Tufts University. Dr. Henry J. Willett, Superintendent of Schools, Richmond, Virginia, serves as chairman of the Committee on Educational Policies of the Council. Under the aegis of this project, the National Council for the Social Studies has examined promising practices in civic education in a number of school systems throughout the United States, while the Survey Research Center undertook a nationwide study of political behavior and attitudes of thousands of high school seniors. The University of California has focused upon teaching about the due process of the law and related teacher-education programs, and the Lincoln Filene Center has responsibility for working committees in the area of curriculum and materials and in research and theory, all in civic education. It is hoped that the Council's present and future activities will do much to strengthen the relationship between the social studies in the schools and the behavioral goals for American students.

(1) John Gardner, "National Goals in Education", in *Goals for Americans: The Report of the President's Commission* on *National Goals*. Englewood Cliffs, N.J.: Prentice-Hall, 1960, p. 81.

THE PHILOSOPHER–TEACHER

Ralph C. Preston

Frequently, teachers and other educators develop, out their often frustrating and futile attempts to make meaningful use of objectives, a skepticism toward the value of overtly identifying instructional purposes. This writer —from his full experience as a teacher, teacher educator, curriculum consultant, and analyst of social studies instruction —provides here a thoughtful and practical recognition of the problem and suggested solutions for teachers. Although his writing is directed ostensibly to elementary teachers, it is clearly applicable to those at the secondary level. Omitted here are portions of the original analysis that appeared in the numbered subsections.

FROM *Social Studies in Elementary Schools*, John Michaelis, ed., Thirty-Second Yearbook, Washington, D.C.: National Council for the Social Studies, 1962, pp. 256–262. Used by permission. Dr. Preston is a professor of education at the University of Pennsylvania.

A TEACHER works toward goals only if he is disposed to think in terms of goals. A person who thinks in terms of goals is a philosopher. Therefore, a goal-conscious teacher is a philosopher.

This syllogism forms the theme of this section of the present chapter. The section will develop the proposition that purposeful teaching requires that the individual teacher take personal responsibility for directing his teaching toward worthwhile objectives and that he become something of a philosopher. In using the word "philosopher," however, the writer does not mean to imply that each teacher should develop his own philosophy of education. Such a practice would lead to chaos. (1) The philosopher-teacher referred to here is simply a teacher versed in, and devoted to those beliefs, values, and principles of conduct which reflect society's purposes.

The section will raise serious doubts concerning the validity of the traditional effort of schools to bring about more purposeful teaching through relying upon lists of objectives. While the listing of objectives is an excellent experience for those engaged in the work, and stimulating to those few who seriously consult the lists, it has not had an important impact upon teaching in general.

Social studies teaching has made greater strides in its methodology than in its purposefulness. The progress in methods may be due in part to the stress upon the "artist-teacher"—the teacher who is able to make learning attractive and whose management of children is smooth and efficient. The artist-teacher, while a worthy ideal, is an incomplete one. Finesse of method is of no value if the teacher's goals are unclear or ignoble. Teachers who have a clear sense of direction as well as a grasp of how-to-do-it are more than artist-teachers; they are also philosopher-teachers.

THE INSUFFICIENCY OF STATEMENTS OF GOALS

Let us survey very candidly and critically the first stage of the standard American practice of curriculum revision. It consists of defining objectives. The thinking behind this approach seems logical enough. Not until we know why we are teaching (so runs the reasoning) can we select detailed content or devise methods to reach reasonable goals. The reasoning is plausible—but the practice itself has proved futile and ineffective. Why has this been the case? An examination of some of the reasons will point up the need for self-generating philosopher-teachers.

1. If goals are to direct instruction they must be creatively formulated. They are not transferrable from one person to another. Hence, a ready-made list of goals has but limited meaning to those teachers on a faculty (usually a majority) who have not helped in their formulation. Although an entire faculty might participate in formulating goals, this is not usually feasible. The full import of a list of goals is known only to those on the committee who

thought through goals together, who argued about them, and who struggled for the best language in which to express them. The unfamiliarity of the majority of the faculty with the full meaning of the goals can be reduced, to be sure, by having meetings of the entire faculty devoted to discussing them. However, seldom is discussion of a ready-made list of goals a sufficiently creative experience to arouse the fire and to cause the deep probing without which goals become more the objects of lip service to a teacher than the mainsprings of his practice.

2. Lists of goals throw some teachers on the defensive. These teachers are probably as anxious to improve their teaching as are others, but involving them prematurely in the study of goals only frightens them and confirms them in their staid habits. They tend to rationalize their practices to conform to the statement of goals. This is done because teachers tend to believe strongly in what they are teaching and are reluctant to change. Statements of goals, handed to teachers by administrators or supervisors, on the other hand, seem strange and cold to them. The type of teacher now under scrutiny usually respects a statement of goals, but he respects his own experience and practice more—because he understands them better. It is not difficult for him to reconcile his practice with the goals when called upon to do so. . . .

3. Lists of goals have regrettably been rejected by some teachers because they have not helped at the points where they have felt the greatest need for assistance. Many teachers tend to be more concerned with questions of method than with questions of direction.

4. Some teachers have an intuitive sense of proper goals and resent the inclination of administrators and curriculum consultants to belabor them. . . .

Defining goals can be just as tiresome and futile as defining education. Obsession with "spelling out goals" is sometimes a symptom of pedantry, sometimes of mediocrity. Fromm points out that today we profess the same values that have been preached for a thousand years. "We, today, who have access to all these ideas," he writes, "who are still the immediate heirs to the great humanistic teachings, we are not in need of new knowledge of how to live sanely—but in bitter need of taking seriously what we believe, what we preach and teach. The revolution of our hearts does not require new wisdom—but new seriousness and dedication." (2) An increasing number of teachers, too, are keenly aware of the enduring human values and goals. They react negatively to suggestions from principals or supervisors that these goals be reviewed, refined, revised, restated. They feel strongly that their energy and time might better be directed to the study of ways and means whereby the goals will infiltrate their day-by-day teaching.

How Goal-Consciousness Develops

How are goals formulated in life? How does the college student, for example, determine his goals for college? How does the young person entering upon his career determine his career goals? If we understand the process whereby life goals are established we may find clues for the development of goal-conscious teaching.

Few persons are able to formulate their goals at the outset of any important experience—college, marriage, business, teaching, or any other career. There is actual danger in the premature structuring of goals. To be sure, we sometimes hear of the head of a corporation who as office boy at age fifteen decided that he would some day be president of the firm; or of a beginning teacher who decides that by forty he will be a superintendent of schools and who fulfills his ambition. Fixing one's eye unswervingly upon a goal in this manner is rare and is not even necessarily healthy. (3) Most individuals are too normal and flexible to harbor such singleminded and self-limiting goals.

The typical young person has short-range or vague goals when he starts out. At the outset he may simply want to earn his weekly salary; or he may want to convince his employer that after the trial period for which he has been employed he should hire him on a permanent basis. When such transitory and short-viewed goals near fulfillment, they become broadened. The young person now may wish to provide the best possible service to his customers. He may wish to increase the security of his family. The beginning teacher's first objective may be to be liked by his pupils; soon he may add to that an aim to keep them in order. The desire to have them become informed and responsible citizens may be a theoretical and visionary goal during the first year of teaching, but it becomes sharpened and more central as he continues teaching and becomes a more mature person.

If this analysis of the development of goals is correct, then the usual "take the bull by the horns" approach to curriculum revision and teacher education is questionable. Teachers' first goals are probably limited and nebulous. Efforts to force teachers' growth through precipitating them prematurely in goal-formulating activities will be largely wasted and will be destructive in that some promising teachers will form a hearty dislike for supervisors, faculty meetings, and perhaps even teaching. The wisest course is to have faith that goals will broaden and deepen with experience and maturing.

A NEW APPROACH TO GOALS

Teachers who wish to improve their sense of direction and supervisors who wish to have teachers become more goal-conscious can profitably begin by focusing upon what the teacher is currently doing. This was the basis of the curriculum improvement program in Maine undertaken in the 1940's by William H. Burton.

Burton abandoned the dramatic, radical type of curriculum revision which had characterized the work of so many states in the 1930's and which attracted so much national attention. His principles were simple. First, the work of the classroom teacher was taken as the starting point. Aid was given to the teacher in whatever he was currently doing. Second, the program was voluntary. Teachers were not even strongly urged to participate. Third, local conferences and workshops were arranged as the need arose. Informal reports to the writer indicated that many teachers through this program took significant strides toward becoming philosopher-teachers.

A second example is furnished by the approach of the late C. Leslie Cushman during the late 1940's and early 1950's in Philadelphia. The social studies curriculum was revised over a five-year period. The first year was devoted to stimulating teachers to improve their teaching, or to inaugurate teaching, about the city or about communities within the city. During the second year emphasis was laid upon the improvement of unit teaching in general. The third year was devoted to defining scope, the fourth year to sequence, and not until the final and fifth year were objectives developed. The writer can testify from firsthand acquaintance with the program that this program, too, promoted among those directly involved the development of philosopher-teachers.

TEACHING GOALS AND LEARNING GOALS

A hasty reader may at this point conclude that the writer does not believe that teachers need bother with goals. Nothing could be farther from the truth. When teaching children, it is imperative, if we wish success, to establish learning goals for each unit, each division of a unit, and each day's lesson. Furthermore, the goals of learning should be made as explicit and attractive to the children as possible. each learning activity should be systematically planned so that children will easily and naturally acquire a sense of direction.

The reader may ask: "How can this be done if the teacher has not thought through the larger teaching goals?" Paradoxical though it may appear, it is entirely possible—and extremely common. Consider the teacher who establishes as a learning goal for his class that Columbus utilized certain forces and phenomena of nature in his use of sailing vessels, compass, and astrolabe. He has not yet thought much about many other implications of man's use of nature; e.g., that nature has conditioned where and how men live, that man has not controlled all phases of the physical environment, that man's knowledge of nature has freed him from many superstitions, and other of the thirty-eight implications brought out by the aforementioned report of the Committee on Concepts and Values. Nevertheless, the teacher grows toward the broader understanding, however slowly, in proportion to the degree that he works intelligently and conscientiously at his daily teaching chores. Indeed, this is how teacher growth took place over the centuries before education became professionalized. Today's principals and supervisors may either help or hinder teacher growth. They help to the extent that they respect the teacher, assist him when he asks for assistance, and gently challenge him when he needs stimulation.

(1) This point is trenchantly developed by Myron Lieberman in his *The Future of Education*. Chicago: University of Chicago Press, 1960, p. 27–31.

(2) Fromm, *op. cit.*, p. 344.

(3) Saul, Leon J. *The Hostile Mind*. New York: Random House, 1956. p. 171–72.

OBJECTIVES

Shirley H. Engle

Numerous analysts, including many teachers, have often found weaknesses and inutility in typical statements of objectives, goals, or purposes for the social studies. The author of this selection goes beyond routine criticism to analyze carefully two major emphases in objectives and a range of viewpoints *within each emphasis. Omitted here are more specific data, regarding each emphasis, that appeared in the original selection. Readers may be interested in relating Engle's criticisms of objectives as identified by Wesley to the latter's illustrative specification of aims for world history (page 181).*

THERE is confusion, if not open disagreement, about the nature and hence the purpose of the social studies. On the one hand are those, principally the academicians, who see the term social studies as no more than a general name for a collection of separate, but somewhat related, disciplines—history, sociology, economics, political science, etc. To many at this extreme, the very name social studies is anathema because it does not refer to a particular subject. At the other extreme are those who see social studies as a discipline in its own right, intermingling knowledge from all of the social science disciplines and dealing directly with social ideas and problems as these occur to the average citizen.

Efforts to bridge the gap between these extreme positions, though frequently attempted, reveal, on closer scrutiny, that they have not resolved the basic issue. According to Wesley's now famous definition, "The social studies are the social sciences simplified for pedagogical purposes" (1958, p. 3). Recent general statements of aims of the social studies, notably those of the Ad Hoc Committee on Social Studies of the National Association of Secondary-School

FROM "Objectives of the Social Studies," by Shirley H. Engle, pp. 1–3, 15–19, in *New Challenges in the Social Studies*, eds. Byron G. Massialas and Frederick R. Smith. © 1965 by Wadsworth Publishing Company, Inc., Belmont, California. Reprinted by permission of the publisher. Dr. Engle is an associate dean for graduate development and professor of education at Indiana University.

Principals (1961, p. 4) and a Committee of the National Council for the Social Studies on the "Role of the Social Studies" (1962, p. 315), begin by accepting the Wesley definition and then proceed to interpret this definition as implying no particular curriculum organization but rather as referring to all the educational activities systematically planned by the school to improve human relations. As Metcalf (1963a, p. 930) has sagely pointed out, detailed listings of social studies aims based upon such statements usually differ little, if at all, from the statements of aims of general education. To such eclecticism in aims, Metcalf (1936b), who would narrow the aim of the social studies to the single one of fostering reflective thought in the "closed areas," has this to say:

> The suggestion that the social studies limit its purposes to the fostering of reflective thought in the closed areas will not be popular with those who call themselves eclectics, and who value equally a variety of instructional aims. The trouble with many of our eclectics is that they have not included consistency as one of their philosophical criteria. A careful reading of their stated purposes leaves one with the feeling that they are not really for anything at all, since their lists of impeccable purposes are shot through with contradictory and incompatible destinations. It is fair to say that a person who wants to ride off in all directions is essentially aimless in his equestrian activity (p. 198).

Equally forthright in an opposite direction is Keller (1961, pp. 60–61), who dismisses the claims of the Ad Hoc Committee (and by implication the Council Committee too) as extravagant and harmful. Keller lays what he refers to as the "present unhappy situation" at the feet of the social studies, which he says is not a subject but rather a "federation of subjects often merged in an inexact and confusing way." Keller decries the fact that "too many social studies teachers have emphasized the creation of good citzens rather than the content and discipline of their subject." He would begin the "revolution" by eliminating the term "social studies," which is vague, murky, and too all-inclusive; he would substitute for it the terms "history" and "the social sciences," which are exact and hence "meaningful." Claiming that good citizenship is a by-product of the discipline of the mind which comes from the study of subjects, Keller would have students "study subjects and become acquainted with the facts and ideas" therein as the best preparation for citizenship.

Keller's position is echoed by Berelson (1962, p. 6). Purporting to summarize the thinking of the scholars commissioned by the American Council of Learned Societies and the National Council for the Social Studies to formulate basic objectives for the social studies, Berelson says, "The scholars will accept preparation for responsible citizenship as the goal only if they can dictate the means, which is the presentation of each subject, for its own intellectual sake, in the spirit of the liberal arts." This, it is argued, is the "best preparation for responsible citizenship." With more insight into the necessary complementarity of means and ends than is exhibited by the committees, Berelson, in effect, says: Yes, I agree, if by social studies you mean the separate teaching of the social sciences. Thus, it is clear at the outset that no real agreement exists, except in terms of platitudes, as to the objectives of the social studies.

Two basically different positions with respect to the nature—and hence the objectives—of the social studies are already obvious. To some educators, the social studies are essentially the same as the social sciences. To another group of educators, the content of the social studies is directly related to its goal of developing the attributes of good citizens. Within each major position a variety of alternatives may be found, each predicting a somewhat different end for social studies instruction. Efforts to reconcile these positions have not proved entirely successful. No one has really taken up the challenge to the social scientists thrown down by Robert Lynd in 1948 under the exciting title "Knowledge for What?" Confused and even contradictory aims for social studies instruction persist. . . .

CONCLUSIONS

A variety of sometimes contradictory aims is ascribed to the social studies. The contradictions run so deep that they are impossible to arrange on a single continuum, but we can get some idea of the differences which exist if we consider them on two separate continuums, one of which we shall call the "content" continuum and the other the "process" continuum. On the content continuum, we see the social studies varying at the extremes from the study of separate subjects, with no claim to any direct bearing on the broad problems of citizenship, to the direct study of broad areas and problems taken from the "life experience" of citizens. The latter is an enterprise held to be clearly separate from, if not over and above, the study of subjects. The clear aim at the first extreme is knowledge, by which is meant the ability to recall multitudinous facts and principles in each of several of the social sciences. If, indeed, one studies a subject to the point of being able to abstract from experience and to discover a model of human behavior (i.e., a model of economic man, of sociological man, of political man, etc.), such a model is necessarily incomplete, because it is detached from real-life problems, which always appear in complex and patterned configurations requiring whole, and not piecemeal, solutions. At the other extreme of the continuum the clear aim is the possession of valid ideals and values as these relate to broad areas of human experience drawn from a wide range of subjects.

On the content continuum Keller (1961) and Berelson (1962), representing essentially the traditional academic position, are at one end. Hanna (1963) and Johnson (1963) are at the other. Wesley and the members of the Committees are essentially unclassifiable because their writings are so clouded in platitudes.

On a second continuum, the "process" continuum, the extremes vary from those who see the central process in social studies instruction as the mastering of subject matter to those who see it as a problem-solving process. To master subject matter is taken to mean to fix in one's mind, memory, and understanding in meticulous order the facts and principles which form the separate content of each social science discipline. Problem solving emphasizes the function of synthesis and imagination as ideas from a variety of related sources are tested in the context of broad areas of social experience. The goal in the first instance is the ability to recall arbitrary associations from each of the social sciences as well as diligence in the process of committing these facts to memory. The goal in the second is a continual development and refinement of the ability to solve problems and arrive at valid answers to the perplexing circumstances which confront citizens. On the process continuum, academicians are at one extreme, just as they were on the content continuum. Metcalf (1936b), Griffin (1942), and Oliver (unpublished manuscript), and possibly Engle (1963) and Massialas (1963) are at the other extreme, with Bruner (1962) somewhere in between.

Perhaps all of the philosophical positions are to some extent worthy of consideration. The difficulty with general statements of goals, like those of the committees cited above, is that they encompass indiscriminately all of the goals mentioned, with the result that the reader is likely to take out that to which his bias inclines him, relegating other goals of equal or even greater importance to limbo. Future studies should focus on operationalizing the objectives of social studies instruction by relating goals to curricula, to methods of instruction, and to more specific student behavioral outcomes.

Berelson, Bernard. "Introduction," in American Council of Learned Societies and the National Council for the Social Studies, *The Social Studies and the Social Sciences*. New York: Harcourt, Brace and World, Inc., 1962.

Bruner, Jerome S. *The Process of Education*. Cambridge, Mass.: Harvard University Press, 1962.

Engle, Shirley H. "Thoughts in Regard to Revision." *Social Education*, XXVII (1963), 182.

Griffin, Alan. "The Subject Matter Preparation of Teachers of History." Unpublished Doctor's dissertation, Ohio State University, 1942.

Hanna, Paul R. "Revising the Social Studies: What is Needed." *Social Education*, XXVII (1963), 190–196.

Johnson, Earl S. "The Social Studies versus the Social Sciences." *The School Review*, LXXI (1963), 4.

Keller, Charles R. "Needed: Revolution in the Social Studies." *Saturday Review*, September 16, 1961, p. 60.

Larrabee, Harold A. *Reliable Knowledge*. Boston: Houghton Mifflin, 1945.

Lynd, Robert. *Knowledge for What?* Princeton, N.J.: Princeton University Press, 1948.

Massialas, Byron G. "Revising the Social Studies: An Inquiry-Centered Approach." *Social Education*, XXVII (1963), 185–189.

Metcalf, Lawrence E. "Research on Teaching the Social Studies," in N. L. Gage, ed., *Handbook of Research on Teaching*. Chicago: Rand McNally, 1963a.

————. "Some Guidelines for Changing Social Education." *Social Education,* XXVII (1936b), 197–201.

National Association of Secondary-School Principals. "Social Studies in the Comprehensive Secondary School." *Bulletin of the National Association of Secondary School Principals,* XLV (1961), 1–17.

National Council for the Social Studies, Committee on the Role of the Social Studies. "The Role of the Social Studies." *Social Education,* XX (1962), 315–318, 327.

Wesley, Edgar B., and Stanley P. Wronski. *Teaching Social Studies in High Schools.* Boston: D. C. Heath, 1958.

PART TWO
SOCIAL SCIENCE DISCIPLINES AS SCHOOL SUBJECTS

A major share of recent efforts to improve the social studies has been devoted to closing the gap between the social sciences and the social studies. Readings in this Part deal with the field of the social sciences, the disciplines of the field that are emphasized in the secondary school curriculum, and other subjects among the social sciences that are represented in the social studies. The articles are written by social scientists with definite interest in the school program and by social studies educators who have special competence in the teaching of particular subjects.

The social sciences are said to be undergoing marked and significant changes. What changes are underway or prospective, and what is their import for social studies? Can the social sciences serve the practical needs of a viable society and, at the same time, seriously devote themselves to the search for scientific truth? Several authorities address their attention to these and related questions.

What are the characteristics and status of history at this time of blossoming behavioral sciences? Can and should history maintain its prime place in the secondary school social studies program? And what of geography, a subject that often receives stepchild status, at least in the senior high school? Should geography be integrated with history, recognizing the danger that most of geographic interpretation may become lost as a result? Is modern geography of such a nature that it more properly belongs in the physical sciences than in the social sciences anyway?

How should the social studies react to advancement of such other social sciences as economics, political science, sociology, anthropology, and social psychology? Do these disciplines really have distinctive values applicable to adolescents' learning about society? Is it practical to offer special courses in each social science subject?

It is evident that teachers and other curriculum-makers in social studies cannot wait for social scientists collectively, or for the specialists in particular disciplines, to agree fully on their purposes, the scope of their common and special areas of study, and the findings from their investigations. Nevertheless, the social studies teacher must be a constant and continuing student of the social sciences if he is to help his students become accurately acquainted with the social world. For those who work on the forward edge of knowledge regarding human relationships constitute the most adequate and valid sources of up-to-date and reliable data about society.

The Field of the Social Sciences

THE SOCIAL SCIENCES
IN THE TWENTIETH CENTURY

Peter Odegard

A major reason for lack of consensus on the purposes of the social sciences is the problem of communication. It arises basically from the fact of an increasingly huge output of findings and interpretations in the field. Here one social scientist relates the problem to his view of desirable aims for the field. Assuredly some readers will disagree with the writer's assessment of the role of the social sciences in society. In any case, his vigorous and thoughtful statements illuminate consideration of purposes that the field should serve.

N OT THE least of the problems created by this age of analysis with its attendant knowledge explosion and one that goes far to explain the tension and conflict within the world of science and scholarship is the problem of communication. The so-called gap between the natural sciences, the social sciences, and the humanities, to which C. P. Snow refers in his essay *The Two Cultures and the Scientific Revolution*, (1) is mainly due to a failure of communication. "I believe," says Snow, "the intellectual life of . . . western society is increasingly being split between two polar groups . . . : at one pole we have the literary intellectuals, . . . at the other, scientists."

Failure of communication, however, is found not only among the great branches of human knowledge but increasingly within them. To "keep up," I'm told, one would have to read 125 specialized periodicals in mathematics, seventy in psychology, and heaven knows how many in other disciplines. In addition to 100,000 government reports, there are nearly 500,000 papers each year in American technical journals, plus an estimated half million in other languages, 30 to 40 per cent of which, it is said, are trivial, repetitious, or redundant. The problem of retrieval from this avalanche of scientific literature

FROM *The Social Studies: Curriculum Proposals for the Future*, pp. 33–40, by Odegard, Hanna, Quillen, Bellack, and Tyler. Copyright © 1963 by the Board of Trustees of Leland Stanford Junior University. Used by permission of Scott, Foresman and Company, the publisher. Dr. Odegard is a professor of political science, University of California, Berkeley.

has become so burdensome that "several industries follow a rule that if a research project costs less than $100,000, it is quicker and cheaper to work out the problem in the laboratory than to plow through the literature to find whether it already has been done." This duplication of work already done has been referred to as "rediscovering the wheel," a process that is perhaps more common in the social sciences than in the natural sciences. President Kennedy's Science Advisory Committee has only recently reported (January 10, 1963) that "science must be unified if it is to remain effective. . . ." (2)

Science and technology can flourish only if each scientist interacts with his colleagues and his predecessors and only if every branch of science interacts with other branches of science. . . . The ideas and data that are the substance of science . . . are embodied in the literature; only if the literature remains a unity can science itself be unified and viable. Yet because of the tremendous growth of the literature, there is danger of science fragmenting into a mass of repetitious findings, or worse, into conflicting specialties. This is the essence of the crisis in scientific and technical information.

The situation in the social sciences and even in the humanities is only slightly less complicated and ominous. "We are like soldiers," says Stuart Chase, (3) "lying in isolated foxholes without means of communication. . . . Yet the social sciences are concerned with the same critter—man, and the notion that we can abstract the economic or the psychological aspect of his behavior without regard to the rest is nonsense." (3) To solve this problem, the President's Science Advisory Committee suggests a centralized scientific depository—a kind of knowledge bank with an elaborate retrieval system to make any existing knowledge readily available. The committee also suggests that authors refrain from unnecessary publication. Universities and foundations could contribute to this end by easing the pressure of the "publish or perish" policy upon scholars and scientists. Equally important would be the rediscovery of some common goals for scientific research.

"Science for science' sake," no doubt, is as easily justified as "art for art's sake." But it is by no means clear that taxpayers who now provide the vast bulk of funds for scientific research will continue to do so simply to satisfy the curiosity of scientists. Nor are governments always likely to accept on faith the claims of scientists that what they do adds significantly to our knowledge of man and his universe. Already one hears mutterings in Congress about the well-nigh cosmic waste in space research and development. Outside the context of the cold war and without the rationalization of national defense, it is extremely doubtful that the tens of billions currently appropriated would be forthcoming. Can we find what William James would call a moral equivalent for war in seeking support for science and scholarship in our society? In the allocation of a nation's limited resources of manpower and materials, there are outer limits to the justifiable claims even of scientific research and development, especially when so much of it is repetitious and redundant. To provide for better communication among the various disciplines, the President's committee urges greater emphasis on the so-called "mission-discipline duality." That is to say, more interdisciplinary research upon common goals.

We are, in fact, confronted in all this with a central paradox of modern times. The very specialization and analysis that have been pulling man and his world apart have at the same time made men everywhere more interdependent. That each man is his brother's keeper is no longer a question but a condition. Disintegration through analysis has made integration not only inevitable but urgent if we are not to fly apart. Indeed the rediscovery of a sense of direction and purpose has become a matter of life and death for the human race. Central to this rediscovery is a continuous restudy of those basic concepts that lie at the core of human knowledge.

Concepts, like other things, come in many shapes and sizes and with varying degrees of significance. They also play different roles. Some merely seek to describe and define what *is*, some to outline what *ought* to be, and others to *predict* what will be or *could* be under certain circumstances. In general, contemporary hard-nosed social scientists, in their zeal to be value free, eschew the use of concepts of what *ought* to be or even of what *might be*, if people were of a mind to have it so, in favor of concepts of *what is*. What this posture overlooks is that neutralism and indifference toward what *ought* to be not infrequently align the scientist with values and social forces least compatible with the freedom without which science itself cannot survive. Moreover, it tends to reduce the scientist to the role of technician and to sacrifice a philosopher's crown for a servant's cap.

It is obvious, of course, that a value-free science—a science without goal or purpose—becomes merely a form of random behavior which makes a mockery of the term. A scientist without values is like a fanatic who redoubles his effort after he has lost his aim. Nor is it enough to say that his values are merely methodological or procedural, concerned with means and not ends, except only the objective pursuit of truth. For truth wears many faces and, except as it is arbitrarily defined in terms of meter readings, can be as elusive as liberty, equality, and fraternity. Moreover, to discover what is true or false is not unrelated to the discovery of what is good or bad. A scientific concept can be true or false in the degree to which it corresponds to the norms or standards of science itself—i.e., to meter readings. So, too, it may be good or bad in the degree that it contributes to or corresponds with the basic needs and goals of human life. Unless science is merely random behavior or idle curiosity without purpose, it has a responsibility to discover and to serve these basic human needs.

This lays a special obligation on the social sciences because they are by definition concerned with man and society. So-called behavioral science, whether hard-nosed or soft-nosed, has no mandate to be indifferent to human goals or values. One of its major assumptions is that human behavior is goal-directed, and in striving for these goals, men choose among alternative modes of conduct. It assumes also that in choosing, they are conditioned not merely by the physical world and the pressures of appetite and instinct but by formal education in rational modes of thought and behavior. Rationally induced changes in human behavior thus become as reasonable, i.e., as scientific, as rationally induced changes in the physical environment. There is nothing unscientific in social scientists who seek to change those conditions of character and environment that impair man's ability to make rational choices among alternative modes of behavior.

There is nothing sentimental or sloppy in social scientists committed to the rational analysis and eradication of poverty, pestilence, and war, ignorance, fear, and hate. There is nothing unscientific in economists who are as much concerned with the components as with the size of our Gross National Product. Moreover, I suspect that integration of the social sciences and better lines of communication with the natural sciences will come as quickly through cooperation on problems of this kind as in conferences on scope and method.

Not less important is the task of social scientists, by precept and example, to encourage in every way possible and in every one they can reach a conscious and continuous reflection on the human condition and on alternative roads to the basic goals for which all men strive. This continuous and rational reflection on contemporary patterns of thought and behavior is but another definition of social ethics, without which men become but creatures of custom and habit, little better than beasts. Scientists are not immune from the responsibilities of other citizens. They need to be reminded that their attitudes of olympian indifference and skepticism toward moral and ethical problems in a society that has all but canonized the scientist can issue in apathy and cynicism among others; attitudes dangerous alike to science and a good society.

In a daring book called *Daedalus*, published forty years ago, J. B. S. Haldane said:

I think that the tendency of applied science is to magnify injustices until they become too intolerable to be borne. . . . I think [also] that moral progress is so difficult that any developments are to be welcomed which present it [i.e., moral progress] as the naked alternative to destruction, no matter how horrible may be the stimulus which is necessary before man will take the moral step in question. (5)

Have we now reached a point in history where the alternatives to moral and political progress are so horrible that we may at long last be willing to put forth the effort necessary to guide mankind into a more orderly and humane society? Unless we do so, we shall surely die.

(1) Cambridge: Cambridge University, 1959. See also F. R. Leavis, *Two Cultures?* (New York: Dutton, 1963), essay by Michael Yudkin, p. 51.

(2) *Science, Government, and Information.* Report of the President's Advisory Committee, 1963. (Washington, D.C.: U.S. Government Printing Office, 1963.)
See also digest in *Current Magazine*, May 1963.

(3) Stuart Chase, *The Proper Study of Mankind* (New York: Harper, 1948).

(4) Roger Blough of the United States Steel Corporation in 1957 commented: "I have studied the economists' differing definitions of 'administered prices'; I have sought to comprehend that stillborn concept called 'zone of relative price indifference'; I have struggled with that impossible paradox . . . 'monopolistic competition'; and pursuing my research even further into the semantic stratosphere of economic literature, I have encountered 'atomistic heteropoly' and 'differentiated polypoly.' "—*Steel and the Presidency*, 1962, by Grant McConnell. Copyright © 1963 by W. W. Norton & Company, Inc., New York.

(5) J. B. S. Haldane, *Daedalus*. (New York: Dutton, 1924), p. 86.

THE OBJECTIVES AND METHODS OF THE SOCIAL SCIENCES

Pendleton Herring

For a number of years the author of this selection has occupied a prime position from which to view developments in the social sciences. His breadth of view, incisive insight, and forthright analysis provide a valuable assessment of the field. Here he deals with major trends, purposes, and conceptions—both public and professional—of the social sciences. Omitted here is a fuller discussion of research methodology that appeared in the original publication.

THE OBJECTIVES AND METHODS OF THE SOCIAL SCIENCES

THE social sciences are too fluid and too varied to warrant neat generalizations about their nature and methods. The social sciences are not a single, ordered body of fact and theory, operating through an internally consistent and generally accepted uniform methodology. One must turn, rather, to the distinctive disciplines of anthropology, demography, economics, political science, psychology, sociology, and statistics, and to the contributions of history, geography, law, and other closely related fields.

FROM *New Viewpoints in the Social Sciences*, Roy A. Price, ed., Washington, D.C., 1958, National Council for The Social Studies, pp. 1–2, 7–11. Used by permission. Dr. Herring is longtime president of the Social Science Research Council with offices in New York City.

Social scientists, moreover, even within their respective disciplines, have varied approaches. Some stress the importance of experimental or quantitative methods of data gathering and analysis. Others may be more concerned with practical application and with the bearing of their studies on policy alternatives. Some, absorbed with the critical interpretation of social phenomena, draw added strength from philosophical and humanistic studies. A frequent interplay of methods and approaches is found. There is no relish here for offering tidy definitions; to recall the words of L. J. Henderson, "To define is to offer a fiat."

As scholarly and research activities become more specialized, the task of interpretation is more difficult. This growth of specialization, and the tendency for those of an analytical cast of mind to dissect perhaps more often than to synthesize, explains why the seams in our common intellectual fabric are often more prominent than the mesh itself.

Perhaps a semantic confusion may be eliminated at the outset. Those critics who worry about the dominance of science over society must first create their own dilemma; to wit, reify the abstraction "society" and then create an imaginary monster in a white laboratory coat to manipulate "man"—another abstraction. The social scientist cannot study scientifically "man" and "society" in the abstract sense, any more than the natural scientist can study "matter" and "space" viewed as metaphysical abstractions. Scientific methods can be applied to the extent that individuals can be observed or the behavior of social groups examined. Moreover, there is reason to question the utility of efforts to compare the social sciences in general with the natural sciences in general, with the intent of applying the word "scientific" as though it were an accolade.

The Problem of Method

The problem of method in the social sciences (and perhaps in any other field) is best understood in relation to purpose. The more scientific the bent of the investigator, the less is he concerned with over-all social problems or broad dilemmas that invite speculative thinking. His quest is for the concrete, the observable, the measurable, the definable. Fact gathering and observation lead to the classification of types or the search for uniformities of reaction or patterns of behavior. Hypotheses are framed in an effort to bring greater coherence to the raw data and to point the way toward further data gathering, with perhaps a sharper sense of relevance. It is appropriate to recall here Alfred North Whitehead's insistence that science is a way of thinking. It provides frames of reference for the analysis of aspects of observed reality. The methodology of the social sciences is best understood in these terms. Much dispute among social scientists and argument about the social sciences could be eliminated to advantage if Whitehead's basic point where kept in mind.

In baldest terms, social scientists share a common concern in the development and use of methods for ordering data systematically and analytically, and for interpreting their findings as objectively as possible. . . .

Misunderstandings About the Social Sciences

Some critics are prone to offer flat assertions about social science objectives and attitudes. Hence, the topic brings to mind a crude miscellany of charges and contradictory criticisms. Some social scientists may be guilty as charged; but there is no firm basis of facts for reporting the personal creeds, partisan loyalties, or political views of social scientists any more than for lawyers, veterinarians, or florists. To consider briefly some of the current criticisms may serve to indicate at least what the social sciences are not—dealing, here, not so much with social science objectives as with public misunderstandings.

There are no data for reporting in quantitative form what public attitudes may be. Should a survey of such opinion ever be undertaken, it might well consider the following categories. The critics, who might be classified as: the dogmatists who say there should not be a scientific approach to social problems; the scoffers who say there can be no such approach; and the skeptics who say, "Show me." These three categories of critics may present fewer difficulties of analysis than the well-wishers, some of whom expect too much too soon on problems that transcend the grasp of science, and a second group who look to the social sciences for pat answers to questions better left to the judgment of responsible individuals. The chief hope for understanding must come from those laymen sympathetic to experimentation and even trial and error. Some critics assert there can never be a completely adequate "Science of Man," and then conclude by predicting with relish all the tyrannical discomforts that would ensue were this millennium to dawn. Others embroider the fallacies of the "economic man" or the "sociological man" as though these logical constructs were live ogres. Still others picture a moral awakening that is seemingly delayed by the already wide awake efforts of men to study mankind.

Yet it is on such grounds that charges of "scientism" are based. This curious "ism" is a word of no relevance to the scientist pursuing his research. It is in current polemic use as a device for berating those individuals alleged to regard the objectives and methods of science as embracing the whole aim and purpose of mankind. This footless argument is only worthy of mention as further indication of the need for getting to more laymen an understanding of the scientific approach to reality, of what the scientist attempts and what he, as a scientist, is simply not concerned about. The social sciences in objectives and in methods are disassociated here from the philosophic embrace of any "ism": albeit humanism, positivism, relativism, empiricism, pragmatism, or idealism! The individual working in one of the social science fields may prefer any one of these "isms" as a guide for his own life and work, or he may prefer Methodism or Congregationalism. The point is that the objectives and methods of the social sciences do not, in whole or in part, rest on a creed—a single, articulated value system or philosophy. And, least of all, on "scientism."

Some scientists may find in the nature and methods of science itself ground for a personal philosophy which they may take from their laboratory and use as an ethical guide or system of values. This is an intensely personal matter and the individual's own private business. The "ism" that may most appropriately provide some degree of ideological support for scientific endeavor in the United States may be "individualism." This is hardly to be treated as a formal ideology or philosophic system of values. It is, rather, an American habit of mind, rooted in historical tradition. Though none the less significant for this reason, it is too disparate in character and too widely shared, to be treated as a distinctive ideology for scientists as such.

Paradoxically, some critics argue that the social sciences have a deleterious influence because they ignore individualism and proceed upon mechanistic assumptions that rule out the possibility of human choice. "Determinism" is said to be the philosophic foundation stone; the human being is treated as no better than a machine and the doctrine of free will is denied. From the discussion so far, the irrelevancy of this line of discourse should be apparent. In the practical, nonmetaphysical sense, freedom is enhanced as our knowledge of limiting factors, or of cause and effect relationships, is increased. Thus, in this sense, the engineer has more freedom to exercise his will with nature than the craftsman; or the doctor than the medicine man. But the social sciences have nothing to offer, pro or con, on free will as a doctrine. This concept belongs to another universe of discourse; it is part of a different frame of reference. Its meaning must be sought in metaphysical or theological, not in scientific, terms. Nor are the limited empirical objectives and quantitative methods of analysis of the social scientist to be pitted against philosophies of history. Each has its place.

The effort to discover antecedent-consequent patterns in behavior based on particular and repeated observation of nursery school children, or to identify variables and determine which are independent and which function as dependent or intervening variables, or to work out correlations in thousands of responses to opinion survey questionnaires, may seem mechanical in method and the results trivial to readers accustomed to grand judgments about the fall of the Roman Empire, the decline of the West, the causes of war, or the future of civilization. It is not that the one or the other approach is the more significant but, rather, that separate skills are needed in building different structures of meaning. While the learned doctors squabble over historicism, and relativism, or ask: "If we had to choose, would we be better and wiser with Shakespeare and without psychology and sociology than we should be with them but without Shakespeare?" is the listener to conclude that less scientific method in human affairs will mean more moral strength or better poetry? The plea here is for simple tolerance of a division of intellectual labor.

Some critics express concern about what they sometimes call cultural relativity, or even ethical relativity, in the social sciences. They have the impression that to describe, for example, the customs or behavior of people in a different culture in a straightforward fashion, or to display a sympathetic appreciation of the rationale that underlies such behavior, is either to preach an "ethical neutrality" or actually to embrace the tenets of the system described. To dispose of these fears bluntly: the moral for our society from such studies of other societies is basically a reminder that the human being has a wider range of possible routines, reactions, capacities, and inhibitions than are revealed or provoked by the culture and customs of any one society. From the standpoint of ethics or morals, the reader could conclude that God works in diverse ways His wonders to perform or, from the standpoint of personal choice, that one man's meat is another man's poison. Ethically, cultural anthropology can fortify a scientific humanism or in terms of religion it can be turned to the enforcement of a belief in Christian charity and the brotherhood of man. Of course it imposes none of these implications.

The Social Sciences As Contributors

The social sciences are not the rival, but rather the auxiliary, of moral purpose, and of normative judgment. They are contributory to policy decisions, and to enhancing man's capacity to cope with life's problems. They can also offer him that ultimate in wisdom—a healthy humility. This gift can be gained from varied sources but the social sciences are not the least rewarding.

Social scientists may be greatly aided by specialists trained in philosophy. The value premises implicit in empirical inquiry often need to be clearly stated and critically examined. Much naïveté, from a philosophic standpoint, might be thereby revealed. Moreover, the philosopher with his training in logic and his flair for abstract thought has much to contribute in the erection of models or systems that would provide a more meaningful structure for empirical investigation. There is much talk of synthesis; scattered and piecemeal inquiries do not add up to any larger whole. How can the cumulative element be introduced? The skilled experimentalist, the ingenious research designer, the statistician—all can gain from the model-builder, the theoretician, and the philosopher. On the other hand, theory, as moral philosophy, is often so rhetorically phrased and vaguely conceived as to be incapable of ever being reduced to propositions that can be tested.

Need for More Effective Data Analysis

Social scientists may be sometimes thought of as facing a choice between (1) verifying empirically propositions of limited range and perhaps no particular novelty or (2) propounding statements that seek to convince through their eloquence, insight, or challenge. There is no dearth of editorial-izing or of free-floating, unrelated theories. The literature is likewise replete with bits and pieces of empirical research. How can greater coherence be achieved? The answer lies in the further development of distinctive skills in analysis. Able young research men are today very alert to any such advances. Acquiring a new research skill seems more appealing to them than absorbing a novel doctrine. A sense of workmanship and the command of distinctive methods for examining human relationships point the way to progress. Joined with this is need for the more orderly accumulation of data to which improved methods can be applied.

In the face of these difficulties, some social scientists prefer to hazard interpretations and pass judgment on large questions, even though the evidence available is far from conclusive. Others seek to perfect their methods even though their actual findings are of very limited utility. We can only hope for a better balance of objectives, namely, theoretical formulations testable by the methods and data we have; and improved methods and larger-scale empirical inquiries consonant with the problems of great social significance that call for study. Research skills, together with the adequate time and money, are essential.

That men of learning still share tastes and sympathies for research and scholarship, however diverse the subject matter, is a valued tradition. Recog-nition of the hazards of parochialism in scholarship is a real safeguard in itself. To be aware of the problem is half the battle. But is there not a larger problem?

Toward a Better Public Understanding

Of serious present concern is the need for bridging the gap between scientists and scholars and the general public. The common aspirations basic in the learned world today need to be stated and restated with eloquence and convic-tion for the man in the street to hear. The welfare of the community of learn-ing is dependent upon understanding and support by the larger community of our democratic society. Have we not been coasting along on popular support of science for the gadgets and comforts it produces, and on public tolerance of scholarship because education is good for the young? Support for research, sympathy for higher learning, confidence in the value of intel-lectual pursuits—all these must rest upon a general public understanding of their objectives and methods.

The basic objective of the social scientists is the same as the aim of the earth scientists and the life scientists and the physical scientists, and of the humanists and the philosophers. It is the objective of all men of goodwill, seeking the good life: It is to release the best of mind and spirit to realize human potentialities. The methodology of all learning is subordinate to the purposes sought and to be vital must be changing and developing. The plea is for pluralism of intellectual effort and shared respect for varied methods of inquiry and forms of knowledge. It is this universe of discourse that needs to be understood and appreciated by our fellow citizens as never before.

AUGURY FOR THE SOCIAL STUDIES

Robert V. Hanvey

The "explosion of knowledge" heavily involves the social sciences as well as several other major fields of human knowledge. Recent and continuing splurges in the amount and diversity of findings in the social sciences hold great and pressing implications for the social studies. The nature of these advances and the potential, desirable reactions of the social studies are considered by the writer of this selection.

THE nature of the urban society in which more and more of us live acts to strip subcultural insulation away from the individual. He is ideologically exposed. Bombarded by massive doses of information and varied interpretations, the young person finds no solace in his immediate circle or in the larger world around him. He is terribly aware that he lives in a society of dissent. This is a crucial fact of his social situation—the extent to which the adults of the society do not agree in their perception and interpretation of social phenomena. We may trumpet the glory of a world whose heterogeneous groups and facile communication destroy provincial viewpoints and challenge every traditional authority, but the situation for the child is most difficult. Children growing up in these circumstances spend a great deal of themselves in the search for valid interpretation.

The dangers of sensitizing the young to a profusion of events and conditions (and can one block their view of the headline or keep them from television?) while withholding adequate explanation will become, I think, ever more obvious. How many Northern high school students, after a hundred headlines, stories, and television newsreels about school-integration crises, have any better explanation for the intransigence of some Southern whites than the glib concept of prejudice? Yet because they have occasional if tenuous contact with more sophisticated explanations of human behavior, many students sense the superficiality of such interpretation.

REPRINTED FROM The School Review, 69:18–24, Spring, 1961, by permission of The University of Chicago Press. Copyright 1961 by The University of Chicago. Dr. Hanvey is associate director of the Anthropology Curriculum Study Project of the American Anthropological Association.

Social scientists have proffered theories that help to explain the cultural inertia of the South, the special dependence of certain socio-economic groups on the maintenance of traditional class structure, the psychological dynamics that underlie the appeal of a Faubus. Exposure to these ideas can at least begin in the high school. When young people lack access to the best explanations that a society can offer, education is tantamount to subcultural indoctrination.

Surely the implicit explanations of human action characteristic of our history textbooks will seem increasingly inadequate. The textbook writers perhaps cannot be blamed; they have so little space and so much to tell. But in their neatly packaged and curiously similar treatment of events and personalities all sense of honest inquiry is lost, deftly disposed by the journalistic assurance of the prose.

Textbooks, of course, cannot provide sufficient data for real student inquiry nor in fairness should there be such an expectation. Happily, the last few years have seen the publication of excellent documentary and case-study materials suitable for high school use. The availability of such materials represents a major step in escaping the dependence of the social studies on textbooks. But such materials are only a partial answer. As long as the theoretical resources available to high school students remain implicit, sparse, or obsolete, access to data is an empty promise.

The prospects, I think, are good. The crucial reaction to anachronistic explanation will come, of course, not from students but from better-educated teachers. Among the signs on the current scene that suggest better days ahead is the strong movement, well financed, toward improved teacher education. Such efforts to extend and enrich the preparation of teachers will have a major impact on the nature of the social studies. Actually, the title of the course, its formal content and organization, its place in a sequence—all are relatively minor concerns when measured against this question: Is the teacher thoroughly enough educated to begin the job of acquainting young people with the wonderfully rich perspectives and theoretical resources potentially available to them?

The maturing of the social-science disciplines, the increased number of graduates in these fields, the rising status of high school teachers, and the major effort being made to upgrade the scholarship of teachers in their subject-matter fields will complement one another in the production of such teachers.

Two other characteristics of our times promise to support a larger role for the social sciences in the social studies: the rate at which new knowledge is being produced and developments in the technology of documentation and information-handling.

In all fields of disciplined research, knowledge is being produced at a rate quite beyond the compass of any one man's imagination. Every professional is aware of the time, energy, and expense of simply keeping abreast. (An electronics firm in the Chicago area assigns one of its engineers full-time to the job of keeping up with the literature.) Specialization has been one form of adaptation to the situation, a solution which unfortunately both contributes to the original problem and creates new ones.

It is difficult to see how we can slow or stop this mass production of information and ideas. There are no signs of an inclination to shut down, and it may be that, as with wheat, butter, and eggs, we shall have to do some storage and work on ways to increase consumption. These tasks we are increasingly well equipped to undertake.

As a matter of fact, as our society's fund of knowledge has grown, so has our capacity for handling it. The accelerating rate of data and knowledge production is bound up—in a not necessarily vicious circle—with increasingly effective techniques for documenting, counting, searching, transmitting, and interpreting. While there is some lag in our ability to fully exploit production, it is not inevitably a serious one.

The technologies involved in documenting and transmitting words, numbers, sights, and sounds have been long marked by a drive toward ever more speed, miniaturization, versatility, and economy. Punch cards, film, and records have been the common tools of recent years. These continue to make significant contributions even as they to some extent give way to more powerful electronic tools.

Today, magnetic tape has become the ubiquitous parchment. On this modern scroll are frozen the perceptions of the television camera and the microphone—and the binary digits that constitute the lingua franca of the computer age. Speed, versatility, and compression are the advantages of the computer. Durability, flexibility, and economy are the promise of video tape. Computer, sorter, video tape—all play their part in the accelerated evolution of the ways in which we document, inquire, determine, and communicate.

The major stimulation for this movement has come from business, government, and the mass media. The academic world has been a fortuitous beneficiary. But the advantages have been no less real, and the burgeoning financial resources of public education now make possible the serious exploitation of such tools by the schools.

Facilities, after all, invite use. The invitation is especially attractive when the new tools are compatible with a society's priority motives. In a society that prizes efficiency, devices that accomplish the hitherto impossible or more effectively perform the commonplace offer a strong temptation. For Americans, innovative facilities not only invite use but stimulate the search for new uses. One possible result is the eventual centralization of scholarly resources for precollegiate education.

The growing affluence of organized education, new perceptions of educational needs, and the excitement that Americans feel when confronted by new devices may, before long, combine to create a definite movement toward such centralization of materials and communication facilities. The technology is available. And there is some experience to indicate that what an American's tools can do, he will want to do.

If this Sunday magazine prediction should come to pass, perhaps we shall see the book and film libraries of schools and school systems augmented by the much richer resources possible in regional centers. Access to library material would be easy and rapid through the use of facsimile and photocopy equipment, video tapes, and closed-circuit TV systems. The regional libraries themselves would have much of their material abstracted, coded, and stored in the memory banks of computers, where they would be subject to rapid search.

If every school's resources should come to include—through the opportunity provided by regional library and communication facilities—a vast storehouse of films, back issues of major newspapers, government documents, cross-cultural records, and sound transcriptions—real inquiry would be possible for the secondary school student.

It may not happen this way—through the development of regional resource centers. And then again, it may. In any event the schools before long will face an embarrassment of riches in the form of content resources. Wealth of resources will provide many opportunities—and create its own demands. Foremost among these demands will be the demand for teachers who can realize full gain from the opportunity, who can draw wise inferences from aggregations of data and help students to do the same, teachers whose inventories of concept and theory are sufficient to impose meaning and order on an otherwise bewildering miscellany.

To reject the employment of a wide range of theory from the social sciences will seem, in this situation, increasingly absurd. To be sure, theory in the social sciences lacks articulation and solid authority. But to withhold rich explanations, tenuous and narrow though they be, on the grounds that they are not ready for general distribution will be, to a large degree, casuistry. The perspectives and hypotheses of the social scientist have not been stamped "classified." These ideas are abroad in the land. The extent to which they have been distorted reflects the extent to which the schools have failed to make scholarly and systematic use of them. But poverty of concept and theory in secondary education is passing.

The physicists have accepted "complementarity." And we quite shamelessly expose high school students to the fact that two theories—wave and particle— are necessary to satisfactorily explain light phenomena. There are signs that before long many of the persons interested and influential in the development of the social studies will admit that a complementary-theory, multiple-perspective approach is just as appropriate in the task of helping the young develop a valid comprehension of the social milieu. All the social sciences will have a contribution to make to this enterprise.

COMMUNICATION OF VALUES
IN TEACHING HISTORY

Walter Rundell, Jr.

Various statements of objectives in the teaching of history indicate the potential values of that subject for students. Rarely has a recent statement so lucidly delineated the discipline's values, in terms of its basic and multi- *faceted characteristics, as does this one. The historian speaking here reflects a broad and sensitive appreciation of practical and desirable returns available from investment in the pursuit of history.*

WHEN we come to the problem of communicating values in teaching history, we are beset with numerous difficulties. Initially, we have the question of what we mean by history itself. We can examine a few representative uses of the term to demonstrate the difficulty of definition. From time to time, we have heard Nikita Khrushchev appeal to history as his witness. Another man might say "history tells us" or "history teaches us." Still another will vouchsafe that "history justifies." And how often have we heard earnest politicians insist that "history will prove" their party, platform, or actions to be correct? So, obviously, history means different things to different people.

Usually when teaching history we don't bother with a precise definition—though perhaps we should. We just sort of take for granted that the students and professor will have some tacit understanding of their common ground. Furthermore, trying to come to a mutually agreeable definition of history, considering the above divergencies of usage, might prove even more baffling to the students than the assumption that we share a common ground! . . .

History is not one of those recondite subjects where the student gains admission only through the ministrations of the professor. If ever there was an open field in the academic curriculum, it is history. We have no mumbo-jumbo which the initiates have to learn to be intelligent practi-

FROM *The Social Studies*, 54:243–247, December, 1963. Used by permission. Dr. Rundell is the director of the Service Center for Teachers of History, American Historical Association.

tioners. There is no password required for admission to the inner sanctum. There is no ritual to be performed. Unlike the chemist, we do not light votive flames nor juggle elements from the periodic table in equations. We have no symbols like the mathematician with which to dazzle the uninitiated. Unlike the psychologist, sociologist, and economist, we have developed no special vocabulary with which to impress the tyro. In these fields the practitioners demand that the students approach discipline on the terms of the practitioners. To be initiated, one must first master the special lingo. Naturally presenting a discipline in these terms gives the practitioners an immense advantage. The students must approach on terms foreign to them if they are to gain admission to the sacred portals. In the field of history, on the other hand, we have not provided ourselves with any arcane trappings. We have been willing to communicate without requiring any specialized technical equipment of those who would learn. Now in this regard maybe we have missed the boat. Perhaps history would be an infinitely more attractive field of study if it, too, could boast the sacerdotal hocus-pocus. If entrance to the field were limited by requiring the mastery of a disciplinary jargon, we might have more novices clamoring for admission. Sometimes it seems that exotic pastries lend more enchantment than does our daily bread. But for better or worse, history does strive to communicate on the level of general understanding. This is why the gap between the teacher and learner of history is probably narrower than in any other field. As one of my professors at the American University said in class one day: "After all, the difference between us is merely one of degree." At this, some wiseacre who didn't feel quite the fraternal bond the professor had indicated retorted: "No, the difference is three degrees." . . .

Why do we say that an active interest in mankind is a requisite? Merely this—history, in its most fundamental terms, is the story of man. We have no better illustration of this fact than the French word for history— "l'histoire." It is also the word for story. In German, "Geschichte" is both history and story. The Italian "storia" further exemplifies this community between history and story. Basically, any kind of history deals with man's activities. Therefore one of the salient values to be communicated in teaching history is that history *cannot* be dull! If a person thinks history is dull, the judgment is upon the individual, not history. For history is the story of man. And surely the person who thinks the story of our race is dull is utterly devoid of imagination or intellectual curiosity. I'm not contending that we don't have such persons among us, but I am demanding that we not take their judgment as authoritative. By saying that history can never be dull, I'm not trying to imply for one instant that history teachers or history books cannot be dull. We all know only too well that they can. But I am submitting to you that because of its very nature—the dynamic story of man on this earth—the subject is vital and immensely exciting. If history is dulled by inept teaching or writing, the loss is doubly great, for someone's enthusiasm for the story of some intensely human activity is blunted and the event itself is given less than its due. We realize that the fault lies not with the story, but with the way it was told.

When we contend that history, correctly taught and written, cannot be dull, does this mean there is nothing unexciting in this story of man? Certainly not! But this does give us an insight into what we mean by history— at least recorded history. And here again we come to an important value to be communicated in the pedagogy of history. When we speak of history, we almost invariably mean historiography, or the writing of history. True, we can conceive of history in a pure sense, but how much "pure" history do we know? Isn't most of our historical knowledge transmitted to us via the written word? So what we're really dealing with is written history and not the actual sequence of men living in a certain time span. Recorded history implies, then, a process of selection on the part of the historian. In the selection, the historian determines what was significant and pieces his story together so that an intelligible pattern emerges. In the process, the dull and commonplace things are omitted. We do have a few records of the past other than the printed word, such as the graphic and plastic arts. But their contribution to our knowledge of the past is indeed slight in comparison with what we know from books. If, then, for all practical purposes, we equate written history with history, we can see that the historian assumes a role of immense importance. For the preponderance of what we know about the past has been transmitted by historians. The Greeks understood the significance of the historian, for in their mythology they elevated the historian to Mt. Parnassus. Clio, the Muse of History, recorded on her scroll the affairs of men.

Granting the incalculable importance of the historian in recording the past, we now come to the question of what values does the particular historian try to communicate? In recognizing that there are different values to be dealt with, we acknowledge the manifold and multiform nature of history. History, in fact, is inclusive. Some philosophers of history have contended that all knowledge is historical knowledge. Certainly no historian could be ambitious enough to do justice to the full scope of human experience. So he must choose some segment of history to treat. He might wish to deal with a limited period in its multiple aspects, or with a special emphasis through a longer period. In any event, he must look at the past and select what he wishes to emphasize. Therefore history is not a total reproduction of the past, but the past as seen through the eyes of an individual. Naturally this reduces history to intensely personal terms. And it makes us aware of the need to understand the historian's background, outlook, and prejudices. Similarly, the student of history should be aware of his teacher's conditioning, for inevitably this conditioning will color his conception of history.

When we approach any particular phenomenon of history, either as a writer or teacher, we should make every possible effort to understand the context in which we find this phenomenon. . . .

Before the student of history renders his judgment, he should investigate his evidence as thoroughly as possible. He must look at his facts from every angle and try to visualize the situation in life's roundness, even though the facts themselves seem flat. Here the historian's interpretive training is brought to bear. He must be careful not to distort, but he must project his research data into life situations before his writing or teaching have relevance. This is probably the most demanding task for the historian, for it requires real artistry. Those historians who are able to vivify their material by relating it to human needs and concerns are the genuine artists. Their work is timeless. That is why we remember Francis Parkman, William Prescott, and Frederick Jackson Turner, while all but students of historiography have forgotten Timothy Pitkin, Jared Sparks, and John G. Palfrey. Among contemporary American historians, one who has conceived of his subjects in the most intensely human terms is Walter Prescott Webb. Because of his relating his history to life concerns, it seems likely that he, too, will take his place among our historiographical giants.

The student of history, whether he be the most celebrated or humble, should look at facts with the least possible degree of preconception. He should be as free from biases and governing assumptions as possible. If the records seem to show less than the full picture, the historian should be aware of that fact and compensate therefor. If they engage in special pleading, the historian's perspective should enable him to recognize it and adjust his reaction accordingly. The historian should examine his subject in depth and from all directions. One notable segment of current American historical writing fails in this respect. That segment is business history. The failure is a very human and most understandable one. Enterprises put up money to have their histories written and it would be an ungracious historian who would present his patron as a "bête noire." And here Clio is traduced. Too often company histories are nothing but publicity blurbs, not even deserving the proud name of history. . . . Business histories indicate to me that the "official" historian runs grave risks. The most meaningful history is that which is beholden to nothing save truth. It is this truth that the writer and teacher of history must serve with the full courage of his convictions.

In writing and teaching history, then, many values are to be communicated to the student. Whether history is conceived of as an expression of God's will; example; experience; a pack of lies agreed upon, as Voltaire contended; fiction badly written, as G. B. Shaw commented; or a conspiracy against the dead, it is vital to understand the prejudices of the historian. As much as von Ranke tried to make an exact science of history by insisting that it be written "wie es eigentlich gewesen," Clio has managed to elude the scientists.

Fortunately, Clio has also escaped those who used to insist that history was nothing but past politics. With greater recognition of history as the total story of man's past, newer emphases have arisen. Social, economic, intellectual, diplomatic, and military history have come to the foreground for they, too, contribute as much understanding of man's existence as does unadorned political history.

As historians have become more sophisticated, they have striven to graduate from mere chronicle or narrative to analytical history. No longer are we content to say what happened—or present our understanding of what happened, but now we want to explain *why*. The historian's emphasis today is on the significance of the phenomena before him. This is why history can afford to be so selective. Those events which are so ordinary that they differ not one jot from something before or after are of no interest to the historian. The differences and contrasts are the motivating factors in history. Today's historian isn't content just to describe the change, but he wants to explain it. A further evidence of increasing sophistication in history is the interest in the philosophy of history. Now some historians attempt to fit all historical phenomena into various types of grand designs. For instance, Benedetto Croce proclaimed that history is the story of liberty—that only man's striving for freedom is the mainspring of history. Marx has said that the only driving force in history is economic need. Carlyle insisted it was the hero. Reinhold Niebuhr says that history is essentially paradoxical and that it remains morally ambiguous to the end. Spengler and Toynbee have traced the rise and fall of civilizations. Nicholas Berdyaev contended that history is moving toward man's ultimate salvation—that in the eschaton, history will be culminated by the Kingdom on Earth. Other Christian philosophers of history say that history has already been fulfilled with the incursion of God into history in the person of Jesus Christ, and that we're just biding our time until Gabriel blows the final trump.

Regardless of one's tastes in history and one's personal philosophy of history, this remains the field where all who would might enter, yet where the challenges and responsibilities are tremendous. The professional with the Ph.D., the dedicated secondary school teacher, the amateur with an active interest, the layman with a knowledge of research techniques and literary ability, and the alert student meet on this field and communicate freely. There are no admission requirements other than a perceptive mind and a concern with the story of man. This most egalitarian of disciplines is obliged to maintain its openness. For when society is denied free access to its past, it can never really understand itself. Without a knowledge of our past, we would be totally without perspective. Perhaps, then, the most important value we can communicate in teaching history is that history, as the story of man's past, forms the background and framework whence all contemporary action springs. History is nothing less than the conscience of mankind.

EXPLANATION AND THE
TEACHING OF HISTORY

John R. Palmer

*What kind of history is taught in a
particular course may well depend basically upon the approach to history
previously acquired, perhaps unwittingly, by the teacher. The author of
this selection carefully examines two
fundamental elements of history as a
discipline. He relates each of them to*
*varying, and sometimes widely diver-
gent, approaches to or emphases in
secondary school courses in history.
Omitted here are most of the original
article's references to and quotations
from leading historians' ranging interpretations of the nature of their
discipline.*

HISTORIANS, written history, and the teaching of history are primarily
concerned with the analysis of change over time. The matter is
uniquely central to history as a field of social study. There are two essential
aspects to the study of the human past—the establishment and verification of
the succession of events and the explanation which accounts for the occurrence of these events.

The first of these tasks has been assiduously undertaken by several generations of scholars and, as a consequence, there is now a generally agreed upon
set of techniques appropriate for the verification of the occurrence of past
events. However, the matter of explanation—of establishing why things
happen as they did—is an open question which is currently the subject
of considerable debate. The debate, primarily involving philosophers with
some contributions by historians, is being conducted in the main in journals
not generally read by social studies teachers. But the issues central
to the controversy are of the utmost importance to the development of the
individual social studies teacher's positions regarding what to teach and how
to teach it. Many of the basic questions which confront the teacher can
be approached through a study of the problems involved in the explanation
of social events.

It is all but impossible to teach a history class for one hour without going
beyond description to explain, cite causes, and analyze. Even the mere listing
of events in chronological order tends to convey the notion that those
earlier in time somehow caused what followed. The student is attempting to

FROM *Educational Theory*, 12:205, 209–211, 214–217, October, 1962. Used by permission.
Dr. Palmer is a professor of the history and philosophy of education at the University of
Illinois.

learn *what* happened and *why* it happened, but the more fundamental of the two is the *why*, the explanation, for it contributes most to his understanding. What a student learns in this regard through his study of history depends not on his knowledge *that* an event occurred but upon his understanding of the dynamics of the situation in which the event took place. It appears, then, that the analysis of the dynamics of the social context provided by the textbook and the teacher is crucial. . . .

Certain salient features of the deductive model have particular significance for the teacher and learner. Universal laws or scientific hypotheses are essential to the model. If there is not an adequate storehouse of these as yet (as many argue), then it is essential that historical study work toward them. If they do exist in quantity, then they must be taught, examined, used, and understood. These universals must, of course, be taught and learned within the context of and in relation to history conceived as a science. The contention presumably is that the only room there could be for saying that something has a causative relationship to something else is knowledge of a law linking events of the first type with those of the second. Although there is some variation in the conception of the place of generalization in explanation on the part of the adherents of this view, all insist that some kind of law is required by the explanation. An explanation is not complete unless the appropriate law or laws have been specified, and it is not tenable unless these have been verified by an empirical procedure.

In this view, classification and attention to kinds or categories of events are very important in the study of history. The emphasis is on establishing similarities between and among events rather than stressing their unique characteristics. Hempel emphasizes that it is universals, not particulars, which are "the object of description and explanation in every branch of empirical science." (1) The notion of the absolute uniqueness of historical events must be discarded, for it precludes the possibility of formulating either concepts or general laws.

Use of the deductive model clearly demands a familiarity with formal logic and scientific method. These require of both teacher and learner skill in the formulation and clarification of hypotheses, the use of induction and deduction, an awareness of logical fallacies, skill in hypothesis testing, and the like. A much greater concern for precision in the use of language than is now common among social studies teachers is demanded, for precise concepts are essential to generalization and logical processes. (2) In contrast with the "common sense" use of language now typical in the field, concerted efforts at clarification are essential if the rigor of the deductive model is to be maintained. Gardiner, content with very loose generalizations, is quite happy using words as the man on the street uses them, but history conceived of as a science would require more uniformity and rigor in use of terminology.

Perhaps it is not too much to say that the logic (though not necessarily the method) of history teaching becomes quite analogous to that of science teaching. The emphasis in the classroom is on generalization, the scientific method, logical processes, concept formation, and the formulation and testing of hypotheses. The individual historical event achieves importance according to its usefulness in carrying out these processes. The teacher attempts to so structure the course of study that the student gains as wide a store of empirically verified generalizations as possible, skill in the use of the methods of science, and a sensitivity to the careful use of language. Obviously, other skills and knowledge are involved, but these appear to be of special significance.

It is unlikely that a history course organized for these purposes would follow the traditional chronological approach. More appropriate would be the study of a particular time and place in history, the formulation of hypotheses suggested by such a study, and the careful scrutinizing of the rest of history in order to correct the suggested hypotheses. Or courses might be organized around an ordered sequence of established generalizations illustrated and supported by historical data. The comparative study of two or more segments of history appears to be another possible approach.

In any case, the learning of particular facts, events, dates, names, and the like is distinctly incidental to learning generalizations, testing hypotheses, practicing correct application of logical processes, and so forth. Items of historical information are useful only when they can serve as data, and they are to be remembered primarily as exemplars. . . .

Attempts to pattern history after the physical sciences have not gone unanswered. Because the formulation of a theory of explanation has been fundamental to the entire debate, the respondents have devoted a major portion of their effort to clarifying their position with regard to explanation schema. As might be expected, there is much less commonality in point of view among the opponents than among the advocates of the deductive model, and the differences among them are certainly not insignificant. It is possible to situate these several theories on a continuum, placing the deductive model in ideal form at one extreme and perhaps "history as an unrelated series of absolutely unique events" at the other. This task is a worthy one but not essential to our present purpose. . . .

While there is wide diversity in the [scholars'] viewpoints . . . they have in common a rejection of the notion that history is a struggling science which must develop or use a theoretical framework of universal laws in order for sense to be made of the past. On the positive side, these theories of explanation suggest at least three elements that can be considered crucial to the teaching and learning of history as a nonscience—the importance of knowing the past as intimately as possible while approaching it primarily as a fascinating narrative, the cultivation of the student's imagination, and the learning of those special skills associated with the proper use of source materials. . . .

The charge to the teacher and curriculum maker is quite clear. Students should learn all they can of the past. This may mean teaching some survey courses but the emphasis must be on detailed study of as much of the past as time permits. There is no substitute for knowledge of individual events in all their complexity and uniqueness. Because little generalization is possible and comparative studies are of limited value, each nation, each age, each event must be examined in order to be comprehended. In classroom terms this implies emphasis on extensive reading in primary and secondary sources and stress on factual recall in recitations and testing.

This experience of immersion in the stream of the past will eventually produce within the student a "sense of history" as a gradual accretion to his understanding. Students ought to be fascinated by the story of the past rather than primarily concerned for its present meaning or the inferences they might draw as to cause-effect relationships. These may come through prolonged association with history, but there is little to be gained from direct attempts to formulate generalizations, make comparisons, and apply formal logic. The emphasis is on what happened, particularly for the novice. The sequence and the organization of content in the history curriculum has been determined, for the past has written its own story in a particular order which can only be distorted by attempting to tamper with it. The teaching function is primarily one of telling the story as clearly and accurately as possible. . . .

The technical apparatus developed for the examination and verification of sources aids students and scholars as they attempt to reconstruct the past. An elementary acquaintance with these techniques might be introduced in the public schools, but they are useful primarily to the researcher who has already spent many years acquiring historical information and developing his sensitivity to things historical.

CONCLUSION

It seems clear that classroom A, conducted by a teacher convinced that history is a science, and classroom B, conducted by a teacher of the idealist or some other contrasting persuasion, will be filled with quite different experiences for the students. This is not to say, of course, that there will not be many common activities and learnings in any two such classrooms. It is difficult to imagine any history teacher of whatever persuasion denying the importance of historical data and a knowledge of the past. And any intellectual undertaking worthy of the name calls for the exercise of imagination and the use of logical patterns of thought. But if courses of study were organized in accordance with each of these theories of historical explanation, the impact on the student of the total school experience with history would certainly be markedly different. Students would not only learn quite different bodies of subject matter, but, more significantly, their approach to and judgments about the past and the present would also tend to be different. That these judgments will help determine the future of the society appears to be beyond reasonable doubt.

It may be suggested that many teachers of history do not claim to be idealists, scientists, or anything else that might classify them according to the explanation model they follow in their teaching. This is precisely the situation to which this paper is addressed. If, as was ventured at the outset, what students learn about social dynamics is one of the essential contributions history can make to their citizenship training, then it is imperative that teachers be conscious of the ideas they are fostering in this regard.

It was stated earlier that historical study involves two primary tasks—one is descriptive, the other explanatory. Both are necessary but neither is sufficient. Social studies teachers in general and history teachers in particular are usually well prepared to carry out descriptive activities. But if the teacher stops at this point and fails to analyze the *how* and the *why* of the temporal sequences, he is mistaking the initial task for the actual problem. No understanding of causation can come from a mere descriptive statement of sequence.

It appears to this writer that the teaching-learning process which is appropriate for the view of history as essentially an interesting account of the human race in action offers little chance for students to gain an understanding of social dynamics. And it is this view of history which seems to be most prevalent in the schools today. For one thing, the exposure to history provided by the common schools is necessarily too brief and sporadic for the student to achieve the almost mystical "sense of the past" that is the final goal of such historical study. Because he is left largely to his own devices when it comes to explaining why things have occurred as they have, it is likely that he will apply the folklore current in his particular social milieu. He must either accept the fact that things just happen and that is the end of the matter, or he must use the explanatory tools he has learned from parents, friends, and his own experience. A large share of these "common sense" notions are the very ones social scientists have repeatedly shown to be fallacious.

More fundamentally, of course, the issue of which view of historical explanation the teacher accepts resides in the choice between two rival views of social study traditionally held by social scientists and historians, i.e., whether or not social phenomena are susceptible to generalization, causal analysis, and prediction. This is not the place to review this continuing battle. Both positions have their difficulties. What I have tried to suggest is that, beyond the standard arguments for either view, it is worthwhile and revealing to consider the issue from the standpoint of the student, the teaching-learning process, and, ultimately, the effect on society.

(1) Carl Hempel, "The Function of General Laws in History," *The Journal of Philosophy*, XXXIX (January 2, 1942), 35–48.
(2) Sidney Hook and Charles Beard have dealt with this problem in *Theory and Practice in Historical Study* (Social Science Research Council, Bulletin No. 54, New York, 1946), Chapter 4.

FRONTAL ATTACK ON PRE-CANNED HISTORY

Van R. Halsey, Jr.

Secondary school history courses are clearly moving in the direction of inquiry involving original source material. Such an inductive approach calls for reconsideration of purposes, values, nature, content, and method of history courses. The author of this selection describes a purposeful and intensive effort to incorporate the new approach in an American history course at the senior high level. This effort exemplifies the significance of a variety of current curriculum projects in social studies that are now underway, discussed more fully in Part Six of this volume.

CALLING itself The Committee on the Study of History, a diverse group of school and college history teachers has been experimenting since 1960 with the teaching of United States History in the secondary school. Recently awarded a three-year contract by the U.S. Office of Education, our Committee now plans to expand its work. This is not a project in curriculum revision, as such. It is an experiment with a particular method of teaching history over a wide spectrum of ability and achievement levels. Our Committee will not confine itself to research in a particular school system. Trial of the units will take place in a variety of private and public schools across the country. . . .

The Committee's prime assumption is that the essence of the study of history is inquiry, rather than the mastery of a series of facts or "answers"; that in order to contribute to the maturation of the student's intellectual powers, the study of history must be relevant to his own concerns. We are not seeking to train a cadre of junior historians, but we believe that only if the student is allowed to be a historian for a while, can he get some sense of the point of studying history. As Professor Jerome Bruner puts it in *The Process of Education:*

FROM the *New England Social Studies Bulletin*, 22:15–20, May, 1965. Used by permission. Dr. Halsey is a professor of American Studies and an associate dean at Amherst College.

The schoolboy learning physics *is* a physicist, and it is easier for him to learn physics behaving like a physicist than doing something else. The "something else" usually involves the task of mastering . . . a "middle language"—classroom discussions and textbooks that talk about the conclusions in a field of intellectual inquiry rather than centering upon the inquiry itself. Approached in that way, high school physics often looks very little like physics, social studies are removed from the issues of life and society as usually discussed, and school mathematics too often has lost contact with what is at the heart of the subject, the idea of order.

Nowhere more than in the study of history—where the genuine laboratory course is largely unknown—does the "middle language" obscure goals and kill the motivation to learn.

The Committee is experimenting with a series of units designed for approximately two weeks of study which present the student with original historical evidence and ask him to come to his own conclusions. The units are designed for use, either as supplementary material in a course, or as a history course in themselves. They differ not only in subject matter, but in type of subject matter. Some will deal with particular historical incidents, some with topics and some with periods of time in American History. They vary in the approach to the subject, too. In some units the student starts with a hypothesis, while in others he starts with no hypothesis at all, but only with a body of evidence on which he seeks to impose some order.

So far, the units produced by the Committee for experiment have the following common characteristics: (1) All are constructed primarily out of source materials, with author's introductions and secondary accounts held to a minimum. We want the student to grapple with the original evidence of history, relatively free—at least until he has developed some of his own conclusions—of either the authority or the temptation to pick up "easy answers" which come from reading what someone else has to say about the evidence. (2) All are consciously structured so the student may have the opportunity to ask related questions of different documents, and to develop and explore hypotheses as he moves on to further evidence. (3) All subscribe to the post-hole approach. (4) There is an effort in all the units to get the student to see the universals which are present in the particular human events he is investigating. (5) A considerable amount of writing is involved in all the units. Usually short papers are requested about sharply pointed questions. The point of this is to make use of the discipline of writing to get the student to engage his mind in the subject, to commit himself, and to come to appreciate the importance of exactness. (6) A teacher's manual, a few pages in length, is included as an integral part of each unit. Here the author states the central points of the unit as he sees them, summarizes the important readings, gives his reasons for putting them in this particular order, and suggests a number of relevant questions to be asked and papers to be written. (7) All the units include at the end several interpretations of the subject at hand by recent historians. However, the primary emphasis is on source material rather than historiographical conflict in order to avoid "either/or formula" in which the student only has a choice of "right" answers.

This sketchy outline only describes the bare bones. Our central concerns are related to how history is taught and how it is best learned. We are convinced that the coverage or survey type of history course does not answer the needs of today's students. We are not proposing, however, to replace it with an in depth or post-hole approach that treats the material in exactly the same old way. We do not mean to exchange a half-page canned textbook explanation of civil rights cases for a week long study of reprints of court cases and some chapters from Myrdal and Baldwin and call this a new approach. For it would be the same old approach if all the students were asked for was a textual analysis on which they were then to be tested.

Most of our effort in the past four years has been in working out the American History units for the eleventh grade. It is difficult to evaluate their effectiveness, at the moment, because only five of them have been published. Until there is a significant number of these units, they can only be used as supplementary material. We do not know how effective they would be if a teacher were to use twelve or thirteen of these units in one year with a narrative of American History as supplementary reading. So far, our experience indicates that although these units have been designed for the college preparatory students, groups of average ability can also handle them.

The Committee is very much concerned with the problem of how these units may be most effectively taught. Heretofore, our limited resources have meant that we have simply mailed our sample units for trial in a scattering of schools; leaving the presentation of the material up to the local teacher and counting on the teacher's manual provided to give any necessary directions. This summer we plan to bring the teachers who are trying our material to Amherst in order to take them through a sample unit and discuss teaching strategy.

The Committee has one junior high school American History unit in progress at the moment. Its emphasis is on skills in the social studies and it is designed for eighth and ninth grade. Our rationale for preparing this unit is that the majority of school systems teach an American History course at the junior high level, although there is increasing discussion over whether or not a solid American History course ought to be postponed. Our experiment in this area should help to answer the question of whether eighth or ninth graders can profitably talk about concepts and structure in the discipline of history. Since most school systems do not group their junior high school students by ability, we need to find out whether these units will be successful in a classroom with wide ranging ability levels.

Perhaps the most challenging assignment that the Committee has taken on is to experiment with classroom materials for that large group of students variously known as the "track four group," "the basic studies group," "the terminal student," or the "potential dropout." Many of these youngsters resent the school and the teachers. Most of them have reading problems. Many of them are emotionally disturbed. Some of them are highly intelligent, but find themselves alienated from the society within which they are forced to operate. Typically, the material given to these students for study is either a watered down "Dick and Jane" type history book, or it is a workbook which, while the reading assignments may be comprehensible, has no relevance for the student. Can one teach history in a verbal format to this heterogeneous group? Does the course have to be an interdisciplinary humanities course? How much visual material should be used? These are just some of the questions that the Committee will be struggling with in the next year or so.

As everyone is aware, there is a curriculum revolution going on in the secondary schools in every field. Now it is becoming evident that whether one talks about the "new mathematics," PSSC Physics, history or almost any other subject, all these projects have certain common features. The words and phrases that seem to be used most often are structure, concepts, inquiry rather than mastery of facts, active participation rather than passive ingestion, original sources rather than predigested opinions, inductive learning, relevancy. Modern mathematics stresses the principles of multiplication rather than learning the multiplication tables by rote. In science, the student must now design his own lab experiment and reason out his conclusions rather than filling blanks in the lab manual. The art teacher encourages his students to think about differences in color, composition and movement rather than defining for the student the difference between classic and romantic art. The same process is going on in all other fields. The idea of coverage and of the teacher as information giver is slowly being replaced by the notion that students must be active participants in the learning process and that the teacher's role is becoming one of Socratic questioner.

The implications of this change in pedagogy in the secondary schools will be felt soon enough by the colleges. Most secondary school teachers are teachers of history first and historians second, while most college teachers are historians first and teachers second. This dichotomy has been the cause of much misunderstanding between secondary school teachers in front of a classroom and college professors who are designing new curricula for them. Depending on the curriculum builder's notion of what a classroom teacher ought to emphasize, the temptation is to design a "teacher proof" course; one in which every step and every question is outlined in an accompanying manual. Undoubtedly these will be a boon to some teachers, but to others these packaged courses are seen as a threat to their own creativity. The original intention of our Committee was to produce a course in American History that could be transplanted whole into a given classroom. We now believe this would be an unwise procedure. We plan instead to experiment with a variety of material with maximum flexibility.

A related problem, caused in part by the necessary dominance of subject matter specialists in curriculum design, is beautifully illustrated by John Holt in *How Children Fail*:

The more aware we are of the structural nature of our own ideas, the more we are tempted to try to transplant this structure whole into the minds of children. But it cannot be done. They must do this structuring and building for themselves. I may see that fact A and fact B are connected by a relationship C, but I can't make this connection for a child by talking about it.

Our Committee will experiment with various devices to encourage the student to do his own structuring and building; make his own generalizations and conclusions, rather than giving him the generalization or concept at the beginning.

Of crucial importance is the style of teaching implied by the new curricular proposals and by our history materials in particular. What is wanted here is a classroom situation characterized by flexibility, an ability on the part of the teacher to plead ignorance on occasion, more difficult preparation for each class, and a much insecure and highly charged air. Is this a realistic possibility? A seeming need for teacher security and status, and a social dynamics of the school which emphasizes medication rather than conflict makes us skeptical of any wholesale adoption of these new curriculum materials. Teachers will be urged to shift from a direct to an indirect style of teaching. One style (the old style?) is that in which the teacher asks almost all the questions, answers the student's questions, passes judgment, makes evaluations, and raises the critical points. The indirect style will be just the opposite of this. Students will suggest hypotheses, question one another. There will be periods of silence and periods of vigorous and confusing debate over interpretation of data. The Committee wants to investigate these opposing teaching styles to see whether there is a maximum tolerance for indirect teaching. What kind of training and what sorts of materials make for the most effective indirect style? We plan to combine summer writing sessions, briefing sessions for teachers, and closely supervised trial situations in the schools in a three-year effort to learn the answers to some of these perplexing questions.

THE FUTURE OF
HISTORY IN THE SCHOOLS

William H. Cartwright

A long-standing emphasis on history in secondary social studies may mislead the unwary or ill-informed to presume indiscriminately that the subject's future is assured. But a well-known specialist on the teaching of history detects weaknesses in such thoughtless presumption. Here he explains why he regards history's place in the social studies as dependent on improved instruction. Improvement is necessary to elicit the public support that will maintain a significant role for history in the schools. Portions of the original article are omitted here.

THERE is some effort these days to substitute the label "history and the social sciences," as more precise, for the label "social studies." The only difference I see in the terms is that of length. Yet, length of titles in America is important. We are a people in a hurry. Many high school freshmen in America study something called "civics." The authorities in the school I attended wanted a more precise label and called it "Community Life and Civic Problems." We students called it "CLP" when we were in a hurry. Otherwise we called it by more opprobrious terms. I once was required to teach a twelfth-grade course under the pretentious title "An Introduction to the Social Sciences." Like my ninth-grade teacher, I carefully explained the meaning and significance of the title to my students. But I am afraid that the explanation did not take. They called it "sock sigh" in my presence. I don't know what they called it when they had time and inclination to take a deep breath first. At least the term "social studies" has the virtues of meaning and brevity. They are the school subjects that deal with society. I would hate to see our field join the American alphabetical soup as "HSS" or something worse.

I am concerned about the future status of history in the schools. There are several dangers to it. The greatest comes from the fact that the whole social studies field has been largely overlooked in the post-Sputnik curricular reaction. That more students should do more and more effective study of the sciences, mathematics, and foreign languages can hardly be disputed. But we must bring about that situation as part of a broad upgrading of education all along the line. If we do otherwise, we may gain the world but only at the loss of our soul.

FROM "Clio: A Muse Bemused," *Indiana Magazine of History.* 59:122–130, June, 1963. Used by permission. Dr. Cartwright is a professor of education at Duke University.

There is also a danger from the new interest which our sister disciplines are showing in the school curriculum. History has lost ground to other social sciences in the past half-century. Fifty years ago, a four-year high school program in the social studies was at least seven-eighths history. Today it is typically half history and often is even less. When I look at all the demands on the high school, I really do not believe that we can expect to have more than two years of history required of all students. The other social sciences do have much to contribute to the education of citizens. And fields other than the social studies are vital too.

But, as a matter of fact, we never gained a two-year requirement in history in this country. The history program of fifty years ago was largely elective. My worry is that history may be losing ground instead of gaining it today, and not only to science, mathematics, and foreign language. Through most of the past seventy years, and especially during the twenty years following 1892, the historians exerted great influence on the social studies curriculum. No learned society in the other social sciences had anything like the influence of the American Historical Association. But I am not at all certain that this situation will continue. All of our sister disciplines are seeking a place in the curriculum. The economists are well on the road; the political scientists, the geographers, the sociologists, even the anthropologists, have committees at work considering the relationship of their disciplines to school programs.

Do not misunderstand me. As a professional educator I welcome the long overdue interest of academic scholars, especially social scientists, in the world of the schools. I only wonder whether the historians are sufficiently concerned to hold their own. It is not that the historians have shown no interest in recent years. Indeed, it might be argued that they have shown more interest in the past decade than in any previous one. . . .

With increasing help from historians, we will do a better job of instruction. But how much history will there be to teach? The scholars in other fields are campaigning for school programs that will give more emphasis to their subjects. Do historians need to campaign also? I think so. Historians with whom I talk seem reconciled to settling for the two years of history we think we have. But they seem to feel that those two years are not in danger, that the weight of tradition and the force of public opinion will preserve them. There is much reason to hold this belief with regard to the traditional year of high school American history. If the schools should decide to give that up, the legislatures would not allow it. But I suspect that the current pressures for anti-Communist education will, by requiring teachers to spend long periods of time on a topic which should already pervade the curriculum, take more time away from the study of American history than they give to it. And I keep hearing recommendations that we might well give up the junior high school course in American history because we have too many cycles of the subject.

Granted that the year of high school American history is relatively safe. The world history course is in no such secure position. It never became a uniform requirement across the country. Some schools recently have substituted world geography for it, or made world geography an alternate elective. The recent mandate in Pennsylvania that all high school students must devote at least a semester to the study of world cultures may be a portent of the future. And I have not found anyone who yet knows the ultimate content of a course in world cultures. I find little reason to believe that it will be a world history course. But it may become a substitute for the world history course and thereby displace more history than it will provide.

One trouble is that there is general dissatisfaction with a world history course that attempts to cover in one year everything from Pithecanthropus to Souvanna Phouma. At the same time, there is no agreement on what is needed for improvement. We hear a lot of talk about "sinking postholes and stringing a few wires between them." (To an old farmer the idea of stringing wires between postholes seems odd. It is probably one of the results of urbanization.) But we cannot go on adding to a course which is already impossible to teach, and it would be better to teach some parts well than to have a comprehensive but superficial course.

We badly need a study of the world history course, but we also need a campaign for history instruction. Over the main entrance to the library at the University of Colorado are the words, "Enter here the timeless fellowship of the human spirit." There used to be a card by that entrance that read, "When the winds blow and the weather turns cold, please enter the timeless fellowship of the human spirit by the side door." I hope that we do not find history entering by the side door before we recognize the change in the weather.

If we are to have a campaign for history instruction, it will have to be conducted in terms that the American public will understand and support. It will have to be in terms of the usefulness of history to the citizen. Other reasons for studying history are valid, but they will not persuade the American people that history should be required in the schools. . . . Studying and writing history should be enjoyable. But they are worth doing even when they are tedious, as they are bound to be sometimes. It is all very well to . . . study history for the fun of it—if you can make an honest living some other way or if you can find a patron. But the patron of the schools of America is the American public. And I expect that it will not be very generous in its support of school subjects unless it is convinced that they have values beyond the provision of pleasure. History has gained the place that it has in the schools because the American people have considered it necessary to loyal and enlightened citizenship. It will keep, gain, or lose ground there as that belief is maintained, strengthened, or weakened.

The kinds of behavior required of a free people are intellectual in nature. They cannot be brought about by fiat or in the absence of intellectual considerations. Success in carrying them out will depend upon the *knowledge* which the citizen possesses, the *skill* of the citizenry in applying that knowledge, and the *power* of the citizenry to obtain and apply such additional knowledge as is required to meet specific situations. It is toward these ends that the teachers of history must strive.

In the striving, we must put the main emphasis on knowledge and on skill in getting and using knowledge. By this statement I do not mean that we must restore or maintain the traditional ways of teaching traditional subjects. I *believe* in teaching these subjects. They are, as Newton Edwards says, "the funded capital of human experience." Only by wise investment of that capital can we hope for a reasonable return. And, too often, we do not make wise investments.

To be specific, school history is too often an almost meaningless assemblage of the names of persons, states, and civilizations, dates and events, and routes of travel and military campaigns. These items are necessary for instruction in history, but the real content of history has to do with *people* who "lived and felt and had their being." It must treat of how they met and solved, or failed to solve, their many problems. How did they overcome, adjust to, or become overwhelmed by the physical characteristics of the regions in which they lived? How did they force nature to yield its riches, exploit these riches while yet conserving them, or lose the material basis of their society through failure to conserve? How, in modern times, has the dizzying pace of the acceleration of material progress become one of mankind's greatest problems, and what subproblems does that acceleration pose? What ways have men tried for organizing their economic activity, and how well have they succeeded? What systems have been developed for governing people and with what success? Under what conditions has human liberty thriven or succumbed? How have men learned to work together peaceably to their mutual advantage? What causes have led them to conflict, and what means have they employed to eliminate conflict or its causes? How have civilizations developed? What institutions have civilizations found necessary to their existence and strengthening? What forms have these institutions taken and what successes or failures have they had? What personal and societal values have people developed as guides to their activities? What means have people taken to bring up their young so as to preserve and enlarge their heritage? Such questions as these and the search for their answers are the stuff of school history. And in the course of their consideration our students must learn, to some degree at least, how the historian works to find out the answers.

Geography

WHAT GEOGRAPHY IS AND IS NOT

Preston E. James

A number of authorities agree that poor instruction is a major reason for geography's limited role in secondary school social studies. As seen by the geographer who authored this article, inadequacy in the teaching of geography derives significantly from the lack of a full and deep conception of the basic nature of the discipline. Here he explains, both positively and negatively, what geography fundamentally involves. See also Kennamer's article, page 332.

WHAT GEOGRAPHY IS AND IS NOT

G EOGRAPHY is that field of learning in which the characteristics of particular places on the earth's surface are examined. It is concerned with the arrangement of things and with the associations of things that distinguish one area from another. It is concerned with the connections and movements between areas. The face of the earth is made up of many different kinds of features, each the momentary result of an ongoing process. There are physical and chemical processes developing the forms of the land, the shapes of the ocean basins, the differing characteristics of water, soil, and climate. There are biotic processes by which the plants and animals spread over the earth in complex areal relation to the physical features and to each other. And there are the economic, social, and political processes by which mankind occupies the world's lands.

As a result of all these processes the face of the earth is marked off into distinctive areas; geography seeks to describe and interpret the significance of likenesses and differences among places in terms of causes and consequences. Geography makes use of the concepts developed by the behavioral sciences, but it examines these concepts not as they work in isolation, where

FROM "Geography" by Preston E. James in *The Social Studies and the Social Sciences* by The American Council of Learned Societies and National Council for the Social Studies, © 1962, by Harcourt, Brace & World, Inc. and reprinted with their permission. Dr. James is a professor of geography at Syracuse University.

"other things are equal," but as they work in the context of particular places on the earth. Geography makes use of the perspective of history, but it does so by recreating past geographies and tracing geographic changes through time—which is not history. Geography must make a selection of features and processes to use in building up a knowledge of area that is relevant to the basic purposes of formal education—promoting curiosity, predisposing the pupil to accept the rules of evidence and logical thought, and providing training in the techniques of communication. One of the special and distinctive techniques of communication provided by geography is through the language of the map.

Geography is not restricted to the study of the relation of man to his physical and biotic environment. This idea developed in nineteenth-century Germany at a time when the physical sciences were developing rapidly but when the sciences dealing with man were stilll rudimentary. Friedrich Ratzel attempted to bring the treatment of man into line with the treatment of physical features. In the first volume of his *Anthropogeographie* (1882 and 1899) he organized his material in terms of the natural conditions of the earth, in relation to which he examined the cultural features. In the second volume (1891 and 1912) he did the opposite, organizing his material in terms of the human culture, in relation to which he examined the physical features of the earth. Although Ratzel did formulate certain concepts regarding the relation of man to his habitat (physical and biotic environment), he was thoroughly in sympathy with the tradition of Alexander von Humboldt and Carl Ritter. He never lost sight of the need for direct observation of all relevant elements of a situation. Thus, in his classic volume on *Deutschland* he pointed out that two physically similar areas, the Black Forest and the Vosges Mountains, had developed in quite different ways because of the differences in economy and historical tradition.

Some of Ratzel's disciples were not so careful to observe all the relevant interrelated phenomena. Especially those who were trained chiefly in physical geography insisted that a geographic analysis must show a relationship that crossed the border between physical and human phenomena, thus leading to neglect of the relationships on the same side of the border—for example, the relation of language to economic system, or economic system to law. Few geographers ever subscribed to such extreme forms of environmental determinism as suggested by the historian H. T. Buckle and others; but many went forth deliberately to find examples of environmental influence on human activities, and many remained blind to contrary evidence. As a result geography was divided into physical geography (a well-developed field of science) and human geography (a relatively superficial treatment of man's relation to the physical earth). The adjective *geographic* came to refer to the physical character of an area. Thus a "geographic factor" was some condition of the physical environment to which human activities were to be related as "responses" or "adjustments."

Geography as the "science of man-land relationships" persisted longer in the English-speaking world than elsewhere. It found few adherents in Germany, where Alfred Hettner was developing the ideas associated with the main stream of geographic thought. It was effectively attacked by the French master, Paul Vidal de la Blache and by those who followed him. But it was given persuasive support in Great Britain and the United States. The American scholars who developed this theme included William Morris Davis, Ellen Churchill Semple, Wallace W. Atwood, Ellsworth Huntington, Robert DeC. Ward, R. H. Whitbeck, and others. One of the critical problems to be faced in promoting the use of modern geographic concepts in the schools is that so many of the teachers have derived their geographic learning either directly or indirectly from these American exponents of environmentalism. In spite of the vigorous efforts of professional geographers over the past thirty-five years or so to disclaim this deviation from the traditional direction of geographic thought, there are still many teachers and many scholars in other social science fields for whom the adjective *geographic* refers to the physical environment exclusively.

Let us be clear about this. Modern geography does not neglect the treatment of the spatial distribution of the physical and biotic features of the earth as the home of man. In fact, geographers insist on the essential importance of considering human activities in their areal association with the features of the habitat—the resource base. But modern geographers insist on the principle that the significance to man of the physical and biotic features of the earth is a function of the attitudes, objectives, technical skills, and other aspects of the culture of man himself. In other words, the physical environment has different meaning for different groups of people, or for the same group at different stages of development. They insist, also, that geography examines the relationships not only between man and his habitat, but also between man and the various cultural features resulting from economic, social, or political processes. With each change in the culture of a people the meaning of the habitat must be re-evaluated. Geography cannot be divided into physical geography and human geography for separate treatment; and a geographic factor is any phenomenon that—being irregularly distributed over the earth—contributes to the differentiation of the earth's surface.

SUGGESTED GUIDELINES TO THE
CONTENT OF GEOGRAPHY
IN SECONDARY SCHOOLS

Henry J. Warman

It may be granted that geography should receive considerable attention in secondary social studies. It needs also to be recognized that the subject is so broad as to render impractical any serious attempt to cover it adequately. What, then, should be emphasized in teaching geography? Here, a specialist discusses two of the most needed emphases: the concept of culture areas and the essentiality of mapping in geography. The original article suggests stressing also three additional geographic elements.

NO GEOGRAPHER would expect that one unit, one book, or one course could finish the task which has been initiated in the present day surge toward studying the people of the world in such subdivisions as "culture worlds" or "culture regions." A perusal of the public school curriculum today will reveal that at only one grade level, the fourth, where "journey geography" is taught, are our children "introduced" quite deliberately to people and their cultures in truly physical and to a large extent man-made environments. The number of families studied is few and the areal extent of their geographic "regions" are both infinitesimal when compared with the "cultural regions" presently being suggested for the secondary school.

Nevertheless, it seems logical to propose that the high school would be the ideal place for a second cycle in the study of the previously neglected cultural patterns. This proposal is emphasized and sharpened by two questions. Are we in the United States to presume that the smattering of vignettes about family life (Ahmad in the Desert, Nanook of the North, Togo of the Jungle, Wan Li of the Yellow River and such stories, delightful as they may be) studied in elementary school is sufficient background for dealing with the people and problems of the Near East and the Sahara (or the Dry World as it is now labelled), Africa south of the Sahara, the Two Chinas, Union of Soviet Socialist Republics, or the Arctic World? (1) The second question, or group of related questions, strike more close to home. In blocking off the world into "culture areas" a standard procedure is to set up "Anglo-America" as one of them. Just what are the developments and/or elements that characterize our "culture?" How are they related to the physical land

FROM *The Social Studies*, 54:207–211, November 1963. Used by permission. Dr. Warman is a professor of geography at Clark University in Massachusetts.

base? What are the forces which Americans have harnessed, where are they, and how have they contributed to the great advances made? How have the great principles of democracy been used (or abused) in populating our land, creating settlements large and small, utilizing the vast resources and controlling them on the American scene? Do we know ourselves?

Since the United States has been dealt with in some sort of geographic way previously, and usually at the fifth-grade level, it seems that a reappraisal of the human, cultural and physical assets can well be made in starting so-called "culture area" work in the high school. The United States in its world relations thus gets studied in a revitalized manner and becomes a basis for moving to other large culture areas, regions, and subregions. (2)

Howard R. Anderson in the first chapter of the Twenty-fifth Yearbook of the National Council for the Social Studies presents a very strong case for obtaining a clear understanding of one's own culture before attempting to evaluate the way of life in a foreign land. He puts it this way: (3)

"It has been said that if one wishes to know others he must first know himself. Americans need to study themselves and their history to understand better the important and persistent issues and problems with which people of this country have had to deal. They need to know how Americans have coped with these issues and problems at various periods in their history. They need to study the institutions which Americans have created to serve their needs, to sense how these institutions have evolved, and to assess how well they work. Through such analysis of their own history and culture Americans will grasp the great truth that institutions reflect the heritage of a people, are adapted to the *total environment*, (4) and are modified to meet new situations, (5) . . . (and) will be in a better position to understand why other people with a different heritage and a different environment may have developed institutions and ways of coping with persistent issues and problems which differ radically from their own."

What to look for as relevant criteria in the various culture regions becomes a pressing problem. One must be careful to select meaningful phenomena. Walter Isard in his recent book proposes certain culture values, or Goals of Culture groups. (6) These may assist educators in formulating a system and subsystems for the study of culture regions. Under the heading of desired political goals, Isard lists (1) liberty and (2) equality. Under the major heading of social goals are listed (1) full development and education of the individual and (2) high level of individual and group stability and responsiveness, and of community spirit. Under the final major heading, economic goals, we find (1) high level of productivity (and efficiency) improving a sustained rate of growth, (2) equitable income distribution, and (3) cyclical stability.

While it seems to the writer that all culture groups cannot be appraised by using the above measuring sticks, it is nevertheless, clear that land, labor, capital, governmental systems, behaviors and attitudes of people, and locational efficiency (as suggested by Isard) can be used to epitomize culture regions, their folk, and their distribution, as the components vary over the earth's surface. (7) One needs, of course, to see more and more clearly the transmitters of the culture in their particular roles—families, religions, languages and those "intangibles of customs, habits, traditions."

One of the social studies' most important aims is that of enabling students to make intelligent decisions. In aspiring to make the fullest use of any geographic region, be it as small as one's back yard or as large as the biggest "culture world," men must be informed about the functions and/or the restraints which nature and society impose. What are the elements at hand, and what are the limits of choice? What is to be accepted and what is to be rejected? Geographic analysis, then synthesis, and finally prognostication for and in regions may be, indeed, should be, introduced at the high school level. The rigorous discipline of thinking through certain regional projects affords an early training in research. Such training reveals that there are but few easy answers to man's multiple problems throughout the world, and that meetings of the well trained and best educated—no matter what their color, race or creed—are essential to "rub up each other's wits" with the hope that solutions will come, even though at a distressingly slow pace.

At the conclusion of "culture area" studies careful consideration may be given to those world organizations, such as the United Nations, which struggle with the human problems world wide. Geography teachers specifically and other social studies teachers as well can develop an appreciation of the difficulties of working with these problems of long standing. "A sense of perspective is one of the most difficult qualities to develop. Without it there is the danger of a feeling of frustration and disillusion." (8)

If any phase of geography can "liberate the mind," free it, really let it go, it is in the modern trend of blocking off the world into "culture areas." One may be prompted to ask why such culture area studies were not attempted before. A part of the answer is that "there is no stopping an idea whose time has come." Two dreadful wars in the first half of this century, both worldwide in scope, the threat of total annihilation associated with new power resources, increased awareness of our world through new communication and transportation media, the actual increase of firsthand knowledge by world travelers, and last, but not least, the concern of all scientists, natural as well as social, expressed in their writings, seminars, and actions for the answer to the question, "What are people for?"—these seem to be the reasons for urging a re-evaluation of mankind and his world habitat.

The preparation of teachers to carry out the "new" becomes a monumental task. It will not be done any faster than the time needed to switch to the metric system. Advocates of this change indicate the sensible arrangement of our currency, in multiples of ten, and then contrast it with our inches, feet, yards, rods, acres, pounds, tons, quarts, bushels, etc. The advocates of a change in these measurements say a generation will be the minimum time needed. In the social sciences too, we should not forget that the large reservoirs from which we shall draw tomorrow's teachers of geography and social studies, in fact of all subjects, are now before us in our secondary schools. But if we pose for our social science classes today the many challenges growing out of the four guidelines already presented and the fifth one which is to be treated in succeeding paragraphs, there ought to be a strong flow of well-informed, and of gifted (since we are not striving for mediocrity) social scientists in the future.

CORE DEVICES ESSENTIAL TO LEARNING AND EXPRESSING GEOGRAPHIC CONTENT AND IDEAS

It would be *almost* ideal if all students of geography could visit those parts of the earth which they have under study. The word *almost* is used intentionally because the full significance of geography, and certainly of social studies, would not be achieved by the visits only. While an intimate, real picture of the parts observed could be obtained the scale of the area naturally would be restricted to the eyes' range. In addition to this are the more serious limitations that patterns, the correlation of those patterns, and the interpretation thereof would be extremely difficult if not impossible. The most serious shortcoming is apparent, however, when we think of the twin dimensions in which we need to see our world—*areal association and time sequence.*

Geography begins in the field and ends in the field. The beginning is made by leading very young children to observe with purpose that which is around. (9) The end is reached when the well-trained geographer contributes the up-to-date information he has been able to glean on his most recent field trip.

While maps of previously little-known areas are a constantly welcomed delight to laymen as well as geographers, there must be new maps of the *same* areas drawn at fairly regular intervals. The upgrading and updating of the distribution and qualities of pertinent resources, human, cultural, and physical, have been regarded as the responsibilities of cartographers, and cartography always has been the core technique of geography. If it is true that "the photo is a one-eyed man in the kingdom of the word" then the map may be regarded as supplying this one-eyed man with a telescopic lens to broaden and lengthen his insight into the past and present kingdoms of the outdoors.

An impending danger lurks in the recent trend of dealing with geography and history by the regional framework of culture areas. It is that teachers may become so engrossed in the word treatment of cultural attributes of the present selected areas that they may overlook the fact that "in each era the inhabitants of any land have appraised it through their own culture filter and have transformed their surroundings to fit their needs." (10) The transformation through time is quite often recorded most accurately and portrayed most vividly in a map sequence. (11) The "life-motif," or as others have put it, the personality of a region may be gleaned in large part from the study and restudy aligning and realigning, imposing, superimposing and even supposing) map details. Such procedures should not be a quick perusal but a controlled one, as though the interpreter were to be required to take action upon what he is learning. Map analysis and map synthesis call for more than mere location. They imply that a place be associated with all the significant attributes thereof. Throughout the geography curriculum, especially in that phase which calls for an increasing competency in globe and map use, there are two responsibilities placed upon the teachers. One is the search for future cartographers, for those youths with a technical background in mathematics, the patience to draw and redraw, and a flair for the creative. Who will be the teacher of the youth who will create the skyway maps of the future? The other responsibility is to recognize that there is a sequential sense to map use, based upon the ability of the learners at various stages, the materials being taught at those stages, not only in geography but in the other social sciences, natural sciences and in mathematics as well.

There is a wealth of material upon which to draw for information regarding specific map learnings and techniques. (12) On the other hand there is relatively little material on the gradation of map concepts, map skills, and map use. Unfortunately, and much too frequently, the same map is used in grades covering a spread of as much as *eight*. Such a situation indicates that one of the greatest forward thrusts which can be made by geography as it performs its role in the social studies is to revitalize the map programs. Such revitalizing can be accomplished by a three-pronged understanding. First, there must be an inventory of what is available. Just a cursory glance at the map and globe companies' contributions will bring out the significant fact that the supplies exceed the demands. The excess is not confined to mere quantity; the quality of the maps in the storerooms and on the display racks of the map makers is vastly superior to most being used in the classrooms. (13) Second, and of much more importance than the mere inventory, is the gradation of maps and globes throughout the curriculum. Just what maps should be available at a definite grade? What maps should be used to bridge from one grade to the next? In other words, what is an ideal *vertically* interlocked map program for a school system? The third prong of the undertaking is peculiarly marked with a social studies stamp for it calls for both appraisals and suggestions regarding the *horizontal interlocking* of a map program with the learnings sought in the related social science subjects.

However, the interlocking goes beyond these limits since the very nature of geography demands that the natural science subjects and mathematics be drawn upon also, if the map and globe program throughout the curriculum is to embody study of systematic patterns (temperature, precipitation, pressure, soils, vegetation and the like), as well as cultural features (agriculture, manufacturing, transportation, language, religion, income, health, literacy and the like) and, not least, to develop cartographic skill. Any committees constituted to make this three-pronged thrust will necessitate careful selection on the part of the persons doing the appointing for these committee members will need in addition to a depth in their own field, a broad perspective of social studies goals in particular, and of the aims and functions of education in general.

(1) These are but a few of the "culture areas" proposed. See Chapter X. "The Use of Culture Areas as a Frame of Organization for the Social Studies," James, Preston E., in Twenty-Ninth Yearbook of the National Council for the Social Studies.

(2) For outstanding helpful material to draw upon for such an endeavor see Kohn, Clyde F., ed., *The United States and the World Today*. Rand McNally & Co., Chicago, Ill., 1957. This publication was created in a workshop consisting of 40 public school teachers and 12 university professors, each of whom is regarded as an authority on the geography of one or more of the world's large culture regions.

(3) Anderson, Howard R., editor, "Approaches to an Understanding of World Affairs." Twenty-fifth Yearbook of the National Council for the Social Studies, 1954, pp. 5-6. This Yearbook also is an excellent source book for content material on culture areas.

(4) Emphasis supplied.

(5) For a device useful in portraying graphically the total environment see *Environmental Impactors* on cover of *Education*, published by Palmer Co., Hingham, Mass., Sept. 1956.

(6) Isard, Walter. *Methods of Regional Analysis*, John Wiley, N.Y., 1960.

(7) James, Preston E., in his book *The Wide World*, Macmillan Co., N.Y., uses the Industrial and Democratic Revolutions as major culture region determinants.

(8) From *Teaching about the United Nations*, Bulletin No. 18, United States Dept. of Health, Education and Welfare, 1960.

(9) See Warman, Henry J. "Some General Criteria for Teaching Local Geography." *Journal of Geography*, Vol. XLVIII, Feb. 1949, No. 2, pp. 77-81.

(10) Broek, Ian O. M. "Progress in Human Geography." *New Viewpoints in Geography.* James, Preston E., editor. Twenty-ninth Yearbook of National Council for the Social Studies, 1959.

(11) Preston James has expressed it this way, "The existing geographic patterns of any period of time are examined as a stage in the process of time." See Chapter II, *New Viewpoints in the Social Sciences, op. cit.*, 2.

(12) (Following are a few source suggestions)
Kohn, Clyde F. "Interpreting Maps and Globes."
Skill Development in Social Studies. Helen McCracken Carpenter, editor. Twenty-fourth Yearbook of the National Council for the Social Studies, 1953.
Odell, Clarence B. "The Use of Maps, Globes, and Pictures in the Classroom." *New Viewpoints in Geography. Op. cit.* 31.
Warman, Henry J. "Map Meanings: A Teacher-Student Guide for Map Learnings in the Secondary Schools." *The Journal of Geography*, Vol. LVIII, No. 5, May, 1959.
Harris, Ruby. *Map and Globe Usage*. Rand McNally & Co., Chicago, 1959.
Espenshade, Edward B., Jr. "Cartographic Developments and New

Maps." Twenty-ninth Yearbook, *op. cit.* 31.

Raisz, Erwin. *Mapping the World.* Abelard-Schuman, N. Y. 1956.

(13) While teachers are expected to caution students to use care in the handling of school materials, a grievous error is made in not ordering new maps constantly. Perhaps it would be better to wear them out fast and order more; but it would be best to keep them in order to compare with future maps.

POLITICAL SCIENCE AND CITIZENSHIP

Evron M. and Jeane J. Kirkpatrick

In social studies the subject matter of political science is often enmeshed in a confusion of various elements. Among these elements are superpatriotic inculcation of loyalty, preaching of no longer workable ideas of democracy, uncritical assumption that citizenship is learned primarily through academic study, and insensitivity to scholarly conception of political science as a discipline. Here, two scholarly specialists *attempt to unravel the hodgepodge. Their interpretations may appear narrow and conservative to some readers who can find broader or otherwise divergent views in this volume's selections on democracy (pages 3–12) and on citizenship education (pages 151–160). Omitted from this selection is much of the original, fuller discussion of political science.*

THERE is a long-standing tradition according to which secondary school instruction in political science, or instruction based upon the knowledge political science provides, has as its main objective the making of good citizens. This tradition appears to be based on the belief that instruction in government, politics, the political process, and the important issues of public policy will produce citizens who will discuss, act, and vote rationally and intelligently and that we may thereby achieve a sane and effective democratic society. Without asserting that education in the field of government, politics, and public policy has no role to play in helping form better citizens, we feel required to state at the outset, in the interests of clarity, that we regard this tradition and the beliefs upon which it is based as mistaken and misleading: First, because it is based on a distorted conception of how citizens are made; second, because it is based on a distorted conception of democracy; and, third, because it is based on a misconception of political science. It is important to clarify these matters;

FROM *High School Social Studies Perspectives*, Erling Hunt, ed., Boston: Houghton Mifflin, 1962, pp. 99–104. Used by permission. Dr. Kirkpatrick is the Executive Director of the American Political Science Association. His wife has co-authored a number of publications with him.

otherwise secondary school time will be spent on tasks foredoomed to failure. We propose, therefore, to devote a few paragraphs to the relationships among political science, democracy, and citizenship.

THE MOLDING OF CITIZENS

Plato and Aristotle were the first but by no means the only great philosophers to point out that the formation of citizens for any type of commonwealth is a task which begins in the cradle and extends to adulthood. It is the whole process of communicating to each new generation the political culture of the community, including the values embodied in its social order and the symbols which express those values and which relate them to tradition on the one hand and the constitution on the other. Here the term *constitution* means the whole interlocking web of institutions, processes, and values that comprise the public order. The process of communicating the values, habits, expectations, and desires which fit particular human beings to particular types of public order is partly conscious, largely unconscious. It proceeds more by imitation and habituation than by instruction. The whole of this process is called political socialization. (1)

There is much we do not yet know about the details of political socialization, but we do know that patterns of political behavior, like other aspects of acculturation, are acquired subtly, almost imperceptibly, from the total environment of the child. Attitudes toward authority, and specifically toward political authority; identification with groups and symbols; expectations concerning adult political roles, including paying taxes, serving in military forces, voting, participating in politics—these are a few of the determinants of the quality of citizenship that are only peripherally influenced by formal courses. They are largely a matter of conscience and character, the product of the long process of political socialization.

It is important to remember, therefore, that academic instruction plays only a minor role, at best, in the process of political socialization. This makes it all the more important that such instruction be based on a clear understanding of what can and cannot be accomplished in the classroom.

THE REQUIREMENTS OF CITIZENSHIP IN A DEMOCRACY

Democracy is government by the people in the sense that "the people" choose their governors from among competing groups of leaders. Democracy requires a set of institutions, procedures, and values that give the community an opportunity to change their governors through regular and peaceful processes. This in turn requires freedom of inquiry and expression, a broad equality of suffrage, and established procedures for replacing those who hold public power with a competing group of leaders whenever some legally determined "majority" of the people is dissatisfied with the incumbents.

Fortunately, democracy does not require that all men be equally expert in their knowledge of politics or public policy. (2) Fortunately—because if democracy required every citizen, or every voting citizen, or even most voting citizens to understand and judge the myriad of complex issues which confront the nation in this age of technical specialization, international involvement, and interdependence, democracy would be impossible. One of the consequences of "big government," which is itself the consequence of mass population and industrialization, is that no one individual can comprehend all the international, fiscal, social, and economic questions on which the government must make policies and act. Problems in all these areas require the joint efforts and coordinated expertise of economists, engineers, military leaders, doctors, historians, statisticians, and political scientists—to name just a few. Like the President of the nation and his chief policy advisers, average citizens must depend on the research, counsel, and judgment of specialists. Again, like the President, the people must judge the experts by the results they achieve.

Does it follow that, realistically conceived, all contemporary government is essentially government by experts? If this is true of democracy then it is also true of autocratic and even totalitarian governments, since these too must depend on experts; and therefore one may ask whether the differences between these forms of government are more apparent than real. But on closer examination it becomes clear that the differences in the forms of government in the industrially advanced nations today are not insubstantial. Experts make policies within the limits and the framework set by their political masters—which in the case of the United States means the President, Congress, and, ultimately, the people. The political leaders of a government determine the goals to be achieved; the experts make judgments about the best ways of achieving those goals, the consequences of alternative policies for achieving them, the social, financial, and cultural cost, etc. In the United States, if the President is dissatisfied with an expert's work, he fires, replaces, or simply ignores him. If the people are dissatisfied with the President's leadership, they replace him and his official family with an alternative group of leaders to direct and watch the experts.

It is important to recognize our dependence on experts, and to disabuse ourselves and our students of the notion that good citizenship requires omnicompetence concerning public policy and the institutions and processes by which it is made. The fact is, of course, that in contemporary society we are almost all experts and all laymen. The doctor is an expert in certain types of medicine or surgery, the garage mechanic or TV repairman is an expert in automobile or TV repair; in all other fields he is a layman. We are almost all laymen about almost all areas of public policy; experts about a few. It is important that students be made aware of the complexity and difficulty of most areas of public policy and of their own incompetence about substantive policy questions. Knowing what one does not know is a most important part of self-knowledge. It is a kind of self-knowledge that has important implications for citizenship. Decent humility about complicated substantive questions of public policy should reduce the dogmatism, demagoguery, and violence that characterize the discussion of so many public issues.

A secondary school teacher who hopes to give students sufficient knowledge to enable them to make rational judgments about substantive questions of policy will be tempted to cram into one term a little information on every aspect of government. The expected result will not be obtained, and time is better spent teaching students how to identify—and influence the resolution of—the questions that must *not* be left to the expert.

What Is Political Science?

The final reason that a survey of political science cannot properly be conceived as a branch of civics is that political science is not a set of maxims about good citizenship. It is an intellectual discipline, a body of knowledge about the political behavior of human beings. Its relevance to good citizenship is approximately the same as the relevance of economics to being a prudent consumer. Fortunately, it is possible to be a good citizen and know nothing about the methods or substance of the study of politics, just as it is possible to buy intelligently without regard to economic theory. Certain types of knowledge about political institutions can be useful to citizens by helping them identify exaggerated, contradictory, or false propaganda, and by giving them reasonable expectations about what may be accomplished by government. Knowledge about the relations between individuals and the state under various forms of government, about the interrelations between the state and society, about the theories of truth embodied in different political ideologies, and about the relations between political means and ends and between freedom and monopoly power—these are topics with which political science is concerned which may be useful to the citizen. But we should be clear that knowledge of these subjects has a tenuous relationship to the performance of the obligations of citizenship and respect for the rights of others. . . .

It is clearly impossible in a single essay to describe, much less discuss, the multiplicity of factors, problems, subjects, approaches, and findings which comprise political science. . . . Further reading of the books listed in the bibliography will sensitize readers to the controversy within the field about its status and future, and go far to correct and round out the abbreviated treatment of the subject in this essay. (3)

Course offerings in political science in almost any large university illustrate the diversity of subject matter and approach that characterize contemporary political science. Choosing a university at random, we note that the catalogue lists the following courses, among others: History of Political Theory, Public

Personnel Administration, Local Government, Conduct of American Foreign Relations, Political Parties, Public Opinion, Constitutional Law, International Relations, Legislation, Social Security, Public Finance, Constitutional History, Political Problems of Africa, Contemporary Public Affairs, Government and Business, and Communism and Democracy. If we ask ourselves what these courses have in common, the only possible answer is that they all relate to what we vaguely conceive as legal government. And it is accurate to say that, regardless of what anyone believes ought to be the proper subject matter of political science, it has been and remains a discipline primarily concerned with the accumulation of knowledge about the history, agencies, processes, structure, functions, composition, rationale, influence, successes, and failures of legal governments.

The several major fields in which political scientists work deal with specific aspects of legal governments. Specialists in political philosophy examine the thought of philosophers relating to the state and the government of men; specialists in comparative government generally examine the political systems of different countries; specialists in international affairs examine the relations among governments; specialists in constitutional law examine the basic, enduring "constitutional" aspects of the laws of a nation; specialists in political parties and pressure groups examine the interaction and influence on government of these paragovernmental institutions; specialists in public opinion examine the formation, communication, and influence of people's opinions about the affairs of government; and so forth.

(1) See Herbert Hyman, *Political Socialization: A Study in the Psychology of Political Behavior* (Chicago: The Free Press of Glencoe, Illinois, 1959).

(2) For a good discussion of the requirements of democracy and the qualifications of citizens, see E. E. Schattschneider, *The Semi-Sovereign People* (New York: Holt, Rinehart & Winston, Inc., 1960).

(3) See, for example: David Easton, *The Political System: An Inquiry into the State of Political Science* (New York: Alfred A. Knopf, Inc., 1953); Roland Young (ed.), *Approaches to the Study of Politics* (Evanston, Ill.: Northwestern University Press, 1958); Charles S. Hyneman, *The Study of Politics: The Present State of American Political Science* (Urbana, Ill.: University of Illinois Press, 1959); Vernon Van Dyke, *Political Science: A Philosophical Analysis* (Stanford, Calif.: Standard University Press, 1950).

A JURISPRUDENTIAL APPROACH
TO CITIZENSHIP EDUCATION

Donald W. Oliver

This selection presents a unique approach to developing students' political understanding and skill. The approach involves both basic elements in citizens' political lives and neglected techniques for teaching social studies. It appears well grounded in the theory of democracy and carefully worked out regarding instructional materials and procedures. A later selection in this volume (page 300) reports attempts to evaluate students' learning through the jurisprudential approach.

FREEDOM inevitably involves controversy. In a society governed by principles of constitutionalism, this controversy is expressed not in physical violence or intimidation but in words. The object of political life is not coercion, but persuasion. As Justice Douglas has said, "The function of free speech under our system of government is to invite dispute."

Much of the dispute centers upon the establishment of man's power relationship to his government: the definition of his rights and the restrictions upon his liberties. There is continuous controversy and redefinition of the words which describe these liberties, as well as the words which justify their restriction. All should have a right to "equal opportunity," "security," "a decent standard of living," "justice," "freedom," and "progress." But the government may restrict these rights "to provide for the general health and welfare of the community," "to prevent crime and disorder," "to provide for the common defense," "to prevent individuals or groups from being exploited," and "to penalize lazy, stupid, or incompetent people." These are the kinds of words we use in our political discussions. The definition of these words which describe our rights and their restrictions evolves through open discussion and application to particular situations and to particular problems.

This process of interpretation and intelligent application of words is not easy. Different people apply different meanings to the same rights. A Negro, for example, may say that it is his basic right to eat in a restaurant with whites. Some white people may say it is their natural right to associate with whom-

FROM *Citizenship and a Free Society: Education for the Future*, Franklin Patterson, ed., Washington D.C.: National Council for the Social Studies, 1960, pp. 215–221. Used by permission. Dr. Oliver is a professor in the Graduate School of Education, Harvard University.

ever they please, and this does not include Negroes. The white owner of the restaurant may say he has a right to control who will eat in his restaurant. Both Negro and white claim it is their right to have freedom, but the word has a different meaning for the two groups.

Often one right seems to conflict with another. One man wants to be free to see that his children get a better start in life than he had. If he has enough money, he will hire special teachers to give them a good education and use his influence to see that they get good jobs. Another who has less money may say that his children deserve equal opportunity. He wants his children to have as good an education as anyone else and to have the same chance to find a good job. The freedom of one may interfere with the equal opportunity of another.

Although we probably never shall solve the problem of defining basic rights to the point of universal consensus, through the process of free debate we continually define and redefine these rights and carry them into public policy. Each time a law is passed or a judicial decision is made, that law or decision defines the rights of people. By encouraging individuals and groups to debate and to work out conflicting definitions of basic rights, we come to conform to, if not to accept, restrictions upon these rights. We rationalize these restrictions by asserting that the government must have certain "police powers" in order to protect health, morals, safety, and the welfare of the community.

One of the most important jobs of a citizen is to reflect upon what he thinks these rights mean when applied to particular public issues. The citizen must constantly act as a judge interpreting the words which describe general moral and legal principles to see whether public action, and hence restriction of liberty, is warranted in a particular situation.

The strategy for teaching such a model of American society might be to build a curriculum—call it a "jurisprudential curriculum"—which would focus upon the earnest use of free speech and open debate for the students to determine what is man's proper relationship to his government. The question would be: To what extent should the government protect or restrict basic rights? The debate should not be carried on in an atmosphere of academic calm, but rather in the midst of that heat and pressure which characterize fundamental societal disputes.

Such a curriculum would focus upon a series of related questions:

1. What is an adequate description of the objective situation which causes the dispute? This refers to empirical, testable questions, though the evidence at hand may, in fact, be scarce. For example, how many labor unions really are corrupt? Exactly what is the nature of the dishonest acts in which some labor leaders engage?
2. To what extent is the situation so pressing that the government can

justifiably use its police powers to restrict personal liberty? Will whites and Negroes, for example, corrupt each other's cultures so that "separate but equal" is a reasonable standard for legislation?

3. To what extent do the rights which we wish to restrict by laws have constitutional guarantees?

4. To what extent do specific checks within the American constitutional system adequately reduce or unreasonably restrict governmental power?

The jurisprudential curriculum would clarify these questions by teaching specific skills and content directed at them. This content would include:

1. Concepts relating to the process of proof.
   For example:
   a. distinction and relationships among definitional, empirical, and ethical problems.
   b. the process of proof and use of evidence for these different kinds of problems.
   c. distinction between inductive and deductive types of proof.
2. Concepts relating to the American form of government.
   a. constitutional checks and safeguards; e.g., rule of law, federalism, separation of powers, checks and balances, judicial review.
   b. constitutional rights; e.g., free conscience and expression, substantive and procedural due process, equal protection under the law, property and contract rights.
   c. rationale for police power; e.g., provide for the general health and welfare, prevent crime and disorder, provide for the common defense, protect groups or individuals from being exploited.
3. Concepts and facts necessary to describe disputes or problem areas. Selection of facts depends largely on problem area being described. Concepts, however, might run across several problem areas. Concepts such as "culture" and "social class" would certainly apply to many problem areas.

The essential skill which would come out of this program is the application of the content characterized as critical thinking and concepts of constitutional theory to actual conflicts and disputes within a free society.

Here is an example of how one content area might be treated within the framework of the jurisprudential curriculum. An immediate and pressing issue in America is certainly the regulation of interracial and intercultural relations. One facet of this broader issue is the school desegregation problem. Returning to the four basic questions, they might be applied to this issue as follows:

1. What is the objective situation that creates the problem?
   For example:
   a. To what extent has differential legal treatment of Negroes and whites injured the Negro?
   b. To what extent are there intellectual, physical, and moral differences between the races that might justify differential educational treatment?

   There is no clear-cut, definitive answer to these questions. Conclusions regarding answers could only be reached intelligently if the student had passed through an active process of claim-testing.

2. Can the government justify the use of police power to restrict liberty?
   For example:
   To what extent are the intellectual, health, and moral differences between the races sufficient to justify segregation in order to protect the health, safety, and morals of the whole community?

3. Are the rights taken away guaranteed by the Constitution?
   In this particular case, at least two areas of the Constitution apply to rights already being restricted: equal protection and due process. But this does not solve the problem. The issue is whether public safety is so acutely jeopardized that these rights should in fact be restricted.

4. To what extent do specific checks within the American constitutional system adequately reduce or restrict governmental power?
   In this case, the fact is that the schools are controlled by the states, which also maintain they have police powers to segregate the races. The Federal Government has the responsibility for upholding and enforcing the rights guaranteed under the Fifth and Fourteenth Amendments of the Constitution. There is an ambiguous division of power and authority between the Federal Government and the state governments which has never been—and probably never will be—completely clarified.

Figure I illustrates four problem-conflict areas and schematically indicates the rights, police powers, and constitutional restrictions that might be discussed within the content of jurisprudential teaching.

Selection of content is, of course, only half the job. Criteria must be developed to define content-style, and procedures designed to present the content effectively. Figure II is an outline of a teaching strategy that [was] under experimental evaluation in Concord, Massachusetts, in the Harvard Social Studies Project.

Styles of content and methods of presentation are briefly described below. There is nothing new or startling about the various styles of content and strategy of teaching presented here. All have been used before. The purpose in giving the description is to clarify ideas suggested above and to show that they are not simply abstract theory. They can be put into practice.

FIGURE I

Illustrative Selection of Content Under Jurisprudential Approach

Broad Problem Area	Subtopic	Constitutional Rights	Rationale for Police Power	Constitutional Checks and Safeguards
1. Racial Conflict	school desegregation	equal protection; due process	prevent violence; protect health and morals	federalism—division of authority between state and national government; separation of powers
2. Labor Conflict	collective bargaining	freedom of association; property and contract rights	prevent violence; prevent exploitation	federalism; separation of powers
3. Business Competition	fair trade laws	contract rights	prevent dishonesty and exploitation	federalism; separation of powers (e.g., F.T.C. vs. courts)
4. Government Defense and Security	federal loyalty-security programs	free conscience; due process; equal protection	national defense and internal security	separation of powers

FIGURE II

Outline of Teaching Strategy

I. Introduction to the Problem.
  A. Narrative text outlining nature of the problem.
    1. Definition of technical terms and concepts.
    2. History of the problem to the point of policy clash.
    3. Discussion of major legal or governmental questions before time of policy clash.
  B. Case Illustrations.
    Dramatic, concrete illustrations of key concepts, e.g., monopoly, poor educational facilities, unemployment, collective bargaining.
  C. Drill on highly probable claims and facts.

II. Analysis of Controversy.
   A. Discussion based on Dilemma cases.
      1. One or two cases illustrating two sides of a value dilemma; use of analogy to illustrate same dilemma with other situations.
      2. Purposes of discussion cases to illustrate value concepts, force use of clear definition, dramatize need for further evidence to prove explanations and generalizations.
   B. Students analyze argumentative dialogue.
   C. Students analyze persuasive documents.

III. Student-Run Discussions.
   Small groups are asked to discuss a specific case and to come to a decision regarding the policy in question.

IV. Writing a Brief.
   Student required to write a brief justifying personal policy decision.

Content and Presentation for the Jurisprudential Approach.

Narrative texts. These include the historical background of a problem area, with some supporting evidence.

Drill materials. Questions based on the text are presented to the student, who has before him multiple-choice answers, one of which he checks as being right. Immediately after each question, the student is shown the answer so that he can find out whether his initial response was correct. This has been found a highly efficient way of teaching the basic facts contained in the text.

Illustrative cases. These are dramatic, concrete stories based on fact used to illustrate or concretize concepts or situations which might not otherwise be understood. The term "poor working conditions," for example, can be illustrated with cases spelling out the experiences of people actually involved in such situations.

Dilemma cases. Dilemma cases dramatize a basic conflict within the unit. The school desegregation issue contains such dilemmas as these: Should people's rights be supported even though public school standards may be disrupted or jeopardized? Should the will of the majority within a state be disregarded by the Federal Government in its interpretation of correct regulation of interracial relations?

The basic characteristic of the dilemma case is that it is fairly concrete, specific, and authentic. The desegregation of schools in Washington, D.C., is used, for example, as a case to illustrate the dilemma of maintaining the right of equal protection versus avoiding disruption of the standards of public schools.

The dilemma case is generally discussed within a Socratic framework; that is, the teacher identifies which horn of the dilemma expresses a "solution" of the problem for particular students and then presses the students to take into account the unpleasant legal or empirical consequences of this solution.

Argumentative dialogues and persuasive documents. When the student has learned to handle dilemma situations in discussion, he is taught to analyze written materials that are very similar to controversial discussion. He is presented with argumentative dialogues (sometimes typescripts of class discussions) and with speeches or articles written for persuasive purposes. The advantage of using such materials is that the level of sophistication of argumentative strategy can be regulated by the teacher according to the ability and training of the students.

Case-play. Group decision making is the critical situation which demands effective use of the skills and knowledge taught in the jurisprudential approach. There are many ways in which to set up a decision-making situation. The one suggested here is based on the case-play written so that students can take the parts of people representing various shades of opinion in their view of the problem being studied. In the play, only arguments are presented, no conclusions. The students are then asked to arrive at some conclusion through open discussion.

The brief. Group decision making sets the stage for individual commitment. Making public decisions demands open defense of one's views. The student should also have an opportunity to commit himself to a decision without the pressure of the group. He can do this by writing a brief in which he presents a careful, reasoned defense of his position. Writing a brief requires an adequate school library containing documents relating to the issue under study.

SECOND THOUGHTS ON
ECONOMICS IN THE SCHOOLS

John R. Coleman

Many thousands of social studies teachers across the nation learned economics from Professor Coleman who was the chief instructor for The American Economy, *a televised film series. Here he takes a hard look at the growing place of economics in the secondary school's program. He identifies signifi-* *cant dangers and difficulties, as well as potential advantages, in the increasing attention to economics. One possible approach to solving the problem of too much breadth in an economics course is through the study of comparative economics; it was discussed in the original selection but is omitted here.*

S UCH a short time ago we were being assailed on all sides for "failing our economic ABC's" and for being a "nation of economic illiterates" (albeit the wealthiest illiterates the world has yet seen). Now, if I read the signs correctly, economics is "in." From many parts of the country, we get evidence of a deeper concern and a firmer commitment to action on the subject of economic education for secondary school students. Indeed, there is even a certain faddishness to the movement, which presents us with new opportunities and new problems too.

Interest in this subject is of course not entirely new. Too many men and too many organizations, such as the Joint Council on Economic Education, have worked too long for us simply to ignore the past. The National Council for the Social Studies did not wait until the 1960's to discover the importance of economics. But no one will deny that the interest has increased sharply since the appointment of the National Task Force on Economic Education in 1960. The Task Force Report (1) came at the right time to have maximum impact: the ferment in secondary school education made this an auspicious time for a plea that we include more analytical, more objective, more de-

FROM *Social Education*, 29:74–77, February, 1965. Used by permission. Dr. Coleman is dean of humanities and social sciences at the Carnegie Institute of Technology.

manding, and more stimulating economic units in the education of tomorrow's decision-makers.

Now that we are past the first burst of this new enthusiasm, it is time to take stock and to sum up some of the early lessons from our shared concern for the education of our students. Here I propose to offer a personal summing-up and then to offer a still more personal suggestion about the most fruitful way in which we might proceed with one part of the job, the economics course at the twelfth grade level.

What then have we learned about economic education since 1960?

1. *While teacher receptivity to economic education is high, teacher confidence in handling economic ideas is low.* No one who has stepped off the college campus and entered the world of the secondary school can help but be impressed with the open-mindedness of so many teachers and administrators towards curriculum revision. (Indeed a college administrator can only look with envy at what he sees in high schools.) There is, in my judgment, far more hunger for economic materials than there is aversion toward them.

But the blunt truth seems to be that this hunger is not matched with feelings of confidence about the use of the materials. We must not delude ourselves here: an understanding of basic economic concepts is *hard* to come by. That surface understanding of these concepts is so widespread is due to the fact that all of us in a free society are economists by definition. That a deeper, more sophisticated understanding is so rare is due partly to the inherent difficulty of precise thought in any complex field; but it is probably due in larger part to a mass of uninspired and irrelevant teaching by the teachers' own instructors, the college economists. In classroom after classroom across this country, tomorrow's teachers (and today's teachers who are seeking advanced credits) are sitting through courses that scarcely lift their sights or their desire to go on learning. They are watching, in all too many cases, a parade of economic ideas better attuned to making the instructor look good in the eyes of his fellow economists than to meeting the needs of students who have no intention of becoming economics majors. Until the economics professors become more concerned about themselves as teachers—and hence more selective in what they do, more imaginative in how they teach, and more aware of what modern learning theory can tell them about their work—the prospects for the economic competence of high school teachers are not too bright.

But, even with the best college teaching of economics, the job will be less than half done. The secondary school teachers must *want* more and more exposure to that teaching if they are to develop that confidence which underlies any rich classroom performance. Our lot as professionals in the last half of the twentieth century is to be caught up in a time when continuing learning has become urgent business. At the moment when we stop exposing ourselves to newer and deeper ideas in our field, we lose our labels as professionals.

Once we could have carried the label for a longer time on the strength of what we learned in the past; now the line between the professional and the hack is drawn in a matter of a year or two. And, given the rate at which knowledge increases, the line once drawn in any man's life is unlikely to be erased.

The moral is clear and relentless. Whatever else we do to seek forward strides in economic education, we cannot move ahead one inch unless the teachers grow in competence and confidence. We waste time and human resources if we try to bypass the teachers and reach out directly to the high school students. No aids—no textbooks, no learning machines, and certainly no television films—can compensate for an insecure teacher; but those aids—those textbooks, those learning machines, and maybe even those television films—can complement the secure teachers.

The urgency then of more and better workshops and in-service programs in economics for teachers of the social studies is great. We have both to make up for the inadequacies in the teaching and the learning of economics in the past and to recognize the exploding interest in new economic concepts and applications. If we would settle for routine teaching by lectures and cut-and-dried texts, it wouldn't matter much whether social studies teachers were well grounded in economics; presumably a teacher can parrot words as easily as a student. But, if we believe in inductive teaching—in leading each student to the threshold of his own mind—then our teachers must have that extra degree of confidence that permits them to lead a discussion where the precise directions can never be set in advance. The inductive method demands more than the skill of keeping the discussion going; it demands keeping it relevant to a few key targets, forcing students to sort out the facts from the value judgments in what they say, and employing the newly acquired analytical tools wherever they are appropriate. This is difficult teaching, inspiring when done by the experts who know their subject and their students, but sham when done by others.

2. *Economic education calls for a deeper partnership between secondary school teachers and college economists.* An alert outside observer who looked in on our world of education would surely be surprised by the extent to which we have compartmentalized our activities. Leaving aside the much maligned colleges of education, the contacts between the box labeled "secondary school" and the box labeled "college" have too often been confined to diplomatic letters between senior counsellors and admissions officers. This gap is more than wasteful; it is now dangerous, because unless the college faculties learn more about the ferment in today's high schools and more about the rising potential of the high school senior, there is every likelihood that college will be a big bore for its new recruits.

But there are some signs that the gap may be closed. You know of advanced placement and curriculum development projects where college and high school faculty members worked together to build more demanding and stimulating courses, and where both parts of the team benefited from their shared insights and experiences. The most obvious gain on the high school teacher's side has been that he returned to his class more confident of his own grasp of evolving ideas in a particular field of inquiry. The most obvious gain on the college professor's side is that he can never again be so complacent about his own teaching once he has seen the best of the high school teachers.

And so it is with economics. Perhaps there are exceptions; perhaps there are secondary school teachers who have worked without the help of professional economists in designing the kinds of rigorous and relevant courses we need. (But I doubt if there is a single professional economist who can design a teachable economics course or unit for the high schools without the aid of the high school teacher who is to use it.) All of the promising projects I know about, however, are joint endeavors. The high school teacher brings to the best of these projects (1) a feeling for what the student is like in maturity, skills and interests, (2) a grasp of the total educational program into which the economic units are to be fitted, and (3) a sense of what he or she can reasonably and comfortably accomplish in the classroom. The college economist brings (1) a richer grasp of the fundamentals of the field, (2) a battery of examples from which the teacher may choose those most likely to hit the target, and (3) a set of expectations as to what the economically illerate high school graduate should know.

Whether this partnership works depends on whether the partners grow in their respect for one another's special skills. Condescending attitudes, rigid convictions of one right way to do things, turning away at the first sign of barriers in the road, unwillingness to challenge one another on the appropriateness of each of the proposed materials—all these things can upset the partnership. But all of these traps are avoidable as men on each side of the artificial line see their mutual stake in getting the job done well.

A last word on this point: just as it is a folly of conceit for the college economist to assume that he is the never-to-be-attained-but-always-to-be-sought-after answer to the high school teacher's prayer, so too it is naïve for the high school teacher to expect that college economists will be coming around in large numbers volunteering their help. The economist has other interests—and his profession has unfortunately not yet made it clear that it will confer accolades for work in secondary school curriculum development. Those who want the help of the economists will have to seek them out. But this is not an impossible task. Attitudes are changing here. One example: Had anyone told me five years ago that Carnegie Institute of Technology, a school without a department of education but with many prospective teachers among its students, would become engrossed in secondary school problems, I would have dismissed the idea as fantasy. Yet today this involvement in curriculum-building is, without any doubt, one of the three or four most exciting thrusts on our entire campus. Economists, historians, English teachers, fine artists, scientists—we are all in it with expanding zeal.

3. *The clearest lesson from the current push for economic education is that we may be trying to do too much in breadth and too little in depth.* If there is any one adverse impact from the landmark report of the National Task Force, it is that it may have seemed to ask too much in describing the minimum literacy that a high school graduate needs. The report was not meant as a checklist, yet it is in danger of becoming one. Witness, for example, the new books and the new courses that proclaim they carefully followed the Task Force Report; they seem to have done a better job of making sure that all of the Task Force's subject areas were touched upon than of heeding the pleas for fundamental understandings and for stimulation in the materials. Then, too, teachers may misread the Report's intent and ask, "How can I possibly do all this?" The answer to these teachers must be, "You can't—and you shouldn't try." What we must do is to settle, not apologetically but gladly, for a few things done well. We must, in short, not confuse coverage with understanding.

Perhaps we could get rid of some of our guilt feelings at leaving a few of our favorite subjects out of the high school curriculum if we remembered the "five-year-out" test. This is the test under which we ask ourselves before each class, "What difference will today's material make five years after the student leaves school?" Once asked, the question becomes a fine winnower; a lot of otherwise important ideas get left in a heap marked "Please discard" outside the classroom door. And then there is a chance to do what the Task Force was suggesting all along: that we concentrate on developing a way of thinking about economic issues.

The critical assumption here is that facts, and even institutions, get out of date rather quickly, but a way of thinking lasts. If sloppy thinking—careless use of data, weak logical constructions, unstated and unexamined assumptions —can survive the economics classes, then it has a good chance of lasting for long years to come. But if the teacher pounds away at precise thought and takes pride in the class period where some of the subject coverage was sacrificed to make a few telling points about sound analysis, there is good hope for the future. Who knows? We may even turn out a generation of voters who, if they do not know all of the institutions around them, at least know a good debate when they hear one. That generation will then be more intolerant than we proved to be in 1964 when confronted with a dreary debate about economic freedom, a debate in which terms were seldom defined, data were seldom offered or called for, and real alternatives were seldom examined. Our goal in economic literacy is not an abstract intellectual exercise; it is the application of straight thinking to complex but real problems.

In the first months of designing an economics project in social studies, the idea of doing one or two things well is probably not hard to sell; the testing period comes a little later when each member of the team says, "But we can't leave *this* entire subject out." (Textbooks have a similar life history. The first edition may be selective in coverage, but before the second edition appears the publisher has thrust irate letters from the field under the author's nose. The theme of the letters is simple: "Why didn't you include . . . . ?") There is no easy answer to this drift. It will only be halted when we discover how little that we thought we had "covered" has any lasting impact on our students.

But the teacher who can discipline himself or herself this way must inevitably ask, "Fine, but *which* few things shall I cover?" I do not think there can be any simple answer here. I propose to offer one candidate for the central theme of the senior course in this paper, but it is only one man's choice. The more important point to make is that the choice should be made on a number of grounds and not on any single one. For each classroom, the right subjects to focus on are probably: (1) those where the teacher is most comfortable; (2) those where the subject matter is most relevant to the students' interests and capacities; (3) those where the chance to use simple analytical tools is clearest; and (4) those where the available teaching materials are both sound and lively. If we use those criteria, we need offer no apologies to anyone for our selectivity or our selections.

4. *Economic materials for the secondary schools are improving in quality and quantity, but still suffer from dullness.* Acceptance of the importance of economics in the education of secondary school students has naturally enough led to a demand for better teaching materials. And there has been a response: We have more textbooks, more supplementary pamphlets, and more economic units in the Problems of Democracy books. The writers or consultants are often good economists. But something is still missing. That something is sparkle.

Where in all of the array of materials, and where in the classroom, is the excitement that is economics? Where is the sense of an unfolding science where new techniques are at man's fingertips? Where is the sense of unresolved issues, of free men grappling with choices that involve trade offs—a little more success in achieving full employment coming at the expense of a little less success in maintaining stable prices, for example?

Most materials that I have seen are antiseptically sterile. Why? If it is because we are frightened of controversy and unsettled issues, then we have given the extremists in our midst a bigger victory than they deserve. Unable to get us to teach their propaganda, they may however have been able to keep us from teaching what is lively and relevant.

Most of the materials seem, too, to be ill-suited to inductive teaching. They follow the old pattern: They tell us what they are going to tell us, tell us it, and then in a neat, closed-door type of summary tell us what they have told us. They bow to liveliness by the welcome addition of good pictures and graphs; but they miss liveliness when it appears in the guise of contrasting ideas and unresolved issues. From such materials, the student is more likely to carry away apparent answers than he is to carry away questions. And this seems deplorable to me when any answer must be somewhat tentative and an inquiring mind seems most worth preserving.

Perhaps one of our weaknesses as teachers, as textbook publishers, or as educational administrators is that we have set our sights so firmly on the high school and college years as a part of *becoming* that we lose sight of them as a part of *being*. The student's years throb with an impulse of their own. Yet we often fail to recognize or build upon his special interests in the classroom. We fail to make the class hours an end in themselves—a joyful end—as well as a means toward the further end of growth.

High school students are surely ready to make their first attempts at coming to grips with issues that will stimulate them again and again in later years. They are participants in a society that:

1. Tries to combine the pursuit of incentive and risk with the pursuit of minimum security for all.
2. Tries to keep alive the game of competition with its unique rule that every competitor should try hard but no one should win the whole prize.
3. Tries to keep free choices dominant by expanding, not restricting, government's role in our lives.
4. Tries to unlock secrets in science—physics yesterday, mathematics today, biology tomorrow—and to promote technological breakthroughs that make many of our ways of running our economic affairs out of date and that challenge man's very ability to live with the change he pursues so relentlessly.

These issues must come into the classroom, and they will come in if we are more imaginative in the materials we prepare together. We should be working now in building case materials from the real world that confront students with the dramatic, unfolding issues around them. We should be building class units that demand that students use primary data, tables for example that have no accompanying text saying, "As the Table shows . . ." and thereby stopping discussion right on the spot. We should be developing films that do more than describe; they should raise more "how" and "why" questions than they answer. (Some of our current materials proceed on the assumption that they should "lay it out cold"; but it is unclear whether the antecedent of "it" is the subject matter or the student body.) We should be using classroom debates, disciplined not by the stultifying rules of the debate societies but by the ceaseless asking of the question, "What is the evidence?" We should be using economic examples to construct exercises in logic that challenge the ability to think more clearly than the student—and maybe the teacher—has ever had to think before.

In short, we should prove once and for all that dullness and economics are not synonymous.

(1) *Economic Education in the Schools,* published by the Committee for Eco- nomic Development, 711 Fifth Avenue, New York, in September, 1961.

EXAMPLES OF ECONOMIC ANALYSIS

John E. Maher, John P. McIntyre, Roy A. Price, and Stowell Symmes

The broad scope of economics encourages indiscriminate attempts to survey the subject in high school courses. Here a team of writers proposes an alternative approach, a solution to the problem of too much breadth and too little depth. What is really needed, they say, is instructional emphasis on the way in which economists approach a problem. And they immediately set about to exemplify what they mean by economic analysis. Others may well argue that the initial point is overstated —that is, that the subject matter of economics does have some distinguishing characteristics—but there is still much value in recognizing that the methodology of economics suggests a needed emphasis in instruction.

M OST people know that economics deals with population, natural resources, income, tariffs, money, prices, and a host of other matters. Indeed, the list of topics can become greatly extended.

However, it is not *what* economics deals with that makes it a distinctive social science. Rather, it is *how* it treats its materials. The *method* of treatment, the *how,* is economic analysis.

To show that it is *method* (*how* it analyzes) rather than what it discusses that sets economics apart from other studies, we need only reflect on the fact that sociologists are as much, or even more, concerned with population and

FROM *Suggestions for Grade Placement and Development of Economic Ideas and Concepts,* Joint Council on Economic Education, 1964, pp. 41–48. Used by permission. Dr. Maher is on the staff of the Joint Council; Dr. McIntyre, director of learning resources in Dade County, Florida, Schools; Dr. Price's biographical note is on page 368; and Dr. Symmes is located at the Watchung Hills, New Jersey, Regional High School.

natural resources; political scientists, with income and tariffs; historians, with money and prices.

In this section, we shall look at several diverse illustrations of the economic method of analysis. We shall see that every economic problem has certain features in common with every other economic problem. It is the recognition of these common features and of the common method of their interpretation that is economic analysis.

The illustrations set forth below provide practice at recognizing what is— and what is not—an economic feature of a problem. Practice of this kind is the best way to achieve economic understanding, to enhance our capacity to analyze in economic terms, and to convey to others those special insights which are economic science. As we shall see, these insights apply to an understanding of an enormously wide range of personal and social problems.

Common Features of Economic Problems

If the core of economics is not encompassed by an understanding of terms like population, natural resources, income, tariffs, money, and prices, what is at the core?

If we can state what is the core of most economic problems, we shall be well on the road to identifying what economic analysis is. With no exceptions that come readily to mind, every economic problem involves the use of *resources* to achieve various *objectives*. The objectives may be such social goals as national income and full employment, or, in smaller-scale problems, such goals as an hour's rest or a new suit of clothing. Similarly, the resources employed to attain the objectives may be such broad resources of the social economy as land, labor, and capital, or, at a lower level, a piece of paper and a pencil. These two ingredients then—the ends (or objectives) that are sought and the means (or resources) of their attainment—are two features common to all economic problems.

It is, however, not enough merely to identify major features of economic problems. Analysis requires that relationships be established among the ends on the one hand and among the resources on the other, and among the resources and the ends as well.

One of the most common relationships tells how much of one resource is the equivalent in production to how much of another. Thus, a gallon of regular gasoline may be equal to four-fifths of a gallon of higher octane gasoline in moving an automobile twenty miles. This relationship also tells us how much of the *objective* of locomotion we can get from each *resource*. A final relationship tells us something about costs: how much must we pay for each resource? . . .

Virtually all economic problems, then, reveal the use of resources to attain objectives in most efficient fashion. To reach such efficiency requires knowledge of the relationships among resources and objectives. Decisions must be made among alternative objectives and among alternative uses to which resources may be devoted.

ILLUSTRATIONS

A series of diverse illustrations of economic problems should help clarify our thinking with respect to the essentials of economic analysis. As a beginning we may take the time-tested economy of Robinson Crusoe. Crusoe, you will recall, for a time was isolated on an island with no means of supporting himself except his own labor and wits. His objectives included rest and food as a minimum. The resource available to him initially was his own labor. These, then, are the two features earlier listed as ingredients of any economic problem: objectives and resources. It is at once clear that the more time spent in rest (that is, not working) the less time there is available for gathering food. And so there is a crude relationship, such that one hour spent gathering berries or attempting to catch fish is one hour less than can be spent in sleep or other activity.

Early in his career on the island, Crusoe discovered that he would probably attain a high standard of living if, instead of gathering berries and catching fish with his hands, he were to fashion some kind of tool for catching fish. This, of course, is an instance of capital formation: the creation of instruments of production. Here a new relationship is introduced, namely, the relationship between a man working with a spear to catch fish and a man trying to catch fish with his hands. The economist calls different ways of achieving objectives, different production functions.

In order to spend his time fashioning a spear. Crusoe must neither sleep nor gather berries nor catch fish with his hands. Therefore, because he must give up time spent in sleep or in gathering food, he is interested in knowing what the "payoff" will be. Will the present sacrifice of food or sleep be worthwhile in terms of the greater consumption of fish he may enjoy after having created a more efficient instrument of production?

The question as to whether he should so devote his time to making a spear hinges upon how great a value he places on the higher consumption he will in the future realize. Perhaps he would rather have but the one fish and the pint of berries he lives upon rather than tighten his belt, reduce his consumption, and fashion the spear; that is, in terms of modern economics, he "discounts" very heavily the value of future levels of consumption. We shall leave this illustration, satisfied with having identified our categories and some of the relationships among them, since we cannot answer the question we have raised without more specific information.

In summary, even a one-man economy exhibits resources (Crusoe's labor and the prospective spear) allocated to attain objectives (sleep and food). The most efficient or optimal allocation is the one that yields the most satisfactory combination of objectives from the limited resources available.

The simple example of Crusoe's economy and the problem of trying to raise living standards through the creation of better tools of production applies to the teaching of history and of contemporary problems. Alexander Hamilton's financial policies were aimed in large part at providing incentives to business to build up America's manufacturing capacity and thereby to raise the level of national production. His successful efforts to establish the credit of the Federal Government had a similar purpose. Industrialization, the creation of factories, machines, and equipment became possible only when the stability of government and the reliability of public and private credit could be counted upon.

The founding of the Bank of France, after the French Revolution, was designed to cope with problems similar to those experienced by the United States. In France, too, the need to promote commercial and industrial development required stable currency and banking facilities. Unlike the United States, France promoted a national, central bank with increasingly monopolistic powers over credit. In both countries, much of the nineteenth century was dominated by investment in transportation systems—canals and railroads. Like the rudimentary economy of Robinson Crusoe, national economies have had to divert their resources from satisfying immediate wants to investment in facilities that yield returns only after a period of time.

The developing economies of the modern world further illustrate the investment process. Egypt with the Aswan Dam, India with steel mills, and middle-eastern states with irrigation projects have come to symbolize dramatically the process of capital formation, the necessity of foregoing present consumption, and the need of creating a climate hospitable to long-term investment. . . .

Like our first illustration, this second one also has its social counterpart. In American history, the especially hard decisions made during wartime are rich illustrations of the problems of social choice. During the Civil War, and in all periods of armed conflict, the allocation of resources to war production coupled with the quantity of those resources largely determined the outcome of the struggle. Teachers may ask their students to tackle the following kinds of question: What were the populations of the North and South at the time of the firing on Fort Sumter? How important were manufacturing and agriculture in each section? How great was the reliance of each on foreign trade? How well developed were the systems of transportation? Finally, how do answers to these questions shed light upon the outcome of the war between the states?

In somewhat the same fashion, the World history course may study both World Wars from the viewpoint of economics. The questions raised above are equally appropriate to measuring the strength of each side in these global conflicts.

A third illustrative problem whose solution has been worked out only in recent years is the so-called waiting-line (queuing) problem. Detailed analysis of waiting lines is highly complex yet the elements of the problems are extremely simple to spell out and applicability is wide. The problems are whenever people wait in line—teller windows in banks, doctors' offices, super-market check-out counters, highway toll booths, and so on.

Suppose that at a repair facility at a Naval base, there are two classes of workers. One class is highly paid ship repairmen; the other class is stock clerks who get the tools required by the repairmen. Suppose, further, that the repair technicians are paid $5.00 an hour and the stock clerks $1.00 an hour.

Now imagine that there is one tool shed to which the repairmen must go to get tools. If we observe that, usually, there is a long waiting line of repairmen whose needs for tools are being met by one stock clerk and, further, that the repairmen, on average, wait in line for a total of eight hours each day before receiving tools, we might well draw the inference that this operation of the repair facility is inefficient. Especially would this be the case if by adding another stock clerk we could cut in half the total waiting time of repairmen. This is true because the repairmen who are waiting in line for eight hours (and receiving a wage of $5.00 an hour) are being paid $40.00 a day merely to stand in line and not for repairing naval vessels. Adding another stock clerk would (in the case of an eight-hour day) only add eight dollars to labor costs and would save $12.00 by cutting waiting time to four hours.

The mathematics of this "simple" problem is intriguingly complex, but without going into this mathematics we may identify the relationships that are crucial to an understanding of the analysis. First, we have implicitly set as an objective the minimization of labor cost; that is, we said it would be wise if we could reduce cost by increasing the employment of stock clerks and de-creasing the waiting time of repairmen. The two resources with which we are concerned here are the two kinds of workers. The relationships we must under-stand before we can attempt a solution are those between the employment of additional clerks and the average waiting time of repairmen. If we were to press further in this problem, we would need to know the rate of arrival at the stock bin of repairmen, the average length of time it takes to get the tools into the repairmen's hands, and so forth.

Probably the best applications of the analysis of waiting lines are to current problems. While detailed studies are generally beyond the abilities of high school students, definitions of problems are easily accessible. Some of the processes amenable to study are those earlier mentioned: banks' teller win-dows, doctors' offices, store check-out counters and toll booths. In addition, aircraft take-off and landing processes, ticket counters, theater box offices, and restaurants provide examples. Teachers of both current history courses and Problems of Democracy courses may adapt these problems to their special needs. Students who see how pervasive are these problems will come to appre-ciate the analysis that underlies their solution. Since waiting lines are readily simulated on modern electronic computers, there are opportunities to show how this new technology has contributed to our knowledge. . . .

Contemporary history and problems courses both provide excellent opportunities for studying the importance of the dependence of one industry upon another and the relations to whole economies. . . .

We may conclude our illustrations by showing a noneconomic approach to a question that, properly construed, can readily be made to yield to economic analysis. Suppose some one says he wants the "best possible education" and then asks, "How can I get it?" A flippant answer might be this advice: study for ten years each at Harvard, M.I.T., Michigan, Berkeley, Oxford, and Cambridge; then study for twenty years at the Institute for Advanced Study, five years at the Center for the Study of Behavioral Sciences, and eight years at the Congressional Library.

What is wrong with this answer? Nothing. It is the question that is at fault. *For no one seeks* the "best possible" anything. Humanity is constrained to live within various limitations. Our appetites are limited; we cannot study endlessly; we do not live forever. We must eat, sleep, and play. We cannot afford, for these and other reasons, to devote all our resources to the attainment of any single objective. As a consequence, the question, How may I obtain the best possible education? needs severe qualification. While we cannot attempt it here, an answer can be devised to such a question as this: Given my interests, aptitudes, intelligence, age, income and family responsibilities, how may I obtain the education most satisfactory to me?

Conclusion

The illustrations developed in this section suggest the following conclusions about the application of economic analysis.

1. The economic problem, and therefore economic analysis, is not to be understand as consisting of certain kinds of subject matter—money, population, banks, and so forth.
2. All economic issues and problems look alike in certain crucial ways. They all involve resources, objectives, relationships among these, and a principle of allocation to attain efficient results.
3. In a world of conflicting objectives and alternative uses for resources, the need for choice results in our getting satisfactory efficiency if we are wisely rational. We never get, and indeed we should never want, the most of any one objective.
4. Economic problems do not arise because human wants are *unlimited*. Problems arise because resources are limited in relation to the objectives we seek and because there are more and less efficient ways of using resources.

Other Social Sciences

ANTHROPOLOGY, SOCIOLOGY, AND SOCIAL PSYCHOLOGY

Meyer E. Nimkoff

Secondary school social studies have made fullest use of subject matter from history, with some additional content from geography, and political science, and recently from economics. The other social or behavioral sciences have been largely neglected. Here, a sociologist illustrates the importance of approaches and ideas in anthropology, sociology, and social psychology, as he discusses three highly significant concepts on which those disciplines focus. Omitted is part of his discussion of each concept and some of the other material in the original selection.

THE WRITER has assumed an ambitious task: to set forth in a single chapter a number of the leading concepts or "big ideas" of cultural anthropology, sociology, and social psychology which high school students of the social studies ought to know. From a pedagogical standpoint it would be better to devote a separate chapter to each discipline, and better still to deal in a single chapter with just one or two significant ideas, but space considerations prevent this. The teacher, with a semester or term at his disposal, would do well to consider the advisability of presenting in each class session only one or two "big ideas" treated as fully as time permits. This is the way to build up in students "a sagacity for the significant."

At the outset, a word of caution may be desirable about the discussion that follows. The writer is a sociologist. In dealing with anthropology and social psychology he may be subject to some bias, although he trusts not. In any case, let the reader beware.

The warrant for listing the disciplines in the order given in the title of this chapter is historical. Anthropology is the oldest, and social psychology the youngest, of the three. However, no rigorous attempt will be made here to

FROM *High School Social Studies Perspectives*, Erling Hunt, ed., Boston: Houghton, Mifflin, 1962, pp. 29–32, 36, 42–43, 50. Used by permission. Dr. Nimkoff is the chairman of sociology at Florida State University.

treat the three disciplines separately, since our interest is primarily in some of the many concepts which are shared by anthropology, sociology, and social psychology.

The warrant for treating anthropology, sociology, and social psychology apart from economics and political science is that the first three are general sciences of man, whereas economics and political science are special sciences. The political scientist deals only with the political process and with political institutions, whereas the cultural anthropologist and the sociologist are concerned with a wide range of social institutions—familial, religious, legal, educational, and economic, as well as governmental. The reason for this broad interest is that the anthropologist and the sociologist are seeking general principles applicable to social organization. History is also a general subject, but it is set apart by its special descriptive emphasis on unique events and movements from the other social sciences, which are characterized by a quest for generalization. The boundaries between the disciplines, however, are hard to draw. Originally anthropology concerned itself mainly with the study of primitive or nonliterate societies; but recently it has been focusing on small groups and villages in modern societies. Social psychology developed as an offshoot of both psychology and sociology and, as the name implies, its primary concern is the way the group affects the behavior of the individual.

CULTURE

The Culture Concept

The central concept of all three disciplines is *culture*, a phenomenon so vast that the student could examine it for a lifetime and still not encompass everything there is to know about it. One way to understand culture is to learn how it began and developed. Culture, as we experience it in the middle of the twentieth century, is the result of nearly a million years of living and learning on the part of mankind, and of transmitting what has been learned. Herbert Spencer called culture the *superorganic*, a useful term because it is readily differentiated from *inorganic* and *organic*. The planet on which we live, however it may have originated, had at first no living thing upon it. In the beginning all was inorganic matter. Then, in the course of a long period of time, life appeared. To the inorganic, the organic was added.

In the earliest animal life there was little or no learning from other animals. Instead, behavior was regulated by simple response to stimuli, as in the response of the moth to a bright light. More complicated behavior was regulated by a built-in mechanism, or instinct, exemplified by the wasp, which builds a nest, lays its eggs, provides food for the young, and seals up the nest whether or not it has ever seen another wasp do these things.

Eventually some animals developed the capacity to learn not only in a random manner from experience but systematically from others of their own kind, through imitation and communication. A familiar example is the way a mother cat teaches her young to catch and kill mice. The capacity to learn is a function of the nervous system; hence the capacity is highly developed among the vertebrates, which have a highly developed nervous system with a central cord. The monkeys and apes have the best learning capacity except for man, but they are limited by their inability to develop true speech or language. There is probably a biological basis for this difference, although its exact nature is obscure. In any case, language provides a medium for transmitting culture, and, especially in its written form, a method of preserving culture from generation to generation.

To the inorganic and the organic realms, then, there was added the superorganic, behavior learned by man as a member of society and persisting through tradition.

Of central importance in the culture concept is the idea that such behavior is learned from the group and that it is not inherent or biological. There are essentially two modes of adaptation to environment, the biological and the cultural. The polar bear has made an adaptation to the Arctic region in part by developing a coat of fur, a biological adaptation, whereas the Eskimo, who lives in the same frigid region, has learned to protect himself by building an igloo—and, we might add, by appropriating the skin and fur of the polar bear. The Eskimo has made a cultural adjustment to his environment.

The cultural adjustment is in many ways superior to the biological. For example, the polar bear has biologically adjusted to the cold North but will fare poorly in the temperate or tropical zones. Man is the only large animal found in all zones and parts of the earth, and this is because he has learned to adjust to the requirements of the various regions by developing an appropriate culture. . . .

GROUP INTERACTION

A prerequisite to culture is group interaction. This is evident from the fact that culture is the social heritage and a heritage is not social unless it is shared. Culture is learned by the individual from the group and is kept intact in part by being transmitted from generation to generation. Some of those who wish to draw formal lines of distinction between sociology and anthropology say that sociology is the discipline which concerns itself with the nature, conditions, and consequences of group interaction, whereas anthropology is the science of culture, one of the products of group interaction. Another product of group interaction, personality, is the concern of social psychology. In actuality, these formal distinctions are not always observed and practitioners who are regarded as sociologists, anthropologists, or social psychologists, as the case may be, often deal with problems which overlap the boundaries. . . .

PERSONALITY

The social psychologist is interested in how human beings learn and how their personalities are shaped. The three principal determinants of personality are the constitutional, the social, and the cultural factors. By constitutional factors we mean the biological causes, centering in the genes as they mature in a variable environment. One such constitutional factor, for example, is intelligence, which is both a part of personality and an influence upon other facets of personality, such as habits and attitudes. The social factor has to do with one's relations to other people, and it has to do specifically with the *nature* of these other people—whether they are more or less intelligent, kind, articulate, and so on. The kind of associates one has, especially during the early, formative years of one's life, has an important bearing on the kind of personality one develops. Kimball Young, sociologist at Northwestern University, has called these influences "personal-social," to differentiate them from the third set of influences, the cultural. The latter are the codified behavior patterns, the customs and ideas of how to do things which exist in the society and constitute the social tradition to which the growing individual is exposed.

The culture offers the individual a choice among a limited number of roles. Thus he chooses an occupation, influenced both by constitutional factors, including intelligence, and by the opinions of his associates: his parents, his friends, and his teachers. Once he enters into an occupation, whether he has actively chosen it or whether it has been to some extent chosen for him, he will follow it with an individual degree of success or efficiency. There may be tension between the demands of the role and one's interest or skill in it. Edward, Prince of Wales, became King of England but abdicated the throne in order to be free to marry the woman he loved, Wallis Simpson. He had been prevented from marrying her because she was a commoner and a divorcee. Although the role conflict, between occupation and marriage, is apparent, there are some who wonder whether he was temperamentally suited to be King. There are many individuals playing roles in society for which they are not suited, either because of some constitutional factor or because of attitudes derived from interpersonal experience. Especially important in the latter category are self-images. . . .

Are anthropology, sociology, and social psychology studies or sciences? The anthropologists, sociologists, and social psychologists who are engaged in research want to make their disciplines as respectable as the physical sciences by using the same means, namely scientific method, exact and quantitative. In the view of many of these researchers, philosophy, ethics, values, and means and ends of social action have no legitimate place in the social sciences, since they cannot be supported by incontrovertible evidence.

There are also those who think the completely scientific position is unrealistic and even dangerous. Precision in knowledge, they say, is undoubtedly a laudable objective; but if precision is the sole criterion, then we shall often be limited to dealing only with irrelevant and trifling matters, because scientific knowledge is lacking or incomplete on many basic problems. Meantime, many urgent social problems press for solution. Intelligent students of society cannot afford to abdicate their responsibility as citizens and leave decisions entirely to those who have power but who may be less well informed. We must often make decisions on the basis of incomplete, imperfect knowledge, striving all the while to improve our knowledge of society. We must recognize, too, that scientific knowledge about man is more difficult to come by than knowledge about the atom. Einstein was once asked why progress in physics was greater than in sociology. "That is easy," said Einstein. "Society is more complex."

There is a greater investment of money and effort in research in natural science than in social science. If as much money and support were given to the social sciences the results would be impressive. In terms of priority, our society has yet to be persuaded that Alexander Pope is right, that "the proper study of mankind is man."

THE BEHAVIORAL SCIENCES AND THE SOCIAL SCIENCE CURRICULUM OF THE AMERICAN HIGH SCHOOL

Eldon E. Snyder

Do the "newer" social sciences really deserve a major role in the social studies? The writer of this selection argues that they are fundamental to a basic understanding of human relationships. Furthermore, he suggests, they potentially furnish half of the desirable content for the social studies. Even if he is only partly correct in the implied prediction that the social studies will use more extensive content from these disciplines, teachers will do well to gain greater familiarity with them.

T HE POST-SPUTNICK era of American education has witnessed public and professional concern and debate in many areas of secondary education. The focus of attention was first directed to the physical and biological sciences and mathematics. Now it is apparent that other curriculum areas will be scru-

FROM *The Social Studies*, 56:5–9, January, 1965. Used by permission. Dr. Snyder is a professor at Kansas State Teachers College at Emporia.

tinized and subjected to critical analysis. The social sciences will be no exception. . . .

In spite of history's continued dominance of the social sciences many social scientists contend that it is not a social science at all. Stuart Chase has pointed out that, "History deals with events which have gone into limbo. . . . and can never hope to measure living phenomena or use the full scientific method." (1) Hunt and Metcalf suggest that, "History as a field of inquiry *is not a social science except in so far as historians use their understandings of past events to develop if-than-always generalizations."* (2) Few such generalizations about human behavior, according to Hunt and Metcalf, can be supported with historical evidence alone. (3)

Whether history be considered a social science or not, there are signs of a trend toward the greater use of concepts from the behavioral social sciences of cultural anthropology, sociology, and social psychology in the high school curriculum. These are the new social sciences. The traditional social sciences of history, political science, geography, and economics have too often been taught as if they existed apart from man; as if there was nothing alive about them. The need in American secondary schools and colleges today is to gain a fuller understanding of man himself, and man's interrelationships. The behavioral social sciences are most directly concerned with this need. The conceptual areas of the behavioral social sciences would contribute a great deal to the ultimate achievement of many of the objectives of social education and the revitalization of the entire social science curriculum (history notwithstanding).

One hazard in the study of the concepts suggested in this paper is that they frequently deal with areas that have traditionally been closed to reflective thinking and surrounded by bias and folklore. (4) Traditional social science subjects have often not been faced with this problem. Patterson points out that, "Whatever else school history instruction today is, it is *safe;* tiresome, mechanical, and shallow, perhaps, but wonderfully inoffensive, except to social scientists and a few other students of society." (5) This characteristic of the behavioral social sciences to focus on "closed" areas (they tend to be "closed" because of their concern with the immediate, personal, and behavioral aspects of social relations) is, of course, actually desirable. Reflective thinking and critical analysis of subject matter in behavioral terms is thereby promoted.

The increased consideration of these newer social sciences has been recognized by several leading authors of textbooks and by the National Council for the Social Studies, as reflected in the Twenty-Eighth Yearbook, *New Viewpoints in the Social Sciences.* (6) In the latter publication, chapters were devoted to new viewpoints in eight social science disciplines; three of these eight were anthropology, social psychology, and sociology. At least two leading textbooks in the field of secondary school social studies have recognized the inadequacy of the social sciences and the need for greater usage of concepts from the behavioral social sciences. Earl S. Johnson stresses the sociological approach as the means of synthesizing the social science disciplines. (7) Hunt and Metcalf point out that, "The relative status of the social-science field is . . . changing. The core of modern social science will probably soon consist of the fields of cultural anthropology, sociology, psychology and psychiatry." (8)

CONCEPTS PRESENTLY NEGLECTED

A review of concepts embodied in the behavioral social sciences will be presented below. This review might serve two purposes: (1) to emphasize the present inadequacy of the high school social sciences and, (2) to provide suggested areas for future curriculum development. The reader is challenged to note how infrequently these concepts are presented in the secondary schools, yet how vital they are for a real understanding of man's social behavior and critical citizenship.

These conceptual areas likewise should be thoroughly incorporated into the teacher preparation program of the social sciences. Present curriculum inadequacies are in part attributable to the previous academic background of the teachers. The behavioral social sciences should be an integral part of the academic background and in-service training of high school social science teachers in order that concepts from cultural anthropology, sociology, and social psychology might assume their proper perspective in the high school curriculum.

The following conceptual areas are admittedly overlapping and interrelated. This is inevitable. Man's social behavior is very complex and interrelated.

1. Personality. The personality structure of man is not inborn. Man becomes human through interaction with others within the society (and the culture of that society). The personality is a microcosm of the groups in which the individual participates. The behavior of individuals ultimately is determined by their personality. Consideration should be given in the high schools to the social processes involved in personality development and the socializing agencies of the society.

2. High school students should have the opportunity to study the group structure of our society. This would include the study of group norms, ingroups, out-groups, primary and secondary groups, social status, and social roles. Within the framework of the group structure of our society social institutions should be considered. This would include the contrast of social institutions in the urban society from those in the primitive society. Social institutions should be viewed in terms of their functionality (and possible dysfunctionality) to the society. Of particular importance would be the economic, political, educational, religious and familial social institutions and the personal and social needs they satisfy.

3. An understanding of the culture concept. An understanding of culture necessitates the study of the variability and uniformity of culture, how culture

changes, and the relationship between culture change and the major social problems of our era. Ethnocentrism, or the tendency of a society to consider its own culture as best, is instrumental in bringing about much misunderstanding and mistrust between societies and ethnic groups today. Significant contributions could be made toward improved group relations by the realization that cultural elements must be studied in context of the cultural setting and caution must be practiced in a moral evaluation of cultural practices of one society with another society.

4. The psychological and sociological analysis of prejudice, scapegoating, and discrimination. Students should become familiar with the "authoritarian personality" theory of prejudice and how economic deprivation and socialization are fundamental in the instigation and spread of prejudice, discrimination, and scapegoating.

5. Social stratification. In the above discussion it was suggested that students should study the group structure of our society. One specific aspect of the social structure is social stratification. This conceptual area includes the manner in which social status is correlated with "styles of life," ethnic, racial, religious, occupational groups, and political behavior. The functionality and dysfunctionality of social stratification should be considered, and particular emphasis might be given to the relationship between social status and educational opportunities and how social status may limit such opportunities even though this is contrary to democratic ideology. These phenomena can readily be observed within the immediate environment of high school students.

6. The importance of population changes and human ecology in our society. Population increases, composition, and shifts are having multiple effects on the social relationships in our society. The effects of the population structure and changes might be illustrated in the major social institutions of the society, e.g., school enrollments, and economic and political implications (such as legislative reapportionments). Emphasis should also be given to the importance of the general shift of population from rural to metropolitan areas.

High school students would also benefit from the studies in the area of human ecology that indicate the relationship betweeen geographical areas (particularly in the city) and human behavior. In light of the increasing urbanization of our population, students should be knowledgeable about the theories concerning the manner in which cities grow, and the overall effects of the trend toward suburbanization.

7. The study of human behavior under stress and when the usual patterns of behavior have broken down. This would include the consideration of crowd behavior, publics, public opinion, emotional contagion, propaganda, and mass behavior. It would also encompass the knowledge of social movements, how they develop, mature, become institutionalized and conservative. Ample case illustrations of the above types of human behavior may be drawn from the disciplines of history and political science.

8. How power is distributed and used in local and national realms. Power is

interrelated with the study of community structure, social stratification, and racial and ethnic groups. Students in our secondary schools should understand the necessity of power in their community and the nation, as well as the possible ill-effects of the usage of power. The consideration of the power concept would, of course, be directly related to the institutional configuration of our society, the population changes, and the effect of mass media in the usage of power in our society.

9. The family. Our secondary schools have the obligation to familiarize students with the importance of the family, how it is a significant socializing agency, and the manner in which it is interrelated with other social institutions of the society—political, economic, religious, and educational. Of course the family is closely related to the social stratification structure of the society, and the study of changes in family life is important in understanding the present and future family disorganization. Likewise, the contrast of our family organization with that of primitive societies will illustrate the similarities and differences of the family in all societies in meeting the basic human needs of people.

10. Social change. Implied in many of the above-suggested areas of study is the concept of social change and the transition and adjustment that most societies, including the newly independent countries, are facing. This includes, in particular, the effects of change on the major social institutions, and the effects of urbanization and industrialization. This concept of social change should be understood, not only in terms of changes in the institutional relationships, but also its effects on individuals and primary groups.

Summary

The above conceptual areas, drawn primarily from cultural anthropology, sociology, and social psychology are personal, immediate, and relate to behavioral aspects of the social environment. The knowledge and understandings that might be achieved would allow the students to observe social behavior in a way not previously possible.

Many of these concepts could be incorporated into the existing subject matter. For example, the rise of Nazism in Germany and communism in Russia in a history or political science course could be more fully understood by the knowledge of social movements, crowd, and mass behavior. Social movements of American history include the American Revolution, the Abolition, Populist, and Suffrage movements, and the American Indian Ghost Dances. Too often these movements have been considered only as events and the cultural and social psychological aspects have been neglected. To study events of the past in this way more nearly allows for the understanding of similar happenings of the present. Likewise, changes in the functions of the social institutions of our society can be traced within existing social science offerings by the incorporation of concepts from the behavioral social sciences.

On the other hand, it may be desirable to establish new course offerings within the high school curriculum in order to fully present the suggested concepts. Perhaps in this way the social sciences can get beyond the structural aspects of human relationships. We have long emphasized events that occurred far away and a long time ago. We have taught only one half of the concepts that are the rightful domain of the social sciences. Our present reappraisal of the high school social science curriculum would do well to incorporate the remaining half of the social sciences in order that students might have a more holistic view of man's relationships with his fellow man.

(1) Stuart Chase, *The Proper Study of Mankind*, Harper and Brothers, 1948, p. 48.

(2) Maurice P. Hunt and Lawrence E. Metcalf, *Teaching High School Social Studies*, Harper and Brothers, 1955, p. 195. (italics in the original).

(3) *Ibid.*, p. 195.

(4) *Ibid.*, p. 6.

(5) Franklin Patterson, "Social Science and the New Curriculum," *The American Behavioral Scientist*, 6:28–32, November, 1962, p. 29.

(6) Roy A. Price, editor, *New Viewpoints in the Social Sciences*, Twenty-eighth Yearbook, 1958.

(7) Earl S. Johnson, *Theory and Practice of the Social Studies*, Macmillan Co., 1956, p. xi.

(8) Hunt and Metcalf, *op. cit.*, p. 193.

PART THREE

MULTIDISCIPLINARY ELEMENTS IN THE SOCIAL STUDIES

Despite the distinctive place in social studies achieved by some of the social science disciplines, there are others that have not fared so well in the school program. Their advancement as social sciences, however, has led to increasing attention from school people. And the solution to the problem of what to do about them has typically involved the offering of one or more interdisciplinary courses. Geography has been given special attention in courses that may continue to emphasize history; and civics has commonly expanded to include elements of sociology and economics as well as political science. It is the problems course that has achieved the fullest integration of subjects in the social studies.

Meanwhile, on additional bases, the social studies have become multidisciplinary to a considerable degree. The reality of multifaceted social problems and complex human affairs has led curriculum makers often to recommend a direct study of aspects of society that do not fit clearly into subject categories. Such topics as conservation, communism, international relations, and contemporary affairs generally elicit a multidisciplinary approach.

This Part opens with consideration of the often overlooked historical development of the present-day program in secondary social studies. It includes attention to the current status of, and trends in, the social studies curriculum. From this it proceeds to a discussion of such multidisciplinary elements as citizenship education, controversial issues, current affairs, international and intercultural relations (including teaching about communism), and other facets of social studies that cut across subject lines.

Issues involving the social studies and the various disciplines that contribute to the field are numerous and a variety of them are treated in these selections. For example, diverse views are presented on whether citizenship education needs to involve more than political education. Some specialists consider the question of whether, and if so how, why, and to what extent, controversial issues should be taught. What attention should the social studies accord cultures beyond the United States and world affairs generally? Should American students study communism and, if so, how should such instruction be handled? Is history the best framework into which the other social sciences should be integrated? Or should students study contemporary problems directly? Thoughtful analyses and challenging suggestions in answer to these and comparable questions regarding the social studies curriculum follow in these readings.

1

The Social Studies Curriculum

CHANGING, PERSPECTIVES IN THE SOCIAL STUDIES

Erling M. Hunt

Conscious as they are of values in history, social studies teachers should be particularly aware of the need to examine the historical development of their own field. In this selection an authority examines the evolution of social studies in American schools with regard to underlying bases and the nature of changes in the curriculum. Omitted here are citations of numerous early and recent references on social studies.

HIGH schools in the United States have developed programs in social studies that, in spite of some spreading influence, are still unique. We attempt to teach the history and cultures of the world as a whole. We insist that textbooks be recently published and include almost contemporary developments, and then supplement the textbooks with weekly publications that summarize current events in the nation and around the world. We either teach the social sciences directly—government, economics, sociology, sometimes anthropology—or draw on the social sciences in the study of problems of American society. We give continuing attention to new needs, and to corrections and reorganizations that may give youth a better understanding of the national and the world society of which they are members and in which they must discharge their responsibilities as citizens.

One result of the unique elements in our program is that the social studies include controversial subjects and become subject to many organized pressures. A further result is that we must constantly check our perspectives and adjust our instruction to new knowledge, new social needs, and new instructional resources.

Yet, although we constantly review and revise the parts that make up our social studies curriculum, we rarely reconsider the basic assumptions on which

FROM *High School Social Studies Perspectives*, Erling Hunt, ed., Boston: Houghton Mifflin, 1962. Used by permission. Dr. Hunt is head of the Social Studies Department, Teachers College, Columbia University.

we have built our courses for elementary and secondary schools, and for nearly half a century we have not systematically considered the program as a whole.

BASIC ASSUMPTIONS

The assumptions on which our social studies teaching rests stem in part from our heritage of Western civilization and values, in part from nationalism, and in part from the principles and ideals of our democracy.

Our Western Heritage

Continued teaching of European history, in a variety of secondary school courses, has reflected American identification with the civilization and values of the West. Until recently that identification has resulted in neglect of other peoples and cultures of the world and in an assumption, often all too explicit, of the superiority of Western ways and achievements. But our new world relationships and responsibilities, especially since World War II, have gradually broadened American perspectives. World history in name gradually becomes world history in actuality. This broader perspective directs teachers to unfamiliar histories, to analyses of unfamiliar political, economic, and social institutions, and to newly developed area studies.

Nationalism

We usually associate the use of history instruction to develop nationalism and loyalty to a political regime with the French Revolution and Napoleon, starting in the late 1790's. But the first school textbooks in American history and government appeared even earlier in the 1790's. The teaching of history and civics, the selections in school readers, and school observance of national holidays have consciously fostered patriotism and loyalty to our federal union and our political institutions. Patriotic organizations have influenced legislative requirements, textbook content, and school exercises; and not infrequently differing interpretations of loyalty and changing emphases in school instruction have given rise to sharp controversy. What is to be taught about American traditions and institutions and about those of other nations and peoples still divides the individuals and organizations concerned with education at all levels.

But a divided world and the exigencies of the cold war are influencing perspectives. Responsible voices counsel us that our national interest now requires study and understanding of democracies other than our own, of the needs and potentials of new nations, and of the uncongenial institutions of totalitarian communism. Again, we need the resources of new histories, new or extended social sciences, and area studies.

Democracy

The ideals of democracy—political, economic, and social—have also shaped our school instruction and divided the American public. The extension of the franchise has implied the need for education about the policies and issues on which citizens develop public opinion and on which they vote. Neither education for an elite who will lead and control nor education for masses who will conform, as in a totalitarian state, will serve a democracy. Education that implements democratic ideals must be practical and realistic, must deal with issues that are current and controversial, must avoid teaching *what* to think and emphasize *how* to think.

Obviously, democratic education so defined bristles with difficulties and controversy. Some Americans still insist that the Founding Fathers established not a democracy but a republic, and at least imply that democracy is un-American. Some assert that young citizens of school age are too immature to learn to think for themselves, and should be taught what to think and to believe. Some would fence out of the curriculum particular topics—or at least realistic treatment of them—such as government-management-labor relations, or church-state relations, or racial characteristics and cultural differences, or communism, or international organization. Many individuals and organized groups have special interests, related to political democracy, economic democracy, or social democracy, that they wish the schools to serve, sometimes by omission, sometimes by emphasis, sometimes by selective consideration. Some would concentrate on early American history and traditions, and either bar recent times and controversial issues or treat them only in general and noncontroversial fashion. Some, although for varying reasons, would provide the same social studies curriculum for all, regardless of differences in the backgrounds, interests, and abilities of learners.

The challenges of a divided world and the cold war deepen the need for success in our experiment in democratic education. Clearly, efforts to develop maximum political, social, and economic understanding on the part of all young citizens will continue to receive strong support. Recent developments suggest, moreover, that able students, in honors courses that are already moving into more advanced study of American and world history, may also, if appropriate resources become available, move into area studies, into deeper study within the long-established social sciences, and into the newer disciplines of the behavioral sciences.

THE PROCESS OF CURRICULUM CHANGE

Our method of achieving curriculum change, like the social studies program that has resulted from it, is again peculiar to the United States. Of course we have no national ministry of education to establish practices and courses, and the state departments of education, which hold this responsibility, have followed rather than led as American education has moved toward a practical and realistic social studies program for all high school youth. But state authorities have certainly assented to, and helped to implement, the revisions that have shifted long-established American and European history courses from political and military narrative to increasingly interpretive treatments of political, economic, and social development; that have brought history courses down as near to the immediate present as possible, introduced accounts of non-European peoples and cultures, and supplemented the courses with attention to current events; that have further supplemented interpretive history with the interpretive analyses of geographers, political scientists, economists, sociologists, and anthropologists; and that now look, with rather more than a speculative eye, at the newer fields of the behavioral sciences and area studies.

Public education, inescapably responsive to political forces and processes, can rarely be bold in dealing with controversial issues. Because almost all change in social studies teaching is controversial, initiative often has been taken by college and university scholars, foundations, and special-interest groups that have subsidized the study of neglected areas and the publication of needed resources. Educational organizations and publications, state and local boards of education, and sometimes newspapers and periodicals have served as forums and sounding boards for debate. Textbook authors and publishers have broken new paths, some of which have been ignored, some abandoned, while others have become well worn.

Change, if rarely sponsored by official agencies, requires official acceptance, is made in full public view, and is subject to public criticism. Moreover, such forces as the conservatism of teachers and of college-entrance requirements, and the financial stake of authors and publishers in their investment of effort and capital, serve to check, perhaps more than is desirable, both the speed and the extent of change. In any case, protests that changes come too late and too little partially balance the protests that change has come too fast or at all.

Focus Within Educational Perspectives

Perspectives in scholarship change faster than does classroom instruction. Almost thirty years ago one researcher found that school textbooks in American history lagged a full generation behind fresh scholarship. That gap may have narrowed a bit as established scholars have helped to compile school texts, but it never closes. [Several of the recently identified] developments in the scholarship of history, the older social sciences, the new behavioral sciences, and area studies that, however important now to the United States as a nation and to American citizens as individuals, have as yet gained little recognition in the high school curriculum. They should help teachers and curriculum makers both to bridge the gap between their academic preparation in the social studies and more recent scholarship and to bring into perspective those parts of the world to which most high school (and college) courses still give little attention. But scholarship is only one of the dimensions in the perspectives of social studies instruction that continually require new focus.

Writing thirty years ago for the Commission on the Social Studies, Charles A. Beard noted that "instruction in the social studies in the schools is conditioned by the spirit and letter of scholarship, by the realities and ideas of the society in which it is carried on, and by the nature and limitations of the teaching and learning process at the various grade levels across which it is distributed." (1) Each of Beard's three elements is volatile, ever flashing new facets that change perspectives and suggest modifications in social studies instruction.

Textbooks and teaching reflect, sooner or later, many changes in scholarship, in society, and in the teaching and learning process. But the curriculum framework that has set the boundaries of most of the changes that have been made dates back to the 1916 report of the National Education Association's Committee on the Social Studies. Many of the assumptions and commitments of that report reach back even further, and reflect both the origins and growth of our Western civilization and the development of American nationalism and traditions. Review of some of our experience may be illuminating and useful as we face the need for new or revised patterns.

(1) Charles A. Beard, A *Charter for the Social Sciences in the Schools*, Report of the Commission on the Social Studies, Part I (New York: Charles Scribner's Sons, 1932), p. 2.

THE SOCIAL STUDIES PROGRAM IN THE SECONDARY SCHOOL IN THE TWENTIETH CENTURY

I. James Quillen

Changes have come in social studies not merely from underlying social conditions. National committees and other organizations have typically motivated major trends and shifting patterns in the curriculum. Here one specialist re-

FROM *The Social Studies: Curriculum Proposals for the Future*, pp. 80–86, 92–94, by Odegard, Hanna, Quillen, Bellack, and Tyler. Copyright © 1963 by the Board of Trustees of Leland Stanford Junior University. By permission of Scott, Foresman and Company, the publisher. Dr. Quillen is dean and professor of education, Stanford University.

*views several of the outstanding mo-
tivators of alterations in secondary
school social studies during this century.
Omitted are brief sections on citizenship education and the social studies,
quite recent national organizational efforts, and the writer's recommendations
for the improvement of the social
studies.*

I BELIEVE that some of the criticism of high school social studies, especially as it relates to the teaching of history and government, is overdrawn, if not overwrought. Still it is clear that the present program has many serious defects and has not [during the 1940's and 1950's] received attention and resources in the current educational revolution commensurate with its importance in the education of the young in a rapidly changing, highly complex, free society. Perhaps one of the reasons for this is that social and economic conditions in the 1920's following World War I and in the depression of the 1930's focused major attention on the social studies curriculum as a major instrument in ctiizenship education.

The high school social studies program in the twentieth century has been shaped largely by the recommendations of three national committees: (1) the Committee of Ten of the National Education Association; (2) the Committee of Seven of the American Historical Association; and (3) the Committee on Social Studies of the National Education Association's Commission on the Reorganization of Secondary Education.

The Committee of Ten, under the chairmanship of Charles W. Eliot of Harvard, was appointed in 1892 in response to the demand for a greater uniformity in high school programs and in college admissions requirements. The report of its Conference on History, Civil Government, and Political Economy recommended that American history and government be taught in the 7th grade; Greek and Roman history in the 8th; French history in the 9th; English history in the 10th; American history in the 11th; and an intensive study of a special historical period and government in the 12th. Among the members of the Conference were James Harvey Robinson, Albert Bushnell Hart, and Woodrow Wilson.

The Committee of Seven in its report published in 1899 recommended ancient history in the 9th grade; medieval and modern in the 10th; English history in the 11th; and American history and government in the 12th. The high schools adopted these recommendations almost universally. Some of the members of the Committee of Seven were Andrew C. McLaughlin, Herbert B. Adams, A. B. Hart, and Charles H. Haskins.

The Committee on Social Studies of the Commission on the Reorganization of Secondary Education sought to broaden the content from the social sciences included in the high school program and to stress education for life in the industrial-urban culture that was emerging rapidly in the United States. This Committee, unlike the earlier two, was composed largely of high school teachers and administrators, with a sprinkling of other members. James

Harvey Robinson was one historian on the committee and was able to bring to it his experience in curriculum-making in the 1890's. The Committee in its report published in 1916 recommended geography, European history, and civics in the 7th grade; American history and civics, with related geography, in the 8th; civics and related history in the 9th, and modern European and American history and a new course in the Problems of American Democracy (social, economic, and political) in grades 10, 11, and 12. The Committee viewed the problems of democracy course as an opportunity to bring more content from the social sciences into the high school curriculum. As it stated in its report:

The only feasible way the committee can see by which to satisfy in reasonable measure the demands of the several social sciences, while maintaining due regard for the requirements of secondary education, is to organize instruction, not on the basis of the formal social sciences, but on the basis of concrete problems of vital importance to society and of immediate interest to the pupil.

In other words, the suggestion is not to discard one social science in favor of another, nor attempt to crowd the several social sciences into [a] . . . year in abridged forms; but to study actual problems, or issues, or conditions, as they occur in life, and in their several aspects, political, economic, and sociological. (1)

The Committee's recommendations of the civics course in grade 9 and Problems of American Democracy in grade 12 were adopted widely; and, with a year of American history in grade 11, European history, now usually called world history, was confined to a single year in grade 10. Hence, in the 1920's and 1930's the typical secondary school social studies program became: Geography or old-world backgrounds in the 7th grade; American history in the 8th; civics in the 9th; world history in the 10th; American history in the 11th; and Problems of Democracy or American government in the 12th. Much of this program has continued to the present time.

The 1930's and early 1940's became a period of differentiation in American education. The attempt to make the curriculum serve individual needs more effectively resulted in the proliferation of local school curriculum development projects. Because of the depression and the threat of totalitarianism, a large number of these were in the social studies. The effect in practice, however, was confined largely to the elementary school; and the traditional high school program in the social studies tended to persist, in some cases with rather major changes in content within the traditional subjects.

Among the changes in content were less emphasis on politics and military campaigns and more emphasis on social, economic, and cultural affairs in history, and more attention to the personal-social needs of pupils and contemporary events and problems in the social studies program generally. The major national reports of this era, including that of the Commission on the Social Studies of the American Historical Association published in a series of volumes from 1932 to 1941, did not recommend a sequence of courses for national guidance. The Committee on American History in Schools and Colleges, which published its report in 1944, did recommend the grade placement of content in American history. The composition of both the Commission and Committee shows that noted historians and social scientists continued to be interested in the teaching of the social studies in the schools.

Since World War II, there have been few basic changes in course offerings in high school social studies. However, in spite of the focusing of the spotlight of national attention on other subjects, the importance of history and the social sciences has continued to be recognized, and an increase in requirements has been made in high school social studies subjects.

The changes in the social studies in the late 1940's and early 1950's resulted to a considerable extent from major projects in certain functional aspects of the social studies curriculum. These projects included such areas as citizenship education, international relations, and intergroup education. Since the mid-1950's, there has been increasing attention to needed modifications in the social studies program as a whole and to the place in it of history and the social sciences as academic disciplines.

In conclusion, I have tried to show that there have been extensive efforts to improve high school social studies instruction in the twentieth century. Progress has been made in some areas. Recognition of what is good in the present program should be the first step in attempting to improve it. There are no simple answers; if there were, they would have been found and applied long ago. For a decade or more after World War II, the social studies area tended to be neglected, while major attention was devoted to other subjects in the curriculum. In the past few years, efforts to improve the social studies have increased and will, no doubt, increase more rapidly in the immediate future. As we seek to move ahead, it seems sensible for us to learn all we can from past experience and to utilize as fully as possible the talents of the many able individuals who are already working in the field. The task now is to build on whatever good that has been done, to concentrate more adequate financial resources and creative efforts on the defects that need to be remedied, and to bring to bear on these defects the best intelligence available in history, the social sciences, professional education, and the schools.

(1) U.S. Bureau of Education, *Social Studies in Secondary Education*, Bulletin 1916, No. 28 (Washington, D.C.: U.S. Government Printing Office), p. 53.

THE SOCIAL STUDIES IN THE
SECONDARY SCHOOL TODAY

Howard H. Cummings

In this article a specialist on secondary social studies surveys the central tendencies in school offerings at present. Then he identifies some of the factors, influences, and problems impinging on the social studies and current efforts to im- *prove this field of the curriculum. His analysis should be especially helpful to individual teachers and to groups contemplating or undertaking curriculum revision.*

SOCIAL STUDIES CURRICULUM—THE STATUS QUO

WHILE the general pattern of courses recommended by the Committee on Social Studies [of 1916] can be easily identified by studying contemporary courses of study, the details of the courses have changed and there have been many additions. Perhaps one of the reasons that it is hard to discover bold new departures for a social studies course today is the fact that changes have been made at regular intervals since the year 1916. The social studies curriculum was probably more dynamic than many other areas in the curriculum before the year 1950. In planning a new curriculum or a revision of an existing course of study, most educators like to have a general view of what is going on and what trends seem to be evident. Therefore, a grade by grade summary of practices which were general in the early sixties will be outlined.

Grade 7. It is difficult to name a course which is commonly taught in this grade. Traditionally, in schools in the Northern states, the second year of a two-year sequence in geography was taught in grade 7. In Southern states (which had a seven-year elementary school) the subject was United States history. Today for those students enrolled in junior high schools (statistics for social studies courses in grades 7 and 8 for systems with an 8-4 organization are not available) more than 250,000 are enrolled in a general social studies course, and more than 650,000 study courses in state history, government and geography. The length of these courses is hard to determine.

Grade 8. The course in this grade is United States history. The original laws requiring the teaching of American history specified that the course be

FROM *Social Studies in the Senior High School*, Willis D. Moreland, ed., Washington, D.C.: National Council for the Social Studies, Curriculum Series No. 7, 1965, pp. 3–7. Used by permission. Dr. Cummings is a specialist in social science in the U.S. Office of Education.

taught at both the elementary and secondary levels. In some states where grade 7 was the last year of the elementary school the course remained in grade 7.

Grade 9. The Committee on Social Studies recommended a one-semester course in Community civics to be followed by a one-semester course in occupations. The 9th grade was viewed as a terminal year for the large majority of high school students. Therefore, they should receive their final work in citizenship and an introduction to the job market during their last year in school. In communities which have a high dropout rate this reasoning is still valid. Where the state dropout rate runs to 50 per cent the 9th grade is the last chance to teach about citizenship and job-finding if, in fact, the pupil reaches the 9th grade. In communities which graduate more than 85 per cent of their youth, any course designed as terminal can be left to grade 12. However, 550,000 students were enrolled in a full year course in community civics while an additional 150,000 took a one-semester course. Courses in occupations still enrolled 80,000 9th grade students.

World or global geography is an alternative 9th grade social studies course to community civics and occupations. The increased interest in international affairs brought demand for a course in geography at the high school level to supplement and perhaps consolidate earlier geographic learnings in the elementary grades. The older courses in economic or commercial geography, inherited from the business schools, were not regarded as adequate. The enrollment in 9th grade for a full year ran to 475,000 with an additional 100,000 in a one-semester course. The comparative enrollments in the two alternative courses are about even.

The slow transition from community civics to world geography illustrates the fact that changes in the social studies curriculum tend to be evolutionary. There are reasons for this relative slowness.

1. The usual explanation of teacher inertia is a factor. If a teacher has learned how to teach a course and has collected materials, developed a pattern for field trips, and invented projects for individual and group activity, he may be reluctant to shift to a completely different subject field where he feels his training has been inadequate. If he is doing a good job his principal may hesitate to encourage the change.
2. As indicated earlier, the old traditional course in community civics may meet the needs for civic education in a particular community better than a course in world geography.
3. Textbooks in a new subject are slow in appearing and have not been tried out in a large number of school situations. Teachers have not been trained in the new courses. Reference works have not appeared in large numbers and the work of identifying books suitable for high school readers remains to be done.

Grade 10. The existence of two courses at the same grade level is true to a much less extent in grade 10. Here world history has a large enrollment of 1,400,000 in a full year course. However, the earlier two-year sequence of ancient and medieval history (enrollment 75,000) and modern history (enrollment 55,000) is still reported. This enrollment is small when compared with world history. However, it is well ahead of the innovations launched in recent years. The older courses seem to survive better than new courses in Russian history, Canadian history, Latin American history, etc., seem to grow. In general, what course to teach is a matter for local decision and some local teachers and school authorities, probably in most cases for good reasons, prefer the older, longer and more traditional two-year sequence of European history.

Grade 11. United States history is the standard subject for this grade with a reported enrollment of 1,950,00. Since this course is required either by law or by the ruling of the state board of education in all states, the enrollment will remain approximately the same as the total enrollment in grade 11. It is possible to reduce the one-year course to a one-semester course and still meet the requirements of the law in states where no time requirement is stated in the regulation. However, the strong drive for time for science, mathematics and modern languages, particularly in grade 11 and 12 does not seem to have reduced enrollment in the one-year United States history course in grade 11.

Grade 12. The Committee on Social Studies recommended a course in the problems of American democracy for grade 12. The recommendation was never carried out in all schools. One-semester courses in civics, economics, and sociology were offered as alternatives to the one-year problems course. Since nineteen states required courses in civics, the combination of civics plus a one-semester course retained a large enrollment. The relative positions of problems of democracy versus its competitors is revealed by the following enrollment figures: problems of democracy one semester 82,840, one year 258,000, civics and government one semester 340,000, one year 430,000; economics and economic problems one semester 217,000, one year 75,000; sociology and social problems one semester 175,000, one year 110,000. There seems to be some tendency for the one-semester course in these three areas to expand into one-year courses. A newcomer to the field of 12th grade social studies is psychology which enrolled 88,000 in one-semester courses and 50,000 in one-year courses.

In spite of the persistence of the general pattern recommended in 1916 it would be inaccurate to describe the social studies curriculum as static. Within the subject fields major changes have occurred. A comparison of course outline in history in 1920 with outlines for 1960 reveal an emphasis on recent history in both the American history and world history courses. The new world history courses include more of the history of non-European countries than the earlier courses. Content has changed in all courses and the appearance of global geography and psychology marks two innovations which have attracted sizable enrollments. (1) Nor do the total enrollment figures indicate that social studies is a moribund area. It gives the appearance of health and seems to have maintained its place with English as the two subject fields which between them probably account for seven of the sixteen Carnegie units required for high school graduation. The present state of the social studies curriculum is not a cause for alarm. Improvement is possible and is needed to help improve the total outcome of American education. A look at some of the ways currently proposed to bring into existence a better social studies program will now be examined.

Social Studies Curriculum—The Look Ahead

The first question that must be answered when any new course is to be organized is, who is going to do it? There are several answers to this question today. Some of the answers run as follows:

1. The classroom teacher either alone or with the help of others who are sought out by him should develop his own curriculum, try it out in his classes, revise it and then teach it. To this ideal most educators would subscribe provided that teachers had the ability, the training, the large knowledge of public issues and the energy required to turn out a good curriculum which would produce well-educated end products. Unfortunately this situation does not exist. However, the number of social studies teachers who do not have either a state or local course of study to follow is very large. Many teachers will continue to be their own curriculum makers out of necessity. The good teacher should be encouraged to develop his course by serving as a middleman between his students and the materials which are continually being published.

2. The committee is a logical development from the single teacher as an agency for curriculum development. Two facts operated to bring the committee approach into existence: (1) not all teachers were effective in organizing a course of study, and (2) it was deemed desirable for reasons of administration to have a uniform course of study for a school system and in many instances for an area as large as a state. Teacher participation was desired for the selection and organization of content, suggestions for methods, and decisions on goals and objectives. College professors of history, the social sciences, geography, and education could work with a committee, but their time was too limited for them to reach the large number of teachers. During the past forty years committees have produced almost all of the state and local courses of study which guide the social studies program. The system has its weaknesses. In general, the majority of the teachers were trained in history and lacked competence in geography and the social sciences. The major contribution has probably been increasingly better suggestions for educational

methods. The work of most committees has been carried on with small expenditures. For the most part the end products represented donated time and effort from the teachers and their college-based consultants.

3. The science and mathematics courses produced in the 1950–64 period were not organized and written by secondary school teachers either singly or in committees. For the most part they were the work of university scientists and mathematicians drawing on all knowledge available in the specialized fields for materials which could be used to induct the beginner into a field of study which led to graduate schools. The importance of the subject in the whole field of science and technology demanded that the scientist, the engineer, the technician and the layman should share the basic knowledge which governed scientific and technical operations. Obviously secondary school teachers were unable to make such a synthesis. The pattern used has appealed to the public imagination. The growing trend is to leave all research and development in the curriculum field to the universities. After the curriculum has been planned and the materials developed there may be tryouts in the schools or teachers may simply be retrained to teach the new courses. The role of the teacher in curriculum building is minimized if not eliminated.

The increasing activity of the universities in the field of the secondary school curriculum should be welcomed. These institutions have received substantial federal grants and foundation funds which have made it possible for them to employ the ablest men in the field for full-time work. The work they have turned out in other fields has been widely acclaimed. That these institutions, properly financed, can make a substantial contribution to the social studies curriculum cannot be doubted. However, it is not inconceivable that an intelligent and imaginative high school teacher might come up with a better organization for a social studies course with a more defensible body of classroom-tested materials than a university might produce. The possibility of program development by committees organized by state departments of education has been recognized by making the state departments eligible for federal grants for this purpose in Project Social Studies. The picture of thousands of teachers waiting patiently for the latest word from the university about what to teach is not an inspiring one. It is to be hoped that individuals and groups will continue to work to develop new social studies programs and to revise existing courses.

The second question to be answered is what needs to be done to produce a social studies curriculum which measures up to present day demands? The categories of answers may be outlined:

1. There has always been the answer from some specialists in the disciplines that in all courses in the secondary schools the integrity of the disciplines must be preserved. This point of view holds that this can be done

only by teaching geography and history as such and that it cannot be done in integrated courses such as a core curriculum or a problems course. One desired outcome is geographical-mindedness or historical-mindedness, and it is argued that these patterns of thinking can be formed only by following the fundamental pattern of the discipline. The large number of separate courses if all disciplines deemed most basic were taught, as, for example, sociology, economics, history, geography, and political science would require much more time than a student has in his program for social studies courses. The recent concern over structure as a guide for the organization of instruction has reinforced this traditional position.

2. The second answer is from a generally opposed school of curriculum makers who seek a foundation for social studies in current or recurring problems which face the society in which the student is living. These problems cannot for the most part be fitted into disciplinary boundaries. The very term social studies implies, according to this school of thought, an interdisciplinary approach to a study of society.

3. A third approach which combines some features of one and two is to have the specialists identify the major concepts which are developed in each discipline and to make this list of concepts the basis for the social studies program. This approach has received much attention in recent years, but the problem of identifying the concepts has proved to be difficult and the natural follow-up of selecting materials for each age level to develop these concepts is proved to be even harder. The general idea, however, appeals to many university specialists and secondary teachers and has furnished a forum for an exchange of views.

There are many curriculum experts who ask for a broader and deeper approach than has been suggested by any of the viewpoints outlined here. Some of these critics are not content to confine the curriculum to traditional subjects such as history, geography, political science, economics, and sociology nor are they content with a consideration of social problems which will draw upon these disciplines for content. These critics propose new goals which do not fit neatly into the older social studies objectives. In general, they have an idea of the kind of man or woman the educational experiences provided in the social studies should produce. In addition to the terms of character and personality they talk about personal and social adjustment, style of life and the tone of a society in which individuals may want to live. To reach many of the goals the social studies courses in the high school may have to look to the behavioral sciences and draw more heavily on psychology and social psychology, anthropology, sociology and biology for a curriculum which will explain the phenomenon of man in society.

Another group of curriculum builders look to the humanities as the proper niche for the social studies program. This would lead to a closer relation with

English, an examination of the university programs in language and area study, more attention to the classics and a new synthesis based on related and traditional fields of study.

To review briefly, our national education picture is varied. While 32 per cent of our young people enter college, 20 per cent grow up to be functional illiterates. We are making a great effort to learn more science and mathematics and to improve our ability to use modern languages. We are keenly aware of the presence of social and economic problems which science and mathematics and the ability to speak French are unlikely to solve. We look to the social sciences for some guidance toward solutions but are not entirely convinced that these disciplines or the humanities can supply solutions. Meanwhile our high school graduates spend one period a day for at least three years in grades 9 through 12 in social studies classes. Can we find ways to take them farther toward finding solutions in the future than we have in the past?

(1) See also Bertram A. Masia, "Profile of the Current Secondary School Social Studies Curriculum in North Central Association Schools," *North Central Association Quarterly*, Vol. 38, Fall, 1963, pp. 205–213 and Emlyn Jones, "Social Studies Requirements in an Age of Science and Mathematics," *Social Education*, Vol. 27, January, 1963, pp. 17–18.

RECENT CHANGES IN THE SOCIAL STUDIES CURRICULUM

Bertram A. Masia

The content of social studies courses was recently surveyed in 368 high schools (upper four years), under the auspices of the North Central Association's Foreign Relations Project. Understandably, special attention was given to the place of international and world affairs in the schools. It is noteworthy that private (mostly parochial) schools constituted 10 per cent of those surveyed. The data reported here concentrate on changes in social studies offerings reported by the schools.

FROM "Profile of the Current Secondary Social Studies Curriculum in North Central Association Schools," *North Central Association Quarterly*, 39:211–213, Fall, 1963. Used by permission. Dr. Masia is a professor of education at the University of Chicago.

Recent Changes in the Social Studies Curriculum

New Courses

THE SCHOOLS in the sample were asked to list all courses added to or deleted from the social studies curriculum during the past two years. No change in course offerings was reported by 237, or 64 per cent, of the schools. The dropping of courses could hardly be described as a widespread habit. All told, forty-one deletions were reported by thirty-five schools. By contrast, there was a total of 155 course additions made by 125 different schools. (1) Thus slightly more than one school in every three had recently added a course to its social studies curriculum.

Most of the course additions fall within three rubrics:

1. *Geography*. Added as a social studies offering by 10 per cent of the total sample. This represents a 28 per cent increase in the number of schools offering this course.
2. *International Relations*, including area history and comparative governments. Six per cent of the sample added this course. Thus, of the fifty-nine schools reporting that they offer a separate and distinct course in international relations, twenty-two of them have only recently added this course. This represents a 60 per cent increase in a two-year period.
3. *Economics*. Ten per cent of all schools added this course, resulting in a net increase of 18 per cent during the past two years.

Clearly, interest in all three courses is on the rise, possibly impelled by world events and pressures on the social studies. Jones' surveys reveal between 1953 and 1962, a three-fold increase in the number of large city school systems that require economics, and a two-fold increase for geography. (2)

It is quite evident that the catalogue of social studies courses of a given high school remains fairly constant over a long period of time. Rarely is a course dropped. Staff and enrollment permitting, a new course is added every few years, invariably as an elective.

New Content in Old Course Titles

Simply because course titles do not change overnight it does not necessarily follow that their contents remain the same. To determine to what extent "new" content has found its way into the social studies curriculum, four of the major courses—American history, world history, problems of democracy, and economics—were examined. The major focus in the survey was on course units or topics of at least one week duration or longer which fall, more or less, under the related titles of foreign affairs, international relations, and area studies.

Problems of Democracy

Of these four courses, the problems course is, by very virtue of its stated purpose, most apt to be sensitive to contemporary world and international issues. Of the 368 schools surveyed, 202 either require a problems course of all students or offer it as an elective. Of these 202, only nineteen seem not to be offering any units on world or international problems.

Nine units of study served as the basis of the survey. The proportion of problems courses which include each topic is:

> Communism—75 per cent
> United Nations—72 per cent
> Comparative economic systems—65 per cent
> International relations—62 per cent
> World peace and understanding—50 per cent
> Intercultural relations—50 per cent
> World trade—35 per cent
> Common market—31 per cent
> Underdeveloped countries—27 per cent

The survey indicates that, on the average, each school that offers a problems course includes five of the above nine units.

American History

The content of the American history course is much more defined than that of the problems course. Yet, units on international matters also receive attention in this the universally-required secondary social studies course. Of the 368 schools in the sample, 308, or 84 per cent, do include, on the average, three to four of the following eight units:

> United Nations—72 per cent
> U. S. and contemporary world affairs—70 per cent
> Current American foreign policy—63 per cent
> Cold war—53 per cent
> World peace and understanding—45 per cent
> Comparative governments—43 per cent
> International trade and aid—35 per cent
> Common market—25 per cent

World History

It has often been claimed that world history is a misnomer for a course that is essentially a history of Western Europe with a certain side excursion to the Middle East and to Eastern Europe. Whether a truly world-wide history can be taught with effectiveness in one year is a matter aside. This survey merely attempted to determine to what extent the study of areas of the world other than Western Europe, which has received much impetus recently, (3) has become an integral part of the course called world history.

Of the 320 schools which offer world history, the proportion which includes a distinctly separate unit of a week or longer on the following eight areas of the world is:

> Soviet Union—82 per cent
> Latin America—73 per cent
> Middle East—72 per cent
> China—68 per cent
> Africa—57 per cent
> India—57 per cent
> Japan—53 per cent
> Southeast Asia—50 per cent

In addition, 66 per cent report having a unit on the United Nations.

Economics

Of the 202 schools offering economics, only 10 per cent do not include a distinct unit on some aspect of international economics. Comparative economic systems is at least a week-long unit in 80 per cent of the economics courses. World trade occupies the attention of somewhat less than two-thirds of the offerings. The economic aspects of foreign policy are studied in 47 per cent of the instances, and the Common Market in 46 per cent. Finally, the important matter of the economic growth of underdeveloped countries is considered as a separate unit in economics in one-third of the schools.

Taking all four major courses together, one is impressed with the considerable amount of time devoted to the "newer" content recommended by such national groups as the American Council of Learned Societies, the Joint Council for Economic Education, and the NCA Foreign Relations Project. The United States' role as a major actor on the world stage is reflected in the heavy dosage of international relations and foreign affairs which students receive in the American history and problems of democracy courses, in the devotion of at least a quarter of the world history course to the study of areas of the world outside of Western Europe which have assumed a crucial importance in recent years, and finally, in the increasing attention paid in the economics course to supranational economic matters.

New Procedures

This survey indicates that the recent widespread interest in talent and in the gifted has not bypassed the social studies. If developing provisions for students with varying abilities can be said to represent change, then change has indeed occurred.

Simply on either a "Yes, we are making provisions" or "No, we have not made provisions" response, only one in three of the sample schools has not adopted special procedures for taking individual differences into consideration in instruction. This one-third that does not are the smallest schools. When they become larger and possess more facilities, they too will have their special programs.

The two most commonly used special procedures are closely related to each other. One is the assigning of student to sections on the basis of ability. The other is the keying of instructional materials to the ability level of the student. The latter procedure is the inevitable consequence of the former. Approximately one-third of all schools in the sample have installed the track system in their required social studies courses.

Other procedures that have received much publicity and ballyhoo of late are reported as being used only by a handful of schools. An advanced placement program is installed in only twenty-one schools; accelerated courses are reported by fifty-one schools, and independent study by sixty-three schools. The latter procedure seems to be the solution for the smaller school which cannot afford either tracking or enrichment.

A FINAL COMMENT

Clearly, the social studies curriculum is undergoing some change: Courses are being added; new content is covered; and needs of talented students are recognized. However, because change seems to be occurring within the existing structure, it is extremely difficult to determine either the rate or degree of transformation. Available data support the arguments of critics who maintain that the social studies is static as well as those of its defenders who see an evolution of increasing momentum.

Indeed, this survey has raised a number of questions about the process and direction of change in social studies. Upon what criteria are courses added to or deleted from the curriculum? Who determines when and whether new units should be added to existing courses? On what basis are such judgments made? What roles do the following play in curriculum revision: school administration, faculty, or university scholars; or state or national legislation; the political and economic climate on the local, national, or international scene? How is the direction of change determined?

One can speculate further about various processes used to effect change. What does the committee system accomplish? What would understanding teachers do, given blocks of time for curriculum planning and appropriate compensation? How can universities and high schools cooperate for mutual advantage? What processes are most efficient? Most creative? (4)

This survey provides a general picture of the current status of the social studies in the North Central Association's accrediting area. But if these questions are to be answered—and they must be if social studies is to recover its dynamism—deeper waters must be fathomed.

(1) In 80 per cent of these instances, the courses were added as electives.

(2) Jones, *op. cit.*, p. 19.

(3) Cf. American Council of Learned Societies and the National Council for the Social Studies. *The Social Studies and the Social Sciences* (New York: Harcourt, Brace and World, 1962); Erling M. Hunt (Ed.) *High School Social Studies Perspectives* (Boston: Houghton Mifflin Company, 1962).

(4) These questions are raised because the survey revealed that 164 or 45 per cent of the sample schools are engaged in curriculum study. In 148 of these schools, curriculum studies are undertaken by committees consisting of faculty and school administration. The social studies staff person is, in three-quarters of these curriculum examinations, given no special consideration. His class load is not lightened, nor is he paid extra for the work he does. One in two of these schools have engaged outside consultants to advise on the study; the lay community or Board of Education is rarely involved. Because the information relating to curriculum study derived from the questionnaire is sketchy and inconclusive, it was not included in the body of this article.

2

Citizenship Education

APPROACHES TO CITIZENSHIP EDUCATION TODAY

Franklin Patterson

Much of what is written about preparation for citizenship is markedly exhortative, effusive, or vacuous. It is particularly refreshing, therefore, to have this forthright, critical assessment of the status of citizenship education in American high schools. The writer recognizes the potentialities as well as the needed strengthening, in each approach commonly used or advocated today. His analysis confirms that the social studies can play an essential and leading, although not exclusive, role in citizenship education.

STRENGTHS AND WEAKNESSES OF CURRENT PRACTICE

THE FIVE approaches to civic education in the American high school mentioned in the preceding material have notable strengths and visible weaknesses. Collectively, the greatest strength of these approaches is that they give citizenship education a tested, several-sided structure. A framework exists in the American high school for citizenship education of adequate quality. In a number of examples, public, independent, and parochial high schools have used this framework to build programs of especial vitality and value. On the other hand, inadequacy in high school citizenship education too often exists because this framework of approaches is built upon in cursory, outworn, or uncreative ways. High school leaders have been occupied by many matters other than citizenship; they have been handicapped by the growing pressure of numbers, by increasingly comprehensive civic education purposes whose priorities are unclear, and by a lack of influence from major studies and projects in citizenship education.

As noted, the most characteristic approach in American high schools is that citizenship is learned through the curriculum and subject matter of the regular

REPRINTED WITH PERMISSION OF The Free Press from *High Schools for a Free Society*, pp. 60–64, by Franklin Patterson. Copyright © 1960 by The Tufts Civic Education Center. For biographical note see page 13.

instructional program. The curriculum devised for this purpose has a remarkable uniformity throughout the country. It is based on the recommendations, some conflicting, which were made forty to sixty years ago. It is oriented basically toward the learning of information about American history and civil government. It includes some reference to similar considerations in the development of western Europe, and in certain instances deals with other parts of the world. This curriculum helps boys and girls to gain valuable background on our national history and government, an awareness of some of our fundamental national ideals and traditions, and a sense of our links with the Western world. On the other hand, this curriculum usually treats contemporary history and problems much less than earlier history, and often avoids more difficult and crucial areas of public affairs altogether. The curriculum and subject matter of the social studies—most directly related to citizenship—tend to overlook the social sciences outside of history and government. Economics gets short shrift; in most cases anthropology, social psychology, and sociology get very little attention. *The approach to citizenship through curriculum and subject matter is in need of serious reappraisal in terms of the nature of modern society and the educational background and capabilities that responsible citizens now need.*

The second most characteristic approach to citizenship in the secondary school is that it is learned through conformance to established standards of conduct. Where the total school environment is very powerful, or where students come from a social background equal or superior to that of their teachers, the prescribing of certain conduct standards (dress, discipline, etc.) may not be particularly necessary. In other schools (e.g., a large public high school in a low-income suburb) standards of conduct may be very explicitly prescribed. Whatever the case, in American high schools "good citizenship" is typically equated with good conduct and behavior in the school and community, whether standards of conduct and behavior are set up by implicit understanding or explicit regulation. Failure to meet these standards is generally identified as "poor citizenship" and punished directly or indirectly. Establishment and enforcement of conduct standards in the final analysis are handled by adults, with students only occasionally being given a substantial part in the process. In schools visited during the present study, students who were interviewed expressed little desire to take part in the enforcement of standards of conduct. At two schools, student leadership was actively involved in ending organizational set-ups in which they had been expected to act as arbiters and judges of student conduct. Students expressed themselves as feeling that the judging role was uncomfortable and difficult for the teenager to play in relation to his fellow students, and that this role more properly belongs to adults. While this was true, a number of students interviewed expressed themselves as feeling that high school students should play a more representative part in establishing the standards by which they were to be judged. In a number of schools, practices were observed which made such representative participation possible. *The approach to citizenship through conformance to standards of established conduct appears more effective the more widely and thoroughly students are involved in determining what these standards should be.*

The third most characteristic approach to citizenship in the American high school is through limited student participation in the management of school affairs. This approach in the high school sometimes has an eerie similarity to the kind of government found in a crown colony. Its principal instruments are the student council, which often serves as an advisory body to the principal and as a coordinator of specified student activities under his supervision, and school clubs. High schools assume that student participation through student councils and club organizations affords a practical mode of learning responsible citizenship. In principle, this assumption seems valid. Participating students have opportunities to learn the difficulties and possibilities of individual leadership, the requirements of useful membership in productive groups, committee and parliamentary procedures, and other things that are useful to know as an adult citizen. The proportion of students involved in student council work, however, whatever its quality, is relatively small. Great numbers of boys and girls are recorded as members of club organizations, but it is not clear how many gain substantial experience in responsibility in extracurricular programs. The approach to citizenship through limited participation in the management of school affairs, while sound in principle, in practice is too often narrow and unimaginatively pursued. *This approach has impressive vitality and impact where school leadership actively plans for a maximum number of students to be involved in carrying responsibility, not only in developing policies and in conducting activities, but in sharing in the real work of operating the school.*

The fourth most common approach to citizenship in the American high school is that it can be learned by study and experience in actual community and public affairs. To this end, a wide range of educational practices has been developed. Some of these have their springboard in the classroom and involve students in community study, field investigation, and simple civic action. Others, perhaps more common, involve a limited number of students, usually adult-selected, in simulated civic participation of the "government-for-a-day" variety. Some of these programs are widespread enough and of sufficient continuity and realism to give students a substantial experience. While strongly encouraged by many educators and community leaders, this approach has not become fundamentally characteristic of high school efforts in citizenship education. This approach is overshadowed by the effort to teach citizenship by books, homework, recitation, and testing. *Studies and experience with this approach indicate that its more widespread and wise use could contribute materially to the quality of citizenship education in the American high school.*

The fifth approach to civic education in the American high school is that good citizenship (i.e., basic values, self-respect and discipline, affirmative and responsible social relations, functional grasp of relevant information, etc.) is learned best through the total culture of the school. *This approach is widely affirmed as being desirable, but in practice it is unusual to encounter a high school where the possibilities of this approach are adequately explored or realized.*

Each of the five approaches to citizenship touched upon is found in most present-day American secondary schools. Each approach, depending on how it is interpreted and put to work, can give impetus to a strong, adequate high school program of citizenship development. It is not surprising that there are observable inadequacies in the civic education approaches of a universal system of secondary education which has grown so fast in such a short interval of time. It would be surprising, too, if some of these practices were not obsolescent and inappropriate in an age of accelerating technological, social, economic, and political change. The American high school does not need to seek new fundamental approaches to citizenship development. What is needed is to strengthen and improve the approaches that have already been mapped out.

POLITICS, PATRIOTISM, AND THE TEACHER

David Spitz

Can citizenship education in a democracy be meaningful in the face of sporadic but recurrent pressures toward social conformity and uncritical or even blind patriotism? Can the teacher fulfill an obligation to aid students in the search for truth, promote the cause of liberty, and still remain patriotic? What, after all, is patriotism? Where should the teacher place his loyalty in a democratic society? These dilemmas are analyzed by the author of this selection; he presents a fundamental rationale that should be stimulating to teachers of social studies. Omitted here are several portions of the writer's analysis that appeared in the original article.

EVERYWHERE custom is king, and everywhere men think themselves free even as they bend the knee to it. They mean to get along; they seek approval and success; they comply, therefore, with customary ways and customary expectations. They do not so much submit as behave, for to submit is to yield one's inclination to custom, and they have no inclinations except for

FROM *The National Elementary Principal*, 43:17–22, January, 1964. Used by permission. Dr. Spitz is a professor of political science at Ohio State University.

what is customary. And because *they* behave, and are comfortable in doing so, they are disquieted and irked by those who talk and act otherwise than they do.

What is true of men in general is true of teachers in particular. In the folk-lore of the academy, teachers are the victims of conformist pressures. They are oppressed by governments, harassed by private power groups, and suffo-cated by a climate of opinion which not only punishes them for unorthodox speech and improper behavior but, more importantly, prevents them, by a well-inculcated fear of probable consequences, from embarking on such speech or behavior at all. And as with all bits of folklore, there is sufficient evidence to make the point credible.

But in reality, teachers are as much, if not more, the creators of conformity. For teachers, though they might be expected to know better, are by and large no different from other men. They too have their vanities and their precious dreams. They too want to be appreciated, nay, applauded and esteemed. They too accept the values and the myths of their community. Hence they too are annoyed by those among them who disturb their tran-quility and repose.

Conformity in education, then, is not merely a matter of pressure from without. It is this, to be sure; but it is also a pressure from within. Thus he who would oppose these pressures must be prepared to dwell always under double jeopardy. He must withstand the external pressures of governments and of private powers, and he must withstand the internal pressures of the teaching profession itself. In each case, moreover, he must understand that even where these forces act in the furtherance of their special interests, they speak always in the rhetoric of idealism. And in these difficult times there is no idealism as appealing as patriotism. . . .

POLITICS AND THE GOOD LIFE

Consider first the impact of politics on education. Of the two dominant schools of political thought, one relates politics to the good life, or justice; the other, to a struggle for power. Yet each has, with one crucial exception, similar consequences for the teacher. . . .

The notion of politics as a struggle for power has a redeeming feature. Since, in a democracy, power is multicentered, there are power groups outside the government that insist on their right to carry on their own type of indoctri-nation. (This is one reason why we have denominational schools.) And since those who currently occupy the seats of political power may someday be out of power, and will then want (hopefully sooner rather than later) to be re-turned, they are prepared to accept criticism that is leveled at a particular political party or social or economic group or government. But they are not equally prepared to welcome criticism of the system that enables them to exist in such form and to carry on their activities. Hence the teacher must still indoctrinate, albeit at a more general level. Now he indoctrinates not so much in support of, say, Republicans or Democrats, but in support of the democratic system, or what is alleged to be the democratic system, that makes the rule of both parties—either alone or in concert—possible.

This is euphemistically known as education for democracy, or education for citizenship. For the teacher who believes in such indoctrination, there is, of course, no problem. But for the teacher who holds to an antidemocratic philosophy or who, while himself a democrat (with a small "d"), conceives it his function to subject even democratic principles, or political and social practices popularly believed to be consistent with democratic principles, to the test of reason, there may be no end of difficulties.

For it is still true, on any fair reading of the historical evidence, that men in power are motivated less by abstract considerations of justice than they are by the promotion of their conceived interests. Those who teach things that question the value of the interests pursued, or the pursuit of such interests in the established ways, are often deemed to be enemies—not simply of the power groups but of the social order that makes possible, and in that sense sanctions or approves, their power and conduct. Hence, we return to the point that the teacher is expected to indoctrinate one way or the other—either as a defender of the underlying system or as a protagonist of a particular power group. He is not free to teach what he wants. He must teach as he is expected. . . .

In both theories of politics, there is a demand by society that the teacher become a servant of the power system and not a free and independent thinker. Only in one theory—that which allows a subjective judgment as to the justice of the existing order—can the teacher claim a right to serve as a free critic.

IDEAS ABOUT PATRIOTISM

As there are opposing theories of politics, so there are conflicting theories *about* patriotism and *of* patriotism. All derive from the idea that patriotism means love of nation or of country, but they differ both in what they mean by love of country and in the value they attach to this love. Hence they differ, too, in their consequences for the teacher. . . .

Take, first, the conflict of ideas *about* patriotism. In what I understand to be the dominant (if largely unarticulated) American view, patriotism is that attitude which puts one's nation or country not merely above self but above humanity. It is idle, therefore, to argue—and improper to teach—that unlike dictatorship, where man is said to exist for the state, in democracy the state exists for man. Whatever the claims of individuality, they are less important and less compelling than the claims of nation or country. Whatever the needs of humanity, whatever the democratic teaching affirming the equality of man or the religious teaching affirming the brotherhood of man, the first priority is that of *national* welfare, the first teaching that of *national* superiority. We can see this not merely in the idolatrous worship of national symbols—e.g., the flag, the Constitution, the national anthem—but in the insistence that men go forth to fight, if necessary to die, for the security and glory of their country.

If follows, therefore, from this idea about the exalted value of patriotism—a view which, for purposes of contrast, I deliberately put here in extreme form— that the teacher's duty is to inculcate the primary obligations of citizenship: loyalty to, nay reverence of, the state and obedience to the law. He may, to be sure, have his pupils recite the words, "In democracy the state is for man, not man for the state," for this rhetoric is still esteemed, but he must make certain that they understand (as the citizens of Orwell's 1984 came to understand) that words are not always what they seem.

There is, however, an alternative judgment about the value of patriotism. . . . Under this conception, the teacher is forced to evaluate both our institutions and our policies by an ideal standard. And since, as I indicated before, an actual state can never be more than an imperfect state, this view of patriotism leads the teacher once again to essay the role of social critic.

One need go no further than to refer to our state and national policies concerning our various minority groups or those who wish to immigrate to this country to see that a teacher who is patriotic in the second sense of this term will run afoul of those who are patriotic in the first sense of the term.

THE FUNCTION OF THE TEACHER

As men disagree on politics and on patriotism, so they disagree on education.

According to the dominant view, the teacher is to teach what is perceptibly useful and right. He must, to be sure, develop (or at least try to develop) certain technical skills on the part of his students: they should, it is generally expected, know how to read and write and execute simple computations with reasonable competence; they should even, perhaps, acquire the virtue of occasional silence. But his primary resonsibility is to transmit and thereby to instill in his students a love of—the accepted view of—what constitutes the American way of life. . . .

There is, however, . . . a contrary view of the proper function of the teacher. This derives from the principle that the school is a center of intellectual inquiry and that academic freedom means not only the freedom of the teachers to teach but the freedom of the teacher and the student to learn. What are they to learn? Quite simply, the truth; at the very least they must be free to seek the truth.

Here it is evident, the teacher cannot readily bestride these opposing views. He must seek either to encourage unswerving obedience to the law or invite his students critically to examine the law's moral content and the sometimes distressing consequences of compliance. His model—at least in the questioning —must be Jean Valjean, or Javert. It seems almost superfluous to add that in times of crisis—and somehow we seem to live now nearly always in a time of crisis—the demands of authority are all too easily equated in the public mind with the requirements of justice.

THE TEACHER AS CONFORMIST

The problem of the teacher thus derives—I tend to think fundamentally—from the fact that men hold opposing views of politics, patriotism, and the teacher; and that, in each case, what I take to be the wrong view has moved, by and large, into a position of dominance. This is true not only of those who command positions of power in the realm of politics and of the general state of public opinion with respect to the idea of patriotism, but even, I fear, of those who are teachers themselves.

I would deny, that is to say, the general presupposition that with respect to all these things the teacher stands on one side—the right side (which somehow, in the public mind, is too often construed to be the left side)—and the community on the other. It is my observation that while this conflict between the teacher and the community is very real and never totally absent, it is greatly exaggerated. The fact is that both teachers and community are internally divided; that many teachers think precisely as the dominant sectors in the community think—they share the same values, the same prejudices. Hence the issue is not simply that of teachers versus the community, but of a particular group of teachers who cling to one set of theories, along with a portion of the community that supports them, versus another group of teachers and those in the community who support them.

It is clear, I think, that in the resolution of this struggle, those who cling to the idea of a liberal education are not likely easily to prevail. Not only do they stand today on what may well be the losing side, or at least on that side which is today under the most severe and pressing attacks; what is more important, the opposition to the liberal idea of education is increasingly enlarged by insensitive, because intellectually deficient, products of our schools.

As a result, the essential push of politics and of patriotism on the schools will remain the push to conformity and not the drive for critical and independent thought. We can expect little significant relief from the whole silly business of loyalty or nondisclaimer oaths, of increased censorship or would-be censorship by parent and patriotic and governmental groups, of increased administrative supervision, of released time and religion-in-life week programs, and the like.

What is characteristic of our time is not that these pressures exist, for pressures of this sort have always beleagured the schools. What is distinctive, and disheartening, is the fact that the schools have not succeeded in defeating, or even (by and large) in opposing, these pressures. This is to be accounted for, in part, by the fact that teachers are often timid and respectable men who dislike to sully their hands in "dirty" politics; so they suffer the consequences of having lesser men rule over them. But it is also to be explained by the fact that some of our teachers themselves welcome these pressures and seek to impose them.

I do not wish to enter here into the controversy about the merits of progressive as against other kinds of education, for such an endeavor would require, among other things, the freeing of John Dewey's teachings from the vulgarizations that often impute to him doctrines he never held. I wish only to make one small, but in this context perhaps important, point. This is, that to the extent that the schools accept the notion of conformity, or of adjustment (as it is more pleasingly and popularly called), they help to destroy their own intellectual and moral foundations; they deny their very *raison d'être*.

For to make conformity or adjustment the goal—to believe that it is most important to produce men who are like other men, who are popular or at least accepted, who belong—is to make a travesty of the idea of education itself, which is to produce a man, a whole man, an individual with a personality and a mind and judgments of his own. To produce a whole man, an educated man, is to produce a reflective and critical intelligence. It is to place a premium on uniqueness; it is to value differences. If the schools abjure this and succumb to the mania for conformity, what will emerge is not the *autonomous* but the *anonymous* man. What will emerge is not a man at all, but a cipher.

I cannot emphasize this point too much, for what is vital is not simply adjustment to life, important as this undeniably is; for life includes the most loathsome forms of hypocrisy and degradation. What is vital is the pursuit of the good life, which includes the life of the mind, the beauties (as well as the agonies) of solitary contemplation, the pursuit of differences which give zest and excitement and bring grandeur and comedy to otherwise drab and penurious lives.

It is indeed a gross commentary on American life—and on its schools—that we have produced a breed of man who values money above beauty, who seeks power and prestige instead of happiness, who dreads the thought of retirement because he does not know what he will do with his time. Is it not a sobering thought that those we have taught to read prefer Spillane to Shakespeare?

The Teacher as Educator

How, then, are we to resist the push to conformity? (I say resist rather than overcome, for we are not likely ever to eliminate what is surely a universal characteristic of human society, even if it appears particularly pronounced or misguided in our own.)

The answer, I fear, is as simple as it may appear innocuous. This is, that we can do so only by remaining true to our calling as teachers, only by educating men in the proper sense of that term.

This is a simple but not an easy prescription, for it implies that as teachers we must be prepared to raise doubts in the minds of our children, to challenge the intellectual nonsense—the prejudices and the stereotypes—that their parents and elders have put there. But such parents and elders are not, customarily, people who are dissatisfied with their own ways of thought, their own patterns of behavior. On the contrary, they can rarely visualize anything better for their children than that they should be taught to think and to behave exactly as their parents and elders do. The teacher, then, who attempts—and if he is a teacher he *must* attempt—to introduce his students to new ideas, to new or different ways of conduct, must possess a degree of courage commensurate with his learning. He must be prepared to live not merely with the dislike of a portion, perhaps of a majority, of the community, but with the disrespect and inadequate rewards consequently given him.

Yet there remains always the consolation that in creating doubt and wonder where previously unreflective certainty reigned, he gives to his students the supreme gift that it lies within his power to confer: the dignity of intellectual freedom.

3

Controversial Issues and Current Affairs

CONTROVERSIAL ISSUES, SCHOOL POLICIES, AND REFLECTIVE THINKING

John P. Lunstrum

Selections appearing earlier in this volume (pages 33–46 and 94–105) have dealt in part with the teaching of controversial issues. In this article, a specialist in social studies education pulls together evidence that authorities in this field are not agreed on desirable treatment of controversial issues. Furthermore, educators' conceptions of the social role of the school and lay and professional policies for schools also exhibit notable divergence. Omitted here is a section of the original article on the social foundations of the controversy, a facet treated more fully by Spitz in the immediately preceding selection.

RECENT accounts in the press and reports from teachers suggest increasing activity on the part of extremist organizations who are apparently bent on making the school and teachers instruments of their own policies. The concern of some NCSS teachers is reflected in the passage by the members of the Indiana Council for the Social Studies on April 15, 1961, of a vigorous resolution asserting in part that "such efforts to use the schools as tools of blatant indoctrination are more representative of the Totalitarian than the Democratic tradition." The unanimous endorsement of a similar resolution by the NCSS during its 1961 convention suggests that teachers in many states are deeply troubled by what an executive secretary of one Midwestern state teachers association has called the "Vigilante impulse." (1) It seems appropriate, therefore, to explore certain basic issues concerning school policy and the educative use of controversy and to raise the question: What practical steps can social studies teachers and school administrators take in their own communities and in the classroom to safeguard the freedom of teaching and learning?

FROM *Social Education*, 26:189–192, April, May, 1962. Used by permission. Dr. Lunstrum is coordinator for school social studies at Indiana University.

Background of the Problem

The significant publications of professional and academic organizations during the last three decades have continuously emphasized the legitimate position of controversial issues in the secondary school curriculum and the freedom of teachers to deal with such topics particularly in social studies classes. Despite the sanction of such organizations as the American Historical Association, the Mississippi Valley Historical Society, the National Council for the Social Studies, and the Educational Policies Commission of the NEA, there is increasing evidence that teachers lack a clear understanding of their proper role insofar as the treatment of controversial issues is concerned. Investigations made concerning teacher attitudes on this subject in several states indicate that many teachers lack insight into the nature of a genuinely controversial issue; these studies also suggest that a substantial number of teachers have no conception of a defensible theory with which they could support the introduction of controversial topics or materials into the classroom. (2)

Factors Underlying Confusion

When questioned specifically on their freedom or willingness to express opinions on controversial topics teachers revealed uncertainty and confusion. For example, in two inquiries conducted in 1953 and 1957 in Ohio and Virginia, teachers were apparently willing to endorse the utilization of controversy on an abstract level, but when confronted with the need for a specific application of this principle, they tended to acquiesce in certain limitations or taboos. (3) . . .

These comments are in no way offered in disparagement of classroom teachers or administrators. That educators have made great gains in public recognition with the assistance of their professional organizations is clearly evident. The difficulties they face in trying to place into practice the ideals of intellectual freedom may be viewed in part as a reflection of the conflicts in values in American education. One has only to examine a number of social studies methods texts to illustrate this point. Some authors advocate extreme caution, particularly with reference to the expression of opinion by the teacher. Emphasis is placed on "presenting facts as they really are," (4) and the teacher's role is seen as one of "neutrality." (5) The author of a pamphlet published by the NCSS entitled, "How to Handle Controversial Issues," advises teachers to avoid stating their beliefs in order to encourage pupils to do their own thinking. These points of view are challenged by other methodologists and social scientists who contend that it is impossible for a teacher to exemplfy reflective thinking in a classroom and conceal his own opinions. (6)

On the subject of the instructor's qualifications to explore the realms of controversy, some writers insist that the teacher must first possess a high degree of scholarship and a mastery of the pertinent facts; (7) others urge the teacher to assume the position of a "learner among learners." (8) To the question as to how much emphasis to assign to the study of controversial topics, there is an equally contradictory array of answers. Only a "few topics" in current events are likely to be controversial according to one ruling (9) while other claims are made that the study of controversial materials is implicit in the social studies (10) and that controversial topics should be deliberately and frequently introduced into class discussion and study. (11)

This conflict in education seems to be part of a larger problem, for there is a growing body of evidence accumulated by social scientists and other students of society that American society is confronted today by a cultural crisis of increasing dimensions. (12) Various symptoms frequently cited as evidence include: (1) confusion and contradiction in values, (2) decline in communication, (3) personal disorganization, (4) discontent of the intellectuals, and (5) an irrationality expressed in the cultivation of myths, absolutes, and a "two-valued" semantic orientation based upon simple "good" and "bad" distinctions. . . .

SCHOOL AND SOCIETY

Underlying a discussion of this problem are undoubtedly a number of differing assumptions about the proper relationship between the school and the society it serves. (12) Some educators may feel strongly that the school is simply an instrument of culture yet powerless to act upon culture; hence the formal educational process under these conditions becomes primarily concerned with preparing the student to make successful adaptation to existing social conditions. Others may agree with Russell Kirk when he insists that "what the twentieth century needs is the check-rein not the goad." (13) If this viewpoint is influential in schools, it means renewed emphasis on the school's function in the conservation and transmission of the cultural heritage and the introduction of controversial topics into the curriculum seems to interfere with the inculcation of basic virtues. Still another interpretation of the social role of the school stresses its operation not only as a means of assimilating traditions but also as a creative force in shaping individuals and modifying beliefs and institutions. (14) The latter view is more compatible with the deliberate introduction of disputed subjects into the course of study.

Social role of the school: a persistent issue.

All of this is by no means new to education. From the time of Plato and Aristotle there have been rival conceptions of the social role of the school—viewed by some as a medium of social regeneration and by others as a defender of the *status quo*. (15) The passive role of the school has been demonstrated also in the political and economic revolutions of the eighteenth, nineteenth, and twentieth centuries. Examination of the curricula, existing laws, and the views of influential persons point to the conclusion that the school then was fundamentally an apologist for the *status quo regardless* of the revolutionary or reactionary nature of the prevailing social order. (16) Even the educational statesman, Horace Mann, struggled on the horns of this dilemma. While espousing freedom of discussion in the halls of Congress, he still found it necessary to endorse some form of introduction and to forbid the introduction of controversial questions into the classroom—particularly the question of slavery. (17)

DEVELOPMENT OF SCHOOL POLICIES

In the face of increasing attacks some school systems in the early 1950's began to formulate written policies concerning controversial issues to communicate to the public the meaning of intellectual freedom in classrooms and the responsibilities of teachers. Support for this move came from several quarters. The American Legion had passed a resolution during its 1949 convention sanctioning the constructive use of controversial topics and providing suggested criteria for the evaluation of instructional materials. (18) In 1951 the Committee on Academic Freedom of the National Council for the Social Studies urged that written criteria should be available to teachers, administrators, school board members, and patrons. (19) By 1952 the superintendents of schools in cities of 200,000 or more population had developed a statement of policy, part of which urged that "instructional policy on controversial issues should be defined by constituted authority in order to protect teachers and school administrators from unwarranted attack by pressure groups. . . ." (20)

(1) Robert H. Wyatt. "The Vigilante Impulse." *The Indiana Teacher*. 106: 159–161; December 1961. Based only on data compiled in one state this inquiry suffers from certain obvious limitations. Nevertheless, in the light of research on the values and attitudes of students, teachers, and administrators, it is not unreasonable to contend that Indiana furnishes a useful case study in the analysis of a national educational problem; a proposition reinforced by the recent marked increase of vocal groups convinced (as Dexter Perkins says of the radicals) of their "own righteousness and, almost equally certainly, of the unrighteousness of others." (Dexter Perkins. *The American Way*. Ithaca, New York: Cornell University Press, 1957. p. 60.)

(2) Calvin Deam. *Opinions of Virginia Schoolmen Concerning the Treatment of Controversial Issues*. Indiana University, 1958. 357 p.; T. L. Hall. A *Study of the Teaching of Controversial Issues in the Secondary Schools of the State of Ohio*. Ohio State University, 1953. 250 p.; M. J. Felsinger. *Investigation of the Study of Controversial Issues of American Democracy in Certain High Schools in Oklahoma*. University of Oklahoma, 1952. 167 p. All three of these studies were completed as doctoral theses.

(3) *Ibid*.

(4) Arthur C. and H. David Bining.

Teaching the Social Studies in Secondary Schools. New York: McGraw-Hill Book Company, 1952. p. 323.

(5) *Ibid*.

(6) Maurice P. Hunt and Lawrence E. Metcalf. *Teaching High School Social Studies*. New York: Harper and Brothers, 1955. p. 439; Earl S. Johnson. *Theory and Practice of the Social Studies*. New York: The Macmillan Company, 1956. p. 50–51.

(7) Edgar B. Wesley. *Teaching the Social Studies in High School*. Boston: D. C. Heath and Company, 1950. p. 16–17.

(8) Richard E. Gross. "How to Handle Controversial Issues." No. 14 of the How To Do It Series. Washington, D.C.: The National Council for the Social Studies, 1958.

(9) Maurice P. Moffatt. *Social Studies Instruction*. Englewood Cliffs, N.J.: Prentice-Hall, 1954. p. 348.

(10) Earl S. Johnson. *Theory and Practice of the Social Studies*. New York: The Macmillan Company, 1956. p. 145.

(11) Hunt and Metcalf, *op. cit.*, p. 21.

(12) R. F. Butts and L. A. Cremin. *A History of Education in American Culture*. Holt and Company, 1953. p. 542–543.

(13) Russell Kirk. "Conservative vs. Liberal: A Debate." *New York Times Magazine*. March 4, 1956.

(14) National Education Association Educational Policies Commission. *Policies for Education in American Democracy*. Washington, D.C.: The Association, 1946. p. 128.

(15) J. S. Brubacher. *A History of the Problems of Education*. New York: McGraw-Hill Book Company, 1947. p. 613–615.

(16) R. E. Potter. *The Role of the School in a Transitional Society*, in *Dissertation Abstracts*. Vol. 15. Ann Arbor, Michigan: University Microfilms, 1955. p. 79.

(17) Merle Curti. *The Social Ideas of American Educators*. American Historical Association, Report of the Commission on the Social Studies. New York: Charles Scribner's Sons, 1934. p. 127–130.

(18) F. L. Haight. "Evaluation of Instructional Materials." *Educational Leadership* 8:349–352; March 1951.

(19) National Council for the Social Studies, Committee on Academic Freedom. "The Treatment of Controversial Issues in the Schools," *Social Education* 15:232–236; May 1951.

(20) National Education Association, Committee on Tenure and Academic Freedom. "What Policies Should Guide the Handling of Controversial Issues?" June 1954, p. 20–22.

HOW TO AVOID BEING HALF SAFE

Kenneth McIntyre

Responsible persons would scarcely deny that effective treatment of controversial issues in social studies is a serious matter. But the pressures and criticisms identified in the preceding selections sometimes carry to ridiculous extremes. The author of this article briefly satirizes the critics by literally applying their ideas to various contents of the curriculum.

FROM *Phi Delta Kappan*, 44:27–28, October, 1962. Used by permission. Dr. McIntyre is a professor of school administration at the University of Texas.

EVERY time a teacher is attacked for dealing with a "controversial issue," other teachers are less likely to take a chance with that issue. Since all issues are by definition controversial, teachers are finding themselves in the difficult position of not knowing which topics will be next to join the untouchables. Social studies teachers in particular are being forced to scurry about like TV criminals in a warehouse, seeking momentary protection behind one barrier after another, only to have the cops strike again from a new vantage point after each brief respite. By following a defensive course of action, the teacher finds that every unassailable position seems to be matched by an ephemeral haven that soon becomes a target for a new assault.

But why be just half safe? Why not launch a bold new approach to teaching that will render content and methods completely beyond attack? In this article I shall present a few illustrative examples of what I affectionately call The McIntyre Plan.

All references to Russia and her satellites will have to be eliminated from the curriculum, of course. Simply avoiding mention of such topics should be easy enough, but certain problems will require special attention. For example, maps will have to be redrawn or altered so that the learners will not come into contact with Communist countries and risk learning to love them. To avoid confusing children by expanding the areas of the freedom-loving countries to fill the void, it would probably be best to cover the controversial areas with advertising, thereby also achieving the concomitant purpose of providing a source of income that should bring much-needed tax relief.

Offensive music, art, and literature should also be removed from the curriculum. Teachers should eliminate not only the products of known communists, but also those of left-wingers, sympathizers, and dupes. The problem of identifying sympathizers and dupes would not be as difficult as one might surmise, for they have already been counted by Robert Welch.

"The Star-Spangled Banner" should be sung daily, provided it is cleaned up to read: "Then conquer we must, *since* our cause it is just," instead of "*when* our cause it is just." On second thought, the entire last stanza might well be omitted entirely, since it not only questions the justness of our cause but also mentions God—a controversial figure if there ever was one.

History books are particularly likely to poison young minds if not carefully written. Because of the difficulty of accounting for twelve years of the American presidency if the New Deal were omitted, FDR will probably have to stay, but his wife must go. If a curious or fellow-traveling child should inquire about her, the teacher should merely say, "There *was* a woman in the White House those twelve years, but we don't talk about such things."

Certain well-known quotations can be retained in history books, provided they are revised to meet current requirements for safety. The following are illustrative of how simple it is to bring history up to date:

1. Woodrow Wilson: "The world must be made safe for democracy."
Suggested revision: *The world must be made safe for republican forms of government.* (This is a republic, not a democracy. Let's keep it that way.)
2. Stephen Decatur: "Our country! In her intercourse with foreign nations, may she always be in the right; but our country, right or wrong."
Suggested revision: *Our country! In her relations with foreign nations, may she always be in the right, as she always has been; but if she should ever be somewhat wrong, I'll go along with her anyway.* (1)
3. Thomas Paine: "The world is my country, all mankind are my brethren, and to do good is my religion."
Suggested revision: *America first, to hell with the rest of the world, and to do good is to be a do-gooder.*

A serious question should be raised concerning the use of the McGuffey Readers. Lurking beneath the surface of McGuffey's ostensibly high moral concepts are some subtle inroads on love of country, in the form of controversial authorship. *McGuffey's New Sixth Eclectic Reader* contains some of the works of Dr. Samuel Johnson, who clearly demonstrated how un-American he was in at least two ways: (1) by being an Englishman, and (2) by making the remark: "Patriotism is the last refuge of a scoundrel."

Teachers should be cautioned against the use of certain words. So that children will not be beguiled by its erroneous doctrines, the word *socialism* should not be mentioned. Also, to be completely safe one should avoid such terms as *social studies, social service,* and *sociology.* The term *evolution* should also be eliminated; an alert teacher will not even speak of the evolution of the tragedy in literary works such as *Macbeth.*

Although nobody objects to the separation of church and state, religion can occupy much of the time freed by the elimination of controversial topics, provided that the Bible is not used. Certain passages, probably inserted by some Communistic amanuensis back in the seventeenth century when King James wasn't looking, are offensive to all right-thinking Americans. Two examples follow:

Matt. 6:19—Lay not up for yourselves treasures upon earth, where moth and rust doth corrupt, and where thieves break through and steal.

Where could one find a more direct assault on our capitalistic virtues of acquisition and thrift? The same leftist forces are at work here:

Matt. 19:22—"He went away sorrowful; for he had great possessions."

It should go without saying that schooling in the future should be rigorous as well as pro-American. Children must be taught to think. Instead of being nurtured on the banalities of *Dick and Jane,* pupils should have to come to grips with such questions as the following, which are both safe and demanding:

How sound was the dollar that Washington threw across the Potomac?

What was the name, age, and home town of Paul Revere's horse?

State whether you are for or against the oppressive, un-American income tax, and support your position with unbiased arguments.

Which one of the following is good:
- a. T.V.A.
- b. N.E.A.
- c. D.A.R.
- d. U.N.

Finally, one should devote a significant portion of his class time each semester to a series of lectures on certain blessings that we Americans enjoy. For example, students should be impressed with the importance of freedom of inquiry, the cornerstone of our structure of American freedoms. In the free time that is created by not readings books, not looking at maps or art works, not listening to music, and not discussing issues, students can be required to write essays on such subjects as "Knowledge Is Power" and "Why Truth Always Prevails."

(1) Teachers should explain that this noble sentiment is not appropriate for enemy nations. The people of enemy nations are stupid for following their wrong leadership.

IMPROVING CURRENT EVENTS INSTRUCTION

Philmore B. Wass

This selection presents a résumé of approaches in the direct teaching of current events. The writer also offers tangible suggestions for improving such instruction, based on his unusually broad experience as a teacher and as an editor of one of the major series of weekly current events papers for schools.

FROM *Social Education,* 25:79–81, February, 1961. Used by permission. Dr. Wass is a professor in the School of Education, University of Connecticut.

S OCIAL studies teachers throughout the United States devote some part of each week's instructional time to teaching current events. Before discussing new techniques it might be well to take a look at some of the practices which seem to be in fairly common use. These practices can be observed by anyone who visits a number of schools. The value of current events instruction has often been judged unfairly because of these methods.

Scatter-gun Method: This method calls for each student, on a specified day of the week, (usually Friday), to bring in a current event. Any newspaper within a school on current events day has an extremely short life span—it is quickly shredded by students looking for brief items upon which they can report.

These reports often are presented in a random series which may jump in a five-minute period from the Congo to the elections, to a severe auto accident, to who won the World Series.

A Current Event-A-Day: Another approach appears in this form: Each day the teacher begins class by saying, "Did anyone hear anything of interest on the news, this morning?" A hand goes up. (Often the same ones go up each day.) The teacher acknowledges a student who then makes a sketchy comment. Little discussion can follow because other students may not have heard the same broadcast. Soon the class turns its attention to the day's lessons.

Paneled News: The class has previously been divided and assigned such news categories as government, United Nations, economic news, sports, etc.

At the beginning of each period a panel—one person from each category—goes to the front of the room. Just previous to this you might see at least two of the panel members looking about them, motioning wildly to classmates for "just a morsel of news."

These panels are often of short duration because the class may know even less on the news items presented than many students. The panel soon ends and regular work proceeds.

The Line-Upon-Line Approach: These classes receive each week a bundle of student news periodicals. The teacher carefully keeps the bundle until current events day—then the package is opened and each student receives his copy and often turns immediately to the jokes.

As the class begins, all students are instructed to turn their papers back to page one. Then there follows a paragraph-by-paragraph oral reading of the text, each student taking his turn. It takes about a period to get through the lead story. When the bell rings the papers are usually stuffed into desks, pockets, or notebooks, not to be retrieved until a washing or general housecleaning brings the long-forgotten papers again to light.

Basically there is nothing wrong with any of these approaches if its full potential is realized and if it is used as part of a varying pattern. But before these techniques can be improved, or other techniques devised, a teacher must have a clear answer to the following question: What is the place of current events in the social studies program?

No reminder is needed that the objective of all public school education is effective citizenship conceived in its broadest sense. And within the curriculum, the social studies have the specific job of training for dealing with present and future civic problems on a local, state, national and international level.

Accepting this aim, the place of current events in the social studies curriculum becomes clear. An understanding of current events, with a focus on the future, should be the aim of the entire social studies program. This can be clearly seen in each social studies area. The purpose of studying history in public schools is to utilize information and ideas from man's past experience for understanding his *present* problems. Geography emphasizes how men's physical environment shapes the way he lives—*in the present*. Economics makes young people aware of the patterns and forces which operate as we strive to meet our *present economic needs*. Political science serves as a guide and preparation for understanding and participation in civic affairs *now and in the future*. Social studies material taken from anthropology draws information from other cultures to enrich understanding of our own *present way of living*.

No teacher who accepts the above need ever be puzzled by whether or not, or how much, current events should be taught in the social studies; rather, we should be concerned with what social science information, and how much is needed to make current events comprehensible to his students.

Current events, then, is not something special but is an integral part of the social studies curriculum. The study of the current world must never be treated as something apart. This is not to say, however, that study of the current scene is only to be done when it happens to fit into an on-going social studies unit. A requisite for applying social science information and concepts to the present is a continuously developing knowledge of the present.

Young people, then, should constantly be encouraged to read newspapers and other news periodicals, listen to news broadcasts and telecasts, and read school news periodicals. They will also need to be taught the skills of news reading, listening and viewing. When the news events are known, the social studies information being gained from daily study can be used to put these current events in their proper perspective.

If the study of current events is to occupy this important place in the curriculum, then every attempt must be made to develop news interest in young people. There are many techniques for doing this.

Evaluating News: One of the basic approaches is to teach young people how to evaluate news. This should involve a study of newspapers and news services. It should also include specific training in evaluating news reports. Young people should learn early to suspect the accuracy of news reports which begin with such phrases as "informed sources say," or "those close to the President report."

Instruction should also be given in deciding the weight to be given the syndicated wisdom of the news commentator and the columnist. Characteristics of a well-qualified person in these fields can be set up in chart form. It should include such things as academic training, experience, travel, and writing. Investigation can then be made of the backgrounds of commentators and columnists and they can be rated according to how many of the desirable characteristics they possess. A part of this process should be monitoring newscasts and reading the syndicated columns for several weeks to discover the pattern of news selection and any biases which might be revealed.

Biographical Studies: The lives of people important in the news have high interest for students. A series of reports or panels on famous world figures, accompanied by bulletin board displays on their activities, should stimulate news reading. At this time such figures as Castro, Eisenhower, Hammarskjold, Khrushchev, Macmillan and Nehru should be of interest.

Role-Playing: Socio-drama or role-playing, valuable in many social studies situations, has much to contribute in current events study. Within each problem on the current scene can be found a variety of viewpoints. These can often be dramatized and delineated by having students assume the roles of the chief protagonists. Many thought-provoking issues from the local to the international scene can be studied in this way.

In preparation, students will need background information so that all viewpoints can be accurately expressed. Simple issues with which students are quite familiar should be tried at first. However, as students grow in skill and knowledge, staged discussions among such groups as U.N. delegates can be tried with profit. Congressional debates, labor-management negotiations— any area in which issues must be resolved through discussion—are suitable for this technique. The greatest value of role-playing is probably in the stimulation for whole-class discussion and the interest aroused in learning more about the problem.

Current Events and Action: The Citizenship Education Project at Columbia University places emphasis on the action phase of social studies education. Action is also an essential in current events instruction. It adds meaning to the study of any current problem, and is, of course, important in itself in creating a climate of not just studying problems, but studying them as a guide to suitable action toward their solution.

The action phase may take many forms. After careful study of a problem, a class may want to report its views to the proper authorities. Or the students may wish to inform others by holding a school or community forum. Another variation might be to set up a class speakers bureau and offer teams of student speakers to town civic and social organizations.

Action might also take the form of raising money to give aid in a needy country through CARE. The final result of such a project would be a growing interest in and understanding of the problems of less developed nations and the realization that even a small amount of money can make a significant contribution.

The number of techniques which can be devised for interesting young people in current events need not be limited to the imagination of the teacher. If she will draw freely upon the imagination of her class in planning current events instruction, a rich program is bound to result.

SUMMARY

In summary these points should be stressed:

1. The purpose of all social studies instruction is to understand the present as preparation for civic action and to prepare for dealing with the problems of the future.
2. Current events is always an integral part of the social studies program. All the thought and resources which go into teaching each of the social studies should be finally focused on interpreting the current scene and preparing for the future.
3. The number of devices for interesting young people in current events is unlimited if the full imaginative powers of the teacher-class team are utilized. Variety of procedure has the same interest-arousing power in current events as in all other subjects.

MAKING HISTORY RELEVANT

James M. Wallace

Many teachers regard the direct teaching of current affairs as unsatisfactory or, at best, insufficient. They employ also, or instead, an approach that relates basic subject matter selected from the social sciences to contemporary events. The writer of this selection provides a specific example of a way in which historical background can be purposely and significantly related to current affairs. Such an approach may well improve the teaching of both history and current events.

MOST history teachers who consider their subject a functional one would probably agree that the study of fairly recent events is of most value to their students. We tell our classes that knowledge of the past—particularly

FROM *Social Education*, 26:17–18, 24, January, 1962. Used by permission. Mr. Wallace is a former social studies teacher now serving as guidance counselor at Rundlett Junior High School, Concord, New Hampshire.

the not-too-distant past—is necessary if we are to understand the present and to influence the future. And yet most of us can think of history courses we have taken (or still worse, taught) in which the class did not complete the planned course of study. Each spring, American history teachers throughout the country can be heard to say, "I'll never make it! We haven't even finished the first World War!"

Usually we manage to bring the students up to date, but this heroic feat is accomplished by skimming the New Deal, World War II, the Korean War, and the cold war. Some ambitious person could make an interesting study comparing the time the average American history class spends on the American Revolution and on World War II.

There are a number of reasons why the recent past is probably the most poorly taught period of history. One is the matter of "textbook lag," coupled with our unfortunate dependence on the text. Our students pick up from us the idea that anything of importance *must* be in the text; if the text ends with Eisenhower's re-election, then obviously nothing of importance has happened since 1956. Another reason is to be found in our poorly developed time sense. In September the months stretch out ahead of us; *this* year we'll do a really thorough job on the colonial period. In February we are pursuing Grant and Lee across Virginia. But in May we are frantically trying to dispose of Harding, Coolidge, and Hoover.

On the college level, I suspect that the reason is often that the instructor feels a compulsion to pass on the results of his research to his "captive audience." In 1927 Professor Snead completed his dissertation on Shays' Rebellion; since then, every history major passing through Ivyhall College has spent three weeks following the activities of Daniel and his unruly friends.

We feel a continual tension between our desire to teach thoroughly and our feeling that we must "cover" (*uncover* would be a better word) the whole period of history included in our course. Unfortunately, we often resolve this problem by teaching most thoroughly those periods of history which are most remote from our students, and of least relevance to the situations which they will face as adult citizens.

The logical solution to this problem is to start our historical study with the present. A course in United States history would begin with a unit on America's current situation. Such a unit may be called "Project 1962," "Current Problems and News Stories," "Events Which Will Change Our Lives," or by some other title appropriate to the age and ability of the class. Whatever the title, the purpose of this introductory unit is to help students develop a clear picture of America as it exists now, with all its successes and problems. Then, as the class shifts back to the traditional chronological approach, the students will have a fairly sound idea of the kind of society which historical developments have created in the United States.

Students are often surprised and pleased to discover that they know a great deal about history as it is being made right now. Whatever else we may say about it, television has done an impressive job of dramatizing recent events in science, defense, politics, race relations, and international affairs. The discovery that they have some understanding of current history often gives students the confidence and motivation to study more distant events with enthusiasm and success.

This unit may be approached in a number of ways. Some students write fascinating essays on "A Teenager's View of the United States," or "A British (or Cuban, or Russian, or African) Student Looks at America." Younger students enjoy writing on "The United States as Seen by a Martian," or "Benjamin Franklin Returns in 1962." Any means of getting students to stand back and look at their country with some perspective is helpful in building this unit.

These introductory activities should lead up to the construction of a list of major problems facing this country. Right now such a list might include:

1. The International Scene.
   a. Congo, Laos, and other former colonies.
   b. The role of the United Nations.
   c. Cuba's revolution and related Latin-American problems.
   d. Communist and Nationalist China—what policy for the West?
   e. Russia and the cold war.
   f. America's defenses and alliances.
   g. World population and food supply.
   h. Trade, aid, and the gold supply.
   i. Disarmament.
   j. The space race.
   k. The Berlin crisis.
2. The Domestic Scene.
   a. Recession and unemployment—the business cycle.
   b. Education and research.
   c. Politics.
   d. The problems of agriculture.
   e. City planning, slum clearance, and other urban problems.
   f. Civil Liberties—freedom and security.
   g. Taxation and government expenditures.
   h. Race relations.

After the class has decided on a list of problems which are descriptive of America's present situation, the topics may be chosen by individuals or committees for study. The purpose at this point is not an exhaustive job of research, but a quick survey in which students define the problem, learn why it is important, determine its background and causes, and find out what some proposed or attempted solutions have been. More mature and thoughtful students can often suggest other solutions from their own study and reflection.

Even a fairly brief study of any of the above problems is enough to show students that these difficulties have not sprung into the headlines overnight. A student investigating the background of present racial difficulties will find himself led back to the Supreme Court's desegregation decision, Negro migrations to industrial areas, Reconstruction, the Civil War, and back to the importation of the first slaves into America. He will begin to see that the solution of any social problem must take into account its historical background and the emotions and ideas which have built up around it.

One value of such a unit is that it gives opportunity to do research work and to use library facilities at the beginning of the year. Students become more familiar with news magazines and other media of current information. Teachers undertaking such a project will find it essential to train classes in the use of the *Reader's Guide*. They will find it helpful to schedule several classes in the school library. Some teachers save magazines and newspapers over the summer for use with such a unit.

When material has been prepared, it is shared with the class by means of oral reports. It is important to group related reports so that class discussion is based upon as wide knowledge as possible. Students can make these reports much more meaningful by imaginative use of the bulletin board and maps. The teacher's role during the reports is to fill in gaps, summarize, ask questions, and in other ways to see that balanced, stimulating reports are given. This is also the time to point out parallels which exist between the problems under discussion and previous events and crises in our history.

Many of our students undoubtedly share Birrell's attitude toward what he described as "that great dust-heap called history." Beginning a course in the way outlined here can help greatly in modifying such feelings. Surprisingly enough, a fairly thorough job on such a unit can be done in two or three weeks. The class can then go back and study history in chronological fashion with much more benefit. Teachers will find that this unit can pay dividends far out of proportion to the time and effort which it requires. In summary, some of its values are:

1. It insures that students have early and continued exposure to those problems and events of most meaning and importance to them.
2. It demonstrates to students that history is continually being made, and that events of the past were as exciting to their participants and observers as present happenings are to us.
3. It provides a basis for studying parallel situations in different historical periods. (For example, the American Revolution and current colonial revolts; present foreign aid programs compared with nineteenth-century European investment in the United States).
4. It creates a background for continued study of current events as they unfold. This can be done by making each committee responsible to report developments in their "specialty" throughout the year.

5. It immediately involves students in research and reports. This often gives students a greater feeling of participation in and responsibility for the material of the course.
6. It accustoms students to dealing with controversial issues and makes them more aware of the disputes and conflicts which they encounter in their chronological study of history.

It can be seen that this approach of "starting history backwards" is applicable, with modifications, to any course, such as world history or European history, which includes the study of recent events. It is a very logical and natural way to begin such courses as civics or American problems. At a time when other, more "practical" subjects are being stressed—sometimes at the expense of the social sciences and humanities—it is essential that history teachers make their courses as interesting, as relevant, and as useful as possible. We can make a very good case for history as a most practical subject. We certainly do not want the next generation to relive our experiences with depression, war, racial violence, and cold-war tension. And yet, as Santayana has said: "Those who do not remember the past are condemned to repeat it." Our students must be helped to develop an understanding of history which will enable them to avoid any repetition of the tragic failures of our generation.

4

International and Intercultural Relations

APPROACHES TO THE STUDY OF INTERNATIONAL AND INTERCULTURAL RELATIONS

James M. Becker

Is is perhaps too easy to accept the "safe" conclusion that world and international affairs should be taught separately or not at all in social studies. The specialist who wrote this article, however, identifies instrumental relationships between world affairs and the social science disciplines. His ideas should help teachers give appropriate stress to other nations and cultures in each social studies course.

A MANNED Gemini spacecraft is launched, a civil rights march takes place in Alabama, U.S. planes bomb North Vietnam, another photo probe of the moon gets underway—These events dramatize the perplexities of our contemporary world.

They also highlight the basic problem of the wide gap between man's increasing success in solving the mysteries of the physical world and his slow, unsteady progress in dealing with the complexities of social behavior. It is a disquieting fact that it is easier to put a satellite into orbit than it is to achieve humane wisdom and insight in thought, feeling, and action.

Scientific and technological developments—the revolutionary developments in communications and transportation—have brought people of differing ideologies, contrasting cultures, and disparate levels of living into close contact with one another. At the same time missiles and nuclear warheads are being perfected, political and economic warfare continues, tensions mount, and at times threaten to split the world asunder. The world seems to be a battle ground of irreconcilable forces. The world agenda of problems demanding

FROM an address delivered by the author in Chicago, March 25, 1965. Used by permission. Dr. Becker was director of the Foreign Relations Project, North Central Association of Colleges and Secondary Schools, and is now with the Foreign Policy Association.

effective concerted action grows more complex and more urgent from day to day.

In such a world there is a need for self-conscious public opinion, which is aware of and concerned about international affairs and willing to help guide international conduct. Any hope of achieving such a condition depends, in part, upon the determination with which individual nations attempt to create it by deliberate effort.

In our own country, a key question is: Can enough Americans learn enough, soon enough, about the problems of international and intercultural affairs to help devise and implement intelligent programs of education and sound public policies? A high degree of trained intelligence is required to make us equal to our responsibilities in the international arena. The task is not an easy one. We work in the breech which exists between man's success in uncovering the nature of the physical world and the frustrations involved in trying to understand man's complex social world.

Many people lack historical perspective and have little faith in the future for mankind; both are necessary if the daily diet of crisis and issues are to have meaning. People seldom have a framework in which to locate data which do not appear directly relevant to their lives. Without a framework of basic ideas about the nature of the international scene, the constant stream of information which bombards us in the mass media is more distracting than instructive. International politics is viewed as ominous, important, and incurable rather than challenging and capable of being understood and influenced. As a result, many people retreat into private life without making the necessary effort to gain some insights into the nature of the contemporary international scene.

As educators we recognize that people will respond not only to fears and false hopes but also to those who can help them make sense of the complex world—to those who can make it interesting and meaningful. This is the task we here today can and must play. How can we help young people comprehend the ways of life, the values, the aspirations of all people of the world? How can we develop a program to achieve an understanding of the requirements for living together on this planet? How can global affairs be made more meaningful?

The tools for dealing with social phenomena are not as accurate, as precise, or as well-developed as those for dealing with the physical world. However, it is heartening to note that significant advances have been and are being made by social scientists working on the frontiers of knowledge. New interpretations by historians, as well as the work of anthropologists, social psychologists, political scientists and others are producing better techniques for observing, classifying, and measuring data. Using methods of inquiry similar to those of the natural sciences, they are seeking to verify some common principles of human behavior. Their work may produce some concepts, generalizations, ideas which can be used to build a framework to bring international affairs into a clearer focus.

What are some of the results of research and study in international relations? What are the implications of these findings for the classroom teacher? Clearly we can all benefit from learning how the social scientist defines and views international relations. The importance of discovering some principles for selecting, simplifying, and organizing the facts is obvious.

What is the nature of the discipline or disciplines dealing with the subject of our concern? Each discipline is a way of analyzing a body of data. The object of discipline is to explain facts and events by exposition of meaningful and useful generalizations. International relations, as a field of study, seeks an understanding of relations among states and governments and people. International relations is concerned with the exchanges that take place across national boundaries. Social scientists point out that the number and frequency of contacts between nations, cultures, and people are increasing. They can be classified as primarily political, economic, social, personal, etc. Sometimes you might ask your students to list all of the contacts which take place between the United States, or your community, and one or more other countries. Then try to categorize these contacts as being mainly *economic*—imports, exports, trade—*political*—diplomacy—*military*, and so forth. Such an exercise should help students see that international contacts are many and varied.

But students might still well say "so what?" You might follow this with questions such as: "Why do we have these contacts?" "What purpose do they serve?" "What needs and wants depend upon these contacts?" If nothing else, such questions will help your students see that you just can't do anything these days without *seeing, buying, using, enjoying, thinking,* or *worrying* about something international.

Another set of questions is related to the problems created by these contacts: "What kind of conflicts and tensions grow out of the connections? Why?" "What means are used in an attempt to resolve conflicts, disagreements, etc?"

The matter of how cultures, nations, and societies influence each other is another aspect to the study of international relations. Still another area of concern is developing deeper understanding of world affairs is: "What rules seem to govern international contact? Who determines the rules? How are they enforced? The role of regional and international organizations might be brought in here."

You might want to consider how different nations or groups see each other. What kind of image do we have of the other fellow? How does he see us? These are the kinds of questions social scientists ask and seek to answer.

The disciplined approach helps us define the area to be studied. As educators we must be aware of the recent findings, changing interpretations, and new insights as we prepare programs seeking to develop international understanding. We need to know more and to keep up with that is happening in this field. The necessity of acquiring some knowledge about the world as a basis for intelligent decisions cannot be over-stressed. Mastery of the subject matter is indispensable to any serious study of a problem. At the same time, knowledge alone is not enough.

In order for the student to understand the role he can play in world affairs, opportunities must be provided for him to make value judgments, to choose among alternative courses of action. It must be recognized that, in areas of public policy, *comparison, contrast, aims, purposes,* and *beliefs* enter in. We need to *search out* the *why* and *why not rather than only* the *what.* Our approach needs to be analytical rather than purely narrative and descriptive. Students need experience and help in finding pathways through complex patterns of elements. They can be stimulated by the need to make choices as they proceed. What would you do? What do you need to know? Where can you get accurate, reliable information?

As teachers, we have an obligation to help students weigh facts, analyze situations and interpret and synthesize available information and values. In this view, subject matter should be used to answer meaningful questions. Education then seeks to produce persons who ask questions, who connect causes to effects and who learn principles. The mere accumulation of facts will not produce such persons.

A noted scientist said recently, "Facts from which no conclusions can be drawn are hardly worth knowing." If we accept this statement, how do we select these facts? *Subject matter* has been defined as that part of *recorded knowledge which is introduced as material for thought in classrooms.* The central concern of the teacher is always that of determining what knowledge is of most worth? If all the knowledge of a field is to be boiled down into one book, or one course, or unit, what is to be included? What emphasized? (Three weeks on Latin America or six weeks on the Soviet Union?) If a unit or course is supposed to deal with or cover a field of knowledge, what is essential? The selection of content depends upon the teacher's purposes and goals and objectives. Each person begins his analysis of the world by a reference to his own area of expertise, and his cultural convictions. . . . Elementary and secondary teachers are not so much concerned with pushing back the frontiers of knowledge in a narrow area, nor in producing walking encyclopedias. Education at this level should not be primarily a process of consumption. Rather it should be concerned with providing road maps to help students through vast, challenging, and sometimes uncharted fields of knowledge. Whet their appetites for a lifetime of learning.

THE POTENTIALITIES OF
WORLD HISTORY IN A WORLD SOCIETY

Edgar B. Wesley

This article exemplifies well the idea of developing an understanding of world affairs through established subjects in social studies. Despite its having originally appeared several · years ago, it is now at least as timely as it was then. The selection complements those in the section of readings on objectives (pages 33–47) as an outstanding selection of major aims for a social studies course.

WORLD history suffers from the burden of abstract and inclusive aims laid upon it by its proponents. The clarification of purpose involves the unloading of some of these nebulous and distracting aims and the restating of logical, tangible, and achievable purposes.

The idea that world history should provide a systematic coverage of the principal events of all ages is a widespread and persistent delusion. Textbook writers, accepting the preposterous pronouncements of historians, have frequently tried to perform this incredible task. The extent to which they have succeeded is a reliable index of the failure of the course. The closer they come to systematic coverage, the greater is the failure of teachers and students. Success in teaching world history involves the complete renunciation of the idea of systematic coverage.

What, then, are the logical, tangible, and achievable objectives which world history should adopt? To select and state the predominant aims of world history is not to deny other values and outcomes. The study of world history will, therefore, continue to promote the general objectives of history. Thus the development of objectivity, growth in critical ability, the acquisition of a sense of chronology, the understanding of concepts, the promotion of civic virtues, and scores of other worthy objectives are neither forgotten nor obscured by drawing up a minimum list of more timely and more pressing objectives.

A restatement of objectives is necessary because many old ideas and explanations are outmoded, because the world of today is so utterly different from the relatively simple situation described in so many of our histories, and because the needs of students are quite extensively different from those of ten years ago. The desirablity of understanding the world gives way to the necessity of understanding. For good or ill, American boys and girls have

FROM *Improving the Teaching of World History*, Edith West, ed., Washington, D.C., 1949, National Council for the Social Studies, pp. 1–5. Used by permission. Dr. Wesley is professor emeritus, University of Minnesota and Stanford University.

become citizens of a new world power. Knowledge of this enlarged domain is a civic imperative.

Communication, transportation, diplomacy, trade, war, and cooperation have brought a great degree of unity to a yet ununified world. The oil of Iran supplies heat for a home in Sioux City; the iron ore of Sweden finds its way into steel products used in Argentina. The windmills of Kendallville pump water in South Africa. While the world is politically and ideologically divided, it is to a considerable extent unified culturally and economically. While racial prejudices, linguistic variations, commercial barriers, political restrictions, and cultural diversities hamper, they do not prevent progress toward unity. In such a world, so different in degree from that of the early twentieth century, the student needs a new orientation.

The first and most obvious purpose in studying world history, then, is to provide an overview of the contemporary world. The achievement of this purpose involves a new appraisal of the historical narrative, and a realization that the narrative itself will fail to present a comprehensive overview. The person who knows the past reasonably well may yet be inadequately informed about the present. History must call upon other areas of knowledge. An understanding of today's world involves a knowledge of resources and their distribution; it involves a concrete picture of the world's population and its relationships to resources; it involves an understanding of the basic economic processes which sustain life; it involves insight into competing political and social ideologies which divide the world into blocs and factions; it involves a realization of the beliefs, superstitions, prejudices, and ignorance which block the road to peace and progress.

The achievement of a comprehensive synthesis involves the re-examination of prevailing theories and explanations. The era of the Europeanization of the world has ended. The idea that the world can be viewed as an expanded Europe is no longer tenable. The student must resist temptation to substitute other inadequate themes and explanations. The triumphant emergence of the United States is an attractive theme for unifying one's view of the world. Likewise, such an oversimplification as the Russo-American conflict, or communism *versus* democracy, is a theme which seems to offer a unifying thread. Some regard the emergence of Asiatic peoples out of colonialism as a movement that may reshape the world. The industrialization of backward areas is a widespread phenomenon which seems to offer a unifying explanation of many developments.

The student of world history must understand and appraise all these and many other theories and explanations. He will find helpful but only partial answers in each one. The course in world history will thus become a search for explanations and synthesis and not merely a survey of the catalogic record of man's political activities.

A second objective of world history, closely related to the first, is to secure an introduction to world problems. To study world history and gain no insight into the problem of contemporary Palestine is merely to escape from reality. To study world history and then laugh at revolutions in Latin America is to exhibit a failure to comprehend. To study world history and have no ideas on how to achieve world peace is to acquire information without understanding. World history, even when enriched by the scholarship of other subjects, will not provide the answers or solutions for these problems, but it does provide the techniques for study, the exposure to pertinent materials, and the chance to develop attitudes which should result in civic action on an international scale. World history thus becomes an introduction to the continued study of world affairs. If the student has acquired any understanding of yesterday he will be in a better position to understand tomorrow.

A third purpose in studying world history is to recognize that culture is international. Stated negatively, this objective involves some lessening of emphasis upon European and American contributions. It means an expansion of the concept of culture and a recognition of the contributions of other groups and nations. The student of world history should learn that Christianity is not the sole upholder of morality, brotherhood, and immortality; that Americans have no monopoly on democratic ideas; that the art, music, and literature of many peoples have values similar to our own artistic productions; that inventive genius has blossomed in countries outside America and western Europe; that the traditions, customs, and practices of other areas are natural and commendable; that progress and development are human rather than European or American qualities. World understanding can be achieved only by the building up of a culture to which all peoples contribute. It is therefore important that students in all countries develop a toleration and an understanding of the actual or potential contributions of all groups.

A fourth objective of teaching world history is to derive and apply generalizations. Desert people tend to war on plainsmen; commerce enriches a city; oppression breeds revolution; inventions ease life and lead to further inventions; discoveries of rich resources cause migrations; an increasing density of population involves more social control. The understanding of these, and hundreds of other generalizations, rests upon one's command of the detailed instances from which they are derived. A generalization which cannot be documented by the student has no value for him. On the other hand, he derives from an understood generalization not only the explanation of a series of developments but also the ability to transfer his insight to new situations. He thus acquires a technique of explanation and the ability to foresee probable developments. For the most advanced students the acquisition of generalizations leads to the formulation of principles and laws. They assist in making man the arbiter of his fate.

From a study of generalizations and laws the student acquires some insight into the future. World history, like all fields of history, should prepare one for the future. To the incisive student of history there can be no major surprises. So a fifth purpose of studying world history is to understand the world of tomorrow. The student who knew the inequitable distribution of land in China was prepared to understand the long and bitter struggle by the agrarians. In fact, he almost qualified to prophesy the eventual victory of the revolutionists. The student of prewar Germany was able to see the coming of World War II; and many did see it. The student of international cooperation was able to foresee the League of Nations, the United Nations, and looks for the eventual arrival of a world government which will assume some of the sovereignty of national states. Insight into the future partakes of the nature of prophecy, preparation, and promotion. Foreseeing the shape of things to come means not only preparation but also a degree of advocacy which helps to bring the prophecy into reality. World history which correctly interprets the past and the present inevitably forecasts the general shape of future developments. The teacher who stresses this objective is providing the basic elements of tomorrow's world. Perhaps a contribution to the building of a better world would be the greatest possible achievement of the teaching of world history.

In brief, it may be said that world history is designed to expand our national horizon to the periphery of the world; to provide an intelligible explanation of world events and trends; to sense the error and inadequacy of many popular theories and beliefs; to acquire an understanding of world problems; to cultivate an appreciation of diverse cultures and to welcome contributions from all groups; to derive and apply generalizations which explain what would otherwise be merely fortuitous; and, lastly, to gain some glimpses into the future. This ambitious program is within the grasp of the able and conscientious student who is directed by an able and conscientious teacher.

IMPLICATIONS OF INTERNATIONAL AFFAIRS FOR THE SCHOOL PROGRAM

Richard I. Miller

Like citizenship education, instruction concerning world affairs and other cultures is not limited to one field of the curriculum. Still, the social studies carry a central responsibility for such instruction. The breadth of education in international affairs and the key role of the social studies are implicit in this selec-

FROM *Education in a Changing Society*, by Richard I. Miller, Project on the Instructional Program of the Public Schools, Washington, D.C.: National Education Association, 1963, pp. 116–120. Used by permission. Dr. Miller was associate director of the NEA Project on Instruction and is now director of the Center for the Study of Educational Change, University of Kentu~~~

tion. Omitted here is a summary of con-   *international affairs that appeared in the*
temporary trends and problems in   *original manuscript.*

WORLD problems have recently appeared to be the foremost concern of the American people. For this reason alone, the public schools should provide students with a background for understanding international relations. In addition, it becomes increasingly evident that participation in civic affairs demands both breadth and objectivity of viewpoint.

All teaching about international relations should stress objective analysis and critical evaluation of the issues. Too often teaching in this area includes an uncritical acceptance of clichés, generalities, and pat phrases.

Take the phrase "international understanding" as an illustration. A critical analysis of the term might consider three questions: Does cultural unity promote peace? Civil wars—wars between the Greek city-states, the Italian wars of the Renaissance, the religious wars of the sixteenth and seventeenth centuries, the War between the States, for example—were fought among nations and states that had common language, education, religion, literature, and art. The weight of history does not seem to support the pleasing generalization that people are less inclined to fight one another as they become more alike in their ways and thinking.

Does a higher general level of education and culture promote peace? Warfare seems to have little relation to the level of education and culture in a nation. The recent history of such nations as Japan, Italy, and Germany—all highly educated and cultured nations—should be contrasted with that of other educated and cultured nations, such as Sweden and Switzerland, both of which have had relatively long periods of peace. Much as one might like to believe that education and culture promote peace, historical evidence does not support such a generalization.

Do wars usually result from mutual ignorance and misunderstanding? Some people contend that if only people of good will could sit down and talk things out, wars might be avoided. This belief is the most misleading of all, for it is based upon an oversimplification. Major wars generally are fought over deep-seated, complex issues, although the specific cause may be a minor incident. It may be argued that misunderstanding between nations prevents or at least delays the onset of wars as often as does understanding. For example, England and France might have acted differently had they clearly understood the motives and the military strength of Mussolini when he went into Ethiopia in 1935. The Allies might have stopped Hitler in 1936 if they had clearly understood the meaning of his move into the demilitarized Rhineland. Demosthenes tried to make the Athenians understand the true nature of the Macedonian threat to the north of Greece; it was too late when they finally did.

Teaching about international relations in the public schools may be approached in three ways:

1. Courses in the so-called traditional subjects, such as geography, history, and foreign languages, can provide knowledge and information that is important at every age or grade.

2. Education for international understanding and competence should follow the concentric-circle concept of learning, beginning with things most familiar and extending toward the unfamiliar. Some educators have argued that this progression is unrealistic in the modern world, when a child can see the world flash across the television screen or can fly across the ocean in a few hours. The significant question, however, concerns what the child actually understands. . . .

3. The international dimension should be used to enrich the instructional program wherever appropriate. For example, classes above the third-grade level might benefit from materials about the United Nations and its related agencies. One Virginia junior high school has in many ways included songs and dances of UN member nations in music classes. A high school in the District of Columbia has utilized FAO, UNESCO, and WHO in enriching home economics courses. A high school in Pennsylvania has found that the work of the International Atomic Energy Agency, the World Meteorological Organization, and UNESCO is useful in physics courses.

An organized approach to teaching world affairs in all subject areas was begun in Glens Falls, New York, in 1957, under the joint sponsorship of the Glens Falls Board of Education and the National Council for the Social Studies, with outside resources. The Program for Improving the Teaching of World Affairs (ITWA) sought to develop in each pupil an increasing understanding of and respect for other peoples, a growing appreciation of other cultures, and a sense of responsibility for his own role and the role of his country in a world of nations.

It became apparent during the study that it was important for all teachers to increase their own knowledge of world affairs. Activities such as committee work, in-service workshops, special courses for teachers, publication of newsletters to inform communities about the project, and some travel experiences for teachers provided opportunities for increased learning.

Large secondary schools may profitably offer a separate elective course on international relations to prepare students for the increasing number of professional opportunities in the field of international relations and many other related professional fields.

One of the thirty-three recommendations developed by the Project on Instruction pertains to teaching about communism. It states—

The school curriculum should include a study of political and social ideologies focusing upon communism. The methods of rational inquiry should be stressed. The study should be set in the perspective of the modern world and be incorporated into the instructional program at appropriate points. *If a special unit on communism is deemed desirable in the secondary school, it should supplement and complement earlier study of these topics.*

As with other areas of the curriculum, decisions about what to teach and how to teach about these topics should be based upon policies developed by school administrators and teachers of the local school system. In the formulation and implementation of such policies, school personnel should utilize the resources of scholarship and be supported in their decisions by the school board and by an informed community opinion.

The discussion of communism in the public secondary schools should be analytical and reasonably objective and should treat communism in a context of other "isms" (capitalism, fascism, and socialism). Teachers should have a solid background for teaching the subject.

Complete objectivity in teaching is probably impossible, but helping the student to reason for himself is crucial. The successful brainwashing of some American soldiers during the Korean conflict attests to the inadequacy of restricting teaching to providing black-and-white answers. Many soldiers were unable to critically analyze and evaluate apparently convincing arguments when they were presented with unfamiliar premises.

Those who fear that American youth will be subverted by knowing the communist point of view underestimate the ability of youth to make intelligent judgments, if given the methods and materials to do so. Furthermore, they underestimate the influence of living in a democratic society. A few speeches or hours of reading about communism will not subvert youth; rather it will provide a comparative dimension that helps them to be come better citizens.

Courses about communism need to be selective, in view of time limitations. They should be developed around basic concepts that serve as a framework of understanding and help to interpret the maze of facts and information about the subject.

The inconsistencies between the theory and the practice of communism and comparisons between totalitarian and other forms of government should be included, in addition to historical material and a survey of Soviet strategy and tactics. A "Day Under Communism" might be used to help students grasp more intimately the realities of the Soviet system. . . .

Thomas Jefferson's familiar sentence—"A nation that expects to remain free and ignorant expects something that never was nor ever will be"—offers a genuine challenge to the teaching profession. Knowledge and understanding of international relations are essential to civic responsibility for the years ahead, and the foundations for competence in this area must be laid in the elementary and secondary schools.

THE CRISIS THREATENING
AMERICAN EDUCATION

Eugene McCreary

The immediately preceding selection suggests specific instruction dealing with communism. There are understandable reasons for the pressures, emanating largely from outside the schools, that have resulted in a widespread offering of such instruction. But there are serious dangers both in indiscriminate yielding to these pressures and in ill-prepared, wholly one-sided, or context-less teaching about communism. These pressures and problems constitute the concerns of this selection. Omitted here is a brief introductory section. Readers interested in McCreary's advocacy of social studies that is both scientifically based and supportive of democracy may wish to refer to related selections in this volume on pages 3-22 and 234-244.

AMERICANS are now an anxious and insecure people. They have suffered many frustrations and fears since World War II, though enjoying an unprecedented material prosperity. The cold war occupies more and more of the emotional life of many people—even as it dominates an important part of our political and economic life and defines our military posture. A sincere concern to defend our freedoms against the encroachment of communism is heightened by Communist victories in China and the Far East, the growth of communism in Latin America and Africa, the frustrating stalemate in Korea, the scientific accomplishments of the U.S.S.R (sputniks, missiles, H-bombs), and the continuing crisis which now threatens world-wide destruction and the obliteration of our civilization. The average citizen is not only frustrated but puzzled and confused by the course of events. He feels helpless and inadequate—powerless to do anything to improve the situation. Karl Jaspers once pointed out that frightened people in times of crisis take a special interest in the education of the young. People who are unable to solve their most vexing problems try to insure that the new generation will be better prepared to settle matters. Americans are now justifiably concerned with how schools can help sustain our liberties and values.

Naturally enough, contemporary anxieties for freedom have led in many places to pressure for stronger programs of citizenship education and changes in the social studies program. There are calls for "pro-American" or "anti-Communist" courses. These well-intentioned pressures have led in some states to new legislation requiring special courses and even special textbooks. In other

FROM *Social Education*, 26:177–180, April, 1962. Used by permission. Dr. McCreary is supervisor of teacher education in social studies, University of California, Berkeley.

states, certain districts are revamping the social studies curriculum to include special courses. In California many districts are taking action, while a special state committee has been named to study the problem and make recommendations. The California Association of School Administrators, in its December 1961 meeting adopted a statement on "Teaching About Communism," which states a point of view, defines the responsibilities of the board, superintendent, staff, and community, and sets up a number of guide lines which ought to be a valuable reference for schools dealing with this problem.

Special courses are no new thing in the social studies. Many special courses were justified in the past by the citizenship philosophy of social studies mentioned above—including driver training, family living, orientation, or problems of living. It is easy to call for a special course each time events emphasize a particular problem. But many of the special courses of the past were later repudiated as a mistake. Certain weaknesses underlie special "anti-Communist" or "pro-American" courses.

A call for such special courses often comes from those unaware of the present curriculum and how it provides an understanding of our own institutions and ideals in contrast to Communist practices. Obviously, no new courses should be undertaken without a serious evaluation of present offerings. A special course might unbalance and hamper an existing program of integrity and depth.

Some pressures for special courses are associated with distrust of and attacks on present programs, texts, methods, and teachers. They represent more than an honest concern for better education. The California Association of School Administrators in its guide warns:

In America today, there is a growing and a desirable public concern relative to the threats of communism and fascism to our American ways of life. This concern has been capitalized upon by individuals and groups desiring to foster upon the schools materials of instruction favoring extreme ideologies of a political, social, and economic nature incompatible with our American ways of life. The public schools of California have for many years conducted an educational program directed toward a belief in the ideals and processes of American democracy. It is recommended that individual school districts bring to the attention of the public the planned sequence of instruction which is directed toward this end in their districts. It is particularly important that materials of instruction used in this program continue to be selected by professional school personnel in accordance with sound educational principles.

Certain extreme right-wing organizations, including the John Birch society, have frankly proclaimed their intention to infiltrate schools, capture P.T.A.'s, and bring their point of view to the fore in classrooms. Such groups in many places across the country have sought to influence textbook selection for their special brand of patriotism, to introduce into schools films and printed materials partisan to their interpretation of Americanism and the Communist threat, and to involve the public schools in anti-Communist programs which emphasize fear, suspicion, and dogma. Surrender to such attacks would compromise our schools, usurp the professional role and responsibilities of teachers, and turn the social studies into subservient propaganda. Any pressure for special courses ought to be evaluated carefully. The establishment of any such courses ought to rest in the hands of competent professionals.

Suggestions for special anti-Commnist or pro-American courses sometimes reflect and unfortunate ignorance about these subjects. Terms are used carelessly and concepts are hopelessly confused. Political systems are confused with economic systems. Theory is equated with practice, both in our country and in the Communist world. Our economic system is described in the naive terms of idealistic theory rather than the reality of deep governmental concern and commitment for the welfare of the people and the health of business. Our political system is seen as a static and perfect product of the founding fathers rather than as the gradual development of a basically liberating and revolutionary approach to man and society. Our country is praised not for its continuing healthy progress toward equality, participation, opportunity and the fuller life for all, but as a model of absolute, unchangeable perfection. Mixed economies are identified with socialism; socialism with communism. Changes in Russian communism are not recognized, nor are internal contradictions in the Communist world understood. Legitimate strivings by hungry and desperate people in underdeveloped countries, which often require revolutionary change, are viewed as Communist plots. All reform or progress is seen as a threat. There is a simplification of reality into two polar absolutes—democracy and communism—overlooking the manifold variety of human institutions, including other dangerous alternatives which might threaten our own people, such as military dictatorship or fascist totalitarianism. There is little understanding of the economic and social realities in this nation and elsewhere; there is an assumption that all demands for reform are Communist-inspired and that free governments are deeply infiltrated by secret Communist agents —the emphasis is not on facts and understandings but on fears and suspicion.

A curriculum built on such ignorance and fear would be a preposterous embarrassment to well-informed social studies teachers and an insult to intelligent students. It would be a repudiation of American ideals and an inadvertent encouragement to the Communist, for it would imply that our freedoms are not dynamic, flexible, and responsive to the needs and desires of our citizens and the welfare of other people of the world. It would distort and compromise the ideals of our free, pluralistic society, open to ideas, and governed by popular consent. It would imply that we, like the Russians, worship an ideology which is divorced from the realities of our national life. It would submerge the true revolutionary content of American history, the establishment of a society of personal freedom under limited government pledged to the ideal and evolving toward the realization of justice, equality, opportunity, and human welfare.

Some suggestions for pro-American and anti-Communist courses reveal an ignorance of how democratic values may be taught. Indoctrination or the authoritarian imposition of viewpoints are appropriate only when the values sought are authoritarian and absolutist. One can be forced to obey, but one can learn cooperation only through working with others in freedom. One is given answers in a totalitarian society, but in a democracy one learns to develop his own answers. There can be only one explanation when there is only one party, one general secretary, one ideology—and the state is supreme. But in a free society, there are often several explanations, several answers, and the action taken may be a compromise, the conclusion may be tentative. Truth, in a free society, is developed progressively and refined gradually by free inquiry and experience.

Critical thinking and problem solving are essential in a democracy—they are our way of finding and testing truth. The study of controversial subjects is essential to citizenship training in a free society. Students need to experience the clash of alternative solutions to vital problems—they need to seek evidence and marshal data. They need to judge between alternative solutions and to evaluate the arguments of partisans. They need to learn to judge and choose. Any attempt to indoctrinate one single viewpoint in controversial areas will alienate the best minds of the young people, who will learn to be skeptical or even cynical of biased or propagandistic teaching. A generous examination of all viewpoints, evidence, arguments, and theories can develop the informed loyalty of free men who have practiced free thought, moral choice, and responsible decision and prefer them over authoritarian indoctrination characteristic of totalitarian systems.

Long ago we made a choice for our nation. Americanism means free and honest examination of facts and objective consideration of alternatives. Americanism means free and respectful discussions of differences and the ability to compromise. Our science and our society reach tentative conclusions which may be modified by experience, changed circumstances, and new evidence.

The concern that young people develop deeper understandings of democratic values and of the various political and social systems which compete and sometimes threaten our own deserves the serious attention of teachers and administrators. Evaluations of existing curricula should not be made hurriedly nor under the pressure or sway of well-meaning but emotionally involved pressure groups. Curricula ought to be examined carefully to assure accuracy, thoroughness, and appropriateness. Evaluations ought to be a cooperative process, including not only members of the professional staff but also lay citizens. Evaluation teams should also include specialists—scholars from recognized institutions of higher learning and other competent authorities.

When evaluations of curricula indicate weaknesses or omissions, new programs ought to be developed. They should be prepared by teachers who will teach the courses, assisted by supervisors and administrators, and *guided by academic specialists* from the colleges and universities. The contemporary renaissance of American education is deeply in debt to academic experts. Programs in mathematics and science, in English, and in the foreign languages, have been redefined, sharpened, and modernized by specialists from higher education. A similar use of recognized authorities is long overdue in the social studies program in secondary schools. Historians, anthropologists, economists, sociologists, political scientists, and geographers ought to play a leading role, in preparing textbooks, devising teaching aids, revising courses, and in in-service training of teachers. Their assistance is indispensable in improving education in Americanism, as their help is needed in many other ways.

Curricula ought to reflect the best available evidence and insights. They ought to contain not the fears and political programs of partisans but the facts and interpretations of scholars. There is no place in the public schools for special curricula designed by pressure groups. There is a desperate need for the best understanding scholarship can provide. Better programs by public schools will reduce the clamor for special "anti-Communist schools" fashioned by partisans, conducted in an atmosphere of pageantry, molded by the temper of religious revivalism, and haunted by fear and confusion.

In any curricular changes, thought should be given to the relative merits of special courses or units on communism versus the treatment of aspects of this subject in context in the secondary social studies program. World history courses can emphasize modern world history and highlight modern culture areas—in such an arrangement, the entire history of world communism becomes a major theme. World geography ought to deal with the whole world, and any such treatment ought to provide opportunity to learn how people live and how society is organized in Communist countries as well as in the newer, underdeveloped nations and in the Western societies.

Civics courses provide the opportunity for comparative government studies —American institutions are best understood and appreciated through comparison and contrast with other systems, both free and totalitarian. American history, particularly in senior high schools, ought to include the most recent period and the genesis and nature of the cold war. Problems courses, particularly at the senior level, offer opportunities to study any aspect of communism and competing systems, including the psychological and sociological aspects. An area of communism which is usually given little attention is that of domestic subversion. The ordinary school and its staff are ill-equipped to deal with this problem, even as they are unable to deal fully with other aspects of crime prevention and punishment. But any penetrating history of the United States will consider why radical alternatives were popular in the early 1930's and how the achievements of the New Deal as well as disillusionment with Communist behavior during the Stalinist period and the Communist alliance with Hitler combined to discredit communism in the United States.

Special courses assure that certain aspects of this important subject are not overlooked—but they may distort the subject matter by isolating it from related materials and understandings. For example, Russian communism reflects Russian circumstances and history and the personalities of Lenin and Stalin as well as the teachings of Karl Marx. Chinese communism has many oriental features and won power in China in a manner peculiar to the Chinese situation. British socialism is typically British, though influenced by the analyses of Karl Marx. American communism exhibited from its inception a schism between native radicalism shaped somewhat by the frontier and doctrines and dogmas shaped under different systems and imported and advanced by immigrants poorly integrated into American life. American communism has suffered from its beginning from contradictions between American reality and Russian state interests which, in the last analysis, have always been forced upon the reluctant domestic movement. There is a danger that special "anti-Communist" courses may fail to define the specific dimensions of communism in various circumstances. Special courses may lack the breadth and depth of a continuing development of understandings through the secondary school years in the context of several subjects. In any case, a continuing review of the entire curriculum is necessary to guarantee that no important elements are omitted.

Whether or not communism is considered a special course or an important theme of several courses, Americanism ought to be taught, not only in the social studies, but in the entire public school experience in all its complexity. Extracurricular programs, student government, assemblies, sports programs, paper drives, milk-fund collections for the needy, and school publications, among other activities, can and should teach lessons in Americanism.

Whatever curricula are maintained, modified, or inaugurated by schools to deepen an understanding of communism and fortify a loyalty to American ideals, it is the responsibility of professionals, advised by scholars and competent authorities, to determine the content and methods—the classroom procedures, textbooks, films, and experiences—which are appropriate for the goals intended. These methods and means must be consonant with scientific and democratic values. They must fit the background and maturity of students. The classroom climate must be one of serious inquiry, mutual respect, and confidence—free of fear and distrust. Students learn values and ideals from teachers they admire. Experiences in democratic classrooms as a part of a democratic school are central to teaching Americanism. Democratic teachers will avoid and reject indoctrination and authoritarian imposition because they respect their subject and their students. Any teachers who attempt to indoctrinate Americanism will defeat their own purpose, for imposed dogmas contradict a free man's loyalty to dynamic ideals he has experienced, understood, and learned to love. We must be certain that in reappraising our social studies programs, we deepen understanding rather than alarm, we develop political sophistication and democratic loyalties rather than mere moral righteousness.

The current crisis in secondary education could lead to subversion of the social studies and their perversion into brainwashing and indoctrination, the prostitution of teachers to the will of impassioned pressure groups, and the substitution for problem-solving and free inquiry of an alien authoritarian prescription of rigid and static ideology. Sensitive awareness of the implications of the present threat can lead to an important reappraisal of social studies instruction, a closer tie between secondary and higher education in the social sciences, a refinement of the secondary program, greater respect for the integrity of teachers and teaching, and a clearer definition of the rights and responsibilities of the professional staff.

INTERNATIONAL RELATIONS

J. R. Skretting, S. A. Arnold, and Robert Weiss

A common objection to giving more stress in social studies to international affairs is that such emphasis is unpatriotic or anti-American. Not so, say the writers of this selection. Rather, by their interpretation, teaching about other cultures and world affairs complements and reinforces direct instruction concerning American society.

As with the role of the school in general, industrialization and the rise of America as a world power have outmoded a social studies curriculum aimed at producing only the national man. A curriculum concerned *only* with American values, life conditions, ideals, and loyalties no longer fits in this age of internationalism nor is such a program an honest reflection of American values themselves. As part of his responsibility, a loyal American citizen must realistically face the facts of world interdependence.

LOYALTY TO AMERICA IS IN FIRM ACCORD WITH WORLD-MINDEDNESS

The national interests and security of the United States are now intimately tied to the welfare of people all over the earth. Since 1945, the cold war and

FROM *Educating Citizens for a Democracy*, pp. 310–312, ed. by Richard E. Gross and Leslie D. Zeleny, copyright © 1958 by Oxford University Press. Reprinted by permission. The authors are professors at, respectively, Florida State University, Colorado State College, and Flint College of the University of Michigan.

international tensions have beclouded this truth for some citizens. Although conditions have changed, there are Americans who still retain the old frame of reference. To these people, internationalism represents a danger rather than an opportunity for the realization of national interests. They fear a loss of national sovereignty. Identification of Americanism with isolationism has led to charges that stress on the international is unpatriotic. Thus, the flying of the United Nations flag alongside the United States flag by some schools came under heavy assault. There have been a number of attacks on the use of the UN and UNESCO material in the public schools.

Early extreme reactions are slowly being replaced by more mature responses. Yet, sporadic opposition to education for international understanding indicates that there remains a pressing need to clarify the compatibility of American and international loyalties. This need will probably persist for some time. It is the task of our nation's educators, particularly teachers of social studies, to help our society bridge the gap between preinternational and international thinking. This entails interpreting the new demands in terms that people already understand and accept. The transition will be made more smoothly when Americans recognize how the ideals of our democracy support internationalism.

At the heart of our American way of life is a belief in the dignity and worth of each and every individual. It is to be noted that the rote way by which this is so frequently expressed stresses 'each and every *individual*,' not only 'each and every *American*.' A faith in man as man, not just as American, is a basic part of our national ethos. A concern for others is at the heart of our way of life. In the words of President Eisenhower, 'We recognize and accept our own deep involvement in the destiny of men everywhere.' As a corollary to this, we prize cooperation as well as competition. It has frequently been pointed out that organization, especially voluntary organization, characterizes the American people. We are known as joiners. Participation in cooperative international organizations which hold dear the faith in man as man and the welfare of others seems a natural outgrowth of these national characteristics.

Cultural pluralism—respect for differences of nationality, race, and religion —lies at the core of Americanism. We are a nation of many groups with many different backgrounds, and we know what it means to expand loyalties. *E pluribus unum* (One from Many): This was our motto in the beginning and remains so today. The United Nations' ideal of diversity within unity merely enlarges the idea which we hold to in our nation so that it embraces all countries. Unity is prized, but it is not a unity of uniformity. It was for this reason that America even discarded the melting-pot concept for one that emphasized respect for differences. 'In union there is strength,' another slogan often repeated in America, is also the essence of international cooperation.

We are a religious people. Although our creeds are diverse, the idea of the brotherhood of man is linked to the fatherhood of God by most of our religions. The original meaning of the word religion, derived from the Latin *religio*, was to bind or to bring mankind together. While it has been argued that religions divide rather than unite men, the American emphasis on religion in its broadest and its original sense not only supports international cooperation, but places a responsibility on us to do so. Mutual security is, in essence, a religious idea.

We believe in representative government. Our nation is founded on the idea that government by the people is the only certain process to secure government for the people. The cry for representation inaugurated our national independence. A continuous extension of the franchise marked our history until universal suffrage was finally achieved. We insist upon the right to select and control representatives at every level of government. It would seem to follow that we should favor representation on an international plane, especially since national policies are now so dependent on what is happening outside the United States. In fact, we increase our sovereignty by extending our sphere of representation so that it includes both a national and an international level. We gain rather than lose in the area of political freedom by having a voice in all policies which affect us.

Americans dislike violence. A democracy wages war only to defend its way of life. War makes man a means rather than an end, and this is incompatible with the democratic ideal. Americans prefer collective bargaining and the mediation of labor-business disputes rather than strikes and lockouts. Emphasis on resolving differences peacefully should lead readily to support of international organs for the arbitration of conflicts among nations.

Participation in world affairs implements American ideas of freedom of expression and compromise. Americans believe in the 'give and take' of life and are willing to modify our concepts across the conference table. During this process of modification, majority opinions and minority opinions are considered. Since majorities are sometimes transient and can be overpowering, minorities need be protected. Minority views can become majority views and the majority needs to consider the time when it may desire to seek protection of its minority opinions. We believe that differences of opinion can be best considered and resolved through open discussion with all views presented. For this reason, we champion a free press and free speech. The General Assembly of the United Nations is a wider arena based on the same principle as our town hall.

The dignity and worth of each individual, cooperation, cultural pluralism, the brotherhood of man, representative government, peaceful resolution of differences, freedom of expression, compromise: these are just some of our democratic ideals which clearly indicate that ideals lend themselves well to extension onto the level of global ideals, thereby supporting internationalism.

5

Other Multidisciplinary Elements

THE "DIM CANDLE" OF MR. BEARD

Robert J. Cooke

For students to develop an appreciation of their own national heritage requires more than the traditional emphasis in high school social studies. More than the standard offering of American history is necessary. This writer suggests broadening the presentation of American life to include elements often classified as the humanities. Teachers of two decades or more experience will recall that the forerunners of the current attention to "American studies" appeared a generation ago with such labels as "common learnings" and "core curriculum." However, readers who are familiar with the writings of the historian and political scientist Charles A. Beard, in reports of the Commission on the Social Studies of the 1930's, may regard even Beard's broad view of the social studies as extending little beyond the limits of the parent social sciences.

A GOOD many volumes have been written in agonized reappraisal of education for another younger generation since World War II. It has failed, we are told, in both descriptive and analytical areas. Little, as yet, has been said of the failure in attitudinal education. That we have failed to communicate the best of our culture from one generation to another is self-evident; that our generation and the coming one hold attitudes inimical to the democratic process we profess to cherish is equally evident; and that we have difficulty reconciling the content of the Declaration with the extension of citizenship to minority groups is amply illustrated by the continuing crisis over civil rights. Indeed the Declaration itself is often considered a museum piece, the charming memento of a glorious past.

In 1958 the National Council for the Social Studies published a report submitted by the Committee on Concepts and Values which has been widely circulated among educators since. Its opening statement sets forth a sweeping and ambitious rationale for social studies.

FROM *Social Education*, 27:216–218, December, 1963. Used by permission. Dr. Cooke is a professor of history and American studies at Southampton (New York) College.

The most inclusive aim of social studies as a part of general education in the United States is to help young people learn to carry on the free society they have inherited, to make whatever changes modern conditions demand or creative imagination suggests that are consistent with its basic principles or values, and to hand it on to their offspring better than they received it. (1)

This appears to be a good and sufficient reason for the social studies to occupy a major sector of public school curricula but when we reflect that the major instrument used to pursue this aim is the American history course it becomes evident that the achievement of this goal is a promise to the ear, to be broken to the hope.

If we have failed to transmit an American tradition it follows that we have failed to fulfill the stated goals of the American history course in the public school. History, as a school subject, is the *one* institutionalized and relatively uniform source of knowledge about America to which all students are exposed. We have had the uneasy feeling for many years that a familiarity with history is not readily distilled by magical process to an essence that is the *geist* of America. Recent evidence confirms our suspicions. Our Peace Corps volunteers must be introduced to the realm of American Studies before going overseas as casual diplomats; Americans traveling in foreign lands have invariably been mines of misinformation; and the most insightful commentaries on the American scene, from Tocqueville to Myrdal, have come from the pens of foreigners.

History has long enjoyed traditional sanction in the American public school and it has long been used as the key to the transmission of our culture from one generation to another. (Historians disagree with this usage but unfortunately cannot control their product once it is on the market.) For all the genius of Wertenbaker, Perry, Turner, Beard, Commager, Nevins, Hofstadter, or Schlesinger, their product, when translated for classroom use, is rather like a condensation of a great novel: the plot remains but the richness and density are gone. Students march reluctantly several times across the plains of America during their public school career but there is little evidence that they are scarred by it.

As Martin Mayer pointed out in his recent work on social studies in American schools the American history course "doesn't work."

At best, the result is a vague flow essentially homogenous with recognized raisins, the knowledge of a few dates and a few names. There is almost no feeling of the texture of life as Americans have lived it, or of the residue of history lying all around. (2)

But the failure of high school history to fulfill our hopes is only one aspect of the problem. A capsule presentation of any great pageant is inherently misleading and we have misled generations of students with the notion that our history obeys the Aristotelian rule in having a beginning, a middle, and an end, and that our future, if the student is sensitive to it at all, is in no way related to what came before. Rather than being a con- tinuum (which it is), history comes in chunks, neatly packaged and labeled. When, at the end of the term, the student arrives at the present, the tale ends. The present is something else again.

Apart from the absence of a "sense of history" in the survey course, the raisins in the dough, those chunks set aside for special treatment, lead the student toward sweeping valuative conclusions based on partial evidence. Young people, being prone to think in terms of the "good guys" and the "bad guys," tend to classify neatly the men and movements of American existence. Classic examples of a "little learning" are presently held notions of our students who have drunk not too deeply from the Pierian spring: Jefferson, aside from being identified with the Declaration, usually comes off as somewhat of a hypocrite because he professed to be a "strict construc- tionist" but afterwards purchased Louisiana (we call Prometheus a thief); Jackson is best known for the institution of the "spoils system" which suggests (out of context) government-by-crony. Not only is this misleading but we miss the opportunity to illustrate one of the great accomplishments of Amer- ican democracy, that of peaceful succession and the establishment of the concept of "loyal opposition"; Lincoln remains a benign, homey wit; Grant is a great general and only on second thought identified with the Presidency; Theodore Roosevelt is identified by physical appearance only; FDR is whatever Dad says he is, and so it goes, entertaining in spots but no more relevant than the garrulous reminiscences of a member of an older genera- tion.

When we reflect that it is our expectation that all citizens of our country understand and agree on the essence of the American experience it becomes evident that we are asking rather too much of the discipline of history. Unless a program of studies is functionally related to being alive in the twentieth century, in the United States and in the world, there seems to be little justification for its continued existence as a part of general edu- cation.

Thus we have fallen prey to a phenomenon which, for lack of a better term, I have dubbed the historical fallacy. In general terms it is this: that a civilization may be understood, appreciated, and propagated by means of the study of its history, that cultural values are implicit in history and are therefore susceptible of being taught via the vehicle of history, and finally, that functional participation in a culture is readily achieved through the study of its history.

The fallacy was not foisted off on American education but emerged from a set of circumstances peculiar to our national life—an educational lag, as it were. The advancement of learning is not often pursued with an eye to its relevance for general education. Understandably, the scholar, with singleness of purpose, pursues his design without regard for the practical relevance of his studies. On the other hand, educators are hesitant to stray too far from the reservoir of accepted ideas. By the nature of their calling they reinforce the "conventional wisdom" with which the pioneers on the frontiers of every scholarly field must everlastingly do battle. The dissociation of productive scholarship from the more conservative concerns of public education has always haunted the American school.

This is certainly not to suggest that history be disestablished as a school subject or to deprecate its value as an academic discipline. It is rather to point out that history is an insufficient instrument to achieve the purposes we proclaim for it. Most historians are highly sensitive to the limitations of history; indeed, the term "universe of discourse" implies boundaries and, therefore, limits of both scope and purpose. To suggest to many historians that the purpose of their discipline is to transmit values is to invite argument. History is, by most definitions, morally neutral; but the uses of history in the public school are highly valuative. When we speak of what *ought* to be taught or what values young American *ought* to hold we have both feet in the realm of normative ethics.

Beard's mot that "history is a damned dim candle over a damned dark abyss" was keenly insightful. We are indeed posed on the brink of a dark abyss and reliance on history alone to save us is hazardous.

Each generation of young Americans has, more or less, begun anew to develop values and perspectives that are often drastically different from the ones held by preceding generations. It seems to be a characteristic of American civilization to develop new and unique attitudes toward not only our political, social, and economic institutions but the premises underpinning them. We have mislaid our transcendent ideal.

Young America today is both egocentric and ethnocentric. In the twentieth century when the exigencies of both domestic and international events demand, more than ever, a politically literate and socially liberal population, the cumulative effect of our failure to communicate the best of our civilization is being felt. An understanding of that which is peculiarly precious about America to give direction and purpose to national endeavor and to involve the individual citizen in it is wanting.

Americans in general hold many attitudes which are inimical to the democratic process we profess to revere. Outstanding illustrations are: (1) a generalized suspicion of the role of government (The government is considered remote, alien to the society, and so complex as to be incomprehensible. There is, it is thought, no hope of effective individual participation); (2) an ethnocentricity which is the wellspring of hostility toward international institutions for the resolution of conflict such as the United Nations

Organization; (3) a provincial attitude which views all foreign aid as the sheerest idealistic folly; and (4) an attitude which holds material affluence to be the measure of all things. And so forth, *ad infinitum*.

For those involved in the affairs of public school social studies these days the singular agreement among teachers, scholars, and administrators that something must be done is striking. Curriculum revision is in the air. *Social Education* is moved to devote an issue to a symposium on revision in the social studies; the American Political Science Association, the Association of American Anthropologists, the American Historical Association, the Association of American Geographers, represent some discipline interests in curricular reorganization; the U.S. Office of Education under "Project Social Studies" and the private foundations stand ready with millions to endow projects and research which seem likely to "do something." The result thus far has been the expenditure of tremendous energy in incoordinate activity. The "slow learner," the "accelerated student," "area studies," "non-Western culture," "the world view," and "cultural deprivation" are familiar phrases which illustrate the variety of areas of concern.

At present there is a conviction on the part of educators, university faculty, and the general public that a viable program of public education must incorporate forms of instruction that transcend the scope and purpose of the social science disciplines. The accelerated growth of general education is itself evidence of the conviction that instruction must have a philosophical dimension if we are to overcome cultural parochialism that is considered the residue of specialization.

The problem of revision in the area of things American is particularly knotty. In Galbraith's apt phrase, the American history course is part of the "conventional wisdom." In an area where familiarity is the measure of acceptability, history is acceptable indeed and has, therefore, great stability as an institution. If we can be guided by previous experience, major and revolutionary revision, although badly needed, is patently impossible. The number of vested interests that abound in any school system preclude rapid change. As Stephen K. Bailey says, "Changing curricula is like moving a graveyard, you just can't do it."

No more hopeful is the variety of committees and commissions initiated by scholarly professional organizations which seek to establish courses and units of study, or to furnish materials, to establish the relevance of their academic disciplines in public school curricula. The inherent insufficiency of history as a discipline also applies to the other social science disciplines. They are by definition morally neutral and do not, separately, speak to basic principles and values of American society. They furnish accurate and descriptive information which is, in the final analysis, only the raw material with which to illuminate the culture and lead students toward functional participation in it. American education needs gifted generalists much more than patriots of a discipline.

Given the fact that revolutionary curricular change is at best difficult and that "far out" pilot studies (such as replacing, on the first grade level, the friendly trashman with a study of Eskimo culture) lack the essential element of transferability, it would seem reasonable that revision might be accomplished within the existing structure. There is no reason why attitudinal concepts and social science concepts we deem to be crucial to the understanding of American culture cannot be accommodated under present curricular pattern.

What is suggested is that the approach be that of American Studies rather than American history. Since history is an integral part of American Studies it would be relatively easy (considering the alternatives) to establish such courses as "Backgrounds of American Civilization," "American Institutions," "American Culture and Values," and "America and the Community of Nations." Such courses would utilize illustrative materials from American history and the humanities within a conceptual frame that embraces the relevant ideas and values of economics, geography, political science, and sociology, thus combining the best of scholarship from both the social sciences and the humanities. To insinuate into the existing patterns the approaches, insights, ways of working, and perspectives of American Studies would be to reconcile the promise and the hope.

This implies of course, abandonment of the "then-to-now" approach. Chronology would become a simple literary device to place in time and space the great event, the significant turning point, and the influential personality or idea. It also implies the courage to exclude. This process is rather like cleaning an attic. It is necessary to bite one's lip to ruthlessly discard that which is of no consequence for there is a good salting of the sentimental antiquarian in each of us. We frequently finish with a more tidy attic but with little additional usable room.

The necessary first step is essential agreement on what we are about. Reluctantly another "list" is suggested. (American education has been done to death with lists.) This must be a list of expectations in the form of attitudes, values, and concepts from the social sciences, history, and the humanities which has been composed by representatives from all these.

The next step, and that which gives substance to such an approach, is the logical insinuation of these concepts into the materials—historical, literary, and socio-scientific—of the American experience. The goals determine the selection of materials and the attic cleans itself. Jackson is put to work for economics and political science, the Supreme Court emerges from the shadows, Puritanism moves from Massachusetts Bay to be recognized as an instrumental force in modern America, geography and literature team up to explain the fact and influence of the Great Plains, and the student is introduced to the pleasures of discovery.

(1) National Council for the Social Studies. *A Guide to Content in the Social Studies*. Washington, D.C.: The Council, 1958, p. 1.

(2) Martin Mayer. *Where, When, and Why: Social Studies in American Schools*. New York: Harper and Row, 1963. p. 42–43.

SOCIAL SCIENCE ELEMENTS IN HISTORY COURSES

Edith West

Both the proponents and opponents of an emphasis on history in the social studies curriculum recognize the considerable use in history courses of concepts from other social sciences. Here, a specialist on the teaching of world history illustrates the potentiality in the extensively interdisciplinary nature of history course content as it frequently is taught.

S TUDENTS need to develop a body of concepts and generalizations if they are to use the past to help them understand the present. A great mass of data cannot be used without some form of conceptualization. Each historical event, writes Philip Bagby, "is different from the rest but at the same time resembles some others. They fall into classes and categories to which we give names. If they did not do so, we should not be able to describe them at all, for description is nothing more than a pointing-out of the resemblances between the event we are describing and other more familiar events. Every noun classifies and every adjective compares. When the historian uses such terms as 'city,' 'nation,' 'king,' 'war,' and 'revolution,' he is saying that the objects or events he describes fall into certain familiar categories." (1) One of the uses of school history is that it provides concrete examples of concepts from the other social sciences. These are not always made explicit in textbooks, but the teacher versed in the social sciences can help pupils make the applications. A number of historians, moreover, are finding that the use of newer concepts borrowed from the other social sciences provides increased historical insight. (2) History also enables pupils to test generalizations from these other fields. At times they will find that such generalizations are valid only for the present day or for their own culture. If so, they will learn that the generalizations may be inapplicable in the future.

FROM *New Perspectives in World History*, Shirley H. Engle, ed., Washington, D.C., 1964, National Council for the Social Studies, pp. 587–590. Used by permission. Dr. West is professor of education and head of the campus high school department of social studies, University of Minnesota.

Space does not permit a listing of all of the concepts which might be taught in a world history course, but some of the more important ones from the different social sciences can be used by way of illustration. Central concepts of anthropology include race, culture, cultural diversity, cultural universals, cultural configuration, cultural change, diffusion, cultural continuity, social lag, value system, enculturation, and social role. Historians, too, are concerned with the interrelatedness of all aspects of a culture with change, and with factors inducing or slowing down change. History involves value systems of different societies and the impact of values upon all aspects of life. These concepts, important to both anthropology and history, are also crucial in understanding many of the problems of today's world, as can be illustrated by the problems of promoting technical change in underdeveloped areas. These anthropological concepts can be developed best if pupils study cultures of different parts of the world as well as of past eras.

The sociologist is concerned with society as a system, with factors and institutions providing stability in a society and with factors producing change. He is interested in stratification, in social role and in social institutions. Both he and the psychologist study motivation and the impact of society and groups upon personality. All of these concerns must also be the concern of the historian.

The very fact that so much of history is political history highlights the relationship between history and political science. The political scientist is interested in power relationships, in political motivation, in revolution, in political theory, in the impact upon people of different kinds of political institutions, in the reasons for the development of our own institutions, in political decision making, in war, and in other aspects of international relations. These topics are emphasized in most history textbooks. Norton Long, in his recent paper on what should be taught in the schools from the field of political science, argues that a large portion of the content is taught best through history with its numerous examples and narrative approach. (3)

The economist, too, is concerned with many of the same things as the historian. He is interested in the conflict between unlimited human wants and limited resources, in different ways of answering the basic economic problems of any society: What shall be produced and in what quantities? How shall it be produced? Who shall get what? Faced by problems of underdeveloped countries today and by serious problems of unemployment in the United States, he is concerned with factors which promote economic growth. Consequently, he is forced to examine history as well as current data. The historian also must examine economic institutions of every era.

History involves a key idea of geography—that physical environment does not determine the course of events, but rather that it sets limits given the current state of technology. Available resources have different meanings for different societies in terms of cultural values as well as technological know-how. These geographic generalizations can be developed thoroughly if pupils study the use of the environment by many different societies in different ages and cultures. It is obvious, however, that the geography correlated with history in each instance of the past must be historical geography. How did the landscape look in that era? How did people of that era perceive their environment? How were they able to use it? The present-day landscape is relevant only by way of contrast to illustrate how changing technology and value systems affect its use.

This enumeration of key concepts and topics in the social sciences other than history needs to be expanded by those organizing world history courses. However, it is indicative of some of the concepts which can be taught through history in a more concrete fashion than in analytical courses in the separate social science disciplines. History is an integrating discipline; it is concerned with all of the past and so with all of the social sciences. To be useful history, it should help students conceptualize in the social sciences. Alternative organizations of world history courses should be evaluated in part in terms of their potential for teaching these concepts.

Certain concepts about history as a field and about the contents of history should also be taught. Students need to learn the meaning of history as "actuality," "record," "knowledge," and "thought." They should learn something about historical criticism, about changing interpretations, about periodization. In addition to key concepts such as change and cultural continuity, they need to understand multiple causation. The content and organization of a world history course should help pupils develop these ideas.

(1) *Culture and History* (Berkeley: University of California, 1963; paperback edition), p. 53.

(2) For example, see David Potter, *People of Plenty, Economic Abundance and the American Character* (Chicago: University of Chicago, 1954); Thomas C. Cochran, "The Historian's Use of Social Role," in Louis Gottschalk, ed., *Generalization in the Writing of History* (Chicago: University of Chicago, 1963), p. 103–110; and Bagby, *op. cit.*

(3) "Political Science," in *The Social Studies and the Social Sciences, op. cit.*, p. 100, 103.

WHITHER THE PROBLEMS OF DEMOCRACY COURSE?

Leo J. Alilunas

At least ostensibly, the most fully interdisciplinary, widely offered social studies course in senior high school is the problems course. In this article an investigator traces the development of the course from its inception earlier in this century to its present-day controversial status and nature. The selection includes some analysis of the nature and role of the course in today's social studies program.

ANDRÉ GIDE once stated that the present would be full of all possible futures, if the past had not already projected a pattern upon it. His statement has application to the P.O.D. course. This course (now in a stage of ferment along with the other social studies, historical and nonhistorical) had its beginnings in 1916 when it was recommended by the National Education Association Commission on the Social Studies. It was set up as the most striking example of the organization of a secondary school social studies course which correlates or integrates political science, economics, and sociology. Initially it was advocated, in part, because educators believed the overcrowded secondary school curriculum could not make room for required separate courses in political science, economics, and sociology. (In the 1960's we find anthropology added to the list of the social sciences which are knocking on the high school door and asking for entrance in some way.) During World War I educators became aware of the need to teach modern problems to prepare American youth for intelligent and realistic training in democratic citizenship. The same need exists almost fifty years later!

There were problems of determination of content and the dangers of teaching controversial problems. There were problems of limitations of study materials, of having competent teachers, and of articulating the course with the eleventh-grade American history course and the ninth-grade civics course. All of these are still problems, along with the danger of what Erling Hunt has called the "forensic exchange of ignorant opinions." This danger confronts students in other social studies courses!

By 1923 the P.O.D. course had a foothold in American high schools. By 1928 it was taught in 890 high schools in thirty-eight states, and by 1934 it had a place in 12,000 high schools in all of the states. (1) In a recent survey

---

FROM *Social Education*, 28:11–14, January, 1964. Used by permission. Dr. Alilunas is a professor of social studies at the State University of New York College in Fredonia.

Willis D. Moreland has reported that problems of democracy is the most popular required social studies offering in the twelfth grade, with American government next in the frequency of the mentioned required courses for that grade. Dr. Moreland's study also shows that problems of democracy is the subject most frequently reported in combination with American government. Further, he indicates the combination of economics with the problems of democracy course, American government, or sociology seems to be the most common arrangement. He has reported only one case of a full year of economics and no offering of sociology or psychology as full-year separate subjects. (2)

In the first decade of the P.O.D. course textbooks were heavily weighted on the side of government and politics, with little emphasis on economic and sociological topics. In the 1938 editions of modern problems textbooks there were thirty-eight topics as against twenty-seven topics in the earlier editions. (3) The common curricular phenomenon, *proliferation* (addition without subtraction) afflicted this course, as it had history and other social studies courses. It still does!

Stokes reported that Modern Problems textbooks in the 1930's were beginning to discuss economic and sociological topics, and cited as new topics, consumer economics, public opinion, city planning, and recreation. (4) There was little attention to international relations. The United States was still in a mood of "isolationism." And as late as 1950, after examining textbooks published since 1941, Manson Van B. Jennings stated it was too early to tell how far the Modern Problems textbooks would go in their treatment of international problems as they involved the United States. (5) In his study Dr. Jennings did report a definite trend to emphasize the present needs of youth, as evidenced in the new textbook chapters on personality development, vocational guidance, and use of leisure time. This new trend, which brought in the elements of the discipline of psychology, tended to add to the problem of proliferation. Dr. Jennings concluded that the modern problems course in its scope had too many topics and observed that textbook authors had to deal with a large number of topics in order that their textbooks might have sales appeal. (6)

It is interesting to note that a comparison of textbooks over the past quarter of a century reveals a pattern of treatment of persistent, fundamental problems rather than just "current" issues. In the determination of content political science still plays the major role, with economics and sociology following in importance. Critics who charge that the P.O.D. course is primarily a "life adjustment" course (7) lack evidence.

Modern Problems textbooks published during the late 1940's began to reflect the influence of World War II and the changing position of the United States in world affairs. In the decade of 1950–1960 they had interpretations of competitive economic systems, Russian-American relations, the study of war, and the search for peace and order. Twelfth-grade modern problems textbooks have approached a better balance between political science, economics, and sociology than do the ninth-grade textbooks in citizenship. The textbooks at the twelfth-grade level deal less with personal problems and give less emphasis to local communities than do the civics textbooks for the ninth grade.

In his report, *The American High School Today*, James B. Conant has recommended that a course on American problems or American government should be required in the twelfth grade. Further, he has recommended that this course should include as much material on economics as the students can handle. He has advocated that for this course there should be a heterogeneous grouping of students and encouragement of free discussion of controversial issues. (8)

Dade County, Florida, Seattle, Washington, and New York City are among the public school systems which have developed solid, well organized P.O.D. courses. They disprove the charge that the Problems of Democracy course in its structure is inescapably a "hodge-podge" of "evanescent," superficial, "life-centered" material catering to boys and girls who want "glib," "entertaining" study featured by field trips and "snippets of historical data." (9)

Like other courses in the field of the social studies, the P.O.D. course has suffered from proliferation. It needs to be reformed, but not abolished, as its most severe critics would like. In the structure of the course the disciplines of political science, economics, and sociology need to be better organized and interrelated. They might well draw upon the discipline of history for background in the way the New York City program has proposed. This program recognizes that history serves a useful function in the beginning of the study of problems but it is not the end. The P.O.D. course needs a better balance in the treatment of domestic and international topics. It needs a reduction in the number of basic issues that can be studied adequately. (10)

It will be hard to satisfy the most zealous advocates of the doctrine of "separatism" within the field of the social sciences that even a reorganized P.O.D. course will provide what they deem to be sufficient attention to their particular discipline. But in the reconstruction of the secondary school social studies subjects other than the P.O.D. course they will be increasingly challenged in the 1960's to make adjustments in the application of their discipline. The emerging reconstruction movement is encouraging the utilization of the social sciences on an interdisciplinary basis. Undoubtedly some of the social sciences will continue to be taught as separate subjects but others will be taught on the secondary school level as a combination of the various social sciences. Pennsylvania has undertaken leadership in this new direction by converting the traditional course in world history into a course in world cultures. The structure of the new course is interdisciplinary and draws upon the social sciences of anthropology, sociology, history, geography, political science, and economics. (11) As high schools, especially the large ones, expand their elective social studies offerings, they will design area courses, such as the Soviet Union, the Far East, Latin America, etc. These courses are likely to be taught more often on an interdisciplinary basis rather than through the approach of a separate discipline, such as history, geography, political science, or economics. In teaching these courses high schools will use materials similar to those the Human Relations Area Files, Inc. of New Haven, Connecticut, has developed in its series on various countries and world areas. (12)

Each of the social sciences has a right to be a pressure group for the establishment of a separate course at the high school level, but each needs to be realistic in its expectations. In the face of the increasing competition from other subjects such as mathematics, the sciences, English and the foreign languages, the various social studies, historical and nonhistorical, are not likely to be allocated more than a course a year for all high school students. As a matter of fact, the present average amount of social studies taken by high school graduates is little more than two and a half years. (13)

In a well-organized P.O.D. course the various social scientists have opportunity to expose significant aspects of their disciplines to large numbers of adolescents who have need of them in their study of vital modern problems. The P.O.D. course will endure in some form because it provides a good common meeting ground for the various social science disciplines. It will endure because it seeks to meet the needs of American youth in their training in democratic citizenship.

(1) Erling M. Hunt. "Twenty-Five Years of Problems of Democracy." *Social Education.* 5:507–511; November 1941.
(2) Willis D. Moreland. "Curriculum Trends in the Social Studies." *Social Education.* 26:73–76, 102; February 1962.
(3) J. Burroughs Stokes. "The Changing Content of Modern Problems Texts." *Social Education.* 4:338–340; May 1940.
(4) *Ibid.,* p. 340.
(5) Manson Van B. Jennings. *The Development of the Modern Problems Course in the Senior High School.* New York: Bureau of Publications, Teachers College, Columbia University, 1950. p. 116
(6) *Ibid.,* p. 122–125.
(7) Arthur Bestor. *The Restoration of Learning.* New York: Knopf, 1955.

p. 131–132. Arthur Bestor. "History, Social Studies, and Citizenship: The Responsibility of the Public Schools." *Proceedings of the American Philosophical Society.* 104:550–552; December 15, 1960.
(8) James Bryant Conant. *The American High School Today.* New York: McGraw-Hill Book Company, 1959. p. 76.
(9) Madolyn Brown and Jeff West. "A Team Approach to Curriculum Development." *Educational Administration and Supervision.* March 1958. p. 79–84; A Guide to the Teaching of Contemporary Problems. A Two Semester Course for Grade Twelve. Seattle: Seattle Public Schools, Administrative and Service Center, 1960; *Problems of Democracy.* Curriculum Bulletin No. 9. Brooklyn: Board of Education, City of New York.

(10) The National Association of Secondary School Principals has recommended that the scope of the course
be limited to six to ten issues. *Social
Studies in the Comprehensive Secondary School.* Washington, D.C.: National Association of Secondary School
Principals, National Education Association, 1961, p. 8.

(11) Pennsylvania Council for the Social
Studies. *Curriculum Suggestions and
Teaching Aids for World Cultures
for Pennsylvania,* January, 1961. p. 1.

(12) As an example, see Thomas Fitzim-
mons, Peter Malof, John C. Fiske and
Staff Associates of the Human Rela-
tions Area Files, Inc. *USSR. Its
People, Its Society, Its Culture.* New
Haven: Human Relations Area Files
Press, 1960.

(13) *The Social Studies and the Social
Sciences.* Sponsored by the American
Council of Learned Societies and the
National Council for the Social
Studies. New York: Harcourt, Brace
& World, 1962. p. 14.

PART FOUR
TEACHING AND LEARNING
IN SOCIAL STUDIES

The immediate and dominant purposes of the social studies are, after all, instructional. To be successful, then, teachers must give attention to methods, techniques, and procedures for learning and teaching. This Part presents varying views on major aspects of instruction in social studies.

The central role of the teacher in affecting learning has long been recognized. What are social studies teachers really like? What qualities should they seek to develop? How can they best prepare to fulfill their functions?

What is the basic nature of students' study activity and learning process in social studies? How can reading best aid social learning? What rational processes are involved in the study of society, and how can the teacher facilitate their improvement? What other chief types of study skill are useful in social studies, and how should they be organized for instruction?

How well does the unit approach facilitate teaching and learning? What practices are likely to improve unit teaching? Is the extensive use of reading and writing activities appropriate for social studies? Should social studies methodology more fully and faithfully reflect the research methodology of the social sciences? If so, what techniques are most applicable to adolescent learning? How far has the social studies progressed in developing sound and workable means of evaluating students' learning? What improvements are needed?

The foregoing questions reflect the range of considerations in the selections that follow. They have been chosen with the hope of providing stimulus and direction to help teachers guide students' learning in such ways that social studies will really make a difference.

1

Fulfilling the Teacher's Roles

A NATIONAL SURVEY OF HIGH SCHOOL
SOCIAL STUDIES TEACHERS

Ann F. Brunswick

Studies that report data on a representative sampling of the nation's social studies teachers are rare indeed. It is particularly interesting, therefore, to have this recent report based on a carefully selected sample consisting of 2,791 respondents in more than 500 high schools. The findings were secured by the National Opinion Research Center in connection with an investigation of teacher-viewing of the nationally televised series on "The American Economy." Understandably, then, the original, much fuller report gives major attention to teachers and subject matter of economics. Some of the data reported here are necessarily a little outdated in absolute, though probably not in relative, amounts—for example, the figures reporting teachers' incomes during 1963–64.

ABOUT one in three (36 per cent) of all the high school social studies teachers were under thirty years of age and only a slightly greater number (39 per cent) were between thirty and forty-five years old; only one quarter of the teachers were forty-five years or older, with one in twenty having reached the age of sixty. . . . Four out of five of the high school social studies teachers were men. . . .

Slightly better than half of all the social studies teachers (54 per cent) were earning between $5,000–$7,499 annually and before taxes, from their teaching. One quarter of the teachers earned less than this and about one in five teachers (21 per cent) earned $7,500 or more. When this salary distribution is compared with that for all personal incomes in the United States (1), we note that high school social studies teachers fare considerably better than the average. In the total population, seven in ten earned less than $5,000, about one in four earned between $5,000 and $7,499 and only one in eight (12 per cent) earned as much as $7,500. However, fewer of the social studies

---

FROM *Economics on TV: An Evaluation of "The American Economy,"* Chicago: National Opinion Research Center, University of Chicago, 1964, pp. 46–78. Used by permission.

teachers are in the highest income bracket: Three per cent of the social studies teachers compared to 5 per cent in the general population are earning $10,000 or more. . . .

We also asked the teachers to record which income category matched most closely their incomes when they added on any nonteaching income plus income from other members of their families. As would be expected, the entire income distribution shifted upward, with only one teacher in nine (11 per cent) reporting a gross family income of less than $5,000 and slightly better than a third (36 per cent) income between $5,000 and $7,499. Just over half of all the teachers (55 per cent) report gross family incomes of at least $7,500. This is considerably higher than family income reported for families in the general population in 1960, of whom 44 per cent were earning less than $5,000, 25 per cent had incomes between $5,000–$7,499, and 31 per cent had a before-taxes income of $7,500 or more (2). . . .

For the sample of social studies teachers as a whole, 1 per cent were foreign born and 99 per cent were born in the United States; 84 per cent of the teachers had fathers who also were born in the United States. . . .

It is of interest to compare the findings for the high school social studies teachers with comparable data that are available from a national cross-section of the United States population, conducted by NORC in 1955. The national survey showed that 9 per cent of the population was foreign-born and 27 per cent (as opposed to 16 per cent of the social studies teachers) had fathers who were born outside the United States. Thus it would seem that high school social studies teachers, as compared to the general population, are more often native-born and similarly more often have fathers who were born inside this country.

The mothers of these social studies teachers have a slightly higher education level than do the fathers: Almost four in ten (39 per cent) of the fathers never went beyond grade school as compared with three in ten of the mothers. About one in four (26 per cent) of the mothers completed high school as compared to only one in five of the fathers. Just about a quarter of either group of parents had some college experience. . . .

As another measure of the socio-economic backgrounds from which the teachers came, we asked them to indicate which of nine standard census occupational categories best described their father's usual occupation during their teenage years. About one in seven of the teachers (14 per cent) reported a professional career for their fathers. Slightly more (17 per cent) indicated that their fathers had been engaged as proprietors or managers. Almost one in five (19 per cent) had fathers who were farmers or farm managers. Better than two in five (43 per cent) reported blue collar occupations for their fathers. . . .

Hardly any of the social studies teachers participating in this survey (one tenth of 1 per cent) reported that they had no academic degree.

Three teachers in every five (60 per cent) currently have a bachelor's degree and nothing more, but just about half of these (32 per cent of the total sample) are working for another degree.

Almost two in five of all the social studies teachers (39 per cent) have a master's degree, or a fifth-year or sixth-year diploma—advanced education degrees. A fifth of these teachers (8 per cent of the total sample) are currently working toward a higher degree. Not quite one high school social studies teacher in a hundred has a Ph.D. or Ed.D. degree. . . .

Two in five of these social studies teachers are currently working toward some academic degree; a third are working toward a master's degree or its equivalent and about three in 100 social studies teachers are currently working toward a doctorate. The remaining 2 per cent are earning other kinds of degrees, e.g., sixth-grade diplomas. . . .

We analyzed the major subjects of study in two ways. First, we determined the number of teachers who had earned a degree in any of four areas: 1) economics, 2) some other area of social studies, 3) education, including educational administration, 4) any subject area besides these three. Then we analyzed in greater detail the major for the teacher's last earned degree.

Just one in twenty-five of the high school social studies teachers earned a degree in economics, and six out of seven (87 per cent) have a degree in some other area of the social studies. About one in five have a degree for which they majored in education or education administration. About the same number have a degree in some subject other than economics, social studies or education. . . .

Only two and one half per cent (2½%) of all the social studies teachers majored in economics for their last degree, two-thirds of them (67 per cent) majored in some other area of the social studies, a fifth (22 per cent) took their degrees in education or educational administration. (3) The only other major subject mentioned with any degree of frequency was physical education, sometimes combined into a physical education and health degree; about one in nine of all the teachers (11 per cent) had such a major for his last degree. . . .

About one in five (19 per cent) of the teachers has earned a degree within the past two years, 1962–64; almost half (45 per cent) have earned a degree within the last five years, 1959–64. Another fifth (22 per cent) earned a degree between five and ten years ago and just a third earned their last degree ten years ago or longer. Fifteen per cent of the teachers received their last degree twenty or more years ago. . . .

Just under half (48 per cent) of all these high school social studies teachers reported some academic honors for their college undergraduate studies—making dean's list or Phi Beta Kappa or graduating cum laude, etc. One in five of all the social studies teachers reported that he had been in the top 10 per cent of his graduating class and slightly better than half (56 per cent) had graduated in the top quarter. About a third (32 per cent) were in the second quarter. One teacher in nine was in the third quarter. Only one in one hundred teachers reported that he had been in the bottom quarter of his graduating class. . . .

Only one social studies teacher in twenty-five belongs to no professional organizations whatsoever. Roughly a third (35 per cent) belong to one or two such organizations, another third of the teachers (32 per cent) reported membership in three professional organizations, and just under a third (29 per cent) belong to more than this. . . .

About half of all the social studies teachers at some time have held an office in a professional organization. Quite similar proportions indicated that they had held such office once (15 per cent) or twice (17 per cent) and three times or more (17 per cent). . . .

There are few social studies teachers who say they have not attended any professional meeting or lecture during the past year. The majority, 54 per cent, have attended at least five such meetings. . . .

But one in twenty of the social studies teachers reported that he does not read any professional periodicals regularly. Slightly fewer than half, 45 per cent, regularly read one or two. Half of the teachers reported that they read at least three professional publications regularly. . . .

For one in nine of the social studies teachers, this is the first year of teaching. A quarter of the teachers have taught between two and four years. Almost two-thirds (64 per cent) have been teaching at least five years, and better than two in five (43 per cent) have been teaching at least ten years. Slightly fewer than one high school social studies teachers in five (19 per cent) have been teaching as long as twenty years. . . .

A number of these teachers have taught subjects and/or grade levels other than what they are teaching now. For while 11 per cent indicated that this was their first year of teaching, we now find 16 per cent who indicated that this was their first year of teaching high school social studies. And where only 37 per cent had been in teaching less than five years, we now find that almost half of the teachers, 47 per cent, have been teaching high school social studies less than five years. Whereas 43 per cent have been teaching at least ten years, only 30 per cent have been teaching high school social studies for this length of time. And while close to one in five of the teachers has been engaged in teaching for at least twenty years, only one in nine teachers have been teaching high school social studies for this long. . . .

A majority of these teachers, 60 per cent, are teaching one or more classes in American history. The next most frequently taught types of courses are European, ancient, medieval or world history and 42 per cent of all the social studies teachers are teaching one or more of these.

In the total group of teachers, slightly better than a third, 37 per cent, are teaching one or more courses in civics, citizenship, government, or political science; better than a quarter (28 per cent) are teaching at least one course called Social Studies; just fewer than one in five (18 per cent) are teaching a course in Problems or Challenge of Democracy. Just about the same proportion, 18 per cent, are teaching geography, economic geography, earth science or the like. Seventh in frequency of being taught was economics or economic institutions, one in eight (13 per cent) of all the social studies teachers indicating that they were teaching a course in this area. . . .

Somewhat fewer than half of all the teachers (45 per cent) indicated a desire to continue teaching in high school what they are teaching now. . . . About a fifth of all the teachers (19 per cent) say that they would like to be teaching at a college or university and about one in six (15 per cent) say they would like to be working in school administration. . . .

One in six of these instructors teaches in a school in a large metropolitan area—a metropolitan area with a population of two million or more. They are divided about two to one between the suburbs and outskirts, and the central city, respectively. A third of the teachers are located in small metropolitan areas, those with a population of less than two million. In the small metropolitan areas, teachers are equally divided between the urban centers and suburban communities.

About one in ten teachers was in a city with a population of less than 50,000; and three in ten of the teachers were in a small town or rural county, lacking a population center as large as 10,000 in population. These proportions reflect to some extent . . . that the central cities of large metrpolitan areas are somewhat underrepresented in our sample. For this reason the proportion of teachers from small communities in this sample is somewhat larger than the actual population proportion. . . .

About a fifth of all the teachers surveyed were in the Northeast. . . . A third of all the teachers were in the North Central states and about a quarter (26 per cent) were in the South. A fifth of these social studies teachers were in the Mountain and Pacific states. . . .

Slightly more than a third of all the instructors (36 per cent) were teaching in schools where there were no more than two other social studies teachers: 12 per cent were in schools where they were the only such teacher, 11 per cent in schools where there was one other and 13 per cent where there were two other social studies teachers. . . . Another third of the teachers were in schools with three to eight social studies teachers. . . . Over all, 31 per cent of the teachers reported that they taught in schools with nine or more other social studies teachers. . . .

As another measure of school size, we obtained from each school information about the number of pupils enrolled there as of January 1, 1964, or as soon thereafter as such a count was available. It should be emphasized that this discussion, like that in the section above, is concerned with the proportions of teachers teaching in schools of given sizes, and cannot be taken to represent the proportion of schools that there are with these enrollments. . . .

(1) *Current Population Reports—Consumer Income Series*, No. 43, Sept. 29, 1964, p. 34, Table 18.

(2) *Statistical Abstract of the United States*, 1962, p. 330.

(3) If the teacher majored in the education of a particular subject, e.g., social

studies education, it was classified according to the subject area rather than to education. Only if the teacher indicated an education degree, not specified as to a particular study, or education administration, was it classified here.

THE OBLIGATION OF THE TEACHER
TO BE A SCHOLAR

Thomas A. Bailey

Current efforts to close the gap between the social sciences and the social studies make this article an especially timely one. Here a well-known historian sketches scholarly characteristics deemed desirable for teachers. His vigorous specification of the scholarly qualities that have a practical effect in improving instruction constitutes a model that social studies teachers can gain greatly by emulating.

F EW WILL deny that the teacher exercises a tremendous influence on the thinking, attitudes, ideals, and habits of our youth. He has therefore a heavy obligation to be not a time-server, not a propagandist, not a doctrinaire—but a scholar.

The word "scholar" conjures up many images, but perhaps the most common one is that of the man or woman who by publishing the fruits of original research in the form of heavily documented monographs widens perceptibly the frontier of human knowledge. According to this concept, all teachers have an inescapable obligation to publish, if not footnoted books, at least learned articles in which a rivulet of text meanders through a meadow of footnotes.

Within limits this is a praiseworthy practice, provided the subject is significant, which unfortunately it often is not, and provided one's teaching is not neglected, which unfortunately it often is. One of the many battles that the teacher-scholar has to fight with his conscience is where to establish a nice balance between the time devoted to teaching and that devoted to research.

The standard argument is that a judicious amount of research makes for more effective teaching, and with this view I heartily agree. Research can

FROM *Social Education*, 13:355-358, December, 1949. Used by permission. Dr. Bailey is a professor of history at Stanford University.

provide a stimulating antidote to the routine of teaching, just as teaching can provide a stimulating antidote to the routine of research. Much as I love teaching, and much as I love research, I should not want to be condemned to a life of doing the one without the other.

Enthusiasm is the mainspring of successful teaching, and research can assist in keeping this virtue alive. The thrill that came to Balboa of discovering something new; the excitement of treading paths never before trod; the satisfaction that springs from sharing one's findings with others—all this helps the teacher to be fresh and vibrant.

The scholar who drinks deep at the fountain of original sources comes before his students with greater confidence and speaks with greater authority. The class is quick to perceive this and appreciate it, provided he does not ride his hobby horse to death, in which case he becomes the campus joke.

The scholar also finds that constant practice in the art of presenting his discoveries in writing sharpens the precision of his thinking and his speech, and often reflects itself in more effective teaching.

Finally, research is a constant reminder of the difficulty of ascertaining truth. It induces a proper spirit of humility and tempers the unfortunate classroom practice of throwing off sweeping but unsound generalities.

But can a man or woman be a scholar who does not grind out heavily footnoted monographs? I should say yes, decidedly. I should also say that a person can publish heavily documented monographs and still not be a scholar. Not all that glitters is gold, and not everything with *ibid.'s* at the bottom is learning. Scholarship is a state of mind, not a mound of footnotes.

In my judgment interpretative essays, like the best of the historians, Frederick Jackson Turner and Carl L. Becker, represent scholarship in its finest form. I deplore the tendency in some circles to assess scholarship, not on a qualitative but on a quantitative or poundage basis. Turner published only one book, and that under a form of mild duress; H. H. Bancroft published about forty. But shall we conclude that Bancroft was forty times more scholarly than Turner?

I also deplore the common distinction that is made between productive and nonproductive scholars. All teacher-scholars produce *something* in the way of ideas, whether the ideas appear on the printed page or in the classroom. Without wishing in any way to rationalize laziness, I would go further and say that many of our greatest scholars—Lord Acton comes to mind—have published little or nothing. Like unknown soldiers, thousands of scholars in our classrooms today will die unsung, but, like the unknown soldier at Arlington, they will have contributed their lives to a cause larger than self. They at least have the abiding satisfaction of leaving behind ideas and ideals which will be carried on by their students, and which will in one way or another help to shape the destinies of the nation for decades to come. One might almost say that a good idea never dies.

If we may assume that the responsibilities of the teacher are such that he is obligated to be a scholar, we may properly ask: What must one do to be a scholar?

The scholar first of all is humble. He recognizes that both he and his students are learners, but that his ignorance is perhaps less than theirs. He therefore avoids pontification and the magisterial air.

The scholar is thorough. While not a narrow perfectionist, he is satisfied with nothing less than perfection in himself and others. He feels that it is his duty to keep abreast of the findings of current scholarship, so that he will not repeat the discredited old myths. He makes a real effort to find out what is going on in cognate fields of interest, so that he may broaden his frame of reference. Unhurried and imperturbable, he does not go off half-cocked and emit potboilers. Like Vernon H. Parrington, he does not produce until he is ripe for production and has something to say that deserves the immortality of print. The pressure for premature publication is one of the great enemies of scholarship.

The scholar is accurate. He realizes that memory, even that of a Macaulay, is a treacherous crutch. He checks and rechecks the results of his findings. He maintains no double standard: slipshod stuff for the classroom, where the students do not know the difference; meticulously careful work for the outside world, where he may be judged by his peers. He knows that repetition of an error does not make a fact. "Of course it's a fact," a professor once replied to an inquiring mind. "I've been telling it to my classes for thirty-five years."

The scholar is honest. He candidly admits the gaps in his evidence; he gladly corrects his errors of fact and judgment. His pen is not for sale. He does not deliberately color his interpretations to fit the prevailing climate of opinion, whether isolationist or interventionist, Japanophile or Japanophobe. He does not seek popularity at the expense of truth. In fact, he does not seek popularity at all.

The scholar is openminded. Urbane, civilized, tolerant of the opinions of others, he is intolerant only of low standards and slovenly practices. He maintains no vested interest in old or discredited ideas. He eagerly accepts reliable new evidence, even though dug up by young whippersnappers, and even though it may undermine convictions growing out of his birth, upbringing, marriage, study, and forty years of research and teaching. He avoids hardening of the intellectual arteries, and he makes it a practice to re-examine periodically the concepts of which he is most sure. If incapable of doing this, he would serve the cause of scholarship, to say nothing of his own reputation, by retiring in favor of those who can, whether in writing, reviewing, or editing. If openmindedness is the test of a scholar, a Moscow-directed Communist cannot in the nature of things qualify.

The scholar is objective. Jealous of this virtue, he is no propagandist, no matter how worthy the cause. He is not a writer of polemics, though alleged scholars have been. He has no fanatical devotion to any "ism," not even Americanism. He realizes that he has a solemn oath, registered in heaven, to present the truth in so far as he can discover it, to the malleable young minds in his classroom and to the less malleable minds outside. Though he may belong to a church and to a political party, he keeps them out of his teaching and writing. With his calling so noble, and his life so short, he is serene and detached, rising above petty jealousies, whether personal or professional.

The scholar is a thinker. He puts a premium on thought rather than on memory work or the accumulation of trivial details. He does not betray scholarship by confusing the nonessential with the essential. He seeks to develop a creative imagination in himself and in others. He is no scissors-and-paste artist. He raises questions, and answers questions, but frequently leaves unanswered more than he answers.

The scholar is courageous. Unlike the historian in Anatole France's *Penguin Island,* he is not afraid to be original—to challenge orthodox interpretations. He will take unpopular paths if he knows them to be true and significant, even though he brings down on his head the wrath of the cults and other pressure groups organized to suppress the truth. At the risk of unpleasantness or even a broken friendship, he will brand bad books bad when he writes reviews. This may not be gentlemanly, but it is scholarly, and at times a man cannot be both a gentleman *and* a scholar. He has a higher obligation to his calling than to individuals. He does not debunk merely for the sake of debunking, but for the sake of clearing away the rubbish so as to get nearer the truth. He is sympathetic without being adulatory, critical without being cynical. The classroom never rings with his hollow mockery of personalities or of causes. Sincerity is a hallmark of the scholar.

The scholar is helpful. He encourages younger students and shares his wisdom with them. He realizes that there is work enough and glory enough for all, and that the torch of scholarship must be borne aloft by others when he is gone. Rising above selfishness, he is aware that he has received much from others and that he must give much to others in return.

The scholar is intelligible. He is brief, whether in print or in the classroom, recognizing that tedious length kills interest. He knows that scholarship is not necessarily dull, and he makes every effort to clothe his ideas in attractive but unsensational habiliments. His findings, both oral and written, are clearly and understandably presented. He avoids incomprehensible classical allusions (which any fool may filch from a dictionary of quotations); he chooses the simple word rather than the polysyllabic (which any fool may filch from Roget's *Thesaurus*); he shuns the professionalized "gobbledegook" which all too often is the last refuge of shallow minds.

The scholar is constantly growing. He strives for wisdom as well as knowledge. He is dissatisfied with his earlier work, and the extent of that dissatisfaction is the measure of his growth. He rises above the Ph.D. level, and does not grind out a half-dozen successive doctoral dissertations, each of about the same degree of mediocrity as the first. He elevates his intellectual and cultural horizons by learning the languages of other peoples and thus thinking himself into their skins. Without being a rolling stone, he travels enough to recharge his intellectual batteries. Without being too convivial, he leaves his ivory tower to mingle with the outside world, so that he will better know the minds and idioms of those whom he addresses. The recluse who knows books but not people is something less than a man of learning.

The scholar is industrious. Thirsting insatiably for knowledge, he pursues his labors with almost monastic devotion. His work, like the housewife's, is never done: there is always vastly more to be investigated than will ever be investigated. There is no such thing as a lazy scholar. He works because he cannot help it; some irresistible inner dynamo drives him relentlessly on.

These are high ideals, and no man or woman who ever trod this earth—much less the present writer—ever attained them completely. But I think we can agree that not failure but low aim is the real crime. Teachers *can* attain these ideals substantially, if they will, but there are difficulties.

If teachers have an obligation to be scholars, then taxpayers, school boards, school administrators, trustees, deans, and presidents have no less an obligation to *permit* the teacher to be a scholar. Scholarship is a full-time, a lifetime job.

Teachers should not be asked to teach subjects for which they are not prepared. Scholarship is not the process of the blind leading the blind.

The teacher should not be saddled with killing classroom loads and prostrating extracurricular duties. No matter how zealous his devotion to scholarship, there is a limit to his physical and nervous energy. . . .

If our society wants scholars in the classroom—and it apparently does—it would do well to provide large enough salaries so that the teacher can do his job. The lean and hungry scholar may be all well enough in poetry, but he cannot work effectively when worried sick about his accumulating bills.

The American public can have scholars in the classroom, and it can have propagandists, but it cannot have both in the same person. The propaganda that is fashionable today may not be fashionable tomorrow, and the community may find it difficult to retool the minds of the teachers and impossible to undo the damage they have done the youth.

Starvation wages, unfavorable teaching conditions, community pressures, teachers' oaths, and other forms of harassment are unfortunately driving young men and women with scholarly aptitudes into more congenial and remunerative professions. The genuine scholar does not seek monetary wealth. He knows that he is deliberately embracing a life of poverty in things of the flesh, but wealth in things of the mind. He finds partial compensation in serenity, without which he cannot continue his pursuits. But if he is to be denied serenity, he will abandon the profession, leaving behind the bricklayers. Proponents of cut-rate education seldom stop to think that they are often entrusting their precious children to persons whom they would not think of entrusting with their less precious dollars.

A healthy and growing America needs scholars in the classroom. Most teachers and prospective teachers would like to be scholars and maintain scholarly standards. The teacher himself can do much more than he has done, but he needs the cooperation and encouragement of the community.

RESEARCH IN THE EDUCATION OF
SOCIAL STUDIES TEACHERS

Jean Fair

Recent and current research gives special attention to the study of varying roles and approaches in teaching and teacher education. Some, at least, of the findings are suggestive of emerging developments in classroom instruction and teacher preparation. This report includes primarily recent research that is concentrated on methods of teaching, evaluating, and changing instructional practices. Omitted from the original article is an identification of investigations into other aspects of teachers, such as their subject-matter background and social viewpoints. More research on methods is reported on page 355.

VIEWING research findings on the preparation of teachers of social studies may be disappointing if our gaze is limited to what can be seen in our own back yard. The big questions have been around a long time: What patterns of competencies are needed by teachers of the social studies? What kinds of programs? What types of experiences? Which strategies for learning are most effective for developing these patterns? And which students should be selected or recruited for admission to educational programs? To deal with these questions means, in turn, coming to grips with problems about the kinds of social studies curriculums for which teachers are needed today. In the end, of course, it is young people's learning that counts.

For these big questions research at present has no certain answers. Indeed, reasearch focused literally upon social studies teacher education is sparse. Much of it comes from writers of doctoral dissertations who are rarely in a position to coordinate their research with that of others.

If we look beyond our own back yard, however, we can see some promising paths. Changes in teacher education programs, not simply those in social studies, are widespread and stimulating. The *Report* of the TEPS Conference in Columbus (3) includes 30 case studies of changing programs and a careful

FROM *Social Education*, 29:15–19, January, 1965. Used by permission. Dr. Fair is a professor of education at Wayne State University in Michigan.

survey of innovations throughout the country. There are new sources of help to both consumers and producers of research (1, 4, 5, and 6), especially from the American Educational Research Association's *Handbook of Research on Teaching* (2).

Promising, too, are new devices—conceptual, methodological, and technological—for obtaining more objective and concrete descriptions of teacher behavior in classroom situations. The fact is that in much of the data we have had in the past, what is going on has been mixed with what ought to go on. Since what ought to depends both on what we value as important and what is appropriate for particular school situations, research findings have been difficult to apply. Indeed, since much of the data has been collected at the gross level of general practices or in the purified air of laboratories, data were second cousins twice removed from the operational reality of classrooms. If we are cautious, willing to adapt, try out, and revise, new research devices may give preservice and in-service teachers and teacher educators themselves some leads for the systematic examination of classroom behavior in operational terms, the groundwork for evaluation and improvement.

Flanders (5) has made a similar suggestion in speculating upon the results of his own studies in interaction analysis. Of particular interest is *Teacher Influence, Pupil Attitudes, and Achievement* (11). An instrument, "Categories for Interaction Analysis," was developed to classify, not judge, verbal exchange within classrooms. One category, "Teacher Talk," was further subdivided into four subcategories of "Indirect Influence" and three subcategories of "Direct Influence." A second major category subsumed two types of "Student Talk," and still a third indicated "Silence or Confusion."

Probably of greatest interest to those in the field of social studies is the instrument's use in a comparison of eighth-grade mathematics and seventh-grade social studies classrooms, each working on a common and suitably prepared mathematics or social studies unit. Using the categories just described, trained observers decided "at the end of each three-second period which category represented the communication event just completed" (5). Observers recorded the sequences as they occurred, and once classes ended prepared a general description of class activities and whatever else might be needed for identification and recall of the observation. The observers' category numbers were then transcribed on a matrix which could be interpreted to answer such questions as what proportion of teacher talk meant indirect or direct influence or whether teachers responded with direct or indirect influence at the end of student talk.

Worth noting is that social studies classes (and mathematics) in which teachers used more indirect influence than direct scored higher on measures of achievement and classroom attitudes. Indirect teachers were more flexible in the kind of influence they used during the work of the unit. Influence patterns in mathematics classes were different from those of social studies. While there are other findings in this study well worth attention, suffice it to say that the observational device did tap objectively behavior which matters in effective social studies classes.

Moreover, Kirk (14) found that using the Minnesota System of Interaction Analysis did modify the verbal patterns of student teachers in intermediate grade social studies classes.

In *The Logic of Teaching* Smith and Meux (31) have taken another tack in describing teaching behavior by an effort to get at strategies and their tactical elements, that is, logical operations. They recorded verbal interchanges in several high school classrooms of social studies and other academic areas. Discourse was then broken into episodes and classified as: defining; describing; designating; stating; reporting; substituting; evaluating; opining; classifying; comparing and contrasting; conditional inferring; explaining, which is further subdivided; and, outside the logical domain, directing and managing a classroom.

The investigators pointed to differences in discourse from classroom to classroom, although they realized "that teacher and subject variables are confounded." These variations "might indicate to some extent—to what extent cannot be determined from our data—differences among the subjects and areas with respect to the frequency with which the various logical operations occur."

Again there is more in this study than can be reported here. However, we can see an effort to obtain an objective record, available for repeated examination, of the logical as distinguished from psychological operations of the classroom.

The Aschner-Gallagher Category System (6, 8) is still another for classifying classroom verbal behavior, recorded on audio tape. Its categories are routine, cognitive—memory, convergent thinking, evaluative thinking, and divergent thinking. The system has been used in studying the productive thinking of gifted children and student initiative in classroom discussion, both in social studies and other classes. Aschner expects that such investigation can become the base for identifying productive classroom tactics and strategies which can then be learned by prospective teachers.

Hilda Taba's studies in the Contra Costa County Schools (25) are focused primarily upon identifying strategies for developing thought processes in middle-grade social studies and as such deserve a full study elsewhere. In the course of the project, tape recorders were turned on to collect the verbal exchanges in participating teachers' classrooms as one of several sources of data. Investigators could then analyze these recordings, or transcripts, of classroom transactions by a coding system which "brings together the several elements which have so far been studied separately: (1) the teaching acts and their function or effects; (2) the strategy, namely, the accumulative effect of a sequence of teacher acts; (3) the psychological identification of the nature of behavior, such as interpreting, classifying, or applying principles; (4) the logical quality of the content of thought." Taba reported that tentative experimentation with coding the transcripts produced "clear-cut evidence of the enormous influence of teacher behavior in the discussion situation on the thinking of students."

It is significant that built into the project were opportunities for participating teachers as well as professional researchers to study significant operations in their own classrooms preserved by the device of audio recording for objective analysis within a conceptual framework.

David G. Ryans' study of the *Characteristics of Teachers* under the auspices of the American Council on Education (21) aimed explicitly at the problems of describing teacher behavior. The study delineated three significant patterns from observational data obtained by use of a classroom Observation Record. Assessments of secondary social studies teachers were to some extent distinguishable from teachers in other secondary fields on these dimensions. Related to these patterns of teacher behavior is a vast store of material on other personal and social characteristics of teachers and even those of oustanding teachers. The study has also become the basis for Ryans' effort to develop a theoretical framework for teacher behavior as information processing and the teacher as an information system (5).

In considering her own already widely reported studies, Marie Hughes (6, 13) has also pointed to possibilities for teachers' learning more effective classroom patterns through coding and analysis of classroom behavior.

Even though not directed towards social studies, Hunter College's study, *The Use of Television for Improving Teacher Training and for Improving Measures of Student Teaching Performance* by Schueler, Gold, and Mitzel (22) is also helpful. Groups of elementary-grade student teachers were formed to try out three conditions: college supervisors observed and then conferred with student teachers (a) from observational notes only; (b) from kinescopes of student teachers' teaching; and (c) from both observational notes and kinescopes. To study the progress of these three groups, Medley and Mitzel developed a revised Observation Schedule (OScAR 3d, e, f) for analysis of kinescopes made from the televised classrooms of all three groups of student teachers. The OScAR contained about 170 items of specific behaviors in three separate sections. Observers noted their presence in each three-minute segment of recorded teaching. From these data came scoring keys and the identification of eight behavioral dimensions in teaching.

Results of the analysis showed no clear advantages to any one of the three supervisory arrangements, although student teachers and their supervisors preferred the combination of personal observation and of kinescope. Teaching behavior of student teachers did change over their semester's experience and in relation to their reactions to the classroom environment in which they worked. The specificity of the Observation Schedule and the repeatable records of teaching performance were basic factors in obtaining results.

Several other studies rely on similar data-gathering methods and should be mentioned briefly here. Wilk and others at the University of Minnesota (37) investigated admissions data as predictors of the classroom behaviors of elementary-grade student teachers by using an adaptation of the OScAR 3 developed by Medley and Mitzel (18) and Flanders' system of interaction analysis (11). Observers trained in the use of these instruments, but not experts in teacher education, were in substantial agreement with elementary education supervisors using their own methods of rating student teachers; that is, trained observers could collect identified descriptive data on the behavior of student teachers. . . .

Several of the staff of the teacher Education Experimental Project also at Wayne State University (24) have been collecting video tapes of interns in several grade levels and subject fields, including social studies. Episodes of classroom behaviors are to be analyzed under such behavioral categories as "facilitating thinking" and "goal setting."

Turner, Fattu, and others at Indiana (26, 27) have singled out teachers' problem-solving skills as the crucial aspect. They are studying teaching performance on sets of specially constructed teaching problems, so far in middle grades arithmetic and reading, but in other areas, including social studies, now under way. Note that although the tasks are performed outside the classroom, these tasks are nonetheless identified and specific as classroom tasks, shown to discriminate among those with more experience or education in teaching.

By using a scale of dominative-integrative classroom behavior, Nicholson (19) examined relationships between classroom behavior of social studies student teachers and some socio-civic attitudes. . . . In one of the studies of the use of closed-circuit television at the University of Minnesota, Adolphson (7) compared the use of direct observation closed-circuit television, and kinescopes in prestudent teaching secondary education courses. He stated that "the nature and extent of observational experience, rather than media, was the significant factor in differentiating the perception of teacher behavior." Through experiments at the University of Akron with films of classroom activities, Painter (20) found they contributed to courses in educational psychology and permitted discussion of commonly observed classroom situations. Chabe (9) found observation by closed-circuit television in elementary social studies methods courses almost as effective as guided observation in actual classrooms.

None of these, of course, nor the Hunter College investigation reported above, obtained miraculous results. But let us suppose that before student teaching, programs provided opportunities to use some scheme for analysis of teacher behavior in the live stuff of classrooms. Video tapes, kinescopes, films, audio tapes, transcripts or codings of classroom dialogues are all capable of repeated examination. (Hunter College, Stanford, Wayne, Oberlin, Akron, Minnesota, to name but a few institutions, have already begun to use them in teacher education programs.) Mere looking at classroom events seems not, per se, to bring about sufficient learning, but what of systematic looking at situations which students can re-examine until they can actually identify some aspect of classroom behavior within some theoretical framework?

There is widespread agreement on the value of student teaching itself, but not much clarity when it comes to how much, whether it should be full or half time, or what experiences should be available within it. Perhaps student teachers might at times pair off, teach in teams to observe each other for making a record of classroom behavior. Student teachers' classrooms might be "preserved" on video or audio recordings. Cooperating teachers and college supervisors might learn to use analytical schemes. From more objective records student teachers have evidence for their own analysis and interpretation. What kinds of influence techniques are they using? For what purpose and what consequences? At what points, if any, do classroom remarks come to some generalization or explanation or application, and what led to these points? What kinds of reinforcement are being used? What factors led to involvement? A record open to reflection might allow the student to see his own practice in the light of some conceptual framework and the framework within live reality. Perhaps such independent experiences might be more effective than ratings of gross behavior and practices or discussions of fragments of classroom happenings, mixed as these may be by implicit or explicit biases of supervisors.

It might be that in-service teachers could use such schemes. Gage (12) found that when teachers were given feedback on students' opinions of their own and their "ideal" teachers, the teachers seemed to change in the direction of students' "ideals." Flanders' instrument for interaction analysis has been adopted, paired with a manual and training filmstrips, and used profitably with teachers (10). Taba has been developing usable materials in the course of her study (25).

If research has yet no ready answers for the big questions, it does offer better tools, not only for further research but with careful adaptation perhaps for teacher education programs as well.

(1) *Encyclopedia of Educational Research*. Chester Harris, editor. Revised edition. New York: The Macmillan Company, 1960. Still recent enough to be of assistance.

(2) *Handbook of Research on Teaching*. N. L. Gage, editor. A project of the American Educational Research Association. Chicago: Rand McNally and Company, 1963. This volume brings together under one cover a wealth of material, conceptual, methodological, and bibliographical. To both consumers and producers of research, the *Handbook* should prove indispensable.

(3) National Commission on Teacher Education and Professional Standards. *Changes in Teacher Education*. Report on the Columbus Conference. Washington, D.C.: The Commission, National Education Association, 1963. This report, a "Directory of Innovations in Teacher Education," is based on a request for information to more than 600 schools. The "Thirty Case

Studies of Changes in Teacher Education," although not directed to the social studies in particular, are stimulating; at least a few carry evaluative material. The report is probably the most useful single source of material on widespread efforts at improvement of teacher education programs.

(4) *Review of Educational Research.* 33: October 1963. The issue devoted to "Teacher Personnel" includes research on preservice and in-service education, and the assessment of teacher behavior and instruction for the last five years.

(5) *The Journal of Teacher Education* 14: September 1963. This issue contains "A Symposium on Current Research on Classroom Behavior of Teachers and Its Implications for Teacher Education." It consists of a collection of papers whose authors not only report their studies but speculate on their implications for teacher education. The issue also includes the twelfth annual list of doctoral dissertations concerned with teacher education.

(6) "Theory and Research in Teaching." Arno Bellack, editor. New York: Bureau of Publications, Teachers College, Columbia University, 1963. A collection of thought-provoking papers in which researchers explain the conceptual frameworks underlying their studies of classroom behavior.

(7) Louis John Adolphson. "A Comparison of the Effectiveness of Selected Observational Procedures in Developing Teacher Perception." Unpublished doctoral dissertation. The University of Minnesota, 1961. (*Dissertation Abstracts* 22:3933; 1962.)

(8) Mary J. McCue Aschner. "The Analysis of Classroom Discourse: A Method and Its Uses." Unpublished doctoral dissertation. University of Illinois, 1959. (*Dissertation Abstracts* 20:221.)

(9) A. M. Chabe. "Experiment with CCTV in Teacher Education." *Peabody Journal of Education* 40:24–30; July 1962.

(10) Ned A. Flanders. "Teacher Influence: No. 1–5." Five filmstrips available from the Audio-Visual Education

Service, Westbrook Hall, University of Minnesota, Minneapolis. See also Ned A. Flanders, "Helping Teachers Change Their Behavior." Available from the author, School of Education, University of Michigan, Ann Arbor.

(11) Ned Flanders. *Teacher Influence: Pupil Attitudes and Achievement.* Minneapolis, Minn.: University of Minnesota, College of Education, 1960. U.S. Office of Education Cooperative Research Project 397.

(12) N. L. Gage, P. J. Runkel, and B. B. Chatterjee. *Equilibrium Theory and Behavior Change: An Experiment in Feedback from Pupils to Teachers.* Urbana, Ill.: University of Illinois, Bureau of Educational Research, 1960.

(13) Marie M. Hughes and Associates. *The Assessment of the Quality of Teaching: A Research Report.* Salt Lake City: University of Utah, 1959. U. S. Office of Education Cooperative Research Project No. 353.

(14) Jeffery Kirk. "Effects of Teaching the Minnesota System of Interaction Analysis to Intermediate Grade Student Teachers." Unpublished doctoral dissertation, Temple University, 1964. (*Dissertation Abstracts* 25: 1031.)

(15) Shia-ling Liu. "Personal Characteristics in Secondary School Social Studies Student Teachers as Related to Certain Measures of Potential Teaching Behavior." Unpublished doctoral dissertation, North Texas State University, 1963. (*Dissertation Abstracts* 25:1032.)

(16) J. D. McAulay. "Weakness in the Social Studies Methods Courses." *Education* 81:245–46; December 1960.

(17) James Marmas. "Teacher Preparation in Economics at California State Colleges." Doctoral dissertation, Stanford University, 1961. (*Dissertation Abstracts* 22:3536.)

(18) D. M. Medley and H. I. Mitzel. "A Technique for Measuring Classroom Behavior." *Journal of Educational Psychology* 49:86–92; April 1958.

(19) Virgil Nicholson. "The Relationship

between Dominative-Integrative Classroom Behavior and Selected Measures of Socio-Civic Attitudes of Students Preparing to Teach the Social Studies." Doctoral dissertation, North Texas State College, 1961. (*Dissertation Abstracts* 22: 2302.)

(20) William I. Painter. "Production and Use of Classrooms on Film *versus* Traditional Observations in Teacher Education." Akron, Ohio: The University of Akron, 1961. U.S. Office of Education Project 127.

(21) David G. Ryans. *Characteristics of Teachers*. Washington, D.C.: American Council on Education, 1960.

(22) Herbert Schueler, Milton J. Gold, and Harold F. Mitzel. *The Use of Television for Improving Teacher Training and for Improving Measures of Student-Teaching Performance, Phase I, Improvement of Student Teaching*. New York: Hunter College, City University of New York, 1962. U.S. Office of Education Grant No. 730035.

(23) B. Othanel Smith and Milton O. Meux. *A Study of the Logic of Teaching*. Urbana, Ill.: University of Illinois, College of Education. Bureau of Educational Research Project No. 258.

(24) Staff of the Teacher Education Experimental Project, Wayne State University, Detroit, Michigan. See work in progress by E. A. Bantel, R. Ellsworth, J. Fair, S. Mikelson, and I. Sigel.

(25) Hilda Taba. "Thought Processes and Teaching Strategies in Elementary Social Studies." A paper presented at the AERA meeting in February, 1963. See also *Thinking in Elementary School Children*. San Francisco: San Francisco State College, 1964. U.S. Office of Education Cooperative Research Project No. 1574.

(26) R. L. Turner and N. A. Fattu. "Skill in Teaching. A Reappraisal of the Concepts and Strategies in Teacher Effectiveness Research." Bulletin of the School of Education. Vol. 36, No. 3. Bloomington, Ind.: Indiana University, May 1960.

(27) R. L. Turner, K. W. White, E. P. Quinn, and N. Smith. "Skill in Teaching, Assessed on the Criterion of Problem Solving." Bulletin of the School of Education. Vol. 39. No. 1. Bloomington, Ind.: Indiana University, January 1963.

(28) Roger E. Wilk and William H. Edson. *A Study of the Relationship between Observed Classroom Behaviors of Elementary Student Teachers, Predictors of Those Behaviors, and Ratings by Supervisors*. Minneapolis, Minn.: University of Minnesota, College of Education, 1962.

2

Developing Skills and Understanding

THE PROBLEM OF UNDERSTANDING

Edwin R. Carr

Perhaps the special features of social studies that deter students' development of understanding are obvious. Yet the nature of instruction and even some teachers' remarks about their students' learning seem all too often to reflect limited sensitivity to such basic difficulties in social learning. It is helpful, therefore, to have this lucid summary that furnishes reminders of basic impediments to the individual's achievement of social understanding.

THE PROBLEM OF UNDERSTANDING

THE SOCIAL studies are not easy to teach or to learn, yet much school practice seems to be based on the assumption that they are. It is on this mistaken assumption that some college students—perhaps a large number—choose social science majors or elect social science courses. Some school administrators are more likely to assign social studies courses than courses in most other fields to poorly prepared teachers. Only rarely are the so-called boners which appear on examination papers (to the delight of journalists who seize upon them for feature stories) attributed to the difficulty; usually they are offered, and read, merely as anecdotes. Many teachers and parents assume that a high percentage of "correct" responses on an examination indicates a proportionately high level of understanding; actually it may indicate nothing of the kind.

An analysis of the problem of understanding in the social studies was written by Ernest Horn over a quarter of a century ago. Simple and direct, it has never been surpassed. (1) Horn wrote that factors influencing understanding could be grouped in three categories: the inherent nature of concepts in the social studies; the nature of the instructional media through which the student attempts to come to grips with the problem; and the student himself.

FROM *Teaching the Social Studies* by Edwin R. Carr, Library of Education, Englewood Cliffs, N.J.: Prentice-Hall, 1964, pp. 44–47. Used by permission. Dr. Carr is a professor of education at Orange State College, Fullerton, California.

The nature of the concepts. Concepts in the social studies are difficult. It is a rare adult who understands the Age of Pericles, the theory of comparative advantage, imperialism, why the Chinese chose Communism, the Holy Roman Empire, the United Nations, the nature of democracy, the functions of the Federal Reserve System, pre-historic man, the culture of the Eskimos, interdependence among nations. The adult may *recognize* these concepts, but even with his educational background and his mature viewpoint he has little understanding of them, and what little he has may be fuzzy, vague, or even erroneous. Yet the concepts mentioned constitute only a tiny fraction of those which appear in the typical social studies program. Their difficulty is apparent, and it is small wonder indeed that students respond to examination questions about them with "funny" answers or that they retain so little of what they have supposedly learned.

The answer is not to be found in a philosophy of despair, exemplified in such recommendations as postponing the study of the social sciences until adulthood or teaching people to choose good leaders since the issues of the times are "beyond" their comprehension. Nor is the answer simply to improve teaching methods, though such improvement would be helpful, it would not solve the basic problem—that of attempting to teach children and youth too many difficult topics. And this problem points to the curriculum and to the need for selectivity.

The nature of the instructional media. The second factor influencing understanding involves the media through which the social studies are taught. Most of what is taught in the social studies programs cannot be experienced directly; it must be learned through vicarious experience and this vicarious experience must be gained, for the most part, through the written or spoken word. And it is fortunate indeed that this experience can be acquired through language, for the essential function of language is to formulate and convey ideas. An education based solely on direct experiences would be almost no education at all.

But the importance of language and man's dependence on it should not obscure the difficulties it may cause for the learner. Language is a symbol; although it has no meaning in itself, it should guide the learner to meaning. In any social studies textbook which attempts a survey of a considerable area or period of time, a number of ideas, topics, and themes must be compressed into a small space. There is no room for expansion and amplification or for the provision of specifics or color which would round out the ideas and give them body. The more an idea or topic is compressed, the more vague and abstract it becomes, and consequently the more difficult for the learner to grasp.

In American schools the principal source of information for students is the textbook. If it is used alone, as it often is, the students' learning tends to become restricted to learning the textbook or of a paraphrase of it. Sometimes this "learning" may take the form of direct memorization, particularly if the teacher's tests encourage it. In other cases, students may be able to speak or write glibly—even convincingly—on certain topics and not be discovered unless the teacher probes more deeply. Amplification and explanation by the teacher will help some, as will the use of audio-visual materials and collateral reading, but there is too much material to cover for these methods to be practical for more than a fraction of the course. The result is that the student learns words rather than meanings, except as he has had experience or prior learning which helps him to interpret new words properly. If the curriculum has been properly organized and effectively presented, this probability is enhanced. If not, much of the learning falls into the category of verbalization; concepts can be recognized, repeated, or paraphrased, but not understood. It must be emphasized, as Horn points out, that "Books are not used too extensively in teaching the social studies; they are used improperly. There is not too much talk in school; but the wrong kind of talk." (2)

Difficulties within the student. The third kind of difficulty is that which lies within the student. These include differences in academic ability, in work habits, in reading ability, in interests, and in experiential background. The first four differences are commonly recognized and occupy a major share of the teacher's attention. The last is frequently overlooked, though it may be the greatest and one of the most significant for learning in the social studies field.

The writer of a textbook must assume some common experiential background on the part of the students for whom the book is intended, and he must also assume that, if and when there is no such common background, the teacher will do what he can to identify and make up for this lack so that communication may take place. Many teachers do this—particularly those in the elementary school, for they have fewer pupils, are with them all day, and are able to come to know each one as an individual. Teachers in secondary schools, who see some two hundred students daily, rarely find it possible to come to know any one student very well. And the less the teacher's knowledge of a student, the less effective will he be in assessing the student's weaknesses and planning corrective action.

Consider the possible differences in experiential background in an eighth-grade class in American history. Among the thirty students may be some who have never been outside their state and others who have toured the battlefields of the Revolution and the Civil War. Some of the children may have come from homes in which the political complexion is extreme left or extreme right. Some of the children may have had experiences which make democracy seem pretty much of a mockery; others may never have given democracy a thought, simply taking it for granted. Some of them may have come from homes in which public affairs are regular dinner table conversation; others may not know the name of the governor of the state—and care even less. Some may have lived in or become acquainted with the ghettos of large cities, and others are only dimly aware that the ghettos exist. Some may have lived in the mountains, others on the plains, and still others on the seacoast; each group is familiar with some of the characteristics of the culture of one locality, but not with those of the others. Some may have been brought up in the best traditions of our country; others may hardly be aware that such traditions exist. To some, books are to be treasured as the source of endless hours of satisfaction and enjoyment; to others, books other than textbooks are scarcely known.

In any class, then, there are some in whom a brief textbook exposition evokes vivid, meaningful, and essentially accurate images; and others in whom it evokes almost nothing at all. The teacher's problem, and it is a very difficult one, is to bring about a minimum level of understanding of ideas and concepts for all. To do this, he tries to find some common starting place, or minimum experiential background, using verbal explanations, illustrations, audio-visual materials, collateral reading, and such other devices as seem promising in given cases.

(1) Ernest Horn, *Methods of Instruction in the Social Studies* (New York: Charles Scribner's Sons, 1937), pp. 122–50. Essentially the same analysis is in *The Psychology of Learning*, Nelson B. Henry (Ed.), Forty-first Yearbook, Part II, National Society for the Study of Education (Chicago: the University of Chicago Press, 1942), pp. 377–413.

(2) *Ibid.*, p. 128.

THE NATURE OF CRITICAL THINKING AND ITS APPLICATION

Isidore Starr

How can students best develop the ability to consider critically the complexities of human relationships? The author of this selection offers some practical suggestions for so guiding the learning of students in social studies classes. He recommends techniques, recognizes barriers to be overcome, and considers some underlying reasons for the difficulty in developing critical faculties.

FROM *Skill Development in the Social Studies*, Helen M. Carpenter, ed., Washington, D.C.: National Council for the Social Studies, 1963, pp. 45–50. Used by permission. Dr. Starr is a professor of education at Queens College, New York.

TECHNIQUES

VARIOUS procedures generally useful, regardless of whether the question is controversial, merit consideration. An important one is often referred to as the normative problem.

Using the Normative Problem. The most difficult, and yet a most effective technique in teaching critical thinking, is use of the normative problem. This approach requires the highest degree of sophistication and the most thorough accumulation of intellectual capital—the knowledge and the skill needed to examine the dichotomy between the ideal and the real, principle and practice. Although this is generally done most effectively on the college level, good teachers in high schools can also engage in this exercise with better-than-average students.

Every society is based on certain assumptions. The people of the United States believe in the decentralization of power. Politically, this has taken the form of the federal system and separation of powers; economically, Americans prefer a competitive economy based on private enterprise to monopoly and state controls; socially, we favor a mobile society without class distinctions. The great all-pervading norm is the dignity and integrity of the individual, with its inevitable counterpart of equal opportunity for all.

The rub occurs when we are confronted with issues that involve a clash with these principles: socialized medicine, federal aid to parochial schools, welfare programs, and treatment of minorities. How does one close the gap between the *what is* and the *what ought to be?* A recent book proposes a modification of the traditional problem-solving steps for this activity: clear identification of the issues; public examination of the conflicting interests, beliefs, or opinions; analysis of the historic reasons for the norms and their relevancy to the contemporary scene; factual study of the relation of the issue to the norm; attempt to arrive at a consensus for a reconstruction of the norm, if necessary to reduce or eliminate the conflict; relevance of the new norm to the ideals of democratic living; and a proposed course of action. (1)

Analyzing Documents. Great documents in history are often the products of crucial issues. Analysis of these writings gives impetus to reflective thought, for this activity requires a knowledge of the background of the historical source, its meaning at the time it was written, and its implications for today.

In world history, as well as in American history, a comparison of Pericles' *Funeral Oration* with Lincoln's *Gettysburg Address* can help to clarify the meaning of democracy. Classroom study of three important related documents—the Declaration of Independence, the Declaration of Rights of Man and of the Citizen, and the Universal Declaration of Human Rights—will disclose the persistent ideals cherished in Western civilization.

Reading selected excerpts from the Sadler Report, the study of the parliamentary committee which disclosed the abuses of child labor in English factories in the 1830's, will possibly do more to explain the factory legislation of that period than any other approach. In the same way, present-day reports by congressional committees or reputable private sources can serve as invaluable aids in helping students to clarify issues, to evaluate evidence, and to arrive at warranted conclusions.

Eliminating Common Obstacles

Consciousness on the part of teachers and students alike of frequent blocks to critical thinking is progress in itself. Means of avoiding some of the most common pitfalls are suggested.

Failure To Define Terms. One of the simplest steps which can be taken in fostering critical thinking is to insist on a definition and clarification of terminology. Some words have specific meanings; others vary in context. As Stuart Chase has so aptly warned: "Without knowledge of the correct use of words, most of us are defenseless against harmful stimuli." There is a rich literature in this area, ranging from the now famous classic of C. K. Ogden and I. A. Richards (2) to more popular works. (3)

Among the activities which teachers can utilize in clarifying words and their meanings is the definition of certain key words (capitalism, communism, socialism, fascism, democracy, and totalitarianism), as well as an analysis of the different shades of meaning of such terms as reactionary, conservative, liberal, radical, "the right," and "the left." The platforms of political parties or statements by some politicians sometimes offer useful examples of abstract terminology which resists pinning down to concrete cases. (4)

Faulty Comparisons. Teachers of the social studies use the analogy for motivating lessons or for simplifying complex historical phenomena. This process of reasoning by comparisons has inherent dangers which must be identified. Comparing the motives of men, the causes and results of wars may be useful in discovering relationships in situations which are similar. It must be remembered, however, that events in history are unique and that resemblances may be superficial, imaginary, or forced. In the social studies, this reasoning technique must be used cautiously and with scrupulous honesty. Books on logic discuss the appropriate uses of analogy.

Hasty Generalization. The hasty, or careless, generalization is sometimes the result of the need to simplify the "seamless stuff of experience," and at other times it may be the impetuous outpouring of a troubled spirit. The writer remembers an incident in one of his classes a number of years ago which may be helpful in the handling of careless thinking. A student in his American history class had blurted out, "All Puerto Ricans are bad." The teacher wrote the sentence on the blackboard and asked the class to evaluate this all-inclusive judgment. How many Puerto Ricans were there? How many did they know?

As a result of class analysis, this hasty generalization was quickly changed to "Most Puerto Ricans are bad," and then to "Some Puerto Ricans are bad." This latter conclusion was then subjected to further inquiry and, with teacher guidance, there emerged the most meaningful judgment of the day: "Some people are bad."

In attacking the hasty generalization, the teacher should press the class to *prove*—cite data—that what is true in the observed cases is also true in those cases which have not been observed. In testing generalizations, the class must be directed to make careful examination of all the known facts with a view to comparing and classifying them. Exceptions to the generalization must be recognized and admitted.

An interesting analysis of generalizing in the social studies was made some time ago by Dr. Samuel H. Jones, with a number of useful examples of how to penetrate the validity of the all-encompassing judgment. (5) His observation is that there should be inscribed in every social studies classroom William James' famous admonition: "No one can see any further into a generalization than his knowledge of details extends."

Abuse of Statistics. Disraeli is reported to have said that there are three kinds of lies: lies, damned lies, and statistics. Inspired by this quip, Darrell Huff has written an amusing and instructive book entitled *How To Lie With Statistics.* (6) Rich in examples of how statistics can be used deliberately to mislead the unsuspecting public, the volume is an invaluable teaching tool. Laughter and chagrin, the by-products of the book, will help to impress students with the need for skillful dissection of quantitative data.

Economic data often take the form of statistical information. A comparison of labor's view of certain statistics with that of management can be a worthwhile study in how the same material can be utilized for different purposes. Carefully designed exercises in statistical analysis are most helpful in training students in reflective thinking.

The Seven Propaganda Tricks. In the understandable concern of this nation with the importance of literacy, the obvious fact often has been overlooked that some of the most literate people in the world have been the dupes of propagandists. With this in mind, educators in the 1930's began to experiment with techniques of propaganda analysis. Aided by the work of the Institute for Propaganda Analysis, teachers and students studied the application of the "seven tricks of propagandists"—name calling, glittering generalities, transfer, testimonial, plain folks, card stacking, and band wagon. (7) Students were taught to beware of broad, unsubstantiated statements, powerful slogans, and the appeal to emotions.

Experiments in this field indicate that mere memorization of the propaganda techniques is rarely helpful. (8) What is required is a study of the actual content and the applicability of the "tricks" to specific examples in diversified areas of the mass media. Russell relates an incident which illustrates the sensitivity of even the very young to the exaggerated claim of advertisers, as follows. (9)

. . . One boy who had listened to several different radio advertisements extolling the "best" cereal was asked by his father which was best. He replied, "There's probably no best cereal; they're just trying to sell more." This boy was seven years old. . . .

DIFFICULTIES IN TEACHING CRITICAL THINKING

The exhortation to engage in critical thinking is very easily made; the deed is confronted with obstacles requiring a strong spirit, a good mind, and a dedicated person. It is not for the timid, the bigoted, the weak; it is for those who realize that in a democratic society the rulers are the people. If the sovereign power abdicates its responsibility or is inexperienced in intelligent decision making, the vacuum may be filled by those who have nothing but contempt for the American heritage.

There are many obstacles that stand in the way of effective critical thinking. Community mores and the climate of opinion have often closed off certain areas of discussion. It is no secret, of course, that there are *closed areas* where teachers find it dangerous to tread. (10) In some communities it is sectarian religious beliefs; in others, sex and marriage; in some, economics; in others, race and minority-group relations; in some, social class; in others, politics and government. The NCSS has published a number of statements which support teachers in their freedom to teach and students in their freedom to learn. (11) Textbook writers in the methods field have reaffirmed this very important aspect of social studies teaching.

The teaching of critical thinking may lead to carping criticism. Students begin to feel their new-found strength by questioning the textbook, fellow-students, and even the teacher. Teachers must help students to differentiate between well-intentioned and thoughtful criticism and captious and frivolous objections. To permit criticism simply for the sake of criticism is to indulge in a luxury that few teachers can afford. Rules of classroom procedure should include the obligation to suspend judgment pending the gathering and evaluating of pertinent data. Students should feel free to question, provided there is the accompanying obligation that criticism must be tackled in accordance with the accepted procedures of reflective thought.

Other factors which may militate against the teaching of critical thinking are sometimes found in the home and in the school. The influence of the authoritarian home can develop in a child a lifelong block against critical thinking. So, too, of course, can the authoritarian teacher or the school system which decides to play it safe by apotheosizing conformity of thought and memorization without meaning. It is also reasonable to infer that the size of classes and the present infatuation with objective-type examinations may be stumbling blocks on the road to teaching reflective thought.

(1) Burton, Kimball, and Wing. *Education for Effective Thinking.* pp. 317-19.

(2) *The Meaning of Meaning: A Study of the Influence of Language Upon Thought and of the Science of Symbolism.* (Harvest Book). New York: Harcourt, Brace and Co., 1923. 363 pp.

(3) Chase, Stuart. *The Tyranny of Words.* (Harvest Book). New York: Harcourt, Brace and Co., 1938. 396 pp.; and Hayakawa, S. I. (in consultation with Pillard, Basil H.) *Language in Thought and Action.* New York: Harcourt, Brace and Co., 1949. 307 pp.

(4) Ferrell, Frances Hunter. "The Right Word Makes a Difference." *Social Education* 16:107-108; March 1952.

(5) Jones, Samuel H. "Generalizing in the Social Science Classroom." *Social Education* 21:358-62; December 1957.

(6) New York: W. W. Norton & Co., 1954. 142 pp.

(7) Burton, Kimball, and Wing. *Education for Effective Thinking.* pp. 303, 357.

(8) *Ibid.,* pp. 303-305.

(9) Russell. *Children's Thinking.* p. 297.

(10) Hunt, Maurice P., and Metcalf, Lawrence E. *Teaching High School Social Studies: Problems in Reflective Thinking and Social Understanding.* New York: Harper & Brothers Publishers, 1955. 471 pp.

(11) The NCSS Committee on Academic Freedom has published the following reports: "The Treatment of Controversial Issues in the Schools." *Social Education* 15:232-36; May 1951; "Freedom To Learn and Freedom To Teach." *Social Education* 17:217-19; May 1953; and "Action To Uphold Freedom To Learn and Freedom To Teach." *Social Education* 20:371-72, 374; December 1956.

PATTERNS OF STUDENT BEHAVIOR IN REFLECTIVELY ORIENTED CLASSES

Benjamin C. Cox and Jack E. Cousins

About a generation ago an emphasis emerged on critical thinking and the problems approach in social studies. Recently, the stress in these instructional elements has shifted to their intellectual aspects. This selection reports on a group of related investigations that examined classroom procedures for teaching rational processes of problem solving.

FROM "Teaching Social Studies in Secondary Schools and Colleges," by Benjamin C. Cox and Jack E. Cousins, in *New Challenges in the Social Studies,* eds. Byron G. Massialas and Frederick R. Smith, © 1965 by Wadsworth Publishing Company, Inc., Belmont, California, pp. 90-95, 117-120. Reprinted by permission of the publisher. The authors are professors of education at Ball State University in Indiana.

SEVERAL researches have been designed in such a way as to shed light on what actually happens in the social studies classroom. Some of these have accepted or contrived models of classroom management and then attempted to replicate the models within an experimental design. Four researchers at Indiana University, as a part of their design, described and analyzed the methodological procedures followed by a class dealing reflectively with problems. In general, the four studies, recently published as *The Indiana Experiments in Inquiry—The Social Studies* (Massialas, ed., 1963), attacked and confirmed the over-all hypotheses that growth in reflective thinking is produced most efficiently in classrooms where reflective thinking is valued, emphasized, and practical and that the goal of acquiring facts is not sacrificed in classrooms which are oriented toward reflective thinking.

Massialas (1961) and Cox (1961) utilized comparable research designs, which allowed them to divide four classes of tenth-grade world history and four classes of eleventh-grade United States history into experimental and control groups equated on the basis of IQ, sex, socioeconomic status, reflective-thinking ability, and knowledge of world history or American history.

These investigators analyzed the results of their investigation both statistically and judgmentally. Pre- and post-test scores were used for the statistical analysis. The judgmental analysis involved the use of daily anecdotal calendars, kept by each of the investigators for each of his classes, and the logical analysis of transcribed tape recordings made early in the experiment and near the end in each of the experimental sections.

Both investigators based their teaching methods in the experimental groups on the general method presented by Hunt and Metcalf (1955) in their text *The Teaching of High School Social Studies*. Method A, the experimental teaching method in each case, involved the use of springboards, or groups of related and thought-provoking facts in standard textbooks, which could lead to conceptualization of some problems of importance. These conceptualizations took the form of hypotheses or insights whose logical implications the class was to explore. A typical hypothesis might state, for example, that *contact with different cultures results in changed values and desires*. These hypotheses were then clarified, elaborated, and tested. In the testing process the textbook and other available evidence were brought to bear on the problems in order to validate, disprove, or modify the hypotheses. The reaching of conclusions or generalizations was the final step of this method.

Method B, as proposed for each of these studies, was a logical adaptation of a traditional attitude toward learning and the social studies. The prime concern of Method B was to impart to the student a body of factual knowledge relevant to the social science involved.

These two investigators independently constructed models of critical thinking which they used in their analysis of tapes and calendars. Massialas constructed a ten-point model which made reference to specific skills he wished to develop in his students as they learned to deal with materials critically. The model included the following operations:

1. Hypothesizing.
2. Defining and clarifying.
3. Enlarging the students' perspective.
4. Identifying and probing assumptions.
5. Drawing logical implications.
6. Producing relevant information.
7. Generalizing, and distinguishing among different kinds of generalizations.
8. Recognizing material fallacies in propositions.
9. Relating propositions to one another in terms of their consistency and the extent of their explanatory power.
10. Developing a sensitivity to facts and proof.

Cox, on the other hand, devised a six-phase operational model of critical thinking: (1) orientation, (2) hypothesis, (3) definition, (4) exploration, (5) evidencing, (6) generalization.

The third of these studies at Indiana University, conducted by Cousins (1962), involved the use of only one eighth-grade social studies class. Although it was concerned primarily with studying the development of the particular skills of reflection, an integrated pattern of these skills, or a reflective model, was implied.

As a part of his study, Cousins reconstructed his model of reflective thinking from an analysis of two bodies of data. One of these was a daily log kept by the teacher in which changes in thinking skills were noted. The other consisted of evaluations of eight classroom discussions, tape-recorded and transcribed during the semester. The typescripts of these recordings were evaluated by a panel of three judges, the original theoretical model of reflective thinking providing the criteria by which the evaluators categorized each student's response in the discussions.

Cousins' reconstructed model contained four major parts: (1) generalizing, (2) deducing, (3) problem-solving, and (4) sensitivity to values.

The fourth of these Indiana studies was that of Elsmere (1961) who experimented with an eleventh-grade class in United States history at Elmherst High School, Fort Wayne, Indiana. Elsmere confined his investigation to the testing of the learning and retention of historical facts in United States history and the learning and retention of certain steps in problem solving. He hypothesized that a problem-solving approach in teaching United States history produces significantly greater pupil achievement in knowledge of historical fact and in problem-solving ability than does a traditional approach. He determined to test these gains by means of (1) teacher-made instruments purporting to measure the acquisition and retention of historical facts and (2) instruments purporting to measure the retention of and the ability to use the problem-solving steps.

Elsmere defined the problem-solving approach as involving four steps: (1) stating the problem, (2) hypothesizing, or selecting, courses of action, (3) discussing the problem, and (4) drawing conclusions.

The traditional approach was described in the study as having the following aspects: The text is read, the facts are discussed through question-and-answer sessions, and then the pupils are tested to see how much of the factual information has been learned.

In designing the study, Elsmere used matched pairs and a single independent variable, the different teaching methods. He also used two conditions: An experimental group A and control group B. Pairs were matched on the basis of intelligence, previous history grades, achievement on a factual history test, and achievement on a subjective problem-solving test.

Intelligence scores consisted of the mean score computed from two forms of the Otis Quick-Scoring Mental Ability Test. Since there is no standardized test measuring the specific content covered during this twelve-week experimental period or specifically measuring the problem-solving steps devised for this study, Elsmere constructed both instruments for this research.

In the subjective test purporting to measure four problem-solving steps, three problems related to the content of the textbook were developed. The problems dealt with the rights of citizens in a democratic society. Each problem presented two conflicting statements. Within these tests students were directed to follow the four problem-solving steps.

The Indiana studies appear to indicate that classroom behavior of students engaged in reflective thinking falls into a certain pattern. The pattern is represented by these researchers as a model to be replicated in social studies classrooms where reflective thinking is desired. The pattern does clearly present distinct phases in which discriminable critical-thinking skills exist. However, the claims (1) that critical thinking can be pursued in the classroom only paradigmatically, (2) that this particular pattern is clear and sophisticated enough to be considered a universal paradigm, or (3) that enough is known about thinking, knowledge, group interaction, and many other relevant factors to construct such a model can at this point only be called hypotheses. Nevertheless, the pattern has many implications, which should influence teachers in the way they proceed in various classroom situations.

First, in the Indiana pattern, students are oriented to a frame of reference through which they acquire "background" information, establish the validity of this information, and form operational definitions. This phase may involve one or more of a variety of activities, such as watching a film, reading the text, reading books, listening to tapes or recordings, or writing responses to questions. A single historical episode, a series of events, or a case may often be the vehicle used to establish this basis for conceptualization. The essential feature of the opening phase is that the students are involved in a situation in which they acquire a frame of reference or orientation to a material or intellectual problem.

In the second phase, students begin to recognize problems, suggest tentative hypotheses as explanations for puzzling situations, or establish the meaning of propositions contained in the materials they are using. This aspect is characterized by free discussion which follows an inductive pattern. It is stimulated by the teacher, who asks leading questions, provides additional information, and encourages widespread participation, so that all possible ideas are generated. Hypothesizing is always heuristic and often intuitional— that is, there is always a certain amount of "guessing" and discovery involved in forming a hypothesis.

Third, the problems or hypotheses which have been suggested are explored in depth, so that assumptions and logical implications are made clear. Again, the students engage in free and largely deductive discussion, in which they challenge each other's logic and use of factual information. Definitions are subjected to further refinement.

The fourth part of the pattern is made up of the acts of concluding and generalizing. The students come to agree as to which of the hypotheses or which solution to a problem is most acceptable. The statement of the problem or the hypothesis is often altered as they arrive at a consensus.

The important implication for the teacher in these studies is that reflective thinking within the classroom setting can be effectively established through the use of a pattern or a model with distinguishable phases. The teacher can introduce reflection into his classroom, or improve his present attempts at it, simply by recognizing and employing these phases.

As stated above, the precise nature of the pattern and its parts has not been described or examined sufficiently to make more than a warrantable assertion that this is *a* way to engage reflection in the social studies classroom. However, when the teacher begins to use the model to guide the investigations and discussions of his students, he will gain an appreciation and understanding of the utility of dividing it into the various phases.

Obviously, if the teacher is uncertain of the over-all strategy of reflection as prescribed by a reflective paradigm, he may also feel insecure in his use of the several critical-thinking skills that make up the model.

Cousins, Jack E. "The Development of Reflective Thinking in an Eighth Grade Social Studies Class." Unpublished Doctor's dissertation, Indiana University, 1962.

Cox, C. Benjamin. "A Description and Appraisal of a Reflective Method of Teaching United States History." Unpublished Doctor's dissertation, Indiana University, 1961.

Elsmere, Robert T. "An Experimental Study Utilizing the Problem-Solving Approach in Teaching United States History." Unpublished Doctor's dissertation, Indiana University, 1961.

Hunt, Maurice P., and Lawrence E. Metcalf. *The Teaching of High School Social Studies.* New York: Harper & Row, 1955.

Massialas, Byron G. "Description and Analysis of a Method of Teaching a High School Course in World History." Unpublished Doctor's dissertation, Indiana University, 1961.

————, ed. *The Indiana Experiments in Inquiry: The Social Studies,* XXXIX, No. 3. Bloomington, Indiana: Bulletin of School of Education, Indiana University, May 1963.

DEVELOPING A PROGRAM FOR THE EFFECTIVE LEARNING OF SKILLS

Dorothy Fraser and Eunice Johns

Curriculum planners in social studies have typically devoted major efforts to the selecting and organizing of content. The planning of instruction for various courses and grades has often proceeded no further than sketchy lists of instructional materials and types of learning activities. However, if students are to develop the much needed skills of social study, more careful planning is needed. The writers of this selection discuss the problem of planning skill development in a sensible sequence in its appropriate relationship to the rest of the curriculum.

DEVELOPING SEQUENCES OF LEARNING EXPERIENCES

THE actual implementation of a program of skill development comes, of course, in working out sequences of learning experiences in various skill areas. Planning such sequences grows naturally out of any of [several recommended] approaches, but it must rest in the end on information and ideas gathered through all of them.

The interrelation of all types of learnings requires a broad approach to the planning of sequences of experiences for skill development. While it is necessary to focus on one area at a time, it is equally necessary to treat each area as a part of the whole complex of skills, attitudes, and understandings that children are developing. Thus, when learning experiences for the skills involved in interpreting graphic materials are planned, these experiences

FROM *Skill Development in the Social Studies,* Helen M. Carpenter, ed., Washington, D.C.: National Council for the Social Studies, 1963, pp. 303–307. Used by permission. Dorothy Fraser is professor of education and coordinator of social sciences in teacher education at Hunter College in New York. Eunice Johns is chairman of secondary social studies for Wilmington Public Schools in Delaware.

should be part of broad units in which students utilize other skills along with interpretation of pictures, charts, or other graphic representations. The use of graphics goes hand in hand with the development of social concepts and of socially desirable attitudes. This is true whether the study of the community in the second grade or the study of education in American life on the junior college level is considered. In the same manner, learning experiences which develop speaking and writing skills should be presented, not as isolated exercises, but as integral parts of broad units of study.

As a means of providing vertical coordination in the social studies skills program, some teacher groups have selected particular skills or areas of skills to be emphasized at particular grade levels. Thus, in planning the Port Arthur, Texas, social studies program, a comprehensive chart of skills was worked out, and those to be treated in the primary grades, intermediate grades, junior high school, and senior high school were indicated. (1) One part of the continuing curriculum-development program of the public schools of Wilmington, Delaware, and Washington County, Maryland, is the identification of particular skills for stress at a given grade level, with provision for extended development in succeeding years.

Sometimes three or four levels of treatment for specific skills or aspects of skills are agreed upon, such as (a) introduction through planned readiness experiences, (b) systematic development, and (c) reviewing, reteaching, and extending the skill. It is assumed that most skills will be utilized at most grade levels, but that at some place in the program systematic attention to each phase of skill development will thus be assured.

Rigidity and artificiality must be avoided, however, in a plan that calls for emphasis upon specific skills at particular grade levels. Clearly, such prearranged emphases should never be permitted to interfere with the full presentation of any skill at a moment when it is needed in the on-going activities of the class group. If children in an intermediate grade class embark on study of a topic that requires extensive use of periodical material, for example, they may be introduced to the *Readers' Guide to Periodical Literature,* the use of which is not usually begun until the junior high school years. When, as part of their class study, pupils need to consult more complicated maps and charts than they would ordinarily be expected to interpret, they should be helped to develop the needed skills. There must be room in any scheme for flexible treatment of skills to meet immediate needs of individuals as well as of the group. For example, some elementary school students will be ready to use a standard dictionary instead of a children's dictionary long before others will be able to do so. Again, the secondary school teacher must judge how much assistance to give particular students in locating the information needed for a particular project. He should throw abler students more fully on their own resources in finding appropriate materials, while guiding others in their use of the library card catalogue and of various reference indexes. The student who is ready for more mature applications of particular skills than are his classmates must be given assignments that are suitable to his stage of development.

The problem of conflict between the preplanned schedule for presenting skill areas and the immediate needs of the students will be minimized if criteria such as the following are considered as a basis for the prearranged schedule:

1. What skills may be appropriately assigned to this school division or grade level, considering the developmental characteristics of the students involved?
2. What skills are called for or seem most appropriate for development in connection with the social studies center of interest or theme at this grade level?
3. What skill experiences and needs are students of this age group having in classes other than social studies?
4. What skills do children of this age need in then out-of-school life?
5. What prior experiences with skills will students probably have had before they reach this grade level?

As resource units or social studies curriculum guides are developed for the various levels, the allocation of skills can be implemented by treating appropriate ones in statements of objectives, potential learning experiences, and suggested evaluation procedures.

As a second approach to sequence in social studies skill learnings, the teacher group may develop for each major skill area descriptive statements of sample experiences for each age group or grade level. . . . Such an approach requires careful interrelating of the various skill areas within the social studies program.

A third approach to vertical coordination of skill development rejects the advance allocation of skills to particular grade levels. Instead, teacher-pupil planning, with consideration of previous experiences and present needs, is depended upon to provide for sequential development of skills. Such an approach presupposes that the teacher has access to full information about each child's previous experiences and present status with regard to skill development. It may suggest, for example, that each year the teacher will receive for each student a folder containing scores on skill tests, products of student work, a description of units studied by the student in previous years, and other similar material. This approach assumes that the social studies teachers as a group have clearly defined their purposes in teaching skills and maintain close communication regarding activities at various grade levels. This plan requires a high level of teaching skill. But when effectively implemented, it would seem the most desirable of the plans described.

Whatever the approach to vertical coordination of skill development, one fact is clear. In no case can a teacher assume that all students in a class have the same command of skills, nor that they will all gain the same insights from skill experiences. Whatever the plan used, it must be applied flexibly in order to meet the individual skill needs of learners. Diagnostic exercises should be used extensively and frequently as a basis for pacing assignments for individuals and groups. (2) One major criterion would seem to apply in the selection of skill-learning experiences under any of the plans described: What skill experiences does the learner need to help him achieve his immediate, as well as his continuing goals in this situation?

Horizontal Coordination of the Skills Program

Perhaps one solution of the problem of horizontal coordination may be to extend through the secondary school and even into the junior college the broad-unit curriculum—the core-curriculum, common-learnings, or general-education program. Accounts of core-curriculum programs indicate the advantageous situation such programs offer for functional development of skills. (3)

For the great majority of secondary social studies teachers who are working in subject curriculums, however, the problem of horizontal coordination of skill experiences remains a real one. The recent tendency toward the use of special teachers and departmentalization in elementary schools may be expected to intensify the need for specific planning for horizontal coordination of skill instruction at that level. The nature of the problem is obvious. Other school areas share with social studies the responsibility for many skills that are integral parts of the school program—the communication skills, for example, or the skills of critical thinking. Communication and cooperative planning among teachers of all subjects at a given grade level are keys to the solution of the problem.

Various procedures have been used to facilitate communication and cooperative planning among teachers of all subjects at various grade levels. Ranging from informal to definitely structured arrangements, procedures such as the following have been used:

One social studies teacher at the secondary level discussed with his classes the problem of working efficiently, and invited students to keep him informed of opportunities they could see to relate social studies work to work in other classes. As a result, several joint social studies—English assignments were arranged in senior high school classes, some for individuals and some for full-class groups. Several boys carried out industrial drawing–social studies projects involving preparation of graphic materials. The same technique used at the junior high school level results in mathematics–social studies assignments in graph making, and a social studies–science field trip and class demonstration concerning city water-supply and sanitation services.

One group of seventh grade teachers met at an after-school coffee hour once every three weeks to share informal reports on new units begun, progress on continuing units, special activities, and indications of arising needs.

In one junior high school, where each class group moved as a unit through the day, most of the teachers working with a particular class group were scheduled for a free period at the same time. This provided time for cooperative planning during the school day.

One group of eighth-grade teachers utilized a monthly round robin to maintain regular communication. Each teacher submitted for duplicating a brief statement (from one-half to one typewritten page) describing the current work of the class, any new unit about to begin, and other pertinent situations. On reading the monthly statement, teachers who saw possibilities of tying together the work in social studies and English, for example, got in touch for specific planning.

One social studies department, at the secondary level, arranged for representatives of other departments to participate in its planning sessions. Opportunities for cooperative planning across subject lines were thus identified.

In one secondary school, a part of the regular time given to faculty meetings was set aside for reports from each department as to its curriculum at each grade level. Opportunities for coordination of work in various subjects could thus be identified.

In one city school system, the social studies curriculum committee worked cooperatively with English teachers and school librarians as they developed an over-all plan for grade placement of skills instruction. In another, a statement of common practices in all school work was prepared under the leadership of the English teachers, but with the cooperation of representatives from other subject fields. It covered the communication skills and provided a common base from which all academic-subject teachers and students could work.

(1) Julian C. Aldrich, ed., *Social Studies for the Junior High School*. National Council for the Social Studies, 1957. pp. 63–66.

(2) For specific suggestions concerning the use of diagnostic exercises in teaching map skills and time concepts, see Fraser, Dorothy McClure, and West, Edith. *Social Studies in Secondary Schools: Curriculum and Methods*. New York:

The Ronald Press Co., 1961. pp. 178–80, 198–201.

(3) See, for example, the description of the class in Johns, Eunice, editor. *Social Studies in the Senior High School*. Curriculum Series No. 7. Washington, D.C.: National Council for the Social Studies, a department of the National Education Association, 1953. pp. 24–25.

3

Organizing and Guiding Study Activities

BRIDGING THE GAP BETWEEN TEXTBOOK TEACHING AND UNIT TEACHING

Raymond H. Muessig

Although it is nominally popular in the social studies, the unit organization finds considerably fewer full practitioners than advocates. The writer of this selection suggests a means of moving from teaching that depends chiefly or solely on a textbook to instruction that involves a unit's variety of materials and activities. Though the suggested procedure may appear complicated or even cumbersome, it should require less formal effort once a teacher has mastered the process.

THE approach which I am going to outline very briefly is not a panacea. It must be considered as tentative, subject to error, open to revision and improvement. As a matter of fact it is proposed as a *temporary* measure to aid teachers in getting a feeling for unit teaching. Once this feeling has been grasped, I hope that this idea will be discarded and new operational levels sought. I worked out this procedure initially to help a group of experienced teachers, used to single textbook teaching, move into unit work. They reported that the idea "worked." Whether this suggestion is good, right, new, or old, it is at least "pragmatic." . . .

Unit teaching in a more simplified form is not always a radical departure from the most enlightened textbook teaching, nor is it any kind of a final answer; but it does attempt to correct many of the shortcomings of narrowly conceived textbook-centered methodology. Unit teaching at its best can be a thing of beauty, however, and has some unique properties which distinguish it from its more mundane cousin, the textbook approach. Unit teaching attempts to integrate, combine, coordinate, or articulate understandings, skills, attitudes, and appreciations around large significant topics. It seeks

---

FROM *The Social Studies,* 54:43–47, February, 1963. Used by permission. Dr. Muessig is a professor of education at Ohio State University.

wholeness rather than fragmentation, clusters of ideas and data rather than isolated particles, more of a montage than a series of single snapshots taken one by one. The unit approach does not avoid facts, but it does try to build facts into concepts and generalizations which may have more meaning, may be transferable in more situations, and may be more lasting. This method recognizes that any single source of information, however good it may be, imposes unnecessary limitations upon the class and the teacher. Pupil-teacher planning in the drafting of objectives, search for materials, selection of methods of study, and development of evaluative processes is more common. Actual interests, needs, aspirations, and problems of students are tapped and kept in mind, and greater student involvement and identification with objectives of learning tends to upstage intrinsic rather than extrinsic motivation. The unit may deal with material similar in content to that which the textbook approach gives its allegiance, but there is no pressure to cover any given text. Unit teaching encourages creative, independent, critical thought rather than memorization for its own sake. It relies on a variety of evaluation techniques in addition to the typical standardized and teacher-made tests. We could go on, but the basic thing, it seems to me, is that the unit teacher is after more *meaning* in what goes on in a classroom.

I believe that one of the reasons the unit approach has not found its way into more social studies classes is that the distance from basic textbook teaching to full-blown unit teaching is too great to travel all at once. I propose that the teacher already used to the text begin there. The first step is to make the most of the textbook, to get more meaning out of it, to emphasize relatedness. Later, a few added resources may be brought in and some activities with a "unit flavor" blended in. Still later, a simple unit could be worked out with the students, and so on until a complete unit approach is attempted in the spring.

This article begins with and stops at the first stage of this process—using the text as a more unified teaching tool. The steps for the procedure are outlined below:

1. Let us assume for the sake of this illustration that it is a few weeks before the start of the school year. Taking the basic textbook for the course, the teacher might begin by writing the chapter titles on separate 3 x 5 cards. It is sometimes useful to jot down a few of the subtopics under the chapter title just to have a reminder of some of the basic things included in the chapter. The cards should be separated into several stacks by priority. Some chapters which the teacher considers to be of primary importance will fall into the "essential" pile; others of secondary importance will fall into the "helpful" stack; and still others which may have doubtful value for a particular class would go into a "possible," "hold," or "delete" group. (Realiz-

ing that many textbooks try to be all things to all people, the teacher is already beginning a discrimination process by seeking significant aspects of the course for his point of focus.)

2. Next, the teacher works out a rough approximation of the number of teaching weeks in the school year. His purpose for doing this is not to see how much material—regardless of its importance—he can cram into the course but to work out *areas of emphasis* or "unit" topics. Now he roughly divides the total number of weeks into blocks of approximately five weeks. Later, as actual "units" emerge they may vary from three to six weeks in length depending on the teacher's objectives, the interest of the class, and other factors. In a typical school year, there would be from six to eight of these textbook units. Glancing quickly at the 3 x 5 cards in the "helpful" stack and thumbing more carefully through those in the "essential" pile, the teacher tries to list from six to eight over-all problems, topics, or content areas around which the units can be constructed.

3. The remainder of the 3 x 5 cards in the top priority group, probably most of the cards of secondary importance, and perhaps even a few of the cards in the third questionable pile may now be separated under the basic unit copies. This unit distribution may or may not follow the organization of the textbook. The important thing is whether the over-all topics make sense to the teacher and the students. The order of the unit topics can be arranged chronologically, logically, psychologically, or developmentally according to the teacher's perception of the nature of the class and the content discipline. The first unit might be so placed because it is fundamental or foundational in its content, interest arousing, more concrete or understandable, or for some other reason.

4. Now the teacher is ready to build the first of the units. He takes the 3 x 5 cards in the group assigned to the initial topic and notes the chapters they represent. (Each unit would include from about three to six chapters in the typical social studies text.) It is at this point that a rather tedious, but rewarding, process begins. The teacher carefully reads only those chapters which will be used for the first unit. On fresh, additional 3 x 5 cards he writes down the *crucial, basic* facts contained in each chapter, using one card for each factual statement. Just "any old facts" will not do! These must be facts with lasting importance, facts which will lead to significant understandings, attitudes, and appreciations. Altogether, though it is not possible to assign a magic number, the teacher might have from one-hundred to two-hundred essential facts.

5. The "fact" cards are now separated into three basic piles, "understandings," "attitudes," and "appreciations." The "understandings" pile will probably be the largest by far.

6. The cards in the "understandings" pile are again subdivided. The teacher tries to find groups of facts which support a given concept. A concept

is a class of related information, a "basket" which holds a cluster of facts and gives them real meaning. A given unit might contain from ten to twenty concepts each of which would be supported by from five to ten basic facts which "add up to something." One last refinement is necessary, however, to complete the treatment of "understandings." This is the formulation of from one generalization up to five generalizations. A generalization is the interrelationship of two or more concepts and should emerge quite naturally when the teacher analyzes the concepts already developed. One of the most important goals in social studies education is the ability to generalize, to fit particulars into a configuration, to draw inferences from data, or to perceive applications. The generalization, therefore, is the cognitive capstone of the unit. It is the vein of gold which is the product of all of the digging which the students and the teacher do throughout the unit.

7. A single unit may lead to only one or two important attitudes and appreciations. The "attitude" pile may contain only two or three concept cards and the group of fact cards which buttress the concepts, and a similar situation usually exists with the "appreciation" pile. Attitudes and appreciations are mixtures of both facts and feelings, cognitive and emotive elements. They carry the values, predispositions, and aesthetic elements of the unit.

8. The teacher is now at the "blueprint" stage of building a textbook-oriented unit. He takes a large piece of butcher paper and divides it into three columns. At the top and center of each of the three columns he prints "Content," "Activities," and "Evaluation" from left to right, respectively.

9. In the "Content" column the teacher prints a complete structural outline of the material he has gathered on the 3 x 5 cards. A Roman numeral is assigned to each generalization, attitude, and appreciation. Capital letters are given to supporting concepts which go under each generalization, attitude, and appreciation. Arabic numbers are assigned to the facts which undergird their respective concepts. Now the teacher can "see" what he is after, where he is going, what he wants to build. This view can be quite satisfying, for it gives a textbook teacher a sense of purpose which he may have missed before.

10. In the "Activities" column the teacher prints *over-all activities* which will serve the purposes and content of the unit like reading from the text, group discussion, etc. and *specific activities* like student panels, individual student papers, etc. which match up on a one-to-one basis with particular generalizations, attitudes, and appreciations or individual concepts which support them. Later, these more traditional activities may be augmented with procedures typical of a full-blown unit approach. The teacher could begin this expansion process on the second unit by having students write for free and inexpensive materials, by ordering several films, by forming a few research committees, by securing a resource person, etc.

11. In the "Evaluation" column the teacher would again list both general and specific procedures for assessing student growth on the unit as a whole and on given generalizations, attitudes, appreciations, or underlying concepts. During the first trial "unit" the teacher might be contented with just teacher-made essay tests, multiple choice tests, etc. In later units, the teacher may include inventories, check lists, observation, open-ended procedures, etc.

12. The final step in the process is for the teacher to ditto copies of the "unit" for all of the students. A cover with a "catchy" title and a clever illustration can help a great deal to interest the students. The teacher should write a one paragraph overview of the nature of the unit to secure student involvement. A group of basic unit objectives might be listed. This time they will be the teacher's, but later they will come out of class discussion. Also included would be a copy of the teacher's outline of content, activities, and evaluation so the students have a "preview of coming attractions." The first dittoed unit might contain daily assignments with some options for differences in students' interests and capacities. Students will read selectively from the text and use it as a genuine resource. Additional enrichment activities could be suggested too. Culminating, or wrap-up activities might be planned by the students themselves after they have a feeling for this approach. This would also initiate some pupil-teacher planning. Finally, if the teacher has caught the spirit by now, the unit might have a brief bibliography for the students so they could start getting in the habit of consulting other sources.

This has been an attempt to suggest a procedure by which teachers in secondary social studies could bridge the gap between textbook-centered teaching and unit teaching. The "bridge" suggested probably bears a closer resemblance to a log dropped across a creek than a sleek, steel suspension bridge, but it is a beginning. The rest of the construction task is up to the dedicated teacher who wants to do more for the wonderful, unique, challenging young people who walk through his door.

THE UNIT CONCEPT
IN SOCIAL STUDIES:
A RE-EXAMINATION

Donald W. Oliver

The widespread seeming acceptance of the unit approach in social studies may easily mislead the unwary to overestimate the frequency and degree of its actual implementation. Furthermore, there are some who even doubt its basic value, at least as it is commonly described. In this article one authority on social studies education questions much of the doctrine favoring unit instruction.

I N educational circles, the assignment-recitation method of teaching needs little introduction. It is a read-recite method. The teacher assigns students a certain number of pages in the textbook on one day. The next day the teacher tests the students' knowledge of the material by oral recitation. The method is associated with a strong emphasis on day-to-day memorizing of isolated facts.

During the first quarter of this century, a growing lack of faith in the assignment-recitation method spurred an intensive search for new teaching procedures. Several approaches, which their inventors called "unit" methods, were worked out. The methods were very much alike. All of them, for example, set forth a series of steps or phases that the teacher and student were to follow. In preparing a unit a teacher was to draw up a statement of understandings to be attained. The statement was to be followed by an overview of the subject, which was to be used to motivate the students. Next, the teacher outlined the content to be assimilated and drew up descriptions of student activities. Finally, the unit provided for evaluation.

The history and the meaning of the unit concept deserve to be re-examined. A new appraisal at this time should certainly be of considerable importance to educators, if only to illustrate how a concept may insinuate itself into the vocabulary of a profession, even though efforts at careful definition and validation fail.

Henry Morrison is often credited with originating the unit method, though most of the ideas in his major work may be found in the writings of earlier

FROM *Education Digest*, 24:37–39, September, 1958. Used by permission. The article was condensed from the *School Review*, 46:204–217, Summer, 1958, and is reprinted here by permission also of the University of Chicago Press. For biographical note see page 99.

thinkers. Much of Morrison's thinking can be traced back directly to the Herbartians, who believed that thinking proceeds through a series of predictable phases to a given product of learning.

Like the Herbartians, John Dewey analyzed the thought process and developed a concept of the unit based on his analysis. William H. Kilpatrick and Charles A. McMurry contributed their ideas. These educators all believed that they had discovered a cycle through which the thought processes of the student passes. To them, the cycle was inherent in the nature of thinking. Rooted deeply in this concept is the idea that, if classroom situations are manipulated in the right way, the individual will pass through the cycle and arrive at a permanent thought product. The object of classroom instruction, then, is, to allow such an experience to unfold.

Educational literature discussed the unit concept long before 1926, when Henry C. Morrison's *Practice of Teaching in the Secondary School* appeared. Still, his work was the first comprehensive treatment of the unit as an approach to learning, as a specific objective or product of learning, and as a teaching method for the secondary school.

Morrison's educational objectives are at the root of *his* unit theory. He makes careful distinction between what is learned and what is not learned in terms deeper than understandings or organized knowledge. He strives toward a change in behavior which he calls "adaptation." One writer, Herbert G. Lull, speaks of "learning by adaptation," although Morrison himself said that learning *is* adaptation. Like his predecessors, although he differs from them in some of his views, Morrison makes two predictions: First, that a particular kind of classroom situation will facilitate a particular kind of thought process; moreover, that, when this thought process is in operation, it will produce a particular kind of learning outcome. Unfortunately Morrison failed to define explicitly the relationships between thought process, learning outcome, and teaching method. Furthermore, writers of textbooks for secondary schools and for social studies in teacher education failed to ponder over the complexity of these relationships. As a result, each new textbook has its own interpretation of what Morrison meant by "unit."

Robert E. Swindler, author of *Social Studies Instruction in the Secondary Schools,* devoted four chapters to the discussion of the unit. He distinguishes between various types: The Dalton Plan, the Morrisonian unit system, the Winnetka Plan, and the unit system as practiced at the University of Virginia. This classification illustrates the persistent confusion between the unit as a general principle of learning and the unit as a particular teaching method.

The application of Morrison's idea of a unit to practical situations stimulated serious efforts to measure quantitatively the value of the unit method. Investigators usually followed the procedure of roughly matching two groups or classes according to revelant variables, such as age, grade, intelligence-test scores, or academic marks. One group was taught by the assignment-recitation procedure and the other group by some variation of the unit method. All of these experiments were made in an effort to clarify, teach, and measure Morrison's concept of adaptation.

F. C. Macomber—to select but one of the experimenters—carried on a study to compare a contract or unit method with an assignment-recitation method. Twenty pairs of students in two groups were included in the final analysis of data. A special feature of the study was the amount of class discussion in each group. The assignment-recitation group spent a total of 960 minutes in class discussion. Students in the contract or unit group had only 236 minutes of class discussion; most of their time was spent in individual study. Three objective tests were given: One was a geographical place-location test, and the other two asked for general information. The discussion (assignment-recitation) group scored higher on the general information tests than did the contract group but lower on the geography test.

No Superiority

The conclusions reached by experimenters and reviewers of experimental research on the social-studies unit in high school warrant at least one generalization. When factual retention is the outcome measured, unit methods, as defined in various experiments, give no striking evidence of superiority over other teaching methods. This finding perhaps should have punctured the inflated claims made for the unit method by early proponents; actually it did not. In fact, the majority of vocal curriculum-makers continue to expound the values of the unit.

Is it not interesting that although educators do not agree on what a unit is, they continue to use the term? Is it possible that this concept, which has no precise meaning, can still be useful to educators concerned with teaching procedures?

The positive feeling that many curriculum experts have toward the unit raises a second question. Their feelings are based on the assumption that the unit describes a teaching procedure that is superior to other procedures. Evidence indicates that this belief is not necessarily well-founded. Research on the subject is inconclusive. Is it appropriate for educators to act on an assumption surrounded by so much confusion and supported by so little evidence?

Nor is more evidence forthcoming. Although educators and other applied social scientists are showing more and more concern for guiding and changing the thinking process, the literature reflects fewer and fewer attempts to define carefully and validate experimentally teaching procedures designed to bring about such changes. Is there any reason why an observable teaching procedure cannot be subjected to empirical validation?

Our closing questions raise a basic issue: Isn't the unit really a vessel? Isn't the unit like the physician's black bag? Aren't the size and texture trivial compared with the instruments and medicines inside? Are we lost in discussions of structure, when in the end it is the content that really counts?

GUIDANCE FOR
SOCIAL STUDIES READING

Ralph C. Preston, J. Wesley Schneyer, and Franc J. Thyng

The importance of reading skill for success in social studies has been widely recognized. Not so well perceived, however, are the relationships between reading and the nature of the subject matter in social studies. This selection analyzes some of the characteristics of social studies content that make reading difficult for students and challenge teachers to help their students handle capably.

MANY SOCIAL STUDIES CONCEPTS AND GENERALIZATIONS ARE ABSTRACT

THE SOCIAL studies deal in part with concrete human behavior and concrete human institutions. On the other hand, many of the problems and ideas seem to the student remote and detached from human life. An example of this is seen in the boredom reported by some students with the sequence of events in the Roman effort to stem the barbarian conquest of Europe. The barbarians and their primitive way of life as described in most textbooks remain ill-defined and vague, and seem only loosely analogous to the barbarians of the moment. Also drawing yawns are definitions of variously interpreted terms (*cultures, due process,* etc.), descriptions of economic constructs, and terms such as "progress" and "responsibility" which often fail to evoke the kind of imagery that underlies good learning. The yawns in themselves would be of slight consequence were it not for the fact that reading for mastery calls for an alert, questioning (even if not curious) mind.

In other words, portions of social studies content have an element of unreality for the student because he is dealing with times, places, conditions, or perplexities which he cannot know at first hand and which seem to him to lack immediacy. Some of the most important social phenomena are, indeed, quite foreign to his experiences and cannot be demonstrated in the way that phenomena in the natural sciences can be reproduced in the laboratory. To a mature, well-disciplined mind, the factor of physical remoteness or of abstractness is of no moment; such a mind discerns relevance even in the remote. But the typical student is neither sufficiently matured nor disciplined for attaining true intellectual perspective. Moreover, he has been influenced by American infatuation with practicality and functionality.

FROM *Guiding the Social Studies Reading of High School Students,* Bulletin No. 24, Washington, D.C.: National Council for the Social Studies, 1963, pp. 8–13. Used by permission. Drs. Preston and Schneyer are directors of the Reading Clinic at the University of Pennsylvania; Miss Thyng is social studies editor for D. C. Heath Company.

It is not surprising, then, that for many students there is a peculiar lack of satisfaction in reading about ideas which appear nebulous, events which appear shadowy, personalities which appear wooden, situations which appear alien. One high school student asks: "Why can't we simply be taught that the Supreme Court has the power to declare a law unconstitutional? We don't understand that fact any better by reading about the case of *Marbury* v. *Madison* and trying to remember what a writ of mandamus is." Another student writes: "Who cares that an example of the Mediterranean climate can be found in Australia?" Such attitudes breed a poor quality of reading.

The road to inducing greater interest in abstract concepts and generalizations lies in humanizing the content, in providing the raw materials for better imagery, and in sharpening the relevancy of the events or places under study. This was pointed out by Johnson nearly fifty years ago. (1) Johnson recommended "a systematic search of local resources for points from which the pupil may begin his journeys to the past and to which he may return. The result should be an added sense of the reality both of the past and of the present." (2) Museums, monuments, centers of government, models, pictures, and supplementary reading matter can be used far more frequently than they usually are. Thus, the concept of the frontier, if vaguely described in the textbook, can be promoted through pictures and vivid text such as are found in one of the splendid American Heritage publications. (3) Current events can be cited to draw modern parallels to remote events. Charts, diagrams, time lines, and maps can be used to bring out relationships which otherwise might be hazy. For example, a chart or sketch on the chalkboard can show our governmental system of checks and balances; and this, together with a press clipping reporting controversy over recent decisions of the Supreme Court, would lend clarity and contemporary significance to the decision in the case of *Marbury* v. *Madison*. These are examples of details which "may furnish the very touch needed to make the misty immortals of history really human." (4)

MANY SOCIAL STUDIES CONCEPTS ARE AMBIGUOUS

Some students find it difficult to master ambiguous concepts. They become uncomfortable or impatient when confronted with issues of an unsettled character. (5) They search for fixed rules, incontrovertible truths, durable ideas, and stable principles. . . .

The social studies appear to such students as an unsatisfactory field. Courses in civics, government, economics, and problems of democracy are saturated with ambiguous concepts. They contain such dilemma-ridden subjects as international diplomacy, foreign aid, foreign trade, labor relations, race relations, and the role of government as a regulatory agency.

One source of ambiguity is the need for revision of concepts consequent to the discovery of new knowledge. Students who are intolerant of ambiguity find it painful to have to readjust their ideas as they read that oil is changing the desert countries; that recent radioactive-dating measurement has led to a dramatic upward revision of the former estimate that toolmaking man is 600,000 years old; that a recent archeological discovery in Mexico pushes back by 20,000 years the earliest date hitherto reported for man in the Americas; et cetera.

The necessary imprecision of many social studies concepts is another source of ambiguity, and hence of annoyance, to these students. Some facts cannot be pinned down, some questions cannot be definitively answered, some problems admit of more than one solution. Needless to say, every field of scholarship has imprecisions of this sort, but it is probable that they are particularly abundant and vexing in the social studies.

Obviously, social studies teachers cannot eliminate ambiguity. However, there are ways in which they may help these vexed students. They can make as clear-cut as possible those portions of the content which are definite and well organized. For example, there is controversy over Turner's hypothesis, but the frontier which he described had some clear-cut characteristics; an election is controversial, but election laws are usually clear and precise. Students should be asked frequently to identify textbook material which is precise and that which is ambiguous. The teacher can set an example of his own casual acceptance of ambiguity. He can present ambiguity as a challenge to scholarship and thinking rather than as a cause for annoyance. He can help students see that our very survival may depend upon our ability to tolerate ambiguity.

THE SOCIAL STUDIES CONTAIN A LARGE AND DIFFICULT VOCABULARY

The vocabulary of the social studies is enormous. A portion of it consists of technical terms of restricted use and meaning such as *patrician, fief, gold standard, rhumb line, habeas corpus,* and *blitzkrieg.* Another portion of the vocabulary consists of terms which have a general use as well as a technical use. Examples of these are *assembly, democracy, slavery, monopoly, town,* and *imperialism.* Their context discloses whether they are used in a strictly technica lsense or in a popular sense. Sometimes they are emotionally charged as parts of slogans or battle cries such as "Make the world safe for *democracy*" and "Down with *imperialism.*"

The social studies vocabulary is continually growing. Part of its increase is due to new scientific and technological achievements. Outer space, fallout, automation, and computer science have overpowering social implications. They become inescapable elements of social studies and find their way into textbooks. As new nations emerge on the world scene, hitherto obscure place names enter the social studies lexicon. The names of their leaders appear in headlines. Pronunciation alone presents a problem.

The difficulty which high school students have even with the more common social studies vocabulary can be illustrated by citing the test performance of three eleventh-grade classes in United States history. The range of I.Q.'s was well above that of the average high school population. Each class was given a ten-item test of terms drawn from United States history. The students had already encountered five of the items (*charter, secession, federal, impressment,* and *embargo*) in their textbooks and class discussions. They were not due to encounter five other items (*imperialism, reparations, moratorium, arbitration,* and *diplomacy*) until the following semester. The students were asked to write out their definitions or explanations of each term. An average of only three of the ten definitions or explanations were reasonably accurate. The students did not do much better on the terms which they had already encountered than on those which they had yet to encounter: An average of two definitions in the former category was accurate and an average of one in the latter. (6)

Some teachers feel that the solution lies in producing textbooks which are written at a reading level of two grades below that for which they are intended. According to this view, textbooks for eleventh-grade students, for example, should be written at a junior high school level of difficulty. There are several reasons why textbook authors and publishers find this difficult of accomplishment. In the first place, a social studies topic (e.g., the westward expansion, the feudal system, or the Cuban revolution) dictates to a large extent the terminology that must be used. It is doubtful if an author could explain the Taft-Hartley Act, for example, at a child's level. Perhaps he could do it if he had unlimited space, but textbooks are already too bulky and it is unlikely that school boards could be induced to foot the bill for two-volume textbooks. Furthermore, authors and publishers feel a responsibility for stimulating the student to enlarge his command of language; they feel that high school books should introduce him to new concepts and words which go beyond those he has learned in elementary school. Finally, confining a book for high school students to words of one and two syllables would produce monotony and limit the depth of concepts which could be introduced. Needless to say, students with severe reading handicaps must have books with simple vocabularies if they are to profit from their books.

The solution to the vocabulary problem lies in the direct teaching of new and specialized terms. An impressive body of evidence attests to the value of this approach. The purpose of direct teaching should be not only to have the students acquire the meaning of specific words, but to have them acquire the skills whereby they can get the meaning of unfamiliar words without always having to resort to a dictionary.

SOCIAL STUDIES COURSES CONTAIN A HEAVY CONTENT LOAD

Social studies courses are overloaded. This situation and its damaging effects were vigorously presented by Horn a generation ago. (7) . . . An examination of state and city courses of study indicates that the situation has not improved over the years. The objectives which are set up are reasonable, worthwhile, and pedagogically sound. But all too frequently they are followed by a list of topics to be covered of such length that the objectives get lost in the clutter of content. By way of illustration, we turn to the world history course commonly offered in the tenth grade. It must necessarily be a survey course. A survey course can be justified if the topics have been selected realistically in relation to the maturity and background of the students and in relation to the time allotted for teaching the course. This is seldom done. The fact load usually equals a compilation of the content formerly taught in the separate courses of ancient history, medieval history, and modern European history, plus substantial sections on the modern world. The content roams over geography, politics, military science, anthropology, art, architecture, music, literature, and other fields. There is little time for the student to develop real comprehension, appreciation, or interest.

The fault is frequently attributed to social studies textbooks. They are charged with being overly compressed and containing too many topics. It is true that in order to cover the required topics in a one-volume book the textbook author must minimize colorful detail, human motivation and conflict, and other aspects of the richness of social studies content. This is painful to the author, to the publisher, to the teacher, and, of course, to the student. The omission of enriching detail reduces the interest level of the textbook; and the more the interest level is reduced, the more the readability of the textbook is reduced.

On the other hand, textbooks are written as tools to aid teaching. Something is wrong when a teacher looks to the facilitating tool to dictate the scope of content. It is up to the teacher to adapt a textbook to local circumstances— to determine which portions of it the students are to master, which portions they are to skim, and which portions can be omitted without violence to the fundamental structure of the subject. Textbooks are necessarily condensed if they are to serve their purpose as "texts," i.e., books to be used as the *basis* for instruction. The teacher is equally charged with referring the student to other published materials for enrichment.

Many teachers think less in terms of reaching the course objectives than in "covering" the specified ground. Such a teacher wrote to one of the authors of this pamphlet: "How can I make my American History class move faster through my course of study? Spelling lessons, remedial work, time-charts, map exercises, reteaching, etc. have worth but at the close of the year the course of study will not have been completed." Teachers should introduce their students to new facts and ideas at a pace which is consistent with their ability to assimilate them. To be sure, if this principle is followed many classes will not be able to cover the subject as outlined. This need not be catastrophic. Teachers should, of course, be at pains to preserve the subject's essential integrity and structure. But this is not necessarily achieved by rushing a class mechanically through a course of study or a textbook. Teachers have a responsibility to decide near the beginning of the school term what content to emphasize and then to make each teaching period count by informed and inspired teaching. They would do well to heed Whitehead's dictum: "Do not teach too many subjects . . . What you teach, teach thoroughly. . . . Let the main ideas which are introduced into a child's education be few and important, and let them be thrown into every combination possible." (8) A student is actually handicapped by trying to, or by having a teacher try to, cram more information into his head than he can possibly hold. Such a procedure leads to poor learning and kills interest in the subject.

(1) Johnson, Henry. *Teaching of History in Elementary and Secondary Schools.* New York: The Macmillan Co., 1915.

(2) *Ibid.*, p. 204.

(3) Ketchum, Richard M., narrator. *The American Heritage Book of Great Historic Places.* New York: American Heritage Publishing Co., 1957. pp. 142–61.

(4) Johnson, *op. cit.*, p. 218.

(5) Discussion of "intolerance of ambiguity" as a personality type appears frequently in psychological literature. . . .

(6) Preston, Ralph C. *The Multiple-choice Test as an Instrument in Perpetuating False Concepts and in Clarifying Vague Concepts.* In preparation.

(7) Horn, Ernest. *Methods of Instruction in the Social Studies.* New York: Charles Scribner's Sons, 1937. . . .

(8) Whitehead, A. N. *The Aims of Education & Other Essays.* New York: The Macmillan Co., 1929. pp. 2, 3.

WRITING

Lewis Paul Todd

For some time social studies teachers have devoted increasing attention to oral learning activities and less to writing assignments. This tendency may be explained in terms of the predominance of oral messages in most citizens' communications on public affairs; writing has tended to become professionalized in our technological society. But writing still has major value as a means of learning, even if it is less widely used outside schools as a means of expressing ideas about the social world. The following thoughtful article offers valuable suggestions to social studies teachers who want their students to learn through writing.

FROM *Skill Development in the Social Studies*, Helen M. Carpenter, ed., Washington, D.C.: National Council for the Social Studies, 1963, pp. 121–126. Used by permission. Dr. Todd is editor of *Social Education*.

THE ABILITY to "say it," to express oneself with clarity and precision, is not, unfortunately, an inherited talent. It has to be learned, and the learning process involves the mastery of a number of skills. Since skills can be acquired only through practice, the way to learn to write is to write, as we observed earlier. But—and this is the crucial point—the beginner needs guidance and direction in order that good habits may be developed and bad habits can be blocked before they gain the upper hand.

Where does the social studies teacher begin? Here, we submit, his point of view, or frame of reference, is all-important. He should understand that he is not trying to develop professional writers, but merely the competence to communicate in clear, direct language. He should also understand that his efforts will be increasingly effective to the extent that he is able to cooperate with his colleagues in the English department. Such cooperation may involve joint assignments or an arrangement to have social studies papers checked by both the English and the social studies teacher. Regardless of how it is done, however, the student has a right to expect that his work will be evaluated in terms of the quality of the writing as well as the social studies content *and* the clarity of thinking. This, the relationship of language and thought, must, for reasons we have suggested previously, be a matter of special concern to social studies teachers.

With these considerations in mind, the value of brief, carefully assigned exercises for the inexperienced writer should be readily apparent. By *exercises,* we mean writing assignments appropriate to the age level and competence of the students, including letters requesting materials or information, essays and essay questions on tests, items for the school newspaper, book reviews, and reports of work done and articles read—in summary, any activity that requires writing. A properly planned program that has as its goal the development of writing skills should lead the pupil from the simpler exercises of the lower grades to the ability to write a respectable term paper before he graduates from high school. Whatever the dimension of the assignment, however, every bit of writing should be conscientiously evaluated and returned to the student. If individual conferences (the ideal, of course) are not feasible, the paper should contain enough of the teacher's reactions to enable the student to understand what he has done well and where and why he has failed to make his point. All of this takes time. How much time a teacher is prepared to give to the job of evaluation is, to be sure, a question each individual must answer for himself. The responsible teacher will not, however, assign more written work than he is prepared to read and evaluate.

If misery does indeed love company, the already overburdened social studies teacher can take comfort in the fact that at literally every grade level his colleagues are grappling with the problem. A brief look at a few examples of how from the graduate school down to the elementary grades educators are trying to help students to write better may prove encouraging and perhaps even instructive. . . .

In a recent article in *Social Education*, Professor Finkelstein of Union College reported his enthusiasm for—and the students' favorable reaction to—a type of assignment that he first tried out with considerable misgivings. He was, he said, running into a "wall of unacceptance and frustration" with his attempts to get the students to do the assigned reading in source materials. "Almost then of necessity," he turned to what he called the "Two-Page Essay."

Each week, on one of the three readings assigned to them, the students were required to write two pages, or about five-hundred words. The brief paper could be a summary, a criticism, or an enlargement of an idea found in the reading itself. During one of the weekly classes, several of the students were asked to read their papers. "These exercises (for I had no great end in mind)," Professor Finkelstein commented, "became, interestingly enough, the most significant part of the course." The students were challenged by the problem of compressing their reactions into concise statements. Knowing that their essays would be considered and evaluated by the instructor, and in some instances by their own classmates, the students exerted themselves to think critically and creatively and to express themselves clearly.

The author observed in conclusion: (1)

Two pages—but no more. It must sound terribly arbitrary. There are compelling reasons for the built-in limitations. From the student's side, two pages are challenging, stimulating, but not overwhelming. From the teacher's point of view, the simple truth is that we can do no more. From five hundred words, we can have sufficient material to educate and judge without assuming heroic but impossible work loads. . . . The Two-Page Essay is a felicitous compromise, nicely adaptable, of particular use to historians but readily convertible to other disciplines. It has worked well with college Freshmen, Juniors, and even Seniors. I would feel certain of its equal success on the secondary level, and it is manageable for all. Sometimes so simple and obvious a device as the one we have suggested can make a rich and permanent contribution to our teaching.

However much can be done at the college level, the inescapable fact is that the secondary school must accept the major share of the responsibilty for developing writing skills. One teacher makes extensive use of "the daily written summary." (2) As homework, each student is required to write a brief summary of the previous class discussion. At the opening of the next class, the instructor, or a student chairman calls upon one or more of the students to read his statement. This exercise helps to train the students to listen carefully and to separate the significant from the trivial in the class discussion. It provides practice in note-taking and in writing, with the students themselves serving in part as their own critics. It also gives the instructor a measure of insight into the effectiveness of his teaching. Careful evaluation of *all* the papers would, of course, place an inhuman burden on the teacher who attempted to require daily summaries, but the occasional use of the device deserves consideration.

In an article entitled "Writing and Thinking in Historical Study," (3) Virginia S. Deane discusses two different types of writing assignments—the fully developed essay and the exercise. The exercises she recommends include the daily summary of classwork, note-taking and outlining, and the preparation of test questions. "A student can suggest the extent and quality of his learning," she observes, "by the questions he finds to ask about the facts he knows. Designing test questions helps students to figure out what is worth remembering and, incidentally, provides a frontal attack on pre-examination jitters."

"If," Miss Deane argues, "writing is, as I believe it to be, essentially a measure of the quality of thought, then time for it and for its correction must take precedence over other matters. No teacher enjoys pruning his course, but I am convinced that each time we do this our teaching improves. Perhaps history classes should meet, as do many English classes, only four days a week, leaving the fifth period for individual conferences."

Whatever else the social studies teacher may do by way of written assignments, he should not neglect the essay question. There is a great deal to be said for the practice of giving the student several days to think about the question and then having him write the answer during a class period, with or without the aid of notes. However the questions are assigned, they should be constructed with the utmost care. The poorly framed question that encourages loose generalizations and rambling commentary is responsible for much of the criticism of the essay test. Henry Johnson once recalled the boy who was asked what he knew about Alexander the Great. "Alexander," the boy wrote, "rode a fast horse in his youth and died drunk." "You get a zero for that," remarked the teacher grimly. "But I did what you asked me," insisted the boy. (4)

The good essay-type question is one that requires a direct, thoughtful answer. In his excellent discussion of the subject, Henry Bragdon gives a number of examples, including the following: "The Emancipation Proclamation did not free a single slave. Is this true?" This, he points out, requires a more thoughtful answer than if the student were asked to "explain the effects of the Emancipation Proclamation." Responding to the question, "Is that true?" the student should understand that his "yes" or "no" answer is a statement of judgment which requires a supporting body of evidence. In another example, the student is asked to "explain why the War for Seamen's Rights was opposed in maritime Massachusetts and supported in inland Kentucky." Phrased in this way the question requires a more thoughtful answer than the related but inferior question in which the student is asked to "describe what you consider to be three principal causes of the War of 1812." (5) The essential difference between the good and the inferior questions in these examples lies, of course, in the demands they place on the students. One type of question requires only the recall of information; the other compels the student to analyze a situation and to draw from the analysis a body of evidence to support his conclusion. . . .

How much of this writing is good education, how much merely busywork, depends upon why and how it is conducted. It becomes valuable only when two conditions are met: The assignment, whether teacher-directed or self-imposed, must make sense to the student, and the finished product must be carefully evaluated.

(1) Finkelstein, Joseph. "The Two-Page Essay." *Social Education* 26:301–302; October 1962.

(2) Entin, Jack W. "The Narrative Summary." *Clearing House* 34:223; December 1959.

(3) *Social Education* 25:149–51; March 1961.

(4) *Teaching of History in Elementary and Secondary Schools, With Applications to Allied Studies.* New York: The Macmillan Co., 1940. pp. 276–77.

(5) Bragdon. *Atlantic* 204:119; November 1959.

4

Using Researchlike Approaches

A PROPOSED BREAKTHROUGH FOR THE SOCIAL STUDIES

Stanley P. Wronski

This article was a forerunner in the current revival and expansion of efforts to reflect more fully in social studies the methods of the social sciences. This selection challenges present and prospective teachers to break through the traditions in teaching methods and the massive but increasing body of content in the social sciences to a sound, workable, and stimulating approach to the social studies.

T HE ESSENCE of the breakthrough proposed here is that there be a radical shift in emphasis in social studies teaching from the *what* of the social sciences to the *how* of the social scientist. Specifically, there is need for greater awareness on the part of both teacher and student of how the social scientist, *qua* social scientist, operates. On what bases does the economist, for example, make his predictions about recessions, recoveries, or "soft spots" in various sectors of the economy? How does the political scientist conclude that a council-manager form of government would be a desirable, or undesirable, move for a given town? What can the sociologist reliably report about the probable consequences of ethnic group mixing in a public housing development? And how does he arrive at this conclusion?

Specific answers to questions such as those given above will lead students to seek answers to questions that deal with more generalized procedures common to any qualified social scientist. What are the ground rules that the social scientist sets up for himself? What assumptions underlie his investigations? What areas does he mark as out of bounds for his studies? What kind of tools and techniques does he employ? How reliable and valid does he himself consider his generalizations or conclusions? In short, what is the methodology underlying the social sciences? . . . .

FROM *Social Education,* 23:215–218, May, 1959. Used by permission. Dr. Wronski is a professor of education and social sciences at Michigan State University.

Knowledge about the tremendous potential energy contained within the atom has been commonly understood by physicists for several decades. Nevertheless, during most of this time the major source of energy used by mankind has been the relatively inefficient, crude, and finite fossil fuels. Similarly, social studies teaching has been operating at an incredibly low rate of efficiency. There is this difference, to be sure, in the "fuel" used by the physicist and the social studies teacher: In the former case it is approaching zero; in the latter it is approaching infinity. The outlook in either case, using conventional approaches, is not encouraging. The conventional approach in the social studies would be to add to the curriculum more and more new topics relating to the entire area of human relationships. The breakthrough would consist of going to the very nucleus that generates these new topics, new interpretations, new research, and new knowledge—the basic composition of this entity called the social scientist.

Consider the almost hopeless task that now confronts the conscientious teacher who wants to "keep up with new developments" in the social studies curriculum. Among the competitors for greater attention within the curriculum are the following: East-West tensions, international organizations, underdeveloped areas, aviation education, economic education, citizenship education, the Middle East, the Far East, the non-Western world, resources use, global geography, geo-politics, propaganda analysis, intercultural education, and moral and spiritual values. It is little wonder that some teachers and even entire school systems take one look at the myriad possibilities and revert to the safe, comfortable, stereotyped, and sterile subjects of the past. But suppose that such a reactionary solution is rejected. One may still ask, "Why study about how the social scientist operates? After all he didn't create these new topics or problems. They grow out of the nature of our world society." True, but the most important way by which the typical individual learns about these matters is *via* the so-called expert. Rarely is a person's understanding about the United Nations, for example, dependent upon any direct or overt experience. Similarly, one's understanding of how our economic system operates would be very inadequate indeed if it were to rely exclusively, or mainly, upon direct experience and observation. It is inescapable that that *major* source of information, generalizations, and ideas—in other words, curricular content—in the social studies comes to us via the social scientist. This is attested to in nearly all textbooks dealing with the teaching of the social studies; they define the social studies as "the social sciences utilized for instructional purposes."

Assuming, then, that one agrees to place considerably more emphasis in secondary social studies on how social scientists operate, what kinds of understandings about their methodology should be developed? What follows is an extraction of some key ideas concerning each major area within the social sciences. The examples are not intended to be inclusive; rather they indicate the possible scope of such treatment.

Henry Johnson, in his *Teaching of History*, provides several indications of how the history teacher may profitably deal with the methodology of the historian. It is significant that his opening chapter is a succinct review of historiography. And one of the most challenging and exciting chapters, "School History and the Historical Method," contains specific examples of the use of historical criticism even by elementary school pupils. "The author's own faith in the ability of boys and girls to cope with history is frankly greater than that commonly professed in educational discussion." Thus Johnson states his position in the preface, and then proceeds to demonstrate that his faith is well placed.

Here are some of the processes in historical criticism that are capable of being understood on a rudimentary basis by ordinary students: How the historian searches for materials. What kinds of sources constitute the raw materials for historical writing. How the historian determines the authenticity of sources. How materials are selected, classified, and synthesized so as to present a unified story.

Depending upon the grade level, the teacher may or may not introduce such terms as primary and derived sources, original documents, secondary accounts, records, remains, internal criticism, and external criticism. The possibilities for the application of the historical method present themselves at all grade levels. Even a first grader can be led to see that something can be learned about Indians from material dug out of burial mounds, that something can be learned about early white settlers by persons who wrote down what they saw, and that something can be learned about the newly settled country by drawings and maps made by the settlers. The junior high school student can be alerted to discrepancies in two different secondary accounts (such as textbooks), and can then determine whether one or the other, or neither, is verifiable. The senior high school student can experience the excitement and intellectual refinement that is demanded in writing a carefully constructed historical account of some phase of local history. If the student does a conscientious job, he will perforce acquaint himself with some of the basic ingredients of historical criticism.

What of the other social sciences? How would they be taught so as to reflect this emphasis on their methodology? In political science, for example, there has been a considerable amount of maturing within the discipline. It has changed its character considerably from its original concern with the vague and indeterminate area of political economy. According to Evron M. Kirkpatrick, Executive Director of the American Political Science Association, one of the major contributions that the secondary school teacher can make is to teach *about* political science. By this he means an understanding of the limitations that the political scientist puts on his sphere of activities, such as the distinctions between roles of a political scientist as an impartial expert, a policy-maker, and a private citizen. The general public is still very much unaware of the real nature of the job of the political scientist. The citizen is frequently inclined to think of the political scientist as performing the functions of a "brain trust" to elected office holders. But the political scientist is most effective *not* when he says, "This course of action should be taken instead of that," but rather when he says, "If course X is taken, then the probable consequences are A, B, and C; whereas if course Y is taken, the probable consequences are D, E, and F." The secondary school student, in studying the possible roles of the political scientist will thus gain an insight into one of the most basic problems facing an increasingly complex democratic society: How best to utilize the services of the expert and still retain ultimate political power with the people.

The economist offers the student a fascinatingly interesting subject to study. It is of more than passing interest that a . . . best seller in nonfiction is Professor John K. Galbraith's *The Affluent Society*—a book that is addressed to the layman and is essentially about the economist and how he thinks. Whether one agrees or not with Galbraith's many-sided thesis about our affluence, his book is a powerful argument for the need to understand and critically appraise the assumptions underlying contemporary economic thinking.

Sociological literature probably offers the widest range of readings about methodologies underlying a particular social science. More than any of the other social scientists, the sociologist seems to be constantly picking up his newly planted discipline and examining its roots. It is true that some socio-logical studies have a highly sophisticated rationale, involve elaborate hypotheses, and frequently require extensive mathematical understanding. But even the secondary school student can profitably learn to distinguish between a statement that may be subjected to verification and one that is an unverifiable value judgment. And he can see that data that are capable of being presented in quantified form are more amenable to objective comparison than are highly subjective data that may be couched in the imprecise English language. It is rather significant to point out that our secondary school colleagues in the teaching of mathematics have seen fit in recent years to introduce considerably more work in statistics and statistical analysis. Here is a fortunate opportunity for horizontal integration within the total curriculum.

At the moment, geography probably lends itself the least to any radical shift in emphasis from its content to its methodology. This may be attributed to at least two factors: The first is the enormous gap of ignorance about basic geographic understandings that still has to be filled somewhat in most of our population. The second factor is the *comparative* lack of strong disagree-ment among professional geographers as to what constitutes their stock in trade. But this issue is by no means completely settled. Geographers take varying positions, for example, on the relative importance to be attached to the relation of social institutions to geographic development within a society, or the influence of personality configurations on the group life of a people. As an illustration, the geographer may suggest that a sharp reduction in the supply of certain kinds of animals would lead to a more balanced economy and more effective use of limited resources. But what if these animals are highly regarded according to the religious mores of the people? Is the geographer therefore obligated to include the study of religions in order to do a totally effective job?

Some generalizations may now be made about methodology of the social sciences as a whole. Perhaps the most obvious—and still the most significant— is that all profess allegiance to the scientific method. Little is to be gained at this point by engaging in a bootless discussion of whether, in fact, the social sciences are "truly" scientific. It is a fact that all purport to have some degree of scientific validity and that all are committed to the goal of making themselves *more* scientific than they now are. The various elements of the scientific method may be described with varying degrees of intellectual sophistication. In essence, however, it consists of rigorous delimitation of some identifiable segment of the whole area of human relationships, posing carefully worded hypotheses about the segment, gathering verifiable data to test these hypotheses, and reaching some conclusions or generalizations. Of course, there are numerous other related aspects of the scientific method such as the relationship between social values and objective analyses, the advantages of quantified versus qualitative data, the need for a preciseness in communication, and the like. The point is, however, that the essential elements of the methodology underlying the social sciences are capable of being understood by the secondary school student.

It is not surprising that such a radical shift in emphasis in the *content* of the social studies curriculum should also *profoundly* affect the methods of instruction. A person best learns how a procedure is carried out by going through the process himself. If the procedure is an academically rigorous one, the learner should be given numerous opportunities to practice, refine, and demonstrate his learning. The teaching method that best lends itself to these procedures is generally referred to as the problems approach. In the very *process* of carrying out the problems approach the student is involved in basically the same methodology as the social scientist, albeit there may be different degrees of precision between the two. Furthermore, as any teacher who has used the problems approach in the classroom will attest, the students are constantly reminded that the process by which they reach a decision on their problem is just as important as their knowledge about elements of the problem; frequently, it is more important.

Sociologist W. F. Cottrell in a recent address describing the way in which the sociologist works "with his shirt sleeves rolled up," had this to say:

"We seek to learn the ways in which recently-used scientific methods have changed sociology so importantly that all social studies teachers should know about them.

. . . Sociologists have been trying to find categories which they can treat as if they were units of some kind. The reason is that in our culture we have developed ways of handling such units, which can be counted, that are very enlightening. The development of punched card machines, which can count and sort very rapidly, permits us to handle a great deal of data in a short time and at relatively low expense. When these data are fed into an electronic computer we can very rapidly test them by mathematical means. These permit us to test a lot of inferences or hunches about what relationships there are between the categories we have set up. The consequence is that we can learn quickly which are useful and reliable ideas and which contribute little to what we want to know."

The proposed breakthrough has implications for both preservice and in-service teacher education programs. At the preservice level the prospective social studies teacher will need not only the additional depth in the social science that he is currently expected to attain but also a more widespread acquaintance with the kinds of materials that are usually reserved for graduate seminars in the various subject matter areas. This, of course, will necessitate considerable rethinking on the part of college social science departments about their own course offerings. *There is no psychological or academically justifiable defense of the common practice of reserving only for graduate students and a few honor student seniors the opportunity to deal with the very heart of a given discipline, i.e., how its body of knowledge is accumulated.* This core of understanding will have to permeate all college offerings at the undergraduate level. It should not be reserved as an esoteric cell to which only the properly initiated doctoral canditate is admitted.

As for the in-service program, let us be realistic and recognize that the average age of secondary school teachers is past forty, which means that most of them had the bulk of their academic work about two decades ago. The social sciences have moved a tremendous distance since then in content and even more so in methodology. It is certainly to be hoped that a substantial number will keep abreast of new developments in both of these areas, but the more likely possibility is a considerable amount of inertia tending to retain the same pattern of social studies instruction. The major hope, therefore, lies with the teachers now in training and with prospective teachers.

The breakthrough will not be accomplished quickly. It has been estimated that it takes about fifty years for a new idea in education to become reasonably well accepted and practiced after its introduction. Probably no more can be hoped for in this case. Admitted that the road is long and difficult, what are the alternatives? They would consist of well-intentioned attempts to patch up and especially add to the already burdened social studies curriculum. In essence, the alternative is more of the same.

Is the proposed breakthrough unrealistic, visionary, and beyond the capabilities of secondary school students? It is curious but true that our colleagues in science and mathematics rarely let such presumed fears deter them. Within six months of the launching of Sputnik I, literally scores of high school science clubs were experimenting with jet and rocket propulsion. They were in fact dealing with knowledge, understandings, and theories that were generally reserved for college and even graduate courses a mere quarter of a century ago. Is a general knowledge of the methodology of the social scientist any more difficult inherently than the principles associated with man-made satellites? I find this hard to believe.

USING DOCUMENTARY MATERIAL IN THE AMERICAN HISTORY COURSE

John S. Bowes

In this article a specific type of source material is dealt with in relation to one subject in social studies. Mr. Bowes writes in the context of current proposals for making marked changes in the social studies curriculum. He illustrates, by reporting from his own teaching experience, practical ways of using historical documents.

THE embattled teacher of the social studies, wondering how on earth all that needs to be done can be fitted into the slender area of the curriculum allotted to his field, can draw a measure—but only a measure—of reassurance from the symposium, "Revising the Social Studies," which appeared in the April 1963 issue of *Social Education*.

As he saw the sociologists and anthropologists falling in behind the ranks of economists and political scientists massed for a final assault that threatened to carry all before it, he could also be mindful of the inexorable process of history itself, adding in his own lifetime a mass of material that would require another lifetime to assimilate and teach. To many, the writer among them, Jerome Bruner's little book, *The Process of Education*, held out some hope. Here was the promise of an answer to the crushing weight of sheer quantity. Let the teacher concentrate his efforts on structure rather than content—on the "how" rather than the "what."

Noting the advances made in mathematics and the physical sciences by concentrating on the structure of those disciplines, Bruner suggests that there may be lessons here for the humanities and the social sciences. . . .

FROM *Social Education*, 28: 88–90, February, 1964. Used by permission. Mr. Bowes is chairman of social studies at James Wilson Young High School, Bayport, New York.

For those who feel that the structure of the social sciences is something so abstruse that it can be revealed only to those at the graduate school level, Bruner has this to say:

If one respects the ways of thought of the growing child, if one is courteous enough to translate material into his logical forms and challenging enough to tempt him to advance, then it is possible to introduce him at an early age to the ideas and styles that in later life make an educated man. (1)

In his contribution to the symposium mentioned above, Lawrence Metcalf maintained that any effort to apply these principles in the social studies "will probably result in a larger place for the social sciences and a lesser emphasis on history." He explains this on the grounds that history "is totally lacking in structure," and points for justification to the fact that historians are generally suspicious of anyone who tries to construct theories that might explain the causes of historical events. (2)

It would be regrettable if a choice had to be made between history and the exciting new vistas which are opening for the social studies. Should the implication of Professor Metcalf's statement—that history, lacking structure, is incompatible with this new approach—be accepted literally there can be little doubt as to whether the subject matter or the method will prevail. Leaving aside the argument as to whether history should or should not dominate the social studies at the secondary level, he would be an incurable optimist who would maintain that it can be unseated in the near future. The strong historical orientation of those who teach the social studies, the inertia which any such profound reorganization is bound to meet, or the pedestrian fact that the American history course is bolted and riveted into the curriculum by legislative act in most of the fifty states will serve to hold the pace of change to that of a glacier. Desirable or not, the courses in history are going to be with us for a long time at the center of the social studies or close to it. A new approach that cannot be adapted to them will have but a limited usefulness.

Cold comfort indeed for the beleaguered classroom teacher, if Metcalf's prediction, as stated above, were to be taken at face value. Fortunately, it need not be. There are at least two avenues of escape from the dilemma which have been explored to some degree and which demand further attention.

First, as he has stated, there is no accepted "structure" to history, but neither is it a totally formless mass of data. The editors of The Harvard Guide to American History have this to say in their introduction:

There are historical interpretations which concede that perfect objectivity is unattainable but remain hostile to rigid or dogmatic historical theories. This school is pragmatic and pluralistic, assuming always multiplicity of causation, and prepared to use ad hoc whatever general theories may illuminate a particular point. (3)

Later they claim:

Most American historians today operate from this type of interpretation. They agree with the relativists that interpretation is inescapable, they agree with the scientific historians, however, that objectivity, even if unattainable, must stand as the historian's ideal. Accordingly, they foreswear all single-valued or dogmatic theories of history and subject theory itself to the perpetual countercheck of facts. If facts are no longer said to speak for themselves, still historians must speak through them; and the interpretation which can hold in suspension the largest number of diverse facts is that most likely to do justice to the total complexity of a past which can never be fully recovered. (4)

Here then is one possible route—that of historiography. It is interesting to note that the exercises being developed in western Massachusetts by the project which Van R. Halsey, Jr. reported in the May 1963 issue of *Social Education* are in this direction. (5)

A second opportunity lies in those areas where economics, political science, anthropology, or social psychology throw light upon the past. As the historian has appropriated the conclusions from these disciplines, may not the teacher of history "borrow" some portions of their structure as well? Thus no doubt will Professor Metcalf's prediction of a "lesser emphasis on history" be fulfilled. At the same time, high school social studies can be presented within a predominately historical framework as they always have been and, willy-nilly, must continue to be for some time to come.

To learn whether or not anything might be gained from having high school history students emulate Professor Bruner's schoolboy by "centering on the inquiry itself" the writer conducted some experiments at Farmingdale (New York) High School. The students concerned were all of the college preparatory level, and one group was an honors or track one class.

In the three efforts to be reported here, he set out to have his students "discover" for themselves the following ideas:

1. A knowledge of past mistakes can guide men in their future actions.
2. Contemporary observers are not the best guides to the meaning and importance of events.
3. In seeking political solutions to economic problems, people often proceed on insufficient evidence.

Now it may be stated that none of these concepts is very difficult to explain or to grasp, that if they are not, in fact, self-evident, a brief passage in the textbook or a few words in class should be sufficient to encompass them. The writer would point out that the Pythagorean Theorem can be stated almost as succinctly, yet he doubts that even an Einstein could make it part of his permanent intellectual furniture quite that easily. He suspects strongly that the ease with which such generalities as these can be mouthed and parrotted back is at the bottom of much of our frustration in the teaching of history. Their very simplicity makes it difficult to introduce them into the student's thought processes in a way that will make them both permanent and meaningful. . . .

It must also be granted, at least for the sake of argument, that the concepts stated above are something worth knowing—that they help to explain certain phenomena in the past and have a certain cautionary value for the future citizen.

In the first of these efforts the intention was to "teach" the fact that a knowledge of past mistakes can guide men in their future actions. Students were asked to read that passage of Bradford's *History of Plimoth Plantation* in which he describes the dreadful suffering of the colonists during their first winter on the inhospitable New England shore. (6) Following this they were directed to find out for themselves if any other American colonies had gone through such a "starving time," and having done so to make some judgment as to why some suffered and some escaped. In performing these tasks it became evident to most that the worst mistakes had been made in the earliest colonizing attempts, including the unsuccessful ones of Raleigh and others. The inference, all too obvious perhaps in this case, was drawn—that the later colonizers were able to avoid the worst mistakes of the pioneer settlers. It could also be learned, of course, that this "feedback" took not less than thirty years.

If this effort was too simple, the second proved too difficult, at least with the imperfect materials chosen. The fact that *contemporary observers are not the best guides to the meaning and importance of events* was the desired outcome. Two letters of George Washington, written in the fall of 1786 to Henry Lee and James Madison were duplicated for the students along with the summary chapter of Merrill Jensen's excellent study of the so-called Critical Period, *The New Nation*. (7) Whatever may have been gained in the way of acquaintance with contemporary sources or the historian's subtle analysis of the opposing forces in the formation of our federal union, from the viewpoint of the desired conclusion stated above, this exercise was a dismal failure. However, the idea still seems worth another attempt. A clearer contemporary statement on the turmoils of the post-Revolutionary years and a simpler, more explicit statement of the revisionist position may serve better. (8)

The third and final attempt to be reported here was built around the idea that *in seeking political solutions to economic problems, people often proceed on insufficient evidence*. Some overheated statement from one of the disciples of free silver or fiat money who filled the political landscape in the latter part of the nineteenth century seemed the best introduction for this exercise. Eventually a passage from *Coin's Financial School* was chosen. That lively little pamphlet with its evangelistic style, statistical buttressing, and entertaining format, understandably exercised enormous influence in its day. The brief passage chosen for duplication contained amidst its 700 to 800 words the following statement summing up the claims of those who blindly accepted the quantity theory of money. . . .

Balancing this was a reprint (some 1500 words) of an article from the monthly publication of the Federal Reserve Bank of Philadelphia for February, 1962. The piece was a brief, informally written history of United States monetary policy in regard to gold and silver. It was occasioned by President Kennedy's proposal, in January 1962, to repeal existing silver purchase laws and replace silver certificates with Federal Reserve notes, but only the historical portions of the article were used. . . .

Using the *Historical Statistics of the United States,* the information on the population of the United States, the amount of money in circulation, the portion of this money which was silver, and the average price of wheat per bushel was gathered for five-year intervals and presented to students in [a table with accompanying explanation]. . . .

Students were then directed as follows:

Having made the computations indicated on the preceding page, write a brief comment on "Coin's" statement. If you think the statement wrong, try to explain why "Coin" was mistaken.

Gratifyingly, most students, having performed the computations indicated in this simple exercise, were able to place their fingers on the chief fallacy in "Coin's" argument—that many factors other than the amount of silver coinage affected the price of wheat and other farm commodities. Domestic overproduction and world market conditions were correctly identified as being among them.

In conclusion then, these exercises proved to be an interesting supplement to normal class work whose chief advantages may be summarized as follows:

1. Students had an opportunity to *use* (not merely to be exposed to) historical materials.
2. Some insight was gained into the methods and problems of the historian.
3. Data obtained from class work and textbooks were employed in arriving at and testing generalizations.
4. Some portion of class time could be saved from the dull business of factual repetition.

Certainly the writer holds no brief for the particular list of concepts dealt with here. Quite possibly, no definitive list could or should be drawn up. It does, however, seem to him that this is an area where those whose charge or business it is to assist the classroom teacher, particularly the less experienced one, might do valuable service. Curriculum committees, master teachers, and publishers of educational materials could suggest particularly fruitful areas for exploration and assist in digging out and making available the best tools and materials for use by high school students. Needless to say, university scholars in all of the social sciences should be invited—should be importuned—to lend their assistance to this work.

(1) Jerome S. Bruner. *The Process of Education.* Cambridge: Harvard University Press, 1960. p. 52.

(2) Lawrence E. Metcalf. "Some Guidelines for Changing Social Studies Education." *Social Education* 27:200; April 1963.

(3) Oscar Handlin *et al. The Harvard Guide to American History.* Cambridge: The Belknap Press of Harvard University Press, 1955, p. 16.

(4) *Ibid.*, p. 20.

(5) Van R. Halsey, Jr. "American History: A New High School Course." *Social Education* 27:249–252; May 1963.

(6) *Bradford's History "of Plimoth Plantation."* Commonwealth Edition, 1898. p. 11–115.

(7) Merrill Jensen. *The New Nation.* New York: Alfred A. Knopf, 1950. p. 422–428.

(8) Merrill Jensen. *The Articles of Confederation.* Madison, Wis.: University of Wisconsin Press, 1940. p. 239–245.

TEACHING OF SOCIAL SCIENCE AS METHOD

Melvin Tumin

It is perhaps too easy to settle for too little in attempts to emphasize social science methodology. A few documents, statistics, hurried observations, and sketchy reports are scarcely adequate to represent the social sciences faithfully. The difficulties involved should not, however, obscure the basic nature of what is desired. According to this social scientist the complex problem does contain some simple elements. He offers forthright, interesting, and thoughtful suggestions, stressing throughout the close interrelationship of method and content in the social sciences. The selection constitutes part of an address delivered by the writer at a recent conference on needed research in the social studies.

T HE question of how best to explain similarities and differences is really an issue of how to think about human behavior—and that, in turn, immediately directs our attention to the question of how to find out whether

FROM *Needed Research in the Teaching of Social Studies*, Roy A. Price, ed., Washington, D.C.: National Council for the Social Studies, 1963, pp. 47–54. Used by permission. Dr. Tumin is a sociologist at Princeton University.

what we think to be true is or is not true. What is the evidence on its behalf? What is the evidence for contrary points of view? What would we need to know if we wanted to be more sure we were correct or wrong? In short, the *substantive* question about proper explanations of behavior feeds directly and immediately into the *methodological* problem of how to find out.

These reflections lead me to suggest that one does not teach social science either as method or as something else. It seems to me one teaches *social science,* and, in the process, one unavoidably teaches method. That is, one raises issues and questions regarding social behavior. One then asks what one needs to know in order to be able to answer the questions. One then formulates hypotheses that direct one's attention to probably relevant factors. One then concerns oneself with the ways in which these hypotheses can most satisfactorily be tested. One then pursues these methods of inquiry, collects the relevant data, analyzes them, and asks what the data have to say about the hypotheses, and, in turn, what has emerged regarding the question with which one started.

At every point along the line in the consideration of any *substantive* question, methodological considerations are of the highest relevance, and vice versa. Properly, therefore, we should be considering needed research in the teaching of social science, understanding thereby that we mean principles and methods closely intertwined at every stage in our deliberations. . . .

One can easily move in and out of the great range of social science problems starting almost anywhere. If, for instance, we were to begin with race relations, we would quickly move into general problems of heredity and environment; then back to specific problems of individual differences; then onto more general problems of democratic social organization of heterogeneously endowed and interested people; from there on to problems of motivation and their relevance for learning and for feelings of solidarity and loyalty; from there to problems of delinquency and crime and alienation in general; and through those, by a side path, into problems of affluence and unemployment, and on to war and revolution. Start anywhere in that matrix and, sooner or later, one's attention is brought to all the component and interconnected elements.

I for one am firmly convinced that our knowledge on these and other issues of human behavior that are pressing both theoretically and contemporaneously, can be codified and organized far more systematically than at present, and that this can be done in such a way that it can be translated into appropriate and meaningful curricular enterprises at every level of schooling. One doesn't have to look toward another enormous effort at encyclopedic inventory and codification in order to be able to do far more and far better than we now do. There is a great deal more that is known today about problems of human relations, and warfare, and unemployment, and crime, and the like, than is ever transmitted systematically and meaningfully in the schools at any level. We ought to move quickly to translate the best that is known into solid curricular offerings.

In all the foregoing, I have deliberately ignored questions of technique and instructional method, or of discovery of levels of readiness, or of what kinds of projects fit what kinds of texts, or of structure versus content, or of sequentiality. These issues are all implicit in what I have chosen to focus upon. I do not mean to put them aside as unimportant. But I do mean to urge that it is first and foremost important to discover what we wish to achieve through social science instruction; what existing means we have to achieve these ends; what means could we creatively contrive; how we can bring all relevant personnel into satisfactory liaison and communication on these matters; and how, therefore, we may better help the children of the United States to achieve a more profound understanding of who and where they are, and why, and what they can hope to do about enjoying more of what they find good, and about changing more of what they find undesirable and problematic in their lives.

If it could be assumed that a miracle had happened and that the needed research just specified had been accomplished, and all our questions answered, we would then be able to turn to some specific issues arising out of the notion of social science as method. Short of such miracles—and, by definition, miracles are rare and improbable—a good deal of important patchwork has to be done, and done in a hurry, in order to eliminate some of the more egregiously undesirable features of the present levels of understanding and approaches to knowledge about human affairs.

The first, foremost, and most despair-producing problem I see is that of getting across a solid appreciation of how difficult it is to get to know anything with any degree of assurance of its truth. Everywhere it is assumed that reliable knowledge is easy to come by. Even worse, it is everywhere assumed that *systematic*, reliable knowledge is easy to come by. The fact of the matter, of course, as we all know, is that such knowledge even about the most apparently simple dimensions or aspects of human behavior is painfully hard to come by. The question, then, is how can we get a wider appreciation of this fact.

I know of only one way that has a high degree of probability of success, and that is to require everyone concerned to try to answer any one single problem about human affairs by producing reliable, relevant data. This means, unavoidably, that all those for whom this appreciation of the difficulty of securing knowledge is important must themselves engage in research projects, no matter how small in conception, trivial in population size studied, or insignificant in the total bulk of human behavior.

There are many perplexing problems about how best to organize such research projects. There are numerous advantages and disadvantages to every method I have ever tried or know that others have tried. In any event, it would pay us all a good deal of profit to consider at some length how best to produce that indispensable appreciation of the difficulty of securing systematic, reliable knowledge about social affairs.

Apropos of this, one sure thing is that neither school children nor anyone else can get an appreciation of how difficult it is to get reliable information by turning to their encyclopedias for that information. To be sure one can get a lot of information from encyclopedias, and, if they are good encyclopedias, the information is often reliable. But one does not and cannot thereby begin to appreciate what has been required to establish that information as reliable. If it has proven possible in courses in physical science to have children perform simple experiments in order to come closer to understanding the method of science, I see no conceivable reason why this can't be done in social science. Even simple exercises in systematic social observation would do a lot more to bring home to children what is involved in social science than the more usual techniques currently practiced of sending them to the library to index the warehouse of codified information.

The actual involvement in a research project commends itself on grounds other than those stated but implied by them. I think principally of two such grounds. The first concerns the notion of objectivity. The second has to do with the idea of multiple causation.

The desideratum in science, of course, is perfect and total objectivity of the investigator. We all are familiar with a number of the ways in which we fail to achieve this blessed state. There is one path toward objectivity, however, that is open, and that is perhaps not used as often as it could be. This involves that state of mind implied in the words "critical doubt." The cultivation of this state of mind is, of course, indispensable for the *general* education of anyone in a free society. But it is also specifically relevant in the training in science which necessarily involves an unwillingness easily to accept anything as given until there are pretty good evidential grounds for doing so. The task of encouraging this approach in the classroom encounters two primary difficulties. The first is the fact that the schools are charged, as probably they should be, with the inculcation of basic values—at least some values—along with the training of minds and the transferring of skills. Values being what they are, it is extremely difficult to inculcate them and at the same time encourage systematic critical doubt as a general approach of mind. It is, of course, much easier simply to require children to accept things as given to them. With the great power the formal position of the teacher gives to her, it is no trick to have nominal verbal conformity to the teacher's expressed value preferences. It is quite a trick, however, to get a common value base established and, at the same time, communicate a genuine and sincere interest in the manifestation of the critical mind at work. But this is what must be done. And on this, then, we need a good deal of inquiry as to how best we can do it. For critical doubt is the better part of objectivity, just as, in turn, going around the circle, objectivity is the better part of critical doubt. Just how a teacher can maximize both her mandate to inculcate values regarding democracy and the like, and, at the same time, just as deeply institutionalize a critical turn of mind and a constant pressure toward objective dispassionate search for evidence is a very perplexing problem.

The second implied value of engaging in research projects referred to the idea of multiple causation. Earlier in this paper we noted how the untrained mind runs easily toward the simple-minded explanation, which turns out to be no explanation at all. Nor is it enough to shift attention off the biologistic causal thinking on to environmental influences. The further problem is present of getting an appreciation of how complex are the causal patterns connected with any simple behavior pattern. For instance, do boys and girls begin to differ radically in their behavior early in American life? In what ways? Why? And why are they similar in some respects, nevertheless? Since nearly every public school class has both boys and girls who are likely to differ in some patterned ways and resemble each other in other patterned ways, there is a natural matrix of experimental evidence to be researched right in the classroom—if the teacher is up to it. Even a rudimentary inquiry into the similarities and differences among boys and girls would involve the class from the very outset in appreciating that, in addition to the genetic factors that might be at work, there are a host of other cultural variables which make their contribution. This realization of (1) the multiple causation of this everyday fact, (2) the importance of cultural patterns, and (3) the unsatisfactoriness of the "hereditarian" explanation that says "that's the way boys and girls are by nature," might begin to open up a world of understanding that would be extremely valuable. . . .

I have specified some of these examples at length in order to show what must be obvious to most but needs to be made obvious to all, namely, that we have some very basic scientific truths at our command and that these can serve as general guides to observation and thinking about human social affairs, and that, finally, these can be translated into workable, understandable and enjoyable features of the curriculum of our schools even at the most elementary levels.

DEVELOPMENTS IN SIMULATION OF INTERNATIONAL RELATIONS IN HIGH SCHOOL TEACHING

Cleo Cherryholmes

One of the most exciting, and almost surely the most truly new, of the developments on the horizon of instructional method in social studies is simulation of contrived situations. The author recognizes relationships between this technique and certain other procedures used in teaching or research. He illustrates actual operation of simulation in the classroom by describing an experiment in a high school. Further, he reports some of the results in terms of effects on student interest and attitudes. Omitted here are tables that identify the evaluative questions used and the statistics summarizing students' responses to the questions.

SIMULATION, a teaching technique sometimes called gaming, represents a dramatic exploration in teaching international relations to high school students. A simulation of international relations differs from the ordinary model used by social scientists in that the student not only studies it as an observer but becomes personally involved. The simulation to be described has been used to present the basic concepts of international relations—e.g., balance-of-power, sovereignty, international law—and has provided a basis for discussion of decision-making and communications theory.

International games fall into two general categories. First are those which employ real situations and actual nations. These are exemplified by the RAND Corporation and Massachusetts Institute of Technology games. Second are the simulations which use hypothetical nations, compress time, and assign mathematical values to the parameters of the games. This form has been pioneered by Northwestern University. The latter type of simulation was chosen for use at the Lawrence, Kansas, High School as the core activity of a six-week unit in international relations in a college preparatory course in American government. The rationale for this choice was that the *overall structure* of international relations was more likely to emerge and that a greater variety of events would be available for class discussion. This choice necessitated the construction of a game that would accurately represent the

FROM *Phi Delta Kappan*, 46:227–231, January, 1965. Used by permission. Dr. Cherryholmes, formerly a teacher in Lawrence, Kansas, High School, has more recently served as assistant director of the Social Studies Curriculum Study Center at Northwestern University.

major characteristics of the international system and which could be understood easily by the students.

Over a two-year period and eight separate simulation runs involving almost
500 students, the Lawrence simulation evolved into a game that may be used
with fifteen to forty students without the aid of any teacher assistants or
special classroom facilities.

In the Lawrence simulation three students are assigned to each nation;
they occupy the positions of Central Decision Maker, Chief Diplomat, and
Military Adviser. The Central Decision Maker has the final authority to
determine the policies of his nation. The Chief Diplomat is the only official
who may conduct oral negotiations with other nations, and the Military
Adviser is responsible for maintaining the military posture of his nation
and for securing accurate information concerning the military strength and
intentions of other nations.

The unit of basic capability is the gaming concept which represents that
vast category of goods, skills, and services encompassed by a national economy.
These units may be invested internally in basic industry, exchanged in international trade, given to other nations as foreign aid, or used to purchase units
of military capability. There are three types of military force: tactical military
capability, which may be used either to "police" elections or to prevent
revolutions; strategic military capability (non-nuclear); and nuclear military
capability. Each weapons system has its own research and production costs;
even the "time lag" between the research and the use of a weapons system
is simulated. By the manipulation of these economic and military resources
every major strategy available to real nations is an option in the simulation.

An overview of an actual gaming run (spring, 1963) will exemplify the
action which takes place in the Lawrence simulation. During the first session
the ten nations in the make-believe world pursued two basic courses of action.
Two nations, Alphanesia and Lambodia, were secretly planning to take
over one of the smaller nations, Upsilane, by the direct use of military
force. Two other nations, Betaslavia and Delton, were concerned with the
organization of a "United Nations" which would provide for (1) mutual
nonaggression and (2) collective security.

The United Nations movement was successful in drawing all of the
nations of the world into its organization except for the two imperialist
countries mentioned above and for Sigmarainia, which successfully followed
an isolationist policy to the end of the game.

The aggressor nations attacked Upsilane and the United Nations survived
this first crisis by immediately coming to the aid of Upsilane and defeating
the combined forces of Alphanesia and Lambodia. The problem of a post-war
settlement immediately arose and it was very unclear at first what form the
new balance of power would take. The power balance eventually stabilized
between the nations which were competing for leadership and control of
the United Nations.

In the meantime, Upsilane, after being saved by the United Nations, was under the mistaken impression that the UN would support her in an aggressive action. Upsilane declared war on the one neutral nation, Sigmarainia; the United Nations did not give assistance and Upsilane was defeated. Alphanesia and Lambodia applied for admission to the United Nations but were denied membership. During this post-war period militant, imperialistically oriented leadership became more influential in the international organization. Competing factions developed and destroyed the original nanimity of the organization. The rumors which resulted in these factions were later discovered to be false and their origins were never determined. Because of these growing suspicions, however, the United Nations attacked Betaslavia, which was one of its own members. Epsilovia, another member of the international organization, refused to support this action because of the mutual nonaggression clause in the charter. The United Nations declared war on Epsilovia and defeated her along with Betaslavia.

The United Nations not only became militaristically but also economically oriented. After the fourth session, the United Nations was transformed into a rather effective common market and restrictions were placed upon trade with other nations.

As the simulation drew to a close, the world, which had started with ten nations of roughly equivalent size, had been reduced to four nations of dominant strength. There were indications that these four nations would have aligned into two opposing groups had more time been allowed.

Although military actions seemed to dominate the simulation run reported, political and economic actions were not overshadowed. During the course of several simulation runs a balance among these three factors seemed to maintain itself. The variety of events of this simulation run, of which only the more significant are outlined above, provided the basis for many class discussions. The first few simulation sessions followed each other with each meeting of the class until three sessions were complete, then simulation sessions alternated with class discussions and lectures. These latter presentations focused on the conceptual structure of the simulation and of real international relations.

A classroom characteristic of simulation which is very evident to the observer is high student interest. The students approach the simulation with more energy and resourcefulness than they expend on any other part of the course. The students overwhelmingly report a favorable response to the simulation verbally as well as by their actions. In order to determine statistically the nature of student reaction, a number of statements were distributed at the completion of an earlier simulation run . . . to which the students were requested to reply: strongly agree, agree, undecided, disagree, or strongly disagree. . . .

Student response to Statement 1 substantiated the observation of high student interest, since 87 per cent of the students enjoyed participating in the simulation. It is unlikely that such a response could often be educed by lectures or more traditional classroom activities.

Whereas Statement 1 assessed student interest, Statements 2, 3, and 4 were concerned with how the students *perceived* the simulation and what conceptual learnings they *thought* they derived from it. Therefore, when they were asked if the simulation was meaningful in its relation to real international policies, the responses only tell us whether it appeared meaningful to them. If the simulation is to be educationally valuable it *should appear meaningful* to the students; it is the duty of the instructor to *insure* that the simulation is educationally valuable and not viewed as merely a game.

At the end of a recent simulation run . . . the students expressed in their own words their reactions to the game. Representative selections follow:

"The simulation and the country reports were definitely worthwhile. I learned much about making decisions and how to consider the various factors involved. I'm very glad that it ended though, because it was really getting tough to handle. Now I have much more sympathy for the President— I don't think I could stand the strain of a job like that."

"Certainly, I think, the simulation project has served to give us a sharp and perhaps frightening look at some of the complexities involved in international decisions. As such, it serves a valuable function and should be continued as part of the curriculum."

"The basic problem of simulation is that there is no conscience in the game. The human element is not evident in the game and, therefore, there is nothing to stop a nation from being a warmonger. There are no compunctions in the game which may prevent constant war."

Aside from student motivation, a second observation (which has also been reported elsewhere) was the insight which the students received into foreign policy decision making. This was determined by asking students to react, before and after a simulation run, to a number of statements which expressed attitudes concerning international relations. It was noted whether post-test responses were more in agreement or disagreement with these statements. Chi-square analysis was used to determine the significance of changes.

With reference to decision-making attitudes, it was hypothesized that the students would favor a more centralized and efficient policy-making procedure and would appreciate to a greater degree the complexity of foreign policy decision making following the simulation. . . .

Although they are somewhat tenuous, two general attitude changes appeared. First, these students tended to value a decision-making process that was more centralized, following the simulation, by not favoring an increase in the role of Congress in the foreign policy-making process. Second, they displayed an increased recognition of the complexity of the foreign policy-making process. The responses . . . indicate that students seem less willing to generalize about international relations following the simulation than to adopt the view that each foreign policy problem should be decided on its own merit.

Simulation offers the students a grasp of the significant features of international relations because the model aspects of the simulation make it easier to understand than the real world, and because in the simulation the students were able to test information presented in lecture and discussion.

When asked what they considered to be the major features of their simulated nation-state system the students replied:

1. There is a general lack of trust between nations.
2. Sovereignty and competing national interests are the source of many international problems.
3. There is a tendency for nations to seek security through armaments and alliances.
4. Conflict frequently deteriorates into war.
5. International law as derived from international agreements breaks down when vital interests are endangered.
6. The difficulties of inter-nation communication and of securing accurate information upon which to base policy decisions are often quite formidable.

Although these items are not exhaustive, enough important characteristics of the present-day international system are included to indicate that these high school students have grasped some major features of international relations and have a realist frame of reference.

One might question whether the simulation was responsible for these attitudes or whether the students may have held these same attitudes before participating in the simulation. To ascertain whether students did acquire realist attitudes as a result of the simulation, several items in the attitude test instrument expressed idealist-moralist and realist positions.

These findings indicate that students do acquire realist attitudes toward international relations as a result of the simulation. [One statement] illustrates that the students do not value a policy merely because it might be categorized as "right." Thus, for example, the students will not flatly object to allying with dictators, but would favor such a policy to combat the more difficult problem of world communism. This is the position in which the United States finds itself in many parts of the world. In every case of a significant change of attitude the shift has always proceeded from a moralist-idealist position (which has been identified here as a tendency to generalize about international relations) to a realist position (which here has represented an attempt to be explicit about international affairs). It may be concluded, therefore, that the simulation in international relations at Lawrence High School tended to produce realistic attitudes toward international relations.

The results reported above, however, do not comprise an adequate evaluation of simulation. They indicate that attitudinal changes do seem to occur as a result of simulation but they do not determine the extent or persistence of these altered attitudes. Also, present research has not been able to establish the effect of simulation upon factual learning. Therefore, much research remains to be conducted on the pedagogical effects of simulation in addition to the systematic refinement of the simulation model.

The game does not reduce the work of the teacher. In some respects more is demanded, since the teacher must be alert to all of the events of the game in order that each development may be pointed out and student discussion guided into effective channels. The classroom introduction is also very important to the success of the simulation, for otherwise the students may approach the simulation merely as a game and little will be accomplished. Without good teacher supervision, simulation can contribute to classroom disorder, because it is unstructured and allows for greater individual freedom than do more traditional teaching methods. Properly administered, however, the simulation can provide an interesting and worthwhile departure from normal classroom procedures.

No claim is made that simulation is the total answer to instruction in international relations or the social studies generally. It must be combined with other classroom activities, such as lectures, class discussions, reading assignments, and even world area studies to obtain full educational benefits. However, simulation does arouse keen student interest and apparently tends to produce a pragmatic set of attitudes toward international relations. This is accomplished by involving the learner in a relatively new and exciting manner that conveys advanced political science theory to high school students.

5

Evaluating Students' Learning

THE PROBLEM OF EVALUATION IN THE SOCIAL STUDIES

Robert L. Ebel

Rarely has there been a more realistic, frank, sound, and skillful assessment of the status of evaluation in social studies than that in this selection. The author was invited to consult with a group of *teacher's working on one state's plans for the improvement of its social studies curriculum. What follow are his thoughts in regard to evaluating students' learning as related to the stated objectives.*

BOTH the maintenance of good educational programs and the improvement of educational procedures require good evaluation. Good evaluation, in turn, can only be made in relation to the goals of instruction. Too often when teachers make tests they forget their goals and remember only the subject matter they used in trying to achieve those goals.

I should warn you, however, that my answers to your question are going to be more complex and less satisfying than either you or I would wish them to be. The plain fact is that we do not have many evaluation instruments which will do the job you want done. What is even worse, our disappointing experience in trying to measure some of these outcomes is beginning to convince us that part of the job simply *cannot* be done. I even suspect that part of it *should* not be done. On the brighter side, there is much more we can do, and do better, than we are typically doing in evaluating student progress in the social studies.

Three broad categories of educational achievement are reflected in various degrees by the listed objectives:

1. Objectives primarily concerned with knowledge and understanding.
   A. Transmit our cultural heritage.
   B. Teach important historical facts and generalizations.

FROM *Social Education*, 24:6–10, January, 1960. Used by permission. Dr. Ebel, formerly Vice-President of Educational Testing Service, is a professor of education at Michigan State University.

  C. Teach time and space relationships.

  D. Acquaint students with basic historical references.

  E. Provide instruction and practice in locating information.

 2. Objectives primarily concerned with attitudes, values, and feelings.

  F. Promote moral and spiritual values.

  G. Promote the attitude that history is interesting and useful.

  H. Promote good mental health.

  I. Promote aesthetic sensitivities.

  J. Develop democratic citizenship.

 3. Objectives primarily concerned with instruction and practice in intellectual skills.

  K. Writing notes from lectures and references.

  L. Writing essay examinations

  M. Judging the validity of evidence.

  N. Drawing sound conclusions from data.

  O. Working in a group.

  P. Facility in oral expression.

The overlap among these three categories is substantial. Most of us have attitudes, feelings or values attached to much of the knowledge we possess. Conversely, most of our attitudes, feelings, and values have some basis in knowledge and understanding. Intellectual skills are heavily loaded with knowledge, and also have values attached to them. Thus some of the differences among the three categories are differences in the relative contributions of knowledge, feeling and practice to the attainment of the specific goals.

You may have noticed that my grouping omits entirely the second objective in your list, "Provide intellectual exercise for the discipline of the mind." The notion of mental discipline has been the target of considerable psychological criticism. Its most naive form, which assumes that the mind is analogous to a muscle that can be strengthened by exercise in learning anything, especially something difficult to learn, has been generally discredited. Even the notions of general mental *functions* such as memory, reasoning, and will, which were supposed to be separate faculties independent of mental content, have been generally discarded. Modern studies of human and animal learning, and of brain function, suggest that the mind guides behavior by serving as a semiautomatic ready-reference storehouse of ideas derived from experience and reflection. The effectiveness of a mind seems to depend on how many of these ideas are stored in it, how accurately they represent the world outside the mind, and how easily they can be made available for recall and recombination when the occasion demands.

If by intellectual exercise is meant increasing the store of ideas, and if by discipline of the mind is meant improved accuracy and increased integration of these ideas, then this is indeed an important objective—so important, in fact, that it encompasses most of the others. If this is not what is meant, some further clarification may be required. In any case, I cannot suggest any tests which might be used to make a separate evaluation of it.

KNOWLEDGE AND UNDERSTANDING

For the measurement of knowledge and understanding in the social studies a number of excellent tests are available. The Cooperative Test Division of the Educational Testing Service offers social studies tests in its series of Sequential Tests of Educational Progress, and in its end-of-course achievement tests. The World Book Company offers tests in world history and in American history as parts of its Evaluation and Adjustment series. Science Research Associates distributes the test of Understanding of Basic Social Concepts from the Iowa Tests of Educational Development. Oscar Buros' *Fifth Mental Measurements Yearbook* (1) lists sixty tests in the social studies, with critical reviews of twenty-three of them. Not all of the tests listed are of high quality. The reviewers are rather critical of some. While the reader must occasionally discount the idiosyncrasies of particular reviewers, their comments are usually unbiased and always informative. This is the best available guide to educational tests of all kinds. It should be consulted by anyone who seeks better tests for specific goals.

You may have hoped for a more specific recommendation of a few tests exactly suited to measure achievement of the goals you listed. Unfortunately, this is not possible. In only a few cases have these particular goals been made the focus of specific test construction efforts. Even if tests of each goal were available, it is unlikely that the test author would conceive of these goals precisely as you do. So many facts and ideas are involved in our cultural heritage, and there are so many different value judgments that can be made of them that tests from different sources are almost certain to differ widely. Hence, even in this easiest area of educational measurement, you are not likely to find ready-made tests to meet your needs.

What, then, is to be done? One solution is to make tests of your own, based on a very specific definition of each goal in the area of knowledge and understanding. This is a difficult task. In the absence of substantial expert assistance (and liberal finances) it is not likely to be done very successfully.

Another solution is to get along with the published tests that come closest to covering the goals as you have defined them. This will be cheaper, and cost less effort, but may not be any more satisfactory in the end. What is really needed, it seems to me, is some nationwide effort by social studies teachers and other educators to agree on a definition of basic goals in this and other areas of common educational concern. Then the effort to build really good tests of the agreed upon goals would be justified, and we would have a means for making sound evaluations of the achievement of our common goals. Unless a teacher foolishly devoted his whole teaching to the attainment of these common goals, completely suppressing his own special interests and disregarding local conditions and individual pupil needs, this would place no straitjacket on the curriculum. But if we are committed to the defense of the freedom of states, schools, teachers, or even pupils, to define all their own goals in whatever way they think best, then the task of getting meaningful measures of the degree of achievement of these diverse goals becomes almost impossible. The price we pay for what may be an excess of freedom seems rather high.

ATTITUDES, VALUES, AND FEELINGS

Adequate measurement of achievement toward goals in the realm of attitudes, values and feelings present other, and still more difficult, problems. There is the problem of getting agreement on a clear definition of just what is meant by "democratic citizenship" or "aesthetic sensitivities." There is the problem of obtaining valid indications of the students' true attitudes, values and feelings. Direct questions in a test situation indicate mainly how the student thinks he *ought* to feel. Indirect, disguised tests are often low in relevance and reliability. The instability of pupil behavior from time to time and from situation to situation makes any single observation quite limited in significance. Finally, it is very difficult to create a test situation which is realistic enough to give valid indication of a student's probable behavior in a natural nontest situation.

For these reasons, good tests in the area of attitudes, values and feelings are quite rare. I know of none in the realm of moral and spiritual values. Remmers' multipurpose instrument, *A Scale for Measuring Attitude Toward Any School Subject*, might be used to reflect general attitudes toward history, but probably would not indicate specifically the students' attitudes of interest in history and appreciation of its usefulness, and possibly not the students' genuine attitudes. Good mental health is a complex, poorly defined concept. Clinical diagnosis is the best basis for estimating mental health, and even that leaves much to be desired. There are tests of specific kinds of aesthetic sensitivity in art, music, and literature. I wonder if these kinds of aesthetic sensitivity are commonly regarded as goals for a course in the social studies? If not, the concept of aesthetic sensitivity may require further definition. Even when so defined, I doubt that we could do more than measure knowledge of aesthetic principles. There are some tests of civic knowledge. There have been some attempts to predict good civic behavior, but here again the problems of trait definition and test validity have been so troublesome that no existing test can be recommended.

This lack of good, ready-made instruments is bad enough. What is even more discouraging is the lack of any promising techniques for the measurements of attitudes, feelings and values. It is gradually becoming apparent that the difficulties of measuring these traits with paper-and-pencil tests are inherent in the nature of the traits, and in the limitations of formal, written tests. Techniques of testing which are reasonably effective in measuring knowledge and understanding may never be even passably effective in measuring an individual person's attitudes, values and feelings simply because these are specific to situations which cannot be realistically reproduced by any test. Further, deficiencies in these traits can easily be hidden from the prying questions of the tester, behind a mask of conventionally correct responses.

Does this mean that teachers should abandon the pursuit of goals in this area? To some extent, yes. Many widely approved goals with respect to attitudes, values and feelings are generally acceptable only when they are left undefined. What consensus could we get in defining the activities of a good citizen, or the nature of ideal spiritual values? People in different localities, and of different political, religious, or philosophical persuasions would define them quite differently. Is tolerance a virtue or a fault? No teachers can avoid influencing pupils to adopt his own particular attitudes and values, but I doubt that these should become formal goals of teaching, or objects for testing, unless they are the predominant view of the culture, or unless they can be supported as rational consequences of valid knowledge about the world and man.

This suggests that of some of our attitudes, values and feelings are determined by the knowledge we possess. I am persuaded that this cognitive basis for feelings is very influential, and that it constitutes a proper and productive focus for teaching and for testing. Consider the goal of good mental health. How can a teacher promote good mental health? One way is to understand mental hygiene and the causes of mental illness well enough so that most of his acts in dealing with students tend to improve rather than impair the student's (and the teacher's) mental health. Another is to teach a knowledge and an understanding of mental health to the students themselves. Good tests of this kind of knowledge can be built. But no paper-and-pencil test is likely to do an adequate job of assessing mental health or diagnosing mental illness. That is a task for the specialist who knows how to use complex clinical procedures.

Similarly, one could build good tests of knowledge about good citizenship, about aesthetics, about moral and spiritual values and about the uses of history. Imparting of relevant knowledge does not guarantee development of desired attitudes, values and feelings, but it surely must contribute substantially to their development.

The chief alternative to the development of desirable attitudes, values and feelings via knowledge is to develop them by indoctrination or conditioning. Many of our most cherished feelings were developed in this way. As children we learned acceptable social behavior largely through a complex system of rewards and punishments, and only secondarily on the basis of rational understanding of the *why* of the correct form (if indeed it was rational!). Indoctrination is almost the only way of teaching very young children, but it becomes progressively less necessary and less desirable as their minds develop. It is a more appropriate technique in the home than in the school. I seriously doubt that teachers, especially teachers of the social studies at the high school level and beyond, should intentionally have much to do with indoctrination or conditioning. Their attempts to develop desirable, attitudes, values and feelings should have mainly a cognitive, rational base, depending on knowledge and understanding.

This emphasis on knowledge, rather than on attitudes, values and feelings, troubles some teachers greatly. Knowledge alone is not enough, they say. It is what a person does with his knowledge that counts. . . . But . . . [it is erroneous, I think, to] assume that instances of misbehavior are caused mainly by deficiencies in attitudes, values and feelings which the school could correct if it only would try hard enough. Character traits are important determinants of behavior, but so are environmental circumstances. Teachers err if they assume that character is largely independent of knowledge, or that the same techniques of teaching and testing that have served for knowledge will serve also for attitudes, values and feelings. There is little in the experience of teachers or testers to support such assumptions. To evaluate individual achievement in these noncognitive areas we may have to settle for measurement of relevant knowledge of how one ought to feel. We do not yet have good tests to do even this job, but we know how to make them.

For the rest of our evaluation of typical behavior, as influenced by attitudes, values and feelings, we may have to rely on systematic but informal observation of pupil behavior in real, nontest situations. This does not relieve us of defining clearly the traits we wish to observe. It does not promise to yield reliable measurements with little effort. But techniques for observing and recording typical behavior seem to offer more promise than any test-like instrument designed to probe a student's attitudes, values and feelings.

Nearly thirty years ago, Truman L. Kelly, writing on "Objective Measurement of the Outcomes of the Social Studies," stressed the importance of attitudes. (2) His emphasis on developing the basic determinants of behavior, rather than its superficial manifestations, seems eminently reasonable, and he said many true and wise things in supporting his thesis. Social studies teachers could profit much from rereading his words today. He recognized the difficulties of measuring attitudes but was confident that these *could be* overcome, if only because they *had to be* overcome.

Today many of us are less sanguine. The experience of thirty years of generally unproductive efforts are beginning to convince us that we have set ourselves an impossible task, like squaring the circle of building a perpetual motion machine. Kelley himself later reported the unsuccessful outcome of an "Experimental Study of Three Character Traits Needed in a Democratic Social Order." (3) He commented, "This study emphasized the universal difficulty which has been experienced by those who have endeavored to obtain objective character measures of school children." But he did not lose faith in eventual success, ". . . for it still seemed practically axiomatic that traits of character and attitudes and interests are essential determiners of human conduct, independent of intellectual, sensory, and motor abilities and attainments."

Since 1942 an enormous amount of work has been done on personality testing. A great many tests have been developed. Some interesting findings have been reported, and some interesting theories proposed. But much of what goes on in the name of personality assessment is not much better than horoscope casting or tea leaf reading. We still have no personality test of demonstrated value that is practically useful in measuring the effectiveness of learning or teaching in the classroom. We may never have. It may be that our search for the "structure" of personality, and our attempts to "measure" its dimensions will be as fruitless as previous attempts to find the fountain of youth, or the philosopher's stone. Perhaps the problem needs to be reformulated. It may be that the really basic, stable determinants of behavior, so far as behavior is internally determined, are not attitudes, values and feelings, but ideas—rational, cognitive, teachable, testable.

INTELLECTUAL SKILLS

The third category of goals was concerned mainly with intellectual skills. Here again there are no good, ready-made tests that can be recommended. To the extent that these skills rest on knowledge—and this is a considerable extent—they can be tested by conventional paper-and-pencil tests. To the extent that they rest on facility gained through practice, performance tests judged with the help of rating scales offer the most promise. The best solution may be a combination of knowledge and performance tests as a basis for evaluating skills in note taking, essay examination writing, effective group participation, and oral expression.

There are two objectives in this area—judging the validity of evidence and drawing conclusions from data—that may be so greatly conditioned by a student's background knowledge that the influence of generalized skill on his behavior may be relatively unimportant. I wonder if there are broadly applicable rules for judging the validity of evidence, principles which do not depend on the particular nature of the evidence under consideration. I wonder if the interpretation of data is an abstract procedure, like the diagraming of a sentence, that can be applied with reasonable uniformity to all kinds of data. If so, knowledge about these rules and procedures can be taught and tested *as abstract principles*. But I am persuaded that attempts to test these skills by asking a student to judge specific evidence or interpret specific data will reveal mainly how much he already knows about the source of the evidence or data, its meaning, and the problem to which it applies. In short, I wonder if these are important enough as abstract skills to deserve the status of goals of instruction.

RECOMMENDATIONS

What, then, would I recommend for the evaluation of student progress toward the goals of teaching in the social studies?

First, that goals be defined specifically enough so that one can judge how satisfactory a given test will be.

Second, that goals which cannot be defined specifically and with general acceptability, or which hypothesize traits of dubious independence from other more obvious and easily measurable traits, be eliminated or de-emphasized.

Third, that goals which have statewide or nationwide, not just local, validity be emphasized.

Fourth, that command over essential knowledge be emphasized as a primary goal of instruction, even in the areas of attitudes, values, feelings and intellectual skills.

Fifth, that social studies teachers continue to search for, or to construct, evaluation instruments of acceptable validity in terms of specifically defined goals.

Sixth, that the *Mental Measurements Yearbook* be consulted for guidance in judging the usefulness of available tests.

Seventh, that social studies teachers recognize and accept the necessity of building some new tests, whose quality will depend on how much effort and money they are prepared to spend on them, and on how much expert help they get and accept in creating them.

That I have completed this discussion without clearly recommending a single specific test for you to use is something I regret very much. It reflects the complexity of some problems of educational measurement. Even more, it reflects our failure to be realistic in setting our goals, and to be objective and precise in defining them. I am persuaded that the main reason why educational measurement sometimes seems inadequate is that we persist in setting impossible tasks for it to do. But I am also persuaded that if we concentrate on the right problems, and work on them energetically and intelligently, we can improve educational measurement substantially.

(1) Highland Park, New Jersey: The Gryphon Press, 1959.
(2) *Historical Outlook* 21:66–72; 1930.
(3) *Harvard Educational Review* 12:294–322; 1942.

SUGGESTIONS FOR CONSTRUCTING TESTS OF STUDY SKILLS AND CRITICAL THINKING

Horace T. Morse and George H. McCune

The increasing attention paid the development of students' study skills in social studies has led to greater interest in testing their growth in these skills. This selection, from the introduction to a popular bulletin listing many hundreds of such test items as examples, furnishes helpful suggestions for constructing and using such test items. The writers provide also specific reminders of additional (nontesting) procedures for evaluating students' learning skills.

CERTAIN precautions must be followed in making and using study skills test items beyond those ordinarily followed with objective-type achievement test items. It may be helpful to pass along a few suggestions to teachers who wish to construct items of their own for classroom use. These precautions are therefore indicated below in abbreviated form. . . .

1. Directions should be particularly clear and explicit. The form of the exercises may be new to the pupils, or familiar forms may require a somewhat different type of response. It is probably desirable to discuss with a class the necessity for a clear understanding and following of directions before papers containing the test items are distributed.

2. Sufficient time should be allowed pupils to enable them to complete the exercises. Since these involve thought process, responses cannot be reduced to the automatic level of memorized factual information. A study skills test should not be a time test.

3. If factual information is necessary in part to respond correctly to an item, such information should be provided in the item itself. Depending on the maturity and background of a particular class, however, the possession of some common factual information may be assumed. Information in this category might be, for instance, that America was settled by colonists from Western Europe, that the Catholic church is the oldest organized Christian church, and that during the last hundred years or so there have been two major political parties in the United States.

FROM *Selected Items for the Testing of Study Skills and Critical Thinking* by Horace T. Morse and George H. McCune, Bulletin No. 15, Washington, D.C.: National Council for the Social Studies, pp. 20–24. Used by permission. Dr. Morse is dean and Dr. McCune a professor at the General College, University of Minnesota.

4. Items should be phrased so that they are readily understood, and are clear as to what type of response is required. Some check on word frequency by reference to lists of such frequencies would be desirable to be sure that a pupil's possible lack of understanding of a technical or unusual word does not invalidate the item for him.

5. Study skills exercises are probably best if confined to a general area, such as social studies or natural sciences. Some tests are available which are designed to test critical thinking as a general ability, but experimental evidence would seem to indicate that there is not a high correlation between critical thinking in different areas.

6. On the other hand critical thinking is a complicated process, so that a variety of approaches must be taken to measure it in its various aspects. It involves a number of mental processes such as the ability to evaluate, analyze, synthesize, and make new relationships. Therefore no single type of item can be said to be sufficient for testing critical skills, and probably they are best determined by subjective as well as objective means. A paper-and-pencil test measures performance on the test only, and successful test performance would not necessarily mean that the pupil was accustomed to *use* critical skills in a real-life situation.

7. The best educational use of items devised to test study skills is for diagnostic purposes. Their administration should be merely a prelude to classroom discussion which would provide opportunities for pupils to learn more about critical thinking by discussing with each other and the teacher the reasons for making responses as they did. Such tests should never be given as a "final examination," but should be regarded as *exercises* rather than as exact measuring instruments.

OTHER METHODS OF TESTING FOR SKILLS

There are numerous ways to test study skills besides setting up a series of objective test items. In the list at the end of this section, several suggestions are offered to teachers about other methods of testing study skills. The methods are difficult or unwieldy as a basis for the construction of objective test items, although they lend themselves readily to development in individual classrooms. Materials which are immediately available to any particular class are often most suitable for use in constructing exercises of the types described. One of the most fruitful sources of supply would be a local newspaper or the published reports of local institutions, such as the city government, utility companies, or industrial or mercantile concerns. . . .

The alert teacher will construct items with data of his own selection, possibly using the items presented as a basis for form, or will construct different forms which may seem more suitable for the particular material or purpose. He may also foster the development of additional study skills and critical abilities by intelligent adaptation of the exercises suggested below.

1. *Outlining.* Students may be assigned to prepare an outline of some portion of the text, and be given a limited amount of time, such as five minutes. Outlines may then be compared and criticized in regard to form, content, clarity, and completeness. The assignment may be to prepare a detailed study outline, as for reference purposes, or merely a brief sketch outline of main points.

2. *Summarizing.* Students may read a paragraph new to them and then write a summary of it. This may vary from practice in writing a single-sentence summary to a more extended one. When students have finished, their summaries should be discussed and compared in the light of the material in the original paragraph.

3. *Constructing graphs.* The same statistical information may be represented by a variety of graph forms. The teachers may conduct a class exercise or assign as individual projects the conversion of data presented in tabular form into different graphical representations, such as circle, bar, or line. If statistical information is found in descriptive rather than tabular form the process may be carried all the way through from tabulation to construction of one or more graphs.

4. *Taking notes from a speech.* The teacher may suggest that students take notes or an outline of a speech which is to be delivered over the radio or television and which students will have the opportunity to hear outside of school hours. Outlines and notes may then be brought to class for discussion and criticism. The teacher may wish to give a brief lecture which has been clearly organized, and by an examination of pupil's notes diagnose the difficulties they may be having in getting proper perspective, relationship, and form.

5. *Visualizing from a written description.* The teacher may locate a page or so in the text which gives a definite description of a battlefield or a settler's cabin. Students may try to draw a floor plan of the cabin, for instance, including all the furniture mentioned in the description in its proper place. They may then check with each other's plans for the purpose of improving their own or criticizing the given description for lack of clarity or definiteness.

6. *Visualizing from an oral description.* A situation similar to the previous one may be set up, except that the teacher or one of the pupils may read a description from some source with which the pupils are not familiar. They may then try to sketch out the plan of whatever is contained in the description and compare papers afterward for discussion.

7. *Observing.* The class may observe a picture in the text or in the classroom and then list individually how many facts can be observed or inferred from the picture about the historical scene or background which it represents.

8. *Reading.* Students may read a paragraph from the text—then close their books and recall such data as facts, generalizations, arguments, and

illustrations given in the paragraph. This should be a paragraph which the students have not seen previously.

There are many other activities fostering desirable skills which may be developed in a similar fashion. A few in addition to those described above may be listed specifically:

9. *Interpreting cartoons.*
10. *Following directions.*
11. *Participating in panel discussions.*
12. *Taking part in a debate.*
13. *Planning and taking part in dramatic activities.*
14. *Planning trips, diaries, letters, news items, etc.*
15. *Map making.*
16. *Drawing cartoons and posters.*
17. *Constructing models.*
18. *Classifying collections of specimens.*
19. *Planning and preparing exhibits.*
20. *Participating in a mock trial or pantomime.*
21. *Interpreting charts, diagrams, and tables.*
22. *Interpreting maps.*
23. *Analyzing pictures.*
24. *Analyzing tape recordings.*
25. *Evaluating critically models and realia.*
26. *Taking part in an interview.*
27. *Classifying items in a list.*
28. *Performing experiments.*
29. *Making a survey in the community.*
30. *Evaluating events in history.*
31. *Applying principles to new situations.*
32. *Synthesizing from a body of data.*

A wealth of additional suggestive material may be found in comprehensive lists of desirable social studies activities published in one form or another accessible to most social studies teachers. . . .

EVALUATING THE JURISPRUDENTIAL APPROACH TO SOCIAL STUDIES

Donald W. Oliver and James P. Shaver

As is increasingly recognized, an accurate and objective appraisal of students' learning is difficult, complex, and often unattainable. The barriers to successful evaluation should not becloud its desirability. Educators must advance their efforts if improvements are to be made. A useful example of some of the

FROM *The High School Journal*, 46:55–56, 62–63, November, 1962. Used by permission. Dr. Shaver is a professor of education at Utah State University; Dr. Oliver is identified on page 99.

kinds of complexity that may be encountered appears in this selection. The instructional approach is described in an article on pages 99–105 of this volume. *Omitted here is a considerable portion of the description and analysis in the article from which this extract was taken.*

W E have attempted to translate the objectives of jurisprudential teaching into specific learning outcomes which can be described and identified more precisely. It is this . . . effort that we shall describe briefly in this paper. Before doing so, however, we should clarify two points. First, we make no pretense that these outcomes constitute an exhaustive inventory of reflective thinking concepts or skills. Second, they are not general critical or reflective thinking outcomes in the sense that they apply to any content; we are concerned only with their appropriateness in teaching students how to deal with political controversy within the framework of the Western political tradition.

OPERATIONAL OBJECTIVES OF A JURISPRUDENTIAL SOCIAL STUDIES CURRICULUM

A student should be able to:

1. Deal with political controversy at a general analytic level and relate his analysis to specific issues and concrete cases. For example, in a case involving the arrest of a sidewalk orator, the student should see that certain general values are involved, e.g. freedom of speech, the peace and safety of the community, and the property rights of nearby shoppers. If the orator is said to be creating a disturbance, the student should see that the term "disturbance" is a relatively vague one which creates definitional problems. He should see that the assertion about the speech causing a disturbance requires greater specification. Thinking about a particular case in terms of such issues as defining "disturbance" and "free speech," we think, allows the student to deal with the case at two levels: he identifies general problems inherent in this kind of case, and then places the facts of this case within the context of these more general problems.

2. Identify inconsistencies and conflicts between two or more values, empirical statements, or definitions.

3. Deal with inconsistencies and conflicts between values by identifying an array of situations in which the inconsistent or conflicting values are presented in varying degrees of favorableness or unfavorableness in order to delineate at what point he should support one value as against the other. For example, we might support free speech over peace and order if the only danger involved was a sidewalk disturbance. We might

however, reverse our position if such speeches were inflaming riots or an insurrection.

4. Deal with inconsistencies and conflicts between empirical statements by seeking and evaluating specific evidence to support the statements.

5. Deal with the inconsistent or ambiguous use of words by seeking evidence concerning how the words are most commonly used, or how the concepts which the words label may be most accurately described.

6. Distinguish between those factual claims which are relevant to the central value issues in a controversy and those claims which bear little or no relationship to the value.

The level of specificity with which these operations are stated above, we think, makes the problem of assessing a student's ability to perform any of them less difficult than assessing whether or not a student has learned to use some general process called "critical thinking" or "problem solving." Even with generality and ambiguity reduced, however, many problems of measurement remain.

THE ASSESSMENT OF LEARNING OUTCOMES

We have tried a number of ways of translating these learning outcomes into measurable units. All start at the same point. We ask the student to read and analyze, either by himself or in a group, a controversial political situation— a controversial case. In one approach, we then give the student specific statements in the argument, either in written or oral form, and ask him what function they serve. Do they for example, transform the case into a more general problem, or continue to deal with it as an isolated instance of personal conflict? A second approach is to take statements made in the argument, and ask the student to rebut them. This can be done either with open-ended questions, or by presenting series of five or six rebuts from which he is to choose the best and/or the worst.

The approach we have found the most promising, however, is the systematic analysis and categorization of statements made in oral discussions. Some advantages to this approach are obvious. The oral discussion is a more natural situation in which to ascertain the analytical skills of the student. (How many students write about political questions after they leave school?) The oral discussion also provides the student with less structure than objective pencil-and-paper tests. In critical thinking tests of the latter type, for example, the student is commonly presented with a message, parts of which are abstracted for analysis. He is then asked to deal only with these parts in his response, which is already restricted by a multiple choice set. The student thus has a very narrow range of behavior within which he can choose. In the open discussion, however, he must select relevant parts of the controversial case and the ensuing discussion with which to deal. He is thus forced to select from a much broader range of alternative responses which he must create for himself.

This last "advantage" of systematic content analysis is, of course, also its greatest difficulty. Because there is such a wide range of alternative responses which the student can make, all types of responses must be anticipated so that they can be evaluated and scored. Instead of a simple key to a test, the scorer finds himself with a long and complex manual in which hundreds of types of responses may be described and classified. Because of this complexity, scoring is difficult, requiring a long training period. Furthermore the scoring process itself is less reliable. . . .

As an example of the systematic content analysis approach, we should like to present a set of categories we have worked out and used to evaluate the student's ability to handle controversial political issues. . . .

CHART 1—DYNAMIC CATEGORIES

CONFLICT-CONSISTENCY: Statements that indicate explicitly or implicitly that the speaker is aware of a real or possible inconsistency within his own or another speaker's position.

SPECIFICATION and GENERALIZATION: Specification occurs when the speaker gives a specific statement to illustrate or support a more general statement. Generalization occurs when the speaker draws a more general conclusion from one or more specific statements already given.

Example of specification: "Desegregation is not going well. Only 7% of the Negro children in the South are now going to integrated schools after seven years of illegal segregation." The second sentence would be scored as the static operation "specific claim" and the dynamic operation "specification."

Example of a generalization: "After World War II, Russia captured the countries of eastern Europe, helped China to become a Communist nation, and tried its best to take over Greece and Turkey. Russia is the greatest imperialistic nation the world has ever known." Statement two would be scored as a static operation "general claim," and a dynamic operation "generalization."

QUALIFYING: A statement which deals with an implicit or explicit inconsistency or conflict by pointing out under what general circumstances an exception to a general principle is allowable or possible we score as a qualifying act.

Example: Mr. A: Our civil liberties are our most precious asset. To try and restrict them for any citizen is un-American.

Mr. B: If you had been in Germany in the early 1930's, would you have restricted some of the civil liberties granted Hitler when he was conducting mass hate meetings.

Mr. A: I very well might have. I would say that civil liberties should be restricted, however, only when the government which is pledged to protect them is in real danger from an undemocratic and brutal force, which would destroy all civil liberties.

Mr. A's modified position would be scored as static operation "general value judgment," and dynamic operation "qualification."

CHART 2—STATIC CATEGORIES

GENERAL VALUE JUDGMENTS: Statements in which the speaker expresses a preference for a person, object or position in the argument in terms of a general social or legal value, such as: personal privacy, property, contract, speech, religion, general welfare of the group, equality, justice, brotherhood, due process, consent and representations. "Mr. Kohler certainly should have the right to run his property and to make contracts with his workers without union interference."

SPECIFIC VALUE JUDGMENTS: Statements in which the speaker expresses a preference for a person, object or position in the argument in terms of the specific case under discussion. "I think Mr. Kohler should have met the demands of the United Auto Workers."

GENERAL LEGAL CLAIM: Statements in which the speaker asserts that someone has a legal right to do something, expressed in terms of a general legal principle, such as: rule of law, due process, equal protection under the law, constitutional restraints, etc. "He has a right to a fair trial under the United States Constitution."

SPECIFIC LEGAL CLAIM: Statements in which the speaker asserts that someone has a legal right to do something, but does not give a legal principle as a basis for the right. "Mr. Kohler has a right to fire any worker he wants."

GENERAL FACTUAL CLAIMS: Causal, descriptive, or predictive generalizations. "Negroes are just as intelligent as whites."

SPECIFIC FACTUAL CLAIMS: Statements describing specific events delineated in time and space. "The first attempt at integration in Little Rock was on September 4, 1957."

SOURCE: A statement or part of a statement describing the source on which a claim, definition or value judgment is based. "Emergency is defined this way in *Webster's New International Dictionary*."

DEFINITIONAL CLAIM: A statement about how a word or phase is defined or should be defined. It is also a statement of analysis by which several meanings of a single word might be distinguished. "An emergency occurs when one or more people are in danger of being injured or losing their lives and property."

CLARIFICATION: A statement in which the speaker communicates something already stated in order to focus the discussion. It may include single repetition, in that saying something again may emphasize or clarify a person's position.

CASE: A set of statements which describes specific real or hypothetical situations analogous to the one under discussion. Its main purpose is to elaborate the range of situations to which one might apply a value judgment. "Suppose Negroes and whites were given schools of equal quality, teachers of equal quality, books and educational facilities of equal quality: Would Negro schools still be inferior to white schools?"

RELEVANCE: A statement which explicitly deals with the way a statement or group of statements is related to the total argument. "I don't see what that statement has to do with the discussion."

DEBATE STRATEGY: *Ad hominem* or other remarks which explicitly discuss the tactics being used by the opponent. "You're just trying to confuse me."

TASK PROBLEM: PROCEDURAL: A statement directed at controlling the immediate interpersonal situation, and which assumes that everyone in the discussion is trying to do a conscientious job. "Let's take a vote." "Let's give everyone a chance to talk."

TASK PROBLEM: DEVIANCE COUTROL: A statement directed at controlling the immediate interpersonal situation, and assuming that one or more people are violating group norms. "Get back in your seat and sit down." "You don't have to shout."

PART FIVE
USING LEARNING RESOURCES EFFECTIVELY

For too many years the social studies have struggled along in too many, perhaps most, schools with a paucity of instructional resources. Rapid growth of the American economy, expanded production and availability of varied educational materials and equipment, and exploding knowledge in the social sciences have had too few direct counterparts in the form of increased sources of information provided to students. Fortunately, the situation has begun to change. Many teachers are alert to the existence of new materials and are often able to secure them for instructional use. Producers are giving significant, if still too limited, attention to trends in the social studies. Social scientists are entering increasingly into the authorship or editing of classroom material. Matching federal funds are improving the ability of schools to purchase material for some areas of social studies instruction.

The following selections provide an overview of what is available and offer suggestions for the effective use of materials. Several writers make critical analyses of the adequacy of resources available and used—the place of the textbook in social studies instruction, for example, is regarded from varying viewpoints. Other authors deal with the question of how to make the most effective use of reading materials generally. The status and the basic nature of programed material for social studies are also considered.

Has real progress been made in the production of audiovisual aids in social studies? Can the teaching of map interpretation be improved and, if so, how? Is educational television basically a valuable aid or an overrated resource? Can the practical problems involved in use of ETV be overcome? What kinds of classrooms and classroom equipment are needed for instruction that makes maximum use of learning resources? Are community resources outdated as instructional aids, or do they still have value for students in high school social studies? Answers to such questions, suggested by the following readings, should help the teacher become a more effective guide to students' learning. Additional guidance to instructional material appears in the Appendix.

1

Learning Through Printed and
Programed Materials

MAKING HISTORY LIVE
THROUGH READING

Helen McCracken Carpenter and Mary Virginia Gaver

If there is any "royal road to learning" in social studies, it is probably most feasibly traversed by reading. Today's teacher finds much expanded opportunity to help students along this road as the supply of appropriate printed materials continues to increase. There are difficulties, of course, in keeping up with the rapid output of the printing presses and in choosing and securing the materials desired. Fortunately, guidance is available in the professional literature. A prime example is this description of recent materials for students of American history.

OURS is an era increasingly conscious of its past. This characteristic became discernible as the twentieth century moved into its second quarter and the years since have witnessed a quickening interest in Americana. Like the history of many inventions, the idea of the restored community took root simultaneously in more than one place in the mid-twenties. Decorah, Iowa, began the reconstruction of a frontier village as the Williamsburg Restoration was yielding its first fruits. Today there are over thirty restored communities east of the Mississippi alone. In addition, the reconstruction of single historical sites dot our land from fort Mackinac on the north to The Alamo on the south—from the Spanish missions along the Pacific to Fort Sumter and the Saugus Ironworks on the Atlantic Coast. It is a rare teacher in this age of rapid transportation who does not have access to some restorations of our past.

FROM *Interpreting and Teaching American History*, William H. Cartwright and Richard L. Watson, eds., Washington, D.C.: National Council for the Social Studies, 1964, pp. 398–404. Used by permission. Dr. Gaver is a professor of library service at Rutgers University; for biographical note on Dr. Carpenter, see page 3.

The long list of pageants and celebrations presented each summer across our land, commemorating historic events of the locality, further attest our consciousness of the nation's development. The opening of Freedomland indicates that this interest is sufficient to make the re-creation of dramatic events commercially profitable.

Congress, too, recognized the importance of preserving important primary sources when it authorized the establishment of the National Archives and, more recently, of libraries for the papers of each President beginning with Mr. Truman.

Further evidence of the popular appeal of historical themes is to be found in statistics on book production. In the decade between 1946 and 1957, the number of titles in history, and the sister area of geography increased more than one-hundred fifty per cent. No other fields except agriculture and science, exhibited so marked a rise. (1) In children's book publishing, during the same decade, science showed the greatest gain in number of titles, followed in turn by biography and then history and geography. (2) The phenomenal popular reception accorded *American Heritage, The Magazine of History*, since 1954 has pertinency in this connection also.

In addition to the numerous advantages accruing from a dawning awareness of our nation's heritage, the teacher has available today better and more varied materials prepared for school use than ever before. The format of the modern textbook with its use of multiple color, photographic illustrations and devices to intrigue the listless would fulfill Noah Webster's most ecstatic dreams. Nor would this scholarly propagandist for American history be likely to contend that his classic *American Selections* met the needs of its age as well as the content of contemporary texts serves the needs of today. To dramatize, illustrate, and supplement the written word the new medium of recordings exists in abundance and variety. In the past decade the production of both documentary and dramatic sound films has increased at an encouraging rate. The availability of some television programs dealing with historical subjects on film is a fortuitous development for the teacher. The appearance during the 'fifties of plastic maps and globes molded to contour can help make the geographical setting of events more meaningful. The production of inexpensive facsimiles of official papers, letters, money, and correspondence is growing apace and providing the teacher with a new kind of *realia*. As might be expected, in each of these different media more items are being produced dealing with the growth of the United States than with the development of non-American nations. . . .

READING IS GAINING GROUND

Another source of optimism for the teacher, at least at the secondary level where reading constitutes the chief avenue of learning, is heartening evidence that teenagers are reading more books and more difficult books than in decades past. A recent survey of seventy-three school and university libraries and state library commissions across the United States reveals a teenage rush to adult books. In New York City, for example, the 13 to 18 year-olds account for a fourth to a half of the book circulation of adult departments in the branches of the public library. In Reading, Pennsylvania, where population increased little in the two decades between 1938 and 1958, book circulation to young people increased substantially, with a rise in nonfiction from 49,000 to 92,000 and for fiction from 68,500 to 91,250. In Lincoln, Nebraska, population during the 1950's rose thirty per cent but book circulation climbed one-hundred per cent. Increased borrowing by teenagers constituted a noticeable trend. (3) Although statistics are not available to prove it conclusively, librarians assert that works of nonfiction are beginning to outstrip those of fiction in popularity among young people. (4)

The efforts of those outside the academic field to aid in the promotion of reading among children and youth is an encouraging sign of the times which redounds to the benefit of all teachers, including those in American history. The decision of *This Week* magazine to undertake a quarterly feature beginning in September 1960, reporting data from high schools and public libraries under the heading "What Young Americans Are Reading" both reflects the upsurge in reading and also serves to stimulate further book consumption among teenagers. The current community service project of the United States Junior Chamber of Commerce, "Good Reading for Youth," focused on children from five to fifteen is a substantial undertaking with benefits accruing to the 3800 communities which have local chapters. The project includes surveys of the availability of books and knowledge about them, the dissemination of good reading lists, a film on the importance of reading and a traveling book exhibit of four hundred titles. The project is being cosponsored by the Pilgrim Book Society and will have the assistance of professional librarians.

Recent trends in books for children and young adults both mirror and bring to focus these developments in our society. The teacher, hoping to initiate or to keep pace with a reading boom among students, needs to be aware of the trends. The 1950's witnessed the revival and phenomenal growth of publishers' series. Some observers consider this the major trend in children's publishing since World War II although it is not limited to children's books. Series books as developed during the past decade meet uniform standards in format, are written by different authors on different but often related subjects, and are issued by the same publisher under a series name. The practice of publishing books in series received renewed impetus in 1950 with the appearance of the first volumes in the Landmark Books of Random House. Sales of this series alone have totalled more than ten million copies. (5) It is the sole source of selections for the Junior Book-of-the-Month Club. The series field is, however, increasingly competitive. By 1952, ninety-three series were identifiable from the presses of thirty-six publishers. Early in 1958 the number had risen to 148 series from fifty-four publishers (6) and new ones continue to appear. Most of the series books are nonfiction, with American history and heroes serving more frequently than any other emphasis for subject material. The focus of the Landmark Books is entirely that. Other examples of series in which aspects of Americana receive prominent if not total attention include *The Real Books* of Garden City Press; *The First Books* by Watts; *The Signature Books* by Grosset and Dunlap; *The American Heritage Books* by American Book; *The Strength-of-Union Series* by Scribner; and *The American Heritage Junior Library Books* from the Golden Press. The trend is discernible likewise in material for young adults as *Great Lives in Brief* by Knopf, the *American Heritage Series* from the Sagamore Press and the *Rivers of America Series* issued by Rinehart indicate. Clearly the series has become a marketing device. As such it has resulted, unfortunately, in production and consumption that is not always discriminating. A series mark is no guarantee of uniform quality. Within each of the series now deluging the market, wide variations can be noted in accuracy, readability, and appeal among the volumes. Hence no series should be accepted *in toto* without evaluation of specific titles. A particular trademark on books does not assure a standard brand as it does in groceries or household appliances.

Another trend, related to the growth of series books and yet independent of it also, is the explosion in junior biography. Again the majority of the titles treat figures in the development of America so a harvest awaits the teacher willing to make the effort necessary to garner it. Some of the boom in junior biography results from the development of history series. A number of the well-known series contain volumes of biography, such as *George Washington Carver* by Anne Terry White in Landmark Books; *The Real Book About George Washington Carver* by Harold Coy in the series of Garden City and *The Story of George Washington Carver* by Arna Bontemps from the Signature Series. Various publishers of juveniles have series which are entirely biographical. Examples include Abingdon's *Makers of America*; Putnam's *Lives to Remember*; Houghton's *Piper Books*; and Bobbs-Merrill's *Childhood of Famous Americans*. The same need to judge each title in a series individually applies equally to biography as to other works. In addition to the production of biographical books within series, many publishers issue titles independent of series. The following serve as illustrations: from offerings of Crowell, *Restless Johnny, The Story of Johnny Appleseed* by Ruth L. Holberg; *Peter Zenger, Fighter for Freedom* by Tom Galt; and *Tom Paine, Freedom's Apostle* written by Leo Gurko. The biographies of Jean Lee Latham represent books published individually by Harper—*Young Man in a Hurry*; *The Story of Cyrus W. Field*; *On Stage, Mr. Jefferson*; and *Carry On, Mr. Bowditch*. The individual books cited in this paragraph illustrate two developments in the selection of biographical subjects. The marked increase in number of titles has not resulted in a corresponding expansion of lives presented. All too frequently the same persons are treated again and again. The materials on

George Washington Carver above illustrate this point. For statesmen such as Washington, Lincoln, and Franklin the concentration is even greater. At the same time some efforts are being exerted to portray figures not previously studied. The titles of Crowell and Harper suggest this development. Despite the bulge in juvenile biography, many Americans who contributed to our national development still await the researches of children's authors. An area scarcely touched, for example, is the industrial one for figures in management and labor alike.

Another trend which has occasioned some difference of opinion is the increasing appearance of adult books simplified for young people. The changes take various forms. One is directed toward purification for young minds, as illustrated in the abridgment of Guthrie's *The Big Sky*. Another approach to simplification is the cutting of long descriptive passages and verbiage to highlight the main thought as in the young people's edition of Douglas Southall Freeman's *America's Robert E. Lee*. Yet another avenue is to use an earlier published book as inspiration for the creation of a new work as Alice Dalgliesh has done in *Ride the Wind*, based on Lindbergh's *The Spirit of St. Louis*. To those who look askance at any tampering with a work, none of these methods will result in a satisfactory version. On the other side of the question are a goodly number who feel that simplification, done with skill and respect for the integrity of the original, can bring valuable works within the comprehension of many who are unlikely to enjoy the primary version. In this connection the "Harvard Report" observes:

There is a need for versions of the great works cleared of unnecessary and unrewarding obstacles and made by abridgment and reflective editing more acessible to general readers. . . . Great books are being read increasingly in abridgments. If these are not made by scholars, they will be made by relatively incompetent hands. Only the scholar knows enough to distinguish the parts of Homer, Plato, the Old Testament, Bacon, Dante, Shakespeare, or Tolstoy which are essential to their value for contemporary general readers from the parts which concern only the special student. But the scholar, by his training, his competitive position, above all his professional ideal, is as a rule unconcerned with this problem. . . . How far this process of clarification or simplification should be carried is, of course, in every instance the prime question. Nothing but a fine awareness both of the material and of the reader's resources will answer it. (7)

It would be hard to minimize the influence of the reading bonanza resulting from a final trend in books for young people. The rise of the paperback has brought change in book publishing, in mass merchandising, in libraries, in classrooms, and everywhere a reader may consume a book. The statistics on paperback production tell a remarkable success story. Publication figures first became significant in the annual analysis made by *Publisher's Weekly* for book titles published in 1953. In that year four publishers moved into the group of largest houses on the basis of an increase in paperback titles alone.

The number of publishers and paperbound titles each increased steadily until 1958, when figures seem to have leveled at a high peak. An encouraging development accompanying this increase is the appearance of standard works of quality. No longer does the paperback necessarily connote a tawdry story or crude thriller. It has become the means of making the best in writing widely available at a reasonable price. Although there are only about five-hundred good, adequately stocked bookstores for the dissemination of knowledge in hard cover editions, the paperback rack has found space in more than 100,000 outlets frequented by Americans as they go about their daily lives. Another advantage of this kind of book packaging is its use in making available works that are out of print in hard cover editions. Examples of interest to the teacher of American history are Margaret Leech's *Reveille in Washington*; Thomas J. Wertenbaker's *Puritan Oligarchy*; and Henry Adams' *The United States in 1800*. Accepted now by the staunchest supporters of hardback collections among teachers and librarians, the little paperback book, like the little car, has become a familiar object on the American scene.

(1) Robert W. Frase, "Economic Development in Publishing," *Library Trends*, 7:8; No. 1, July 1958.

(2) Rachael W. De Angelo, "Children's Book Publishing," *Library Trends*, 7:229; No. 1, July 1958.

(3) *Publisher's Weekly*, 178:19; No. 4, July 25, 1960.

(4) *New York Herald Tribune*, July 10, 1960.

(5) Rachel W. De Angelo, "Children's Book Publishing," *Library Trends*, 7:229; No. 1, July 1958.

(6) *Ibid.*

(7) Harvard University Committee on General Education, *General Education in a Free Society* (Cambridge, Massachusetts: Harvard University, 1945), p. 114.

HISTORY TEXTBOOKS
AND SOCIAL CHANGE

John R. Palmer

Textbooks have been identified by many educators as the most influential specific determinants of curriculum. Research in education often favors them as a prime source of data because textbooks are regarded as reflecting so fully and accurately the curriculum content. This brief report summarizes one recent study of American history textbooks. The investigator concentrated on their adequacy to reflect social change.

FROM *Social Education*, 25:135–136, March, 1961. Used by permission. For biographical note see page 70.

WHEN surveying the emerging domestic and world scene in recent years, it has been difficult to avoid the feeling that man has set tasks for himself far beyond his capabilities. The explosive quality of the situation as characterized by the hydrogen bomb, the population surge, and the demands of colonial peoples for independence has dominated contemporary civilization. There is more change now than in all previous history, and it is occurring at an ever increasing rate. Science and technology continue to magnify power sources, extend the life span, draw peoples into the baffling complexities of giant urban centers, and accelerate the speed with which men travel.

It is obvious that change is our constant companion, and there are certainly no signs that mankind will suddenly get a reprieve. For the foreseeable future, the educational enterprise, as well as all other human endeavors, will be conducted within this context. If the individual is to act intelligently in such a situation, he must be cognizant of the changing nature of his world and its dynamic content.

Within the typical public high school curriculum, heavy reliance is placed on the history course as a vehicle for conveying understanding of society, its operation and its condition. Formal courses in sociology are not generally found in our high schools, and, where offered, they are usually electives attracting small enrollments. Thus it is in history courses where the great majority of students must gain understanding of society and its rapidly changing character.

High school history teachers, perhaps less by choice than by circumstance, bear a major responsibility for educating youth concerning the changing nature of our present culture and the dynamics of the change process. Unfortunately, there is substantial evidence that many high school teachers of history are inadequately prepared to present a penetrating analysis of society, particularly contemporary society. This means that the understanding of social dynamics which students acquire depends to a considerable extent upon the treatment of the matter in the history textbooks which they use. The case for this view is further strengthened by the frequently asserted contention that in many, if not most, secondary school history courses the bulk of the instruction is highly textbook oriented.

To put the matter plainly, the understanding of social change by high school students depends very largely on the manner in which it is handled in secondary school history texts. Under these circumstances, the treatment of social change in these books is a matter of considerable importance to persons concerned about the education of citizens equipped to deal with the world of the present and foreseeable future.

In order to ascertain the adequacy of the treatment of social change in secondary school history textbooks now in use, an analysis was made of twenty-seven such texts used in a random sample of eighteen large Illinois high schools. The analysis had two purposes: (1) To determine the nature of the explanations of social change contained in the textbooks; and (2) To rate each explanation of social change on an ascending scale of 1 through 5 according to the degree to which it could be said to contribute to an understanding of the processes of social change.

The problem of objectivity was particularly crucial, and two steps were taken to deal with it. The investigator made an extensive analysis of the concept of social change, (1) the various standard theories of social change, and the explanations of change used by American historians. Secondly, a rating technique was devised to determine if persons engaged in the teaching of history and the social sciences who had had extensive graduate training in those areas evaluated passages containing explanations as they had been evaluated by the investigator. Two persons highly trained in the social sciences and the investigator independently completed the rating exercise. Kendall's coefficient of concordance indicated a correlation coefficient of +.859 with the level of significance at the 1 per cent level. There is good reason to believe, then, that the rating device employed was satisfactory for the purposes of the textbook analysis.

Ratings of individual explanations of social change found in the twenty-seven textbooks varied over the full range of the 5-point scale; i.e., from being judged as contributing "very little or nothing" to an understanding of social change to contributing "very significantly" to such an understanding. A textbook passage which was judged as contributing little to the student's understanding stated that "Since Britain had much coal and iron, it became an important manufacturing country after the Industrial Revolution began. . . . " This was the complete "explanation" of this very significant change in the life of the British people.

In contrast, another textbook began its explanation of the same development by noting that "Excellent harbors, located on the leading routes of the world, and an abundant supply of coal, iron, and water power were nature's generous gifts to England." However, the account continued at some length establishing relationships between the development of industry and the decline of feudalism and the guilds, the abundance of cheap labor, the Enclosure Act, the influx of skilled artisans from the Continent, the role of colonial possessions in supplying markets and materials, and the increasing power of business leaders over the monarchy. This explanation was given a substantially higher rating than the first.

The results of the investigation, which were set up in table form, (2) indicated that five of the textbooks had been assigned an average rating for all explanations of social change of 4.00 or more on the 5-point scale. These five books represent a wide range of historical material. However, only these five books of the total of twenty-seven, or approximately 18 per cent, were rated as contributing "significantly" to an understanding of the process of social change. A total of eleven, or 41 per cent, of the sample of textbooks were given a rating of 2.00 or less and were judged to contribute "little," "very little," or "nothing" to the reader's understanding of the dynamics of social change. The average rating of all explanations found in all the textbooks was 2.53, very near the midpoint between the "little contribution" and the "some contribution" categories on the 5-point scale.

The great majority of these history textbooks attempt no systematic explanation of the evolution of civilization. All point out numerous instances of social change, but only a very few could be said to emphasize the changing nature of human society and culture. The writers typically demonstrate no compunction to explain carefully the instances of change which they mention. It is important to note, however, that a few of the textbooks depart quite markedly from this general pattern.

The investigation demonstrated, then, that high school history textbooks can, and in some instances do, provide the student with adequate material concerning the dynamics of social change. However, it appears that in most history classes texts are being used which take note of a great many instances of change but offer little assistance toward an understanding of these changes. From the standpoint of adequate treatment, the most serious deficiencies are in the areas of analysis and interpretation. Typically, the instances of change which are cited are not presented in terms of the political, social, economic, or ideational forces underlying them. Only when events are handled within a context of forces, causes, and consequences does the student have the opportunity to gain a better understanding of the dynamics of society.

It is obvious that these textbooks provide ample opportunities for social analysis, but, if this analysis is to be carried out, it must stem largely from supplementary materials and discussions which go substantially beyond these texts. This will occur only if teachers recognize the importance of carrying through such an analysis with students and if they possess the requisite knowledge. It is open to serious question whether either of these situations obtains at the present time.

(1) The literature and research related to the problem of social change is voluminous. It includes such general studies as Francis R. Allen's *Technology and Social Change* (New York: Appleton-Century-Crofts, 1957) and Newell L. Sims' *The Problem of Social Change* (New York: Crowell, 1939); the writings of such diverse figures as R. M. MacIver, Bronislaw Malinowski, H. E. Barnes, Sigmund Freud, Ralph Linton, and Joyce Hertzler; and the comprehensive theories presented in the works of Karl Marx, Arnold Toynbee, William Ogburn, W. G. Sumner, Oswald Spengler, Pitirim Sorokin, Karl Mannheim, and many others.

(2) Readers interested in securing a copy of the table should send *a stamped, self-addressed envelope* to Dr. John R. Palmer, College of Education, University of Illinois, Urbana.

THE TEXTBOOK AND
SKILL DEVELOPMENT

David Z. Tavel

The continuing popularity of textbooks as a staple of schooling testifies forcibly to their merits. Frequent criticisms to the contrary, textbooks apparently can be very useful in facilitating learning. Although they are most often used to furnish content, they can also aid in skill development. The writer of this selection makes some helpful suggestions along this line.

INSTRUCTION in school involves a large amount of reading. Quite often lack of success on the part of the student is the result not of laziness but of inadequate development of reading and study skills. There are, for example, many pupils who do poorly in their history courses. We tend to characterize them as poor historians, or as poor students. They probably are simply poor readers. Reading involves several skills, and to the extent that an individual has not mastered these skills he has difficulty in reading, hence difficulty in class work.

In view of the fact that the textbook is the most commonly available teaching tool, use should be made of it in skill development. The textbook is employed to a great extent, but usually for the acquisition of factual information. It is widely treated as a watered-down encyclopedia, as a compilation of data. That publishers do not intend it as such is made evident by the nearly universal inclusion of activities at the end of chapters and sections, the widespread use of learning aids in the form of time lines and graphs, and the obvious concern with the learner as revealed by the inclusion of introductions and summaries written *to* the student. What procedures, then, can be suggested for teachers who wish to maximize the value of the ubiquitous textbook? A series of steps is here suggested.

First, select one skill to be developed. (1) This may appear so obvious as to be unworthy of mention, but the fact is that many assignments for skill development unwittingly ask the student to master several skills at once. For example: "Outline Chapter Four by listing the most important ideas of each paragraph. Then in one paragraph summarize what appears in your outline." This is fine *if* the student knows how to select main ideas, develop an outline, and write a summary. If the student receives a low grade on the assignment, the teacher can examine his paper for weaknesses, and after determining them, work on

FROM *Social Education*, 25: 403–404, December, 1961. Used by permission. Dr. Tavel is a professor of education at the University of Toledo in Ohio.

them individually. Giving the student the identical assignment for the next chapter will not overcome these weaknesses. This is only practice, and *practice should not precede the development of a skill.* That fellow who is always on the golf course but never breaks 100 exemplifies what happens when this principle is violated. How to avoid this brings us to the next steps.

Second, start at the beginning; and *third,* increase the difficulty as mastery is achieved. It takes only a few judiciously selected questions to indicate at which skills the student is not adept. If, for example, it is determined that the student is unable to select the main thought of a paragraph, nothing is gained by having him write out the main thought in each of the next ten paragraphs. First he can be given some sentences and asked the "who-what-when-where-why" questions that indicate whether he can comprehend the main thought of a sentence. If success is achieved here, the same type of questions can be used for paragraphs. Then for an assignment the teacher can give the student in multiple-choice form options of a subject and a verb. The student's task is to select from among the options the subject and the verb that best tells the who, what, when, where, or why of each paragraph. After assigning a few paragraphs this way the teacher can then present options consisting of complete sentences. This should be followed by a completion-type assignment in which the student is given only the subject of the sentence which when completed will express the main ideal. (2) Only after the student has performed satisfactorily on these steps does he get the assignment in which he writes "from scratch." In this manner we avoid questions which involve only practice until after there is some development of a skill.

Fourth, recognizing that our purpose is the development of a particular skill, avoid emphasis on lesson scores. When lessons such as have been discussed above are graded, it should be for the purpose of indicating the growth and improvement made by the student. If we have pupils concentrating on the extrinsic grade, they are not concentrating on the mastery of a skill. One of the factors contributing to the lack of development of reading skills has been the tendency of teachers to ask examination questions of such a nature that the student develops poor reading habits in preparing for his tests. He gets questions on trivia, and so he reads for trivia. He amasses a storehouse of details through the painstaking and slow process of reading every word, a procedure which actually makes it difficult for him to read, i.e., get the meaning intended by the author. The teacher desiring a readily available indicator—as grades presumably are—of a student's progress can develop a set of assignments for each chapter. Each set consists of groups of questions at each level of difficulty. Returning to the example given above, an assignment might consist of multiple choice items composed of complete sentences from which the student selects the one which best expresses the main idea of each paragraph (or section of a chapter). Another assignment provides the student with the subject of a sentence, which sentence when completed will express the main idea. For a given chapter a student gets only one type of assignment. When he

masters that particular level he then gets a more difficult or complex assignment for the next chapter. The teacher can thus tell the extent of student
progress simply by seeing which type of assignment the student is working
on. Needless to say, this procedure also contributes to a consideration of
individual differences.

Fifth, on an individual basis avoid being satisfied with less than the student
can do. If lessons are adapted to the level of maturity of the student, the
latter can do a 100 per cent job. It may be open to debate as to whether there
are degrees of mastery, or it is a "you-have-it-or-you-don't" affair. It is, however,
generally agreed upon that students cannot think critically and reflectively
without having mastered more basic skills. Thus, at any given level of difficulty in skill development, the teacher should not be satisfied with less than
a perfect performance by a student. It is recognized that some students will
be unable to master certain levels of abstract thinking, but en route to the
higher levels of mastery each student can get to a particular plateau of learning, and at this particular point the teacher should settle for nothing less than
100 percent accomplishment.

A *sixth* and final point is in order, even though it is not really a procedural
step. This discussion has been concerned with skill development through the
utilization of a textbook. As assignments are developed it should be kept in
mind that students are being guided in the mastery of skills *within the context
of a particular course.* Jumping around in a textbook for material to use in a
"skill" lesson will result at best in mastery for mastery's sake. Although we
here have been stressing skill development, the content of a course should not
be neglected but should be used in a manner that will be meaningful to the
student. Most textbooks have not been organized haphazardly, and teachers
can make the most of that fact.

(1) For a partial list of skills, see David Z.
    Tavel, *Developing Reading and Study
    Skills in the Social Studies: A Guide to
    Lesson Construction.* Denver, Colo-
    rado: Lynn Press, 1960. p. 2. [Order
    from the author.]
(2) *Ibid.,* p. 8, 15.

THE NATURE OF
PROGRAMED INSTRUCTION

Lauren B. Resnick

The efforts in recent years to teach more, and more efficiently, have included a considerable emphasis on the use of programed or automated materials. Thus far, such aids are relatively expensive and available for only a limited scope of social studies content. But the potentiality of such material for *individualizing instruction warrants their experimental use and further development. Here is a specialist's résumé of basic characteristics of programed material. Omitted here is a section of illustrations indicating the nature of the material for automated development of study skills.*

SEVERAL questions concerning programed instruction are pertinent for social studies teachers to consider. First, how adaptable are the techniques of programed instruction to the social studies field? More particularly, are the techniques appropriate to the teaching of social studies skills; and if so, what kinds of skills can be most easily handled? Finally, to what extent can school systems or individual classroom teachers expect to be successful in writing their own programs rather than depending upon commercially prepared materials?

NATURE OF PROGRAMED INSTRUCTION

Since the term "programed instruction" has come to be applied to everything from flash cards to instruction by electronic computer, it will be necessary, before attempting to answer these questions, to define the term more closely. In the definition to be used here, the meaning of the term will be both narrowed and broadened: narrowed in the sense that the term will be reserved for those methods of instruction that represent a serious attempt to apply a well-defined theory of instruction, based on psychological principles; broadened in the sense that many applications of those principles which seem possible, but are as yet untried, will be examined.

Programed instruction may be considered an attempt to approximate without a live teacher certain critical features of good tutorial instruction. The fundamental condition of such tutorial instruction is continual interchange

FROM *Skill Development in Social Studies*, Helen M. Carpenter, ed., Washington, D.C.: National Council for the Social Studies, 1963, pp. 253-257, 272. Used by permission. Dr. Resnick is in the office of research and evaluation of the City University of New York.

between an individual student and his teacher. Participating in this exchange, the student is always active, his attention always on the task at hand because he is asked to respond at every step. The teacher, for his part, is closely "tuned" to the student, speeding up or slowing down as the student does, framing his questions and explanations so that the student will be able to respond appropriately, prompting and encouraging where necessary. As a result of continual exchange with his teacher, the student always knows where he is, never waiting more than a moment or two to learn whether his responses are correct. What is more, the student is likely to be correct most of the time; for effective tutorial instruction does not present the student with a difficult problem and leave him to his own devices. Instead, it attempts to help him along, step by step, each step building on the last, until he is able to solve the more difficult problems or perform the more complex skills.

In approximating the feaures of tutorial instruction, a self-instructional program breaks down the material to be taught into small units, generally called "frames." Each frame of a program presents some information or other material and then requires that the student respond to the material in some way. Having responded, the student is immediately informed concerning the accuracy of his answer or he is presented with the correct answer, which he compares with his own. Only after this evaluation does he go on to the next frame, always proceeding through the program at his own pace. A "teaching machine" is no more than a device for presenting these frames one after another, exposing the correct answer only after the student has made his own response, and maintaining a record of the student's responses at each step. There are on the market and in experimental use a very large number of teaching machines, ranging from simple mechanical devices (the machines most widely in use) to elaborate electronic mechanisms that automatically choose the next frame for presentation according to the student's response. In addition, there are "programed texts," in which programs are bound in ordinary book covers. (1) Thus, programed instruction does not necessarily involve the use of elaborate equipment, although the use of machines, as opposed to paper-and-pencil forms of instruction, sometimes offers an important measure of control over the student's behavior. In any case, it is the quality of the program, not the nature of the presentation device, that will ultimately determine the effectiveness of programed instruction.

Variations in programing style and presentation are numerous and cannot all be described here. However, two broad types of programing, each stressing different aspects of tutorial instruction, should be mentioned. The first is based on Norman Crowder's notion of "intrinsic programming." (2) Intrinsic programs have become best known for their "branching" feature, by which students proceed through the program along different routes: The frame presented at any point depends upon the student's response in the preceding frame. In Crowder's view, learning takes place as the student listens to the tutor or reads the program. The response itself is considered unimportant in learning. It is used principally to inform the tutor how the student is doing, and thus to monitor progress through the teaching sequence. Since wrong answers are as informative to the tutor as right ones, there is no particular importance attached to the student's frequently being correct. Similarly, since the response is only a monitoring device, it is felt that multiple-choice answers can be used exclusively with no harm to the learning process.

"Linear programming," the second major type, derives largely from the work of B. F. Skinner. (3) The term "linear" refers to the fact that, in most Skinnerian programs, all students go through all frames in the same sequence. Actually, however, it is not the linear sequence of frames, but the role attributed to the student's response that is the critical feature of Skinner's theory as compared with Crowder's. For Skinner, accepting the traditional psychological definition of learning as a change in behavior, the response *is* what one learns: One learns, that is, what one does. For this reason, wrong responses are considered undesirable, and, in most instances, responses composed by the student are considered superior to multiple-choice responses.

Skinner's insistence on the critical role of the response derives from a psychological theory developed originally in animal laboratories, but now extended to human learning. Called "operant conditioning," this theory begins with the observation that any behavior that is immediately "reinforced" (with food or drink for animals; with praise, money, or other reinforcers for humans) will tend to occur again. This being so, the trainer or tuter, by giving or withholding reinforcements depending upon what the student does, can gain an important degree of control over the students behavior. By reinforcing certain behaviors, the tutor can increase the likelihood that those responses will be made in the future. He can work toward completely new behaviors by reinforcing closer and closer approximations to the desired behavior. Furthermore, he can teach the student when it is appropriate to make a given response by reinforcing it only in the presence of certain specified stimuli. (4) Skinnerian programs represent an application of these principles of operant conditioning. The immediate confirmation of correct responses serves as reinforcement. The step-by-step progression from a simple to a complex performance serves to shape up new skills and knowledge. In each frame, response is made to specific stimuli—questions, incomplete sentences, diagrams, etc.—so that the student is learning to make his responses at appropriate times.

Specification and Analysis of Social Studies Skills

The systematic application of the principles of operant conditioning in a program depends, clearly, upon the programer's knowing in advance exactly what he wants to teach. The responses desired, the stimuli for securing them, the approximations to the final behavior that will be successively reinforced—

all must be clearly specified. In keeping with the psychologist's definition of learning as an observable change in behavior, terms such as "understanding," "comprehension," and "knowledge" must be redefined by specifying the behaviors performed by the child as he gives evidence that he understands, comprehends, or knows. In addition, the stimuli, or appropriate occasions, for each of the behaviors must be specified. Such a detailed set of statements about a student's behavior in very specific situations constitutes a set of "behavioral specifications" for a program. (5) The techniques of programed instruction will be applicable to the social studies only insofar as behavioral specifications of this kind can be set forth for the various skills and concepts one is interested in teaching.

Programed instruction relies for the development of its teaching procedures on an analysis of the behaviors to be taught such that each of the smaller units of behavior that contribute to or constitute the desired "terminal behavior" is specified. Beginning with a behaviorally stated objective, this analysis asks what other things a child must be able to do in order to do what is stated as the terminal behavior. Five or six sub-behaviors may be identified in this way. For each of the sub-behaviors, the same question is then asked. Using this procedure, it is possible to generate a set of "nesting" behavioral specifications in which several smaller units of behavior serve as components of a larger one, and the behaviors become less and less complex as one describes smaller and smaller units. This analysis will to a great extent serve to determine the nature and ordering of the teaching process. Students will not be asked to perform the more complex behaviors until it is certain that they can perform the simpler component behaviors. The simpler behaviors, depending upon the students, may be either assumed or taught. Teaching begins with the simplest behavior that is not assumed, and proceeds through the "nests," or levels of analysis, to the most complex, or terminal, behavior. The exact nature of behavioral specification and analysis will vary, of course, according to the kind of concept or skill to be taught. For this reason, it will be useful to consider a few examples of such analysis applied to different kinds of social studies skills. . . .

CONCLUSION

Programed instruction as it bears upon the social studies must be assessed as a field of great potential and little realization. While there are presently few programs in social studies, and fewer still on skills, there is every reason to believe that the principles of programing can be effectively applied to the teaching of a wide range of social studies content. However, it should be clear by now that programed instruction is no quick and easy panacea for the ills of education. The task of producing programs both significant in their content and effective in their teaching procedure is an imposing one. For the moment, behavioral analysis and specification are probably the most pressing— and the most difficult—tasks. With the aid of adequate analyses, the techniques of programed instruction can perhaps be applied to the teaching of the most complex skills. Whether or not the goal of complete self-instruction is reached, however, goal behavioral analyses should prove of immense benefit in the design of instructional procedures of all kinds.

(1) For a classification and description of the various kinds of presentation devices, including programed texts, see Stolurow, Lawrence M. *Teaching by Machine.* Cooperative Research Monograph No. 6. U.S. Department of Health, Education, and Welfare, Office of Education. Publication No. 34010. Washington, D.C.: U.S. Government Printing Office, 1961. pp. 4–50.

For a description of machines and a directory of those commercially available, see Finn and Perrin, *Teaching Machines and Programed Learning*, pp. 20–49.

(2) See Crowder, Norman A. "Automatic Tutoring by Intrinsic Programming." *Teaching Machines and Programmed Learning: A Source Book.* (Edited by A. A. Lumsdaine and Robert Glaser.) Washington, D.C.: National Education Association, Department of Audio-Visual Instruction, 1960, pp. 286–98.

(3) See Skinner, B. F. "The Science of Learning and the Art of Teaching" and "Teaching Machines." *Teaching Machines and Programmed Learning.*

(Edited by Lumsdaine and Glaser.) pp. 99–113, 137–58.

(4) Holland, James G., and Skinner, B. F. *The Analysis of Behavior.* New York: McGraw-Hill Book Co., 1961. 337 pp. is a (linear) programed text designed to teach the fundamentals of the operant-conditioning theory. No previous background in psychology is assumed.

(5) Mager, Robert F. *Preparing Objectives for Programmed Instruction.* San Francisco: Fearon, 1961. 62 pp. A branching-style programed text providing an introduction to the process of behavioral specification for programing purposes. Essentially the same process has been discussed with reference to test construction in Furst, Edward J. *Constructing Evaluation Instruments.* New York: Longmans, Green and Co., 1958. 334 pp. For an application in the field of testing, see Bloom, Benjamin S., *et al. Taxonomy of Educational Objectives, Handbook I: Cognitive Domain.* New York: Longmans, Green and Co., 1954. 192 pp.

PROGRAMED INSTRUCTIONAL MATERIALS IN SOCIAL STUDIES

Leonard W. Ingraham

Complementing the preceding selection on the nature of automated instruction in social studies, this article reviews the programed materials that appeared on the market during a recent year. Actually the author also assesses the status of development of such materials as he critically analyzes those that have appeared to date. And his identification of sources will be useful to those who wish to secure from producers information about the presently available self-instructional materials. Omitted here is a list of programed materials published during 1964.

I N 1964 programed instruction in the social studies came under sober appraisal. The zealots among the innovators have had their day, as have the unverified claims for and against programed instruction. The early excitement felt for programed instruction has subsided. Much of the early utilization, research, and claims proved to be more the end results of enthusiasm and curiosity than of knowledge and deliberation. Claims and recommendations were often based on flimsy studies, proving Wilbur Schramm's conclusion to be valid:

> Although the research gives us little reason to be satisfied with the theories and the standards of today's programing and every reason to believe that it will be possible some day to make programs vastly more effective than today's programs, nevertheless programed instruction shows signs of hardening, partly under commercial pressure, into a fixed and mechanized technology, with theories and procedures taken for granted. (1)

Programed instructional materials, which were prepared for social studies classroom use in 1964, tended to be more in keeping with the instructional objectives and subject matter than those materials which had been available previously. Many of the programed materials and devices that flooded the market in previous years have had a deleterious effect on the programing movement. These materials which were rushed into production failed because they overlooked the need for programing techniques and for an understanding of the educational problems to which they applied most appropriately.

FROM *Social Education,* 29:27–28, January, 1965. Used by permission. Dr. Ingraham has served as chairman of the Programed Instruction Committee National Council for the Social Studies, and is an assistant to the superintendent in charge of curriculum, New York City Public Schools.

Again in 1964 science and mathematics teaching gave the most hospitable reception to autoinstructional devices. Studies in depth in the utilization of programed instruction in Denver, the Chicago area, Manhasset (New York) Junior High School, and in a "continuous progress" school in Provo (Utah) revealed that by June 1964 no commercially prepared social studies materials were used. (2) In Denver, a teacher-made program, rather than a "psychologist program" on the Constitution, was utilized. Programed materials reported in 40 situations from 24 school systems indicate recent use of programed materials in English, mathematics, science, reading, and study skills. Social studies programs are conspicuous by their absence.

Two dangers still seem to lie in wait for programed instruction: excessive commercialization, and "educational sclerosis"—a lack of imagination in presenting the materials. The programs and programed textbooks stimulate neither curiosity or the spirit of discovery. They do not fulfill the "noble tasks" of the teacher.

More materials were available for other disciplines than for the social studies, as programs continued to concentrate solely upon the imparting of knowledge. For this reason, the number of teaching machines sold to schools and school systems do not indicate a bright future for them. The programed textbook, which appeared in greater quantity, will probably survive today's teaching machine. Again, machines lacked the programs to be fed into them. And teachers were not, nor will they be, threatened by either usurpation or derogation by this new educational technology.

It is still difficult to judge which is "a very good program," or "a fairly good" one. Teachers can judge the substantive content of a program and can identify the flaws that distinguish a skillful program from an unskillful one. But when it comes to judging the relative effectiveness of two programs that do not possess gross flaws, the only recourse for a social studies teacher or supervisor is to depend upon the scanty research evidence provided by the publisher. Since very few programs come equipped with evaluative evidence, the only alternatives are to test them or adopt one on inspection or a "hunch." Many schools are poorly equipped to "test-out" programs, so the second alternative— "buying on a hunch"—often leads to disappointment and results in a reluctance to try other programs.

Many of the social studies materials of 1964 came with built-in safeguards, thus rescuing some programs from gross abuse. A list of these materials appears in the appendix to this report. Every responsible person associated with programed instruction has sought to find out how well programs function under actual school conditions. Some of the 1964 social studies materials reflect this concern. It seems clear that the great preponderance of programs will have to be made by or for commercial publishers because the process is too costly for individual schools. There is no longer much doubt that many existing programs are efficient, self-contained tools of instruction which can be made part of a total social studies teaching experience.

Schools in 1964 saw more programers operate in their classrooms than ever before. This bodes well for both producers of materials and the consumers— for the classroom teachers as well as the children. No longer will teachers who use programed materials in the social studies have to trust *exclusively* to authority or intuition in making decisions about instructional materials.

We are still dealing with an immature technology. Social studies teachers and supervisors are reminded that "the appearances" of a program may "deceive." Sound advice still is: *Never Judge a Program by Its Title!*

Sources of Programed Social Studies Material

Allyn and Bacon, Inc., Rockleigh, New Jersey

Bolt, Beranek and Newman, 50 Moulton St., Cambridge, Massachusetts

Behavioral Research Laboratories, Palo Alto, California

Coronet Films, 65 E. South Water St., Chicago, Illinois

Doubleday and Company, Inc., 575 Madison Ave., New York, New York

Educational Developmental Laboratories, 284 Pulaski Rd., Huntington, New York

Fearon Publications, Inc., 828 Valencia St., San Francisco, California

General Program Teaching Corporation, P. O. Box 4235, Albuquerque, New Mexico

Fraflex, Inc., Rochester 3, New York

Holt, Rinehart and Winston, Inc., 383 Madison Ave., New York, New York

Macmillan Company, 60 Fifth Ave., New York 11, New York

McGraw-Hill Book Company. Webster Division, 330 West 42nd St., New York 36, New York

Noble and Noble Publishers, Inc., 67 Irving Place, New York, New York

PakDonald Publishing, Stayton, Oregon

Sullivan Associates, P. O. Box 693, Los Altos, California

(1) Wilbur Schramm. *Four Case Studies of Programed Instruction.* New York: The Fund for the Advancement of Education, 1964, p. 114.

(2) *Ibid.* p. 17–96

Utilizing Audiovisual Material

FORTY YEARS OF SIGHT AND SOUND IN SOCIAL STUDIES
William H. Hartley

The past generation has witnessed, among various changes in schooling, a blossoming use of audiovisual aids as picture-projecting and record-playing equipment have become well estab-lished. Here a longtime specialist on audiovisual aids in social studies recalls some of the earlier developments and scans the several types of audiovisual aids that are available today.

FORTY-ODD years ago I first began using audiovisual materials in my social studies teaching. Available were a goodly number of still pictures, some excellent maps, a phonograph and a few records, a 35mm portable DeVry motion picture projector, and a selection of free films, most of which described various industrial processes.

As in all phases of American life, the swift-moving technology of the twentieth century has resulted in great changes in teaching materials and methods. The introduction of the light, easy-to-operate, 16mm projector and the printing of films on safety stock encouraged the use of motion pictures in the classroom. The Yale University Press with its *Chronicles of America Photoplays* gave the history teacher a series of dramatic episodes to enliven American history. The widely disseminated experimentation of Knowlton and Tilton, extolling the use of films, stimulated teachers to use films for educational purposes. The Eastman Kodak's library of silent films added variety to the materials available.

The early 'thirties brought a practial 16mm sound projector. Erpi Classroom Films, now Encyclopaedia Britannica Films, answered the need to "bring the world to the classroom" by producing sound motion pictures especially designed to educate boys and girls. The contributions of such pioneers as Eastman and Erpi (whose name was coined from the first initials of

FROM *Audiovisual Instruction*, pp. 666–667, December, 1964. Used by permission. Dr. Hartley is a professor of education at Towson State College in Maryland.

Electrical Research Productions Incorporated) are hard to overestimate. They did indeed change the nature of the classroom learning environment.

Movies Are Meaningful

Today "movies are better than ever." Encyclopaedia Britannica has been joined by Coronet, Churchill, Contemporary, International, McGraw-Hill, and other film companies. Even the universities have joined in the act, and such productions as the University of Indiana's series on *The American Business System* have provided accurate and meaningful material for the social studies teacher. All this competition has been good for education in general. Today there is a film for almost every purpose, and most of the films are generally very good. Instead of the shotgun approach which characterized many early educational films, today's production deals more thoroughly with a limited area. Color has added to the attractiveness and interest-arousing elements in many films, and in most instances it has been worth the extra cost.

In one area, however, educational films often fall short. They do not make use of one of the unique characteristics of motion pictures: They do not dramatize subject and arouse suspense and interest. Too often they fail to involve the viewer actively, though vicariously, in the action taking place on the screen. Even the old *Chronicles of America* tried to do this. I can remember audiences of junior high school students enjoying Indian raids in *Daniel Boone*. Would Daniel Boone escape in time to warn the settlers? Would the settlers hold the fort? Would help arrive in time? Such suspense helped to make the past real and meaningful. True, not all subjects lend themselves to this type of approach, but those that do deserve good acting, writing, and production.

To help fill the need for films with first-class acting, sets, and costuming, educators have turned to Hollywood. A committee of the National Council for the Social Studies has, over the past fifteen years, worked actively with Teaching Films Custodians in editing Hollywood feature productions for classroom use. This group has cut such films as *Cleopatra, Disraeli, The Oxbow Incident, Brigham Young, Union Pacific, Intruder in the Dust,* and others and has made short versions—usually twenty minutes long—available for schools.

Commercial and educational television has become another source of dramatic films for the classroom. The McGraw-Hill Book Company, for example, distributes such TV films as *Meet Comrade Student, Voice of the Desert,* and the famous "You Are There" series. The National Council for the Social Studies has also succeeded in getting the DuPont "Cavalcade of America" series released to the schools. They are available in edited form, without advertising, through Teaching Films Custodians (1) . . . .

OTHER MATERIALS OF MERIT

The motion picture is, of course, but one of the modern media available to social studies teachers. It serves best when motion is essential to the concept to be taught. When we wish to examine natural or social phenomena in more detail, another type of material or experience may indeed be preferable and more effective. The excellent new *Educational Media Index* published by McGraw-Hill lists materials for geography and history in Volume 12 under the following headings: filmstrips, phonotapes, flat pictures, phonodiscs, videotape, programed materials, slides, models, films, cross-media kits, charts, and maps. Each has its place in the teaching of the social studies and, properly used, each will help to make the social scene more intelligible to students.

Of all the recent developments in social studies teaching materials, I am particularly enthusiastic about the trends in projected still pictures. The improved opaque projectors make possible the effective presentation of current cartoons, news pictures, maps, and other readily available small, flat prints. It is still true, however, that a dark room is necessary in order to use an opaque projector effectively. The recent development of quick and easy methods of transferring pictures, charts, maps, and other graphic materials to sensitized plastic for use in the overhead projector has given teachers a useful and usable device for large-group instruction. Publishers, especially map manufacturers, have recently issued reasonably priced, professionally produced transparencies which add even more to the general usefulness of the overhead projector. With the growth of popularity in the team-teaching type of situation involving sessions attended by sizeable groups of students, the overhead projector or lecture lantern has become a most essential tool for instruction.

Social studies teachers are fortunate, too, in the great number of excellent slides and filmstrips now available. There are filmstrips on practically every unit of work offered in the elementary grades. American history is particularly well covered. Filmstrips suitable to secondary social studies are, it is happy to note, getting better and more numerous. As more and more economic and political concepts are being developed on this level, producers have responded with well-planned and excellently executed filmstrips. Organizations such as the Joint Council on Economic Education, The New York Times, and the United Nations also have prepared special filmstrips for the schools. An increasing number of filmstrips from all sources are now being made with accompanying sound—usually on a long-playing record. Many of these sound filmstrips are very good because they can present an authoritative discussion of the pictured material. They can also add to the realism of the subject by including environmental sounds, voices of the past, appropriate music, and dramatic episodes. On the other hand, some sound filmstrips are simply accompanied by canned lectures of an uninspired nature. There is still a place for the silent filmstrip which allows for pupil discussion on the projected pictures and teacher explanations suited to the needs, interests, and backgrounds of the particular class.

Speaking of sound, the social studies teacher today can present the actual voices of ever president since McKinley. He can present short dramatic incidents from history or music from almost every land on earth. From Folkway Records he can get an album called *American History in Ballad and Song,* and from Enrichment Teaching Materials he can get records which discuss famous documents in our history. Music of the Union or the Confederacy, speeches by presidents of the United States, "You Are There," "I Can Hear It Now," "Sing Along With Millard Fillmore" (campaign songs), and other suitable recordings are available from RCA or Columbia. In addition, the growing numbers of tapes available give the teacher a rich resource of sound.

GRIST FOR IMPROVEMENT

The students of today have the opportunity to get a better social education than did those of forty-nine years ago. Maps are bigger and better—more visible and useful than ever before. Kits of cross-media materials including pictures, realia, filmstrips, maps, and manuals are available. Television, properly used, can enrich and enliven many lessons. The camera seems omnipresent in most parts of the world and at all events of importance. The resultant pictorial material is grist for the social studies teacher's mill. How well this grist is refined and made a part of the mental food for students depends upon the skill of the teachers. From daily observations of today's teachers at work, I have high hope for the future.

(1) *Ed. note:* currently through Encyclopaedia Britannica Films.

DEVELOPING A SENSE
OF PLACE AND SPACE

Lorrin Kennamer

Although films and television receive major attention as instructional aids in the curriculum generally, maps and *globes have a special and almost unique use in social studies. Map makers have made continuing advances in producing*

FROM *Skill Development in the Social Studies,* Helen M. Carpenter, ed., Washington, D.C.: National Council for the Social Studies, 1963, pp. 148–153. Used by permission. Dr. Kennamer is chairman and professor of geography at the University of Texas.

improved representations of the earth's surface. In this selection a geographer sketches the basic significance and nature of maps and globes. Then he delineates the functions of maps that suggest ways of using them instructionally. Omitted from the original selection is a more extensive discussion of factors and approaches for developing students' place concepts.

M ANKIND through the ages has been concerned with the problem of finding and recording position on earth. The question has been how to determine location, measure distance, calculate direction; and then to record these on maps and globes. The early Greeks learned to do these things in theory; modern man, with accurate instrumentation, has been able to apply the theory. The need for man to develop a sense of place and space is even greater today as a growing world population presses on our earth space and a growing curiosity bids us to probe the solar space. However, it is man's concern for earth place and space with which this chapter deals, since the earth as the home of man is a major consideration of social studies teaching.

The Geographic Contribution to the Social Studies

It has been said that within the social studies, history presents the drama of human events in time, whereas geography studies the stage on which those events take place. It should be added that geography is concerned not only with the physical setting of the stage but also with the relations between human events and the stage on which they are enacted. This concept of scope means, then, that a geographically educated teacher will do more than list physical facts about a place; he will do more than compile a list of the stage props; he will, in addition, relate man with the place in which he is found. In continuing this analogy it should be noted that the actors on a stage do have some effect on the disposition of the props and scenery, just as the location of the furniture modifies the action of the players.

Geographic study is focused on the human habitat, a habitat which is composed of both natural and man-made things. It is concerned with the arrangement of things and with the associations of things that distinguish one area from another within our habitat. Geographic study involves spatial interchange, the examination of the connections and movements between areas. When the descriptive elements of human activity and physical environment are brought together in an understandable way, the purpose and result are geographical. To put it another way, geography is a meaningful explanation of the relationships between places and between places and people.

Thus, it is geography, as a field of learning, to which the social studies teacher can turn for meaningful ways to develop skills in spatial relationships. More specifically, we must consider the unique tools of geography, the globe and the map, when we develop a sense of place and space.

Functions of Maps

Maps are systematic representations of the earth or parts of the earth upon a flat, or plane, surface. Upon a systematic network of lines (grid) the map maker arranges in a meaningful pattern the dots, colors, lines, and sometimes words, he has chosen from standardized symbols. To the person who knows how to read these symbols, maps reveal information useful for developing understandings of locational or regional phenomena. In other words, maps may be read and maps may also be interpreted. Map reading, like any other kind of reading, involves the ability to recognize and to understand the symbols on the map. This includes not only the symbols as such but also directions, distances, relative locations, position on the globe, size, or any of the geographical, statistical, political, or cultural information which the map is designed to show. A major objective of map making is to indicate all of these facts in so clear a manner that the map may be easily and accurately read.

Symbol reading, like any other kind of reading, is only the first step toward the understanding of maps. Just as we spend several years learning how to read the printed page, it is necessary also to spend a considerable time learning how to read maps. As a person grows in wisdom and understanding he finds much in literature which in his younger days escaped him, i.e., he learns how to interpret better what he reads. This is true also in the use of maps. What to the child may be a net of lines forming a river and its tributaries is to an experienced map user a drainage basin with flood control, water supply, and hydroelectric potentials. We relate to the map as we do to the printed page in that the more we take to the map the more understandings we obtain from it.

Maps can serve a variety of functions. They are a means of recording information for permanence, for clarification, for comparison, and for communication. A large-scale map of a small region, depicting its land forms, drainage, settlement patterns, roads, or many other geographic and economic distributions, provides the knowledge of relationships necessary for man to carry on many of his activities intelligently. The building of a road, a house, a flood-control system, or almost any other construction project requires mapping. At a smaller scale, maps of soil erosion, land use, climates, population, income patterns, et cetera, are necessary to understanding the problems and potentialities of an area. On the smallest scale, maps of the entire earth indicate generalizations and relationships of broad physical and cultural patterns necessary for us, as the British geographer, James Fairgrieve, says, to imagine accurately the conditions of the great world stage so that we can think sanely and sensibly about social and political conditions around the world.

In geographic instruction, maps have distinctive functions, since they present certain types of information better than any other medium. Their major function is to show certain facts concerning place and man's relations with place and space. The most important of these facts are discussed in the following paragraphs: (1)

Location. Through the understanding and use of latitude and longitude, maps aid in finding the exact or relative location of any place on earth. For example, Seattle, Washington, is at latitude 47° 45' N., longitude 122° 25' W. This is exact location, while facts of relative location include Seattle's relation to Puget Sound, to the Pacific Ocean, to the Cascade Mountains, to the state of Washington and its railroad network, to the United States, and to Canada.

Size and Shape of an Area or of a Feature. Repeated use of maps gives an accurate mental image of the shape of countries, and of natural phenomena, such as continents, islands, and seas. While exact comparisons as to size are not feasible by map study alone, comparisons of size on equal-area maps are possible and do result in concepts of areas. Maps can thus present true areas in perspective.

Distance. By use of the scale of miles or by use of latitude and longitude, distance between points can be read or estimated.

Elevation and Surface. Topographic and physical maps make it possible to learn the elevation above sea level and to judge the slope and surface of the world's land areas. Facts of hydrology can also be determined by studying the patterns of river systems, lakes, oceans, and seas.

Distribution of Natural and Cultural Features. The distribution patterns of many phenomena such as population density, population trends, population characteristics, agricultural commodities, industrial production, minerals, soil types, and climatic types can be shown on maps. In fact, most aspects of human endeavor can be mapped. Often data can be compared more easily and accurately when mapped.

Visualization of Areas and Patterns. Small symbols on maps represent large things of man and nature. Thus, the map is mandatory for visualizing large and distant lands. As an ancient Chinese map maker wrote, "It is as if they were on the palm of your hand."

Relationships. Another function of a map is to provide a basis for noting relationships. This is achieved by comparing two or more maps of different phenomena. For example, comparison of a rainfall map and a map showing agricultural regions can lead to basic generalizations regarding agriculture and climate. Another interesting comparison can be made between a map showing the hydrologic features of a continent and the developed and potential hydroelectric power.

Inferences. By interpreting the significance of facts shown by symbols on a map, important inferences are possible. For example, the location of mountains, direction of prevailing winds, number of cities, transportation networks, location of swamps or deserts, number of rivers and lakes—all help the map reader to make inferences about climate, population density, vegetation, and even the dominant occupations in a region.

Interest. From the teaching standpoint, maps can function in promoting interest in learning about other areas and cultures. They can be used to introduce units of study, to aid in development of units, and to summarize and evaluate the units. All of us are attracted by the suggestions for learning inherent in maps, whether the map be a common road map or a set of maps in an atlas.

Change. One of the most common functions of maps in the social studies is to show change—geographic, economic, social, political. Maps in succession can show the "before" and the "after" of a pattern of change. The movement of peoples, with dates, can be shown, as well as the changed political patterns. Exchanges of goods, development of industries, the spread of crops, the marches of armies—all can be presented dramatically through mapping.

The Role of Globes

Globes are the only true representation of the entire earth. And although maps are more widely used than globes, certain geographic understandings cannot successfully be explained without the proper use of a globe.

The basic quality of the globe is shape, a shape that approximates that of the earth on which we live. Whereas globes may vary in size, they will always represent the complete area of the earth's surface, including both land and water and in the proper size and shape relationships. Only the globe represents the surface of the earth true in all four of the characteristics sought in flat map projections: namely, true *shapes*, true *distances*, true *directions*, and equal *area*. A globe does not need to simulate the spherical relations of the earth we live on: It *has* them.

Understanding the globe is basic to a development of skills and abilities necessary for reading and interpreting maps. The globe must be understood by children before much can done with flat maps, especially world or continent maps. Even if maps of the immediate neighborhood are not so dependent upon global concepts, a complete understanding of the grid of parallels and meridians upon which all maps are based is dependent upon globe study.

A basic function of the globe is the introduction and development of locational concepts. Use of the globe can illustrate most pointedly the need for a framework by which to locate places on earth. For example, have the student place his finger on any point in the Pacific Ocean and ask him to tell where his finger is. Then ask him to give such accurate directions to a classmate that he also can place his finger on the same point. The need for a system of locating places on the earth is made apparent. Through such an activity the student will learn about the earth's grid, rather than memorize terminology about it which is soon forgotten.

Another important function of the globe in the classroom is its use for teaching earth movements and relationships in the solar system, something which cannot be taught well, if at all, with a flat map. An understanding of rotation (basic for understanding daylight and darkness, tides, wind movements, ocean currents, etc.) and of revolution (basic for understanding changing seasons, varying length of daylight periods, etc.) requires the repeated study of the globe. Other concepts dependent upon globe study include time zones, the international date line, and great circle transportation patterns. It should be noted that the study of the globe is not limited to use the elementary grades, since concepts just mentioned are introduced and developed at higher grade levels and need to be reviewed even at the college level.

The functions of globes and maps discussed above suggest that these tools of learning are not to be studied for their own sake; rather, they are vehicles. A truck or freighter is useful only when employed in hauling loads. Similarly, maps and globes are useful in developing a sense of place and space primarily when used for studying the facts of geography, history, and economics as part of the social studies program.

(1) See Thralls, Zoe A. *The Teaching of Geography*. New York: Appleton-Century-Crofts, 1958. pp. 22–23; Board of Education, City of New York.

Teaching Map and Globe Skills. Curriculum Bulletin, 1959–60 Series, No. 6. pp. 2–3.

TEACHING WORLD HISTORY ON TELEVISION

Gerald Leinwand

Early enthusiasm and great promise accompanied the advent of educational television a few years ago. Subsequent experience has yielded some success and helped to identify some problems and difficulties. Here an ETV teacher gives his reactions and those of others involved to their experiences in a social studies course. Omitted from the original article are brief lists of course topics and objectives.

I N THIS article I should like to say something of our aims and plans, my television experiences, and to provide an evaluation of television as an educational medium for high school social studies in the light of those experiences.

FROM *Social Education*, 28:269–272, November, 1963. Used by permission. Dr. Leinwand is a professor of education, City College of New York.

AIMS AND PLANS

During the late spring of 1962 a group of social studies chairmen and I met rather frequently to draw up a series of fifteen programs for the proposed world history course which was scheduled to be given from September, 1962, through January, 1963. The fifteen programs were to make up the series to be known as "Highlights of World History."

In order to achieve maximum viewing by high school students and effective utilization by teachers, substantial publicity was given to the proposed series. The programs, together with a brief synopsis of each, some suggested readings, and some questions and activities were listed in the WNDT *Secondary School Television Guide* and made available to each social studies department. In addition, individual departments often mimeographed the topics and distributed them to individual teachers. The *Bulletin* of the Association of Teachers of Social Studies of the City of New York likewise carried a listing of the topics.

Each television program was to be twenty minutes in length and was to be produced on tape two weeks ahead of viewing date. The program was to be presented three times on a single day (Thursday) so that classes unable to view the program at one hour might be able to do so later in the day. Eventually it was decided to kinescope the series; that is, to place the programs on film so that they would be available through the Bureau of Audio-Visual Instruction in subsequent terms.

Within this framework, I, as television teacher for the course, was free to select those points of emphasis I chose and to make use of whatever methods, materials, and guests, my ingenuity could uncover. For the wide latitude and freedom to experiment with television that I was given, I am most grateful. But this freedom carried with it the responsibility to make the wisest choices of content, to select the best materials available, and to make the most forthright presentation possible.

PROBLEMS AND EXPERIENCES

To the beginner, the problems of appearing before the eye of the television camera are formidable indeed. However, a very fine five-day orientation program which included on-camera practice, make-up advice, and evaluation of the studio's resources, helped overcome the initial feeling of panic and stage fright. Although this feeling never entirely left me (nor any of the other broadcasters, I later discovered), it was sufficiently brought under control so that I could concentrate on attempting to put together effective programs.

At our planning sessions it seemed as if we had a world of materials at our fingertips—films, filmstrips, slides, pictures, guests, and technical equipment of all kinds—resources we had but to tap and each of these would come to do our bidding. But it soon became evident that this was not to be the case. Limitations of space in which to work and time in which to prepare the programs, of funds with which to buy or rent necessary materials and props, of equipment with which to present maps or other data in dramatic form, were hurdles to be overcome if the effectiveness of the series was to be assured. Aggravating these problems was the fact that the School Television Service functioned within the framework of a new educational television station which was itself still groping with its own problems of mustering financial support and community acceptance.

Complicating problems for the television teacher is the fact that all films, filmstrips, slides, illustrations, books, music, and guests must be "cleared for television" in one way or another before they can be used. "Is it cleared for television?" became a question that I learned to ask early and often. Locating materials cleared for TV not only involved a vast amount of time, "leg work," as well as clerical work, but clearance requirements effectively limited the materials that could be shown as well.

For understandable reasons valuable commercially produced films and pictures were not available for television use, as producers were fearful that by making their films or pictures available for television, particularly for a series that was being kinescoped, their future sales of the films or pictures would be curtailed. Adding to my frustrations was the fact that some films that were both available and cleared for television had to be shown in their entirety. On a twenty-minute program it was rare that any show had more than two or three minutes' worth of film. Often, too, films that we would have liked to use were simply too expensive for us. Since there are approximately seventy running feet of film in a two-minute segment, even the special educational television rate of about $2.50 a running foot of film was for us prohibitive in cost.

Museums and art galleries are truly treasure chests of information and materials. But making such materials available for television showing was generally difficult and often impossible. For one thing, museums understandably would not allow items from their precious collections to be taken to the television studio without a representative of the museum standing by. This costs money, money which our budget simply did not provide. We tried, sometimes successfully, to get around this by inviting a representative of the museum to be the guest on the program on which his materials were to be used, but this rarely worked more than once.

All sorts of irritating developments and limitations on what we had hoped to do arose out of conflicts growing out of the contracts governing the work rules under which the unions and the studio had agreed to abide. On one occasion, because models of Leonardo da Vinci's inventions, which had been loaned to us by the International Business Machines Corporation, were delivered in a truck rented by I.B.M. rather than by a theatrical hauler, the prop men refused to handle the models. Only extreme persuasion and "as a special favor" to me "for this one time only" were the men prevailed upon to unload the props and arrange the set. In another case, after I had located a suit of armor, the studio did not allow it to be delivered because, so they said, the prop men "did not have time" to bring the suit of armor from the sidewalk to the studio. On another occasion, the art department had made a model of a guillotine but once again the prop men had to be coaxed into setting it up in its proper place because to them it should have been made in the wood-working shop, not the art shop.

For the program on the French Revolution, two professional announcers regularly employed at WNYE, the Board of Education's radio station, were to play the roles of "defense" and "prosecuting" attorneys at the "trial" of Louis XVI before the National Convention. The announcers were to appear in the costumes of the day. The costumes were rented and we looked forward to a fine program, but at the last minute the use of the costumes was vetoed for fear that costumed announcers would be regarded as actors and so aggravate the already tense relation between WNDT and the television and actors associations. These episodes would have been genuinely humorous were it not for the near calamity with which several of the programs were faced as a result.

Evaluation and Summary

One of the most rewarding experiences of my teaching career was the opportunity to teach on television. My eyes were opened to a new dimension in education, to a new medium of instruction, and to a new industry in general. But what of television as a medium of instruction in the social studies?

As used in New York City television served to enrich and supplement the teaching of world history. No teacher was replaced, viewing was voluntary and generally within a classroom situation. Effort was made to have the television content enrich and enliven the world history classroom, not serve as a substitute for it. However, while potential for growth is enormous and television teaching is here to stay, the fact is that viewing among high school classes was extremely limited.

The problem for high school viewing of school TV programs grew largely out of the programing difficulties within the high schools themselves. Often teachers who would have liked to have utilized the programs were not meeting their classes when the programs were offered; or, when they did meet their classes no world history program was being aired. Aggravating matters was the fact that an insufficient number of television receivers was available and getting them moved into a classroom sometimes presented difficulty and tended to discourage the use of television. Moreover, in classes I observed, and judging from reports of colleagues, TV reception left much to be desired. Sometimes it suffered from technical difficulties. More frequently, however, the difficulties grew out of a lack of window shades with which to darken a room or inadequate care and maintenance of the television receiver itself.

Another obstacle to the effective use of television in high school social studies was the fact that after the novelty wore off teachers had to be cajoled into making use of the medium. In the elementary school, teachers who themselves may not be experts in art, music, or science, may look forward to a television lesson to supplement their own activities. On the high school level teachers consider themselves subject specialists, and are inclined to doubt that a television program can provide any enrichment that they themselves cannot provide. And, given some of the limitations on the use of materials previously suggested, in some cases they are right. It is ironical that a film or filmstrip that can, under ordinary circumstances, be used by a classroom teacher is not readily available to a television teacher.

Nevertheless, teachers should be encouraged to use television because the very nature of the medium provides a built-in motivation for further study. Moreover, it should be remembered, that few teachers, even the very best, can take the time to preview pictures and edit films and exercise the care that goes into the make-up and presentation of a television program.

Technical "know-how" makes possible the production of a host of varied and informative television programs, but often the same technical facilities available to commercial channels or even to the evening offerings of the educational channels are not available to the high school television teacher. To make such technical equipment and skill available to secondary school television teachers is one of the big tasks ahead for school television.

In view of the nature of the high school student, the specialist capacity of the high school teacher, the program difficulties in the high school, as well as the limited number of sets available, efforts should be made to present high school programs after school hours when programs can be viewed at home. In this way, teachers could direct the attention of the students to coming programs, assign suitable homework, encourage family discussion, and provide for follow-up the next day.

Presenting high school programs during and after school hours with a degree of sophistication that would enable them to compete more successfully with the informative programs offered on the commercial networks requires a high degree of sympathetic understanding by the management of educational television. In the School Television Service all in-school programs from kindergarten to twelfth grade were lumped together. In such an arrangement the secondary school is at a disadvantage since preparing programs to meet the learning needs of the more advanced and critical student requires approximately the same consideration lavished on the evening educational offerings.

Forward-looking management of educational television stations must also cooperate more effectively in bringing about "break throughs" that will enable school television services to make programs more exciting. The rules governing the use of films and other illustrative materials may be reasonable for commercial television but they require considerable modification in the area of educational television. Here management of educational television channels should assume the leadership in prevailing upon commercial channels, film producers, and publishers to make their materials more readily and inexpensively available for educational and in-school television broadcasting.

In a similar vein, forward looking representatives of management and labor have both to review their practices and demands so that the work rules under which television personnel work do not strangle educational television in their web. At the present time, in-school television, by no means a "wasteland," seems to be a vast "no man's land" to which the commercial restraints and procedures applied to the use of materials and personnel do not seem to fit but in which no new set of equitable procedures has as yet been found. On more than one occasion, those who would have been eager to make materials available to me found that their hands were tied in that they simply had no precedent or guidelines they could easily follow.

Closely associated with these problems is the question of compensation for the television teacher. Much has been said and written about this subject and its ramifications are many and deep. It seems to me that because programs of the television teacher are likely to be reused in subsequent years some form of additional compensation is entirely in order. Wherever I went in my effort to secure guests or materials for the planned programs this question came up and the sentiment in favor of some form of additional payment for re-use of programs was universal. In all fairness, a fund for modest honorariums to guests should be provided.

In the course of my term of service as a television teacher I had the opportunity of associating with talented colleagues, skillful producers, and magnificent directors. In the course of gathering materials for the programs I had that opportunity of meeting a host of prominent men and women in education, industry, and diplomacy. All of these people were uniformly courteous and helpful in substantial measure. By and large, in all fairness it must be said that the large private corporations were by far the most cooperative in making displays, props, films, and guest experts available to me. Their help was of enormous value and was offered willingly and with "no strings" attached.

The experience to me was particularly rewarding because the School Television Service of which I was a part, was part of WNDT and I was able to be an "eyewitness" to many of the birth pangs of a new educational television channel. And, hopefully, signs of change and progress are in the air. In response to repeated urging that kinescopes of "Highlights of World History" be made available on an evening hour so that the series might be made assigned viewing, this was finally agreed upon for the spring term (1963). Although an early evening hour (5:40 to 6:00 P.M.) on Saturday night is hardly "prime time" even for a high school program, nevertheless it represents a start. While much remains to be done in many areas of producing the programs, utilizing the programs effectively, and making fair and appropriate rules governing the use of copyrights, residual payments, and labor-management relations—rules which meet the peculiar needs of educational television—there is evidence that educational television in general and school television in particular will mature enough to make a significant contribution to the education of youth.

3

Using School and Community Resources

PLANNING SOCIAL STUDIES FACILITIES FOR SECONDARY SCHOOLS

Glen F. Ovard

Social studies educators have seriously neglected characteristics of and needs for classroom facilities that could greatly enhance instruction in this field. The writer of this selection is one of the few who has seriously investigated class-room construction and equipment as related to an effective social studies program. Here he summarizes some trends in classroom activities and available equipment. He then suggests the implications of the current trends for the planning of better social studies class-rooms. Omitted here is his summary of trends in objectives and curriculum, because they were discussed previously in this volume.

TRENDS IN ACTIVITIES

FUTURE activities must be considered when planning a building. The following trends in social studies activities are important:

1. Activities that involve closer contact with the aspects of political, social, and cultural life of today will be utilized (especially those activities which are centered around world affairs) and the study of other nations and cultures. In this regard, the use of current event techniques, radio and television newscasts and tape recordings of public services broadcasts will receive increased impetus.

2. Activities that acquaint individuals with crucial data, relationships and problems which are significant to human welfare will become more important. There will be an increase in the use of critical thinking techniques, problem solving techniques, concrete experiences and use of community resources.

3. Activities that provide for the widespread physical and intellectual capacities of all of the students will continue in importance. There will be more

---

FROM *Planning Social Studies Facilities for Secondary Schools* by Glen F. Ovard, Stanford, Calif.: School Planning Laboratory, Stanford University, 1961, pp. 10–13. Used by permission. Dr. Ovard is a professor of education at Brigham Young University.

grouping of students both by abilities and interests within classrooms to work on projects and units of work.

Providing for the gifted is now being emphasized. A number of programs involving gifted students are now in operation. These programs have a number of special features that involve special type activities. Some of these features are: (a) the class sizes are usually small, ranging from twelve to twenty students; (b) intensive efforts are placed on individual research; (c) the classes are conducted primarily with a college seminar approach in which there is a great amount of critical discussion; (d) the intensive study involves both a study of specific facts and generalizations that are related to present times and events; (e) there are definite needs for many more original and supplementary materials than are presently available to most classes; and (f) there are indications that such activities will involve a greater utilization of all of the audio and visual aids by individuals as well as by the group.

4. Activities that place greater emphasis on student initiative, creativity, and originality are becoming increasingly more important.

5. Activities that teach the democratic process through such procedures as pupil-teacher planning and cooperative activities will continue to be emphasized.

6. Activities that utilize various audio-visual aids will continue to be of prime importance. A number of experimental programs with television and tape recordings indicate greater utilization of these aids in the future. The development of audio-visual centers with twenty-four-hour service (in which pictures, graphs, charts, etc. can be photographed and shown on 2″ x 2″ slides and in which tape recordings can be transcribed) will increase the use of these aids as the service becomes more widespread.

7. There is indication that due to the low cost factor there will be greater utilization of "paperback" books for individual study as well as for total class activities. In this way, many original sources can be brought to class that otherwise could not be utilized.

8. Activities that promote wise use of leisure time will be correlated with the social studies curriculum. There will be a greater utilization of biographies, autobiographies, and historical fiction. Activities that teach appreciation of art, music, and cultural artifacts in both present and past civilizations will be encouraged.

9. Junior high school courses which utilize blocks of time will emphasize more construction activities requiring self-contained features.

10. A trend in our legal processes which has encouraged liability suits to be brought against individual teachers and, in three states, permitted school boards to be legally liable for acts of its members, officers, and authorized agents, has reduced the number of activities that are performed outside of the class where direct supervision cannot be maintained. Halls, cafeterias, and

other unsupervised spaces can no longer be utilized in these schools; thus more of the small-group activities must be carried on, contiguous to other small group activities, in the classroom.

11. In general, there will be a greater number and variety of both individual and group activities in carrying out the social studies curriculum.

12. One additional type of activity should be mentioned. Although it is insufficient experimentation in instruction in large, medium, and small groups to warrant some consideration in planning for the future facilities. If any of the experimental programs become standard practice, it would be necessary to have some rooms which would be capable of handling a large number of students. Flexibility in room size would seem to be an area of consideration in planning for future activities.

Trends in Classroom Facilities

Some of the major trends that are taking place in classroom facilities are:

1. The furniture and equipment are flexible. Student desks can be moved around the room for various seating arrangements. Chairs are designed so they are stackable for ease in cleaning. Flexibility is also being increased through the use of movable cabinets, adjustable shelves, book trucks, magazine racks, folding stages, audio-visual equipment, and removable or interchangeable tackboard and chalkboard.

2. Writing surfaces are of laminated plastic materials which resist scratches and stains.

3. The use of audio-visual aids of all kinds is increasing.

4. The use of educational television is increasing. There are three kinds of educational television: (a) television programs which are carried over commercial stations, (b) television programs carried over the state or community educational television station, and (c) closed-circuit television. All three kinds can be used by the social studies teacher. Closed-circuit television is still in an experimental stage, but many public and private educational institutions are now using it at all levels.

5. There is need for enlarged classroom space in order to accommodate the social studies program. Recent trends emphasize the need for classrooms with floor areas of up to 1200 square feet.

6. Classrooms are being developed which utilize a completely controlled environment. There is no longer a dependence upon natural light. The thermal and visual environment may be completely controlled by mechanical and electrical means. This arrangement also permits greater flexibility as rooms can be enlarged or decreased in size without the age-old questions of the ratios between windows and room sizes being raised. The acoustical environment should be considered in the over-all planning.

IMPLICATIONS OF THE TRENDS IN OBJECTIVES, CURRICULA,
ACTIVITIES, AND FACILITIES FOR PLANNING

The implications of the above trends to planning social studies are: (1) More materials and supplies within the classroom will need to be provided; (2) More adequate provisions should be made for utilities, outlets, hookups, etc. for a wide range of audio-visual equipment; (3) Greater flexibility in classroom furniture will need to be made so that large, immobile furniture will not handicap small group activitiy; (4) Consideration for flexibility in the size of classrooms must be provided by the use of movable partitions so that the classrooms can be enlarged or made smaller, as the need arises; (5) Storage areas for a variety of sizes and shapes of supplies and equipment will need to be provided; (6) The size of classrooms will need to be large enough to include work areas, display areas, adequate storage, and permit as many as five to seven small group projects or activities to be carried on simultaneously; (7) Adequate provisions will need to be made for semipermanent materials such as maps, projection screens, etc.; (8) More self-contained features, especially for junior high schools, will need to be planned within the classroom; (9) The auditorium and other large areas may eventually be divided by movable acoustical barriers and used for large group instruction; (10) A research corner with adequate books, magazines, pamphlets and documents will need to be provided; (11) The control of visual and thermal environment within the classroom will be regulated automatically and there will be less reliance upon the sun and other natural and human sources; (12) All new buildings should be planned to accommodate the eventual use of television. Although all of these features need not be present initially, plans for their eventual use should include:

1. Good acoustics in each room.
2. Indirect lighting.
3. Provision for good ventilation.
4. A good antenna installation.
5. Built-in coaxial cables and antenna lines.
6. Built-in high quality speakers in each room.
7. Built-in television set which is properly ventilated.
8. Central sound system with talk-back equipment.
9. Closed-circuit television equipment.
10. Radio-television studio and control room with the necessary equipment.

THE SOURCES OF LOCALIZED HISTORY

Clifford L. Lord

Extensive illustrations of local historical resources and suggestions of where and how to find them compose this selection. Additional identification and ideas for the use of community *resources in history appear in the booklet from which the selection is extracted. It is the introductory one of a set of booklets dealing with historical resources in each of most of our states.*

THE SOURCES OF LOCALIZED HISTORY

WHAT ARE the sources of localized history? History is where you find it. Localized history is everywhere, and so are its sources.

Background knowledge, if wanted, can usually be found at least in part in several different places. Most states have been the subject of published volumes of state history—sometimes a single volume, sometimes a multivolume set. The index and chapter headings will be helpful in guiding you to pertinent material. Most counties have at least one printed history, often dating to the latter part of the nineteenth century. These, for the most part, are the so-called "mug books," containing a biographical section for which people prepared their own sketches and paid for their inclusion. An extra fee entitled one to one's picture. The biographies are a bit uncritical since each is written by the biographee. The county histories themselves are of widely different calibre. A few are very good, most are quite poor. But good and bad alike will give you some help on a rudimentary background of the history of your community. Many cities, towns, and villages, companies, colleges, and churches have also had their histories written and published. They will be helpful, but may leave unanswered questions of the type you will be exploring. Many local histories have been published, often serially in the local newspaper. The school, or certainly the public library, will have a copy of or at least a reference to, the issues of the newspapers in which these articles appeared. The history of many localities has been written, but not published. These unpublished manuscripts may be found in the public library or the local historical society. Published or unpublished, use these materials only for guidance, not as authorities. They are apt to be filled with the folk-myth and romantic nonsense to which much old-style local history is subject. They are apt to be inadequately researched. They are apt to miss both the wider implications and the real significance of what they record. They are guides, not gospel.

FROM *Teaching History with Community Resources*, Clifford Lord, ed., New York, 1964, Columbia Teachers College, pp. 29–33, 78–82. Used by permission. Dr. Lord is President of Hofstra University.

Many newspapers run, or have run, columns on what happened in the community ten or twenty-five or fifty years ago. These usually carry only a sentence per event, and some events are obviously more important than others. But if they record local, as distinct from national or international, events, they are suggestive. The paper also has probably run at several different periods historical accounts or articles which will be useful.

In addition, the local newspaper is the diary of the community, recording even s as they take place and in considerable detail. What is recorded tends to be simple and dramatic: the coming of the railroad, the opening of a new plant, a fire or flood, an election, the appearance of a national figure in town, the opening of a new bridge, the high school commencement, the repaving of Second Avenue. Advertisements give indication of price levels. Weather forecasts may record a prolonged drought. Job columns indicate salary levels. Legal notices may be important. The local paper seldom does the reflective, background, summary kind of article which is so very useful to the historian, but a lot of raw material for the localized historian lies in every local newspaper.

Government documents can be important sources. Federal and state studies often contain data (economic, geological, statistical, sociological) of significance to your own community; your librarian will be helpful in identifying those of use to you on any particular project. Local ordinances are usually printed when passed (sometimes just in the newspapers). Many official local reports are printed. Particularly helpful, for recent years, are the annual reports of the superintendent of schools (more and more of which are being published each year as school budgets face more intense public surveillance), and the presentations outlining the major features of the community budget.

The more detailed original (manuscript) records in the several major community offices will be even more useful. Land deeds, in the office of the Registrar of Deeds, trace the title to a given piece of property and list the consecutive owners of record of a given tract of land from the beginning of valid title. Tax rolls on a given piece of property are a good index as to when a building first improved the property, or when the initial hut was replaced by a clapboard mansion or a business block. The City Treasurer's office (by whatever title it is known) will have a fascinating picture of the evolution of the community's finances and a detailed record of what the taxpayers' money has been spent for year by year by year. The street department can tell you when Main Street was paved, what sorts of pavement (timber, timber block, corduroy, gravel, cobblestone, brick, macadam, concrete, bituminous asphalt, etc.) have been used consecutively and probably on what streets, and will give you all sorts of information as to the advantages and disadvantages of different types of pavement. The water department can tell you when water pipes and sewers were installed in different parts of the community, and can help on the history of sewage treatment and disposal. The Health Department can give you many vital statistics: the records of births and deaths, morbidity rates, and so forth. And the Board of Education can help you greatly with the history of your school and the school system and curriculum of the community.

The broadsides advertising for a runaway slave, a substitute for a man drafted for the Union forces, a reduced steamship fare, a special lecture at the opera house, the coming of a circus, or the latest attraction at the nickelodeon, may be just what is needed to fill in a particular bit of information. Files are apt to be found at the local library and the historical society.

The magazine article on some event or person of more than local interest may be helpful. So may the printed diary, the printed letter or letters, the memoirs of a local leader, political, industrial, or social. So will be the program of the local event, the dedication, the centennial observance of a local church or the library or the town itself, and the brochures or books printed in connection with such events. Or the program of the local theater or lecture or art show or dance or banquet. Or some other promotional material prepared for the Chamber of Commerce. Check with the library and historical society.

Biographical sketches of prominent figures will appear in the *Dictionary of American Biography, Appleton's Cyclopedia of American Biography, Who Was Who in America, Who's Who in America,* and its geographical children like *Who's Who in the East,* the *Directory of American Scholars,* the whole shelf of who's who type volumes: *Who's Who in Music, Who's Who in American Jewry,* and so on. Professional directories like the *Martindale-Hubbell Law Directory* or P. E. Mohr, *American Medical Directory* may be of limited use.. At least two states, Texas (*Handbook of Texas History*) and Wisconsin (*Dictionary of Wisconsin Biography*), have issued volumes including biographical sketches of men and women prominent in the history of these states. Obituaries and other articles in the newspapers when someone dies are of help. So, too, are the resolutions adopted by the organization or organizations to which a person belonged when he or she dies. So, too, are the self-composed biographical sketches in the county histories already referred to, *if* you remember that the person wrote the sketch about himself and paid for its insertion in the book.

Many basic statistics are obtainable from the published federal census, taken at the beginning of each new decade. Many more are obtainable in the several state censuses taken in many states for many years in the middle of each decade. For localized statistics, the mansuscript censuses, available from the National Archives on microfilm through 1870, are most useful. Here you can find not just the number of people in the community, but the occupation of each, the number of persons in the family, their age and sex. The census also shows the number of industrial establishments, from potash producers or munitions makers in earlier days to automobile plants and sugar refineries today, with the number of employees. The published census statistics give useful summaries. Most newspapers give local summaries when the census appears. City directories, published regularly (every year in many cases), list heads of families and businesses with street address and occupation and may be more readily available.

There will be many handwritten or typed (not printed) sources: the reminiscences of a citizen, an autobiography, a diary, a file of letters, the ledgers and journals of a store or an industry, the minutes of an official body such as the Common Council or of a literary society or a church auxiliary.

Court records, particularly the exhibits, can be extraordinarily revealing of ways of life, of prices and business methods, of social problems in the community at various stages of its history. Unfortunately such materials are not readily usable unless the local county courthouse has a (probably elderly) keeper of the records who really knows what is in his files and how to find it, or there is some member of the bar who has studied the history of the local court. Wills, on file in the probate court, are indicative of what sorts and amounts of property a person in a certain economic and social position (ascertainable elsewhere) was apt to have at any particular period.

There will be oral sources; the people who participated in some movement or event, or who have excellent memories of what happened in the town in other years in politics, or in business, or in other areas. Human memory is highly fallible, and memories must be checked against records. But the memory of participants is often the best clue as to why something was done or attempted when it was, what the motives of various people were in certain situations. If the student interviews a citizen, he should take careful notes; his own memory may be quite fallible. If a tape recording is made, it should be made by someone who already knows a good deal about the topic under discussion so that the person being interviewed can be kept on the track and so that questionable data can be challenged at the time and further explanation obtained.

In almost every community there are one or more people who have made a hobby of knowing the history of the community. Usually they are more than willing to share their knowledge with school children, and usually they are willing to have questions asked as to their sources: not just what they know but how they happen to know it. The local historical society or the local librarian can usually identify such people for you.

There will be physical remains: the photograph, the print, the tool, the forge, the painting, the implement, the vessel, the vehicle, the building, the ruin, the site, the telegraph key, the fire engine, the lottery wheel for the Civil War draft, the abandoned right-of-way, the ditch of the old canal, the mine head and tailings, the sluice and the millstone, the earthworks, the dentist's turnkey, the leech box.

For the more advanced student, this is an appropriate time to introduce the difference between primary and secondary sources, the *primary* source being an original source—a letter, a diary, an account book, a minute book, a personal reminiscence, an unretouched photograph; the *secondary* source being a secondhand, reconstructed account of what happened: a newspaper, a magazine article, a book (other than one of reminiscences), a sketch, print, or painting made after an event.

Between things you can read, things you can see, and people of whom you can ask questions, there are many sources of localized history readily at hand. A little looking, a little probing, will yield a lot.

PART SIX
THE FUTURE OF THE
SOCIAL STUDIES

The recent and current ferment in the social studies is sufficient to indicate that something really is afoot. Despite occasional pooh-poohing from scattered quarters, it is increasingly clear that the social studies have already entered an era of extensive reconsideration, significant experimentation with revised or new elements, and the definite prospect of widespread and perhaps fundamental changes. This section attempts to provide at least the flavor of the changes that are underway and perhaps prospective.

Research in social studies during the past few years has shown signs of making increasingly significant contributions to the field. What is the nature and what are the findings of such research? What weaknesses are found in the previous research on social studies? Although a tremendous amount of additional research is needed, what aspects of social studies should receive high priority? Can sound and useful research be done on the more elusive and intangible aspects of social studies, such as "attitudinal" learning? Are there truly values to be gained from research in the social and behavioral sciences? If so, how can findings be applied to the content and methodology of the social studies? Should those in social studies education devote their efforts to developing their field as a distinctive discpline?

And what of the many proposals, curriculum revisions, and other new elements that appear more and more frequently nowadays? Are current proposals and new programs going too far? Are they going far enough? Is there significant and undesirable waste in the many and varied current proposals and projects? What are the factors that individual teachers and those in curriculum-planning groups should consider in judging new proposals and experiments?

This concluding section of readings attempts to provide a means for the reader to become as up-to-date as practicable on secondary school social studies of the present and the emerging future. Further pertinent information appears in the Appendix. Alert, informed, and diligent teachers are, after all, the resource most basic to any broad and meaningful improvement of their field.

1

The Role of Research

REVIEW OF RESEARCH IN THE
TEACHING OF SOCIAL STUDIES

Sylvia E. Harrison and Robert J. Solomon

An abstract of quite recent research on the teaching of social studies indicates that significant findings are being made. Here is an extract from a fuller review of findings reported during the first third of the current decade. The *section reproduced here involves research on instructional methods and omits the original article's summary of studies on curriculum and on the teaching of controversial issues.*

M ETHODS. In comparing two methods of self-instruction in teaching an eighth-grade social studies unit, one without teacher supervision and one with pupil-teacher conferences, with the conventional class instruction practices, Ingham (13) found that only with high achievers did the self-instruction processes prove more effective in raising achievement. Otherwise, there was no significant difference among the three approaches.

Phillips (21) found that a core-like method of instruction is no more effective in achievement, in developing verbal, manipulative, and computational interests, and in improving social adjustment than a non-core-like method of instruction, and that a non-core-like method used in a double period was more productive of liberal attitudes than a core-like method in junior high social studies classes.

Baughman and Pruitt (1), in comparing the gains on social studies achievement tests in grades seven and eight as a function of (1) supplemental study for enrichment, the assignment of homework designed to encourage exploration in depth of a given area and a creative approach to study, or (2) supplemental study for reinforcement, the assignment of homework of a traditional and routine variety, concluded that the two methods of assigning homework were equally effective in terms of gains made in achievement tests.

FROM *Social Education*, 28:280–287, May, 1964. Used by permission. The authors are staff members at the Educational Testing Service, Princeton, N.J.

Schminke (26) reports that there was no difference obtained on a current events test with the use of two approaches to the utilization of a weekly news magazine: a limited systematic approach characterized by use of the magazine alone and a supplemental systematic approach characterized by the use of the magazine as well as related activities. Results also indicated that, regardless of the method of instruction, a systematic presentation of current events can influence the students' use of news media outside of school.

Cristiani's experimentation (5) into the use of informal dramatizations in the sixth-grade social studies indicated that students gained on a Social Studies Information Test and on a modified Bogardus Social Distance Scale, and demonstrated greater interest and improved attitude toward the social studies all as a function of the use of dramatization.

Forster (11) reports that a significantly higher degree of learning took place as a result of field trips than occurred as a result of classroom activities; and Skov (28) reports that when an elementary school program is structured to promote social learning for democratic behavior, the quantity of learned factual information seems to exceed normal expectancy as judged by standardized test norms, while also resulting in many useful social learnings for democratic behavior.

Lux (18) in his comparison of the teaching methods used by superior and nonsuperior social studies teachers found that both used the same methods and activities but to different extents, the former making more use of outside readings, oral reports, research papers, and a topical approach, and the latter making more use of surveys, community projects, and a chronological approach.

By following the principle that the sophisticated techniques of today's social scientists can serve the teaching of the social studies, Coleman (22, 23) has initiated research that suggests a significant new approach to the methods of social studies instruction. The use of game theory, in conjunction with the techniques of simulation; in which a model is used to reduce a complex construct to a manageable one, has been the basis of Coleman's present research at the secondary level. The research consists of the development of games, and the experimentation and testing of the games in schools in order to ascertain their effect on individual students' motivation, on comprehension of game roles and knowledge of game content, and on the values of the teenage culture relating to scholastic effort. The use of games is an attempt (1) to bring the future into the present, permitting students to play roles in a setting to which they would not be exposed until adulthood, (2) to act as motivating devices, and (3) to eliminate the teacher as the judge since the games themselves are self-judging, the outcome determining one's success. Two general categories of games are planned, socio-economic games and games of scientific discovery, but only one particular game has been investigated experimentally. In an exploratory study, Boocock (2) studied the effects of a presidential campaign game designed by Coleman. The students were given a game *Handbook* and split into teams of "campaign managers" whose functions were to conduct polls, allocate funds, analyze views of voters in their districts, decide what issues their candidates should take a stand on, and plot strategy. The campaign results were refereed by a computer which provided the "simulated environment." It was programed with the actual views and voting intentions of 800 Baltimore residents sampled during the 1960 campaign. Evaluation of this exploratory game session in the form of observations and questionnaires administered to all participants indicated that the major effects of the game lay in the area of changed attitudes and interests rather than learning of specific factual information. In addition to other findings of this first study, the finding that the game presently is not an effective teaching device is to be given special attention in future experimentation.

In a college political science course in National Security Policy, Brooks (34) has introduced a ten-day sequence of "war games" to give students the experience of making decisions under the pressure of time with incomplete information. One of the two sections of this course assumed the roles and functions of the chief military and civilian decision makers for the United States, while the other assumed comparable roles for the U.S.S.R. in a given problem. Although Brooks made no rigorous evaluation of the "war games," they represent one attempt at game construction without the use of computers, which are of limited availability to teachers and which require highly specialized knowledge of programing.

Development of critical thinking and work-study skills. Although a statement of social studies objectives that does not include reference to the development of critical thinking is rare, the teaching of critical thinking proves to be one of the more difficult tasks of the social studies teacher. Fox (12), using a questionnaire administered to teachers of Problems of Democracy courses, found that the methods for developing the higher levels of critical thinking were most difficult for teachers to employ successfully, while those concerning simple information gathering were least difficult. In addition, nearly 10 per cent of the teachers said that they did not have sufficient time to teach the skills of critical thinking. That the more experienced teachers found reasoning and logical skills more difficult to teach than the less experienced teachers was interpreted by Fox as a trend in teacher education towards developing effective teachers of critical thinking.

Scientific inquiry in elementary school children through the use of motion pictures and verbal "experimentation." The Illinois Studies in Inquiry Training, of which Suchman is director, has experimented with the teaching of strategies and tactics of scientific inquiry to children who learn to apply them in question-and-answer investigations.

A considerable amount of research, McGarry (19), Rothstein (25), Wickman (31), and Wallen *et al* (30), has involved defining the optimum conditions for the teaching of critical thinking. Cousins (3), Cox (4), Elsmere (7), and Massialas (20), have set their investigations of critical thinking against the background of our contemporary society and the value decisions demanded of each individual in the society. The primary concern of these four investigations was the matter of "intelligent choice, how it is attained, and in what ways the teacher can contribute to it." In particular, Cox and Massialas experimented with "inquiry-directed processes" in teaching United States history and world history, respectively. Each study involved a control group, a highly structured teacher-centered class, and an experimental group, a less structured inquiry-oriented class. The use of standardized instruments, tapes, and a log of daily activities (the last of which proved a most valuable source of insight into teaching and learning) indicated a comparable or superior performance for the students in the experimental group compared to those in the control group. The former learned as many facts, indicating that the inquiry-centered approach does not lessen the learning of this kind of material. The skills of critical thinking, as defined by Massialas in his model of critical thinking, were identifiable to a greater extent among the students of the inquiry-oriented situation than among those in the more structured situation. Finally the former were less teacher-oriented at the end of the eighteen-week experiment, having reached the point where they could provide themselves with appropriate cues for inquiry, whereas the latter remained teacher-oriented throughout the course of the experiment, with the teacher providing cues for subsequent discussion.

Cousins experimented with an eighth-grade social studies class in which he introduced a carefully defined model of critical thinking, the intention being to review and revise the model in line with the results. His teaching methods and results are similar to those of Cox and Massialas. On the basis of his results, Cousins has proposed a revised model of the development of critical thinking that includes the activities of generalization, deduction, problem-solving, and sensitivity to values, which he holds as an accurate representation of the intellectual development that occurred in his experimental group and would occur in other eighth-grade social studies classes in which similar teaching methods are used. Elsmere's study was designed to examine the effectiveness of the problem-solving approach in aiding students in the acquisition and retention of historical facts and in the acquisition and retention of problem-solving skills. Using methods similar to those of the previous investigations, the experimental group made statistically significant gains over the control group on all measures. Elsmere's particular contribution to this group of investigations was in the systematic preparation of objective and subjective tests for use in comparing educational outcomes.

Another area of critical thinking has been the examination of critical thinking in relation to dogmatism. Ehrlich and Kemp have used Rokeach's investigations of open-closed belief systems as a basis for their own studies. Rokeach's concept of dogmatism is that of (1) a relatively closed cognitive organization of beliefs and disbeliefs about reality, (2) organized around a central set of beliefs about absolute authority, which in turn (3) provides a framework for patterns of intolerance and qualified tolerance toward others (24). Those high in dogmatism presumably have closed systems while those low in dogmatism presumably have open systems.

Using a college sociology class, Ehrlich (6) found an inverse relationship between dogmatism and degree of learning. Kemp's findings (14, 15) indicated that those college freshmen who were low in dogmatism as determined by Rokeach's Dogmatism Scale, were more successful in a test of critical thinking than those high in dogmatism. The latter had a higher percentage of errors in those problems which required the study of several factors for decision and the deferring of a conclusion until each factor had been carefully examined and evaluated. Kemp hypothesizes that the individual high in dogmatism has difficulty in tolerating ambiguities, and is impelled toward a "closure" before full consideration is given to each piece of evidence. Kemp's second study (16) compared the improvement in critical thinking of those low in dogmatism with those high, the hypothesis being that the former would show greater improvement in this area than the latter. The experimental group received special instruction in solving critical-thinking problems. The findings indicated that within the control group there was no significant improvement in performance of either those high or low in dogmatism, whereas in the experimental group both the highs and the lows improved. On the basis of these two studies, Kemp concludes that those classroom conditions that are favorable to improvement of critical thinking are small permissive or "safe" groups in which the usual threats are minimized, and in which the attention given to critical thinking is accompanied by practice.

The objectives of the Cornell Project, Critical Thinking Readiness in Grades 1-12 (8) have been: (1) to answer the readiness question; namely, what are students capable of learning regarding various aspects of critical thinking, and in what grade; (2) to develop instruments for the measure of the two aspects with which this project is particularly concerned, deduction and assumption-finding; and (3) to test the various assumptions upon which the study is based. The emphasis of this current project is less on how to teach critical thinking, and more on what and when children can be taught. To this end, Ennis and Millman (9, 10) have been responsible for the construction of five critical thinking tests, two of which are general, and three of which are specific to deduction.

Witt's studies (32, 33) investigated the effectiveness of certain techniques of reading instruction on developing critical thinking, reading skills, and conceptualization of social studies content. The studies, one with an average group, and one with an above-average group of junior high school students, indicated that: (1) specific skills and techniques stressed in reading; namely, organization through outlining and drawing conclusions from factual materials, relate to social studies achievement, and bring about measurable gains in reading; and (2) the concept approach to the teaching of social studies, focusing on the development of such concepts as health, world interdependence, natural resources, self-government, etc., is a desirable method by which critical thinking can be developed.

Scott (27) found that a gain in reading achievement correlated highest with a gain in social studies and lowest with a gain in science among sixth graders. In particular, the correlation between reading achievement and social studies achievement was high for a low ability group and low for a high ability group which Scott partially attributes to the fact that the social studies test materials may not have been appropriate for the high ability group. In correlating several measures with current affairs knowledge, Kravitz (17) found reading achievement and social studies achievement to have the highest correlations with the amount of knowledge seventh and eighth graders have of current affairs.

B. Othanel Smith feels that "teaching behavior itself must be thoroughly understood from a logical standpoint as a condition for effective work on the improvement of critical thinking in the classroom." To this end, he has made an analytic and descriptive study of teaching behavior (29) and has arrived at a description of the logical structure of classroom discourse in which he defines two aspects in the analysis of teaching behavior: the tactical or logical operations, the forms verbal behavior takes as the teacher shapes the subject matter in the course of instruction, and the strategic operations, the larger movements within which the logical operations are performed. Smith's study of teaching strategies is still only in the formative stage. On the other hand, his study of teaching behavior from a logical standpoint has enabled him to arrive at one major unit of discourse, the episode, which can be characterized as one of several logical operations, such as definitions, designation, classification, comparing and contrasting, conditional inferring, explanation, evaluation, and opining, etc. One tentative conclusion of his study is that differences may exist in the extent to which the logical operations are employed from teacher to teacher and area to area.

(1) M. D. Baughman and W. Pruitt. "Supplemental Study for Enrichment Versus Supplemental Study for Reinforcement of Academic Achievement." *National Association of Secondary School Principals Bulletin* 47:154–7; March 1963.

(2) Sarane S. Boocock. "Effects of Election Campaign Game in Four High School Classes." Report No. 1 of Research Programs in the Effects of Games with Simulated Environments in Secondary Education (James S. Coleman and James L. Kuethe, Co-

directors). Published by Department of Social Relations of Johns Hopkins University. October 1963.

(3) J. E. Cousins. "Development of Reflective Thinking in an Eighth Grade Social Studies Class." *Indiana University School of Education Bulletin* 39:36–73; May 1963.

(4) C. B. Cox. "Description and Appraisal of a Reflective Method of Teaching United States History." *Indiana University School of Education Bulletin* 39:74–113; May, 1963.

(5) Vincent A. Cristiani. "Informal Dramatizations in Social Studies, Grade VI." *Dissertation Abstracts* 21:3375; May 1963.

(6) Howard J. Ehrlich. "Dogmatism and Learning." *Journal of Abnormal and Social Psychology* 62:148–149; January 1961.

(7) R. T. Elsmere. "An Experimental Study Utilizing the Problem-Solving Approach in Teaching United States History." *Indiana University School of Education Bulletin* 39:114–138, May 1963.

(8) Robert H. Ennis. "Critical Thinking Readiness in Grades 1–12." (Appendix A.) Project No. 1680. Revised April 2, 1962.

(9) Robert H. Ennis and Jason Millman. "Cornell Critical Thinking Test, Form X."

(10) Robert H. Ennis and Jason Millman. "Cornell Critical Thinking Test, Form Z."

(11) Edith C. Forster. "Evaluation of the Field Trip in the Foundation of Social Concepts and Generalizations." *Dissertation Abstracts* 22:181; July 1961.

(12) Raymond B. Fox. "Difficulties in Developing Skill in Critical Thinking." *Journal of Educational Research* 55:335–7; April 1962.

(13) George E. Ingham. "Comparison of Two Methods of Self-Instruction in Teaching a Unit in Social Studies." *Dissertation Abstracts* 23:1623; November 1962.

(14) C. Gratton Kemp. "Critical Thinking: Open and Closed Minds with Implications for Social Studies". Paper presented at Philadelphia Meeting of National Council for the Social Studies. November 24, 1962.

(15) C. Gratton Kemp. "Effect of Dogmatism on Critical Thinking." *School Science and Mathematics* 60:314–19; April 1960.

(16) C. Gratton Kemp. "Improvement of Critical Thinking in Relation to Open-Closed Belief Systems." *Journal of Experimental Education* 31:321–25; Spring 1963.

(17) Bernard Kravitz. "Factors Related to Knowledge of Current Affairs in Grades 7 and 8." *Social Education* 26:143–45; March 1962.

(18) John E. Lux. "A Comparison of Teaching Methods Used by Superior and Non-Superior Teachers." *Social Studies* 53:171–174; October 1962.

(19) Eugene L. McGarry. "Experiment in the Teaching of Reflective Thinking in the Social Studies." *Dissertation Abstracts* 22:2721; February 1962.

(20) B. G. Massialas. "Developing a Method of Inquiry in Teaching World History." *Indiana University School of Education Bulletin* 39:1–35; May 1963.

(21) James E. Phillips. "An Appraisal of Social Studies Instruction in Single and Double Period, and in Core-like and Non-core-like Classes in Selected Junior High Schools of St. Paul, Minnesota." *Dissertation Abstracts* 22:3123; March 1962.

(22) "Playing Politics in the Classroom." *Johns Hopkins Magazine* 15:14–17; October 1963.

(23) "Research Program in the Effects of Games with Simulated Environments in Secondary Education." A proposal to Carnegie Corporation of New York from the Department of Social Relations, Johns Hopkins University, June 8, 1962.

(24) Milton Rokeach. "The Nature and Meaning of Dogmatism." *Psychological Review* 61:194–204; 1954.

(25) Arnold Rothstein. "An Experiment in Developing Critical Thinking Through the Teaching of American History." *Dissertation Abstracts* 21:1141; November 1960.

(26) Clarence W. Schminke. "A Study of the Effective Utilization of a Classroom News Magazine in Teaching Current Events." *Dissertation Abstracts* 21:1874; January 1961.

(27) C. M. Scott. "Relationship Between Intelligence Quotients and Gain in Reading Achievement with Arithmetic Reasoning, Social Studies, and

Science." *Journal of Educational Research* 56:322–6; February 1963.

(28) Lyle L. Skov. "The Teaching Learning of Factual Information in the Social Sciences in a Program that is Deliberately Structured to Promote Social Learnings for Democratic Behavior." *Dissertation Abstracts* 22:4283; June 1962.

(29) B. Othanel Smith and Milton O. Meux. "A Study in the Logic of Teaching." Urbana, Ill.: University of Illinois, College of Education, Bureau of Educational Research, 1962.

(30) N. E. Wallen, V. F. Haubrich, and I. E. Reid. "The Outcomes of Curriculum Modifications Designed to Foster Critical Thinking." *Journal of Educational Research* 56:529–534; July-August 1963.

(31) Peter M. Wickman. "An Exploration into the Relevance of Methods and the Organization of Learning Experiences to the Objective of Crictical Thinking in History of Civilization at Greenville College." *Dissertation Abstracts* 21:101; July 1960.

(32) M. Witt. "Developing Reading Skills and Critical Thinking." *Social Education* 25:239–42; May 1961.

(33) M. Witt. "Study of the Effectiveness of Certain Techniques of Reading Instruction in Developing the Ability of Junior High School Students to Conceptualize Social Studies Content." *Journal of Educational Research* 56:198–204; December 1962.

(34) More information on the "war games" can be obtained from Professor Glenn E. Brooks, Department of Political Science, Colorado College, Colorado Springs, Colorado.

RESEARCH PROSPECTS IN THE SOCIAL STUDIES

Byron G. Massialas

In this selection an authority criticizes the research on the teaching of social studies during the past generation or so. His criticisms may not apply fully to current research, but they do provide guides to aid those teachers who try to glean valid findings from reports of research studies.

As EARLY as 1937, in reviewing ten studies conducted in connection with master's theses in the area of social studies methodology, Phillips (18) concluded that (a) most researchers utilized a more or less stereotyped technique in determining variability of outcomes of instruction, the single variable technique being the most frequently used; (b) most researchers conducted investigations of the pretest-posttest variety; (c) most investigators left unde-

FROM *The Bulletin of the School of Education*, Indiana University, 38:20–24, January, 1962. Used by permission. Dr. Massialas is a professor of education at the University of Michigan.

fined certain significant and relevant terms and procedures; (d) many researchers literally abused the experimental and statistical technique, thus producing invalid findings; (e) the social studies were not amenable to the same treatment as other areas of human knowledge and a mere transplanting of a given method or technique of experimentation without adapting it to the peculiarities of the discipline could not yield reliable and fruitful results— a fact which researchers had, generally, failed to understand; and (f) in spite of the various manipulations and treatments of data, studies that had compared teaching methods have, for the most part, failed to refute the null hypothesis of no significant differences in outcomes.

Now, about twenty-five years later, Phillips' remarks and criticisms would be very pertinent and applicable to the studies that have been conducted in the meantime. It would follow that twenty-five years of educational development in the research process has not affected social studies research very much. However, in reviewing the studies summarized above, the same expressions and terminologies as were employed by their respective authors have been used.

1. Most experimenters have utilized the single variable technique (Glaser, Henderson, Quillen and Hanna, Cook and Koeninger, Kight and Mickelson, Peters), although some of them (Quillen and Hanna, Peters) acknowledged the possibility of other uncontrolled variables playing an important role in the experiment. For example, social relations among students, the personality of the teacher and his varying attitudes toward the control and experimental groups, the effects of teachers other than those being included in the experiment, and the like might very well account for differences or no differences in outcomes. Nachman and Opochinsky (15) pointedly entertained the proposition that variance of outcomes is due to many factors, factors which have not been adequately considered by researchers, in addition to the specific methods utilized by the teacher.

2. Most of the experiments conducted in the area of social studies methodology have attempted to compare methods. For example, a "subject-centered" method was compared with a "reflectively oriented" method or an "action-centered" method. It has seldom occurred to the investigators that methods may not be comparable. In order to be able to compare two items, one must be able to find certain dimensions in which they are comparable. Assuming that one finds a dimension or continuum, reflective-non-reflective for instance, one would have to be able to find the component parts comprising the dimension and the dimension criteria. When one compares a fact-centered method with a reflectively centered method, he immediately has two dimensions which are drastically different and which cannot be judged by one set of criteria, for instance standardized tests of factual recall. What has not been realized in the studies mentioned is that the dimension within which the investigation operates should be fully identified and explored. Complex classroom situations would demand investigation on a multidimensional basis, thus necessitating a drastic change in research strategies and techniques.

Downey (5), in an attempt to construct a master conceptual framework for education, touched on the point just developed. He identified three fundamental dimensions in the educative process which he labeled "substantive," "procedural," and "environmental." Within each dimension he identified a number of components or elements. The first dimension was comprised of strategies of inquiry inherent in the given discipline and the content of the various areas of knowledge. In the second dimension the component parts were group climate, teacher guidance and interpolation, and the natural quest for learning. The last dimension was comprised of the organization of personnel, available physical conditions, and technologies. The process of education was the interaction of all these components with consequent outcomes, i.e., changes in the behavior of pupils. A change in one component would inevitably bring about changes in the others and in the total educative process. Thus it would become practically impossible to change one element without changing all of the elements.

To illustrate the above with one example: It is impossible to compare two methods of teaching social studies while holding constant everything else but the methods, for, when the method is changed, changes in content to be studied and the way that content is to be studied automatically occur. Also the social-emotional climate in the class is immediately affected. This interaction constitutes a new configuration which studies in methodology of instruction have not considered as such. Our blindfold stress on relatively archaic methods of investigation has perhaps hindered insightful perceptions into the social educative process.

3. Many investigators have not adequately identified and described the dependent variable and the instrument purporting to measure it. For instance, the Stanford Investigation Study (19) referred to "significant growth" of pupils as being the outcome of the experiment, but, although this was operationally defined, the reader would wonder whether the selection of standardized tests to measure such growth was consistent with the method introduced and the kinds of skills anticipated as the result of employing such method. In other words, the dependent variable seemed to have been identified in terms of existing standardized tests as a matter of convenience rather than in terms of carefully worked out measures which would directly pertain to the teaching method under investigation and to anticipated outcomes. When one was given a certain score as an indication of growth one could not possibly know definitely what he really had and what the score meant. In this respect, the method and the rationale employed seemed to fit the instruments that were available rather than the instruments to be constructed especially to fit the rationale and the method. This observation would apply practically to all studies that have been summarized in this section of the report.

4. In connection with the utilization of standardized tests in experimental studies one would have to admit that most tests were basically tests of factual recall. It would seem rather paradoxical that many investigators who have

operated under a reflective or critical inquiry orientation have accepted, in the last analysis, achievement on factual tests as the determinant of success or failure of the instructional method under investigation (Bayles, Quillen and Hanna, Peters).

Even when standardized tests purporting to measure critical thinking were used (such as the Watson-Glaser Tests of Critical Thinking or the STEP Social Studies Test), one would have to assume that there is a single approach to reflection and critical thinking. But this would not be a valid assumption because reflective-oriented teachers utilize many approaches and instructional practices. Each approach to teaching has its own inherent characteristics and attributes and can be measured only by directly revelant instruments. Nachman and Opochinsky (15) pointed out that different teaching methods have produced differences in learning, but that these effects have been masked in the measurement process.

5. Most researchers based their findings on standardized tests. When other means in evaluation of outcomes were used, such as observations, interviews, questionnaires, anecdotal records, and the like, they were relegated only secondary place. (The use of tape-recordings and video-tapes in objective evaluation of classroom discussion has not been explored in the social studies. Bales and Flanders (1), Carpenter (3), Harris (7), Heyns and Lippitt (9), Medley and Mitzel (12), Moutakes, Siegel, and Schalock (14), Ryans (20), and Smith (21), are just a few among many investigators in areas other than social studies who have attempted to construct objective instruments for observation of classroom interactions.)

Making a case for more descriptive research in education, Carpenter (3) drew a list of restrictions attached to research of the "response-response correlations" and "controlled experimentation" varieties which depend heavily on tests. His main objection to the use of tests was that they failed to get at the dynamics of behavior, and that tests offered very little insight into how learning takes place. Generalizations based on tests would have to be restricted to specific tests; when tests were changed, outcomes would change too.

Cox (4) and Massialas (11), experimenting with reflectively oriented methods of teaching United States history and world history at the eleventh- and tenth-grade levels, respectively, utilized standardized tests to measure differences between each set of their equated groups. Had they depended entirely on the scores obtained from the tests they would have had to conclude that the method of instruction utilized with the experimental group had no peculiar characteristics in the development of reflective thinking. But they employed two other means to obtain data concerning pupil classroom behavior. At certain intervals they taped classroom discussion, and for a semester they kept a daily log of teacher-pupil interactions. Reflective thinking was operationally defined and was broken down into a number of discernible tasks.

Their conclusions based on findings of data obtained through the latter means (tapes and daily calendar) were basically different from those obtained through the administration of tests. On the basis of tapes and the daily log they were able to show significant growth in reflective thinking skills among students in the experimental group. Massialas (11), suggested that standardized tests did not measure reflective thinking as defined and practiced by individual researchers and teachers.

6. Researchers were not careful with the terminology they used. Terms such as "fact," "unit," "teacher-centered," and "gain" were not defined. In several instances the researchers operated under the assumption that there was a common meaning attached to these or similar terms. In view of their usage, however, in social studies research such implicit assumption was not warranted. Also, certain instructional methods utilized in the experiments have not been adequately described and defined. As a rule, investigators attempted to describe only the experimental method, or the "newer" method, loosely referring to the control method as the "conventional" or "traditional," with no additional explanation or elaboration.

7. Although some investigators stated the purpose of their inquiry, the majority of them did not even attempt a statement of objectives of their study. The identity and the background of the researcher and his associates was dealt with even less in all of the studies mentioned. When objectives were stated, they were usually directed to practical and rather vague considerations —for example, to help the teacher of the social studies improve his instructional procedures and curriculum (Peters, Bayles, Meier, Cleary, and Davis). Only one or two seemed to have long-range purposes in mind, i.e., to stimulate further research and experimentation (Glaser; Oliver).

8. One could summarize the comments by saying that investigators of social studies methodology have, for the most part, not been able to construct theoretical frames of reference which would allow them intelligently and coherently to investigate the teaching and the learning process in the classroom. Perhaps lack of an all-inclusive theoretical construct accounted for loose statements of objectives and the obvious inability to link objectives to outcomes, evaluation instruments, and strategies of attack.

(1) Bales, Robert F., and Flanders, Neel A., "Planning an Observation Room and Group Laboratory," *American Sociological Review* 19:771–781, December, 1954.

(2) Bayles, Ernest E., *Experiments with Reflective Teaching*, Kansas Studies in Education, vol. 6, no. 3, University of Kansas Publications, Lawrence, Kansas, April, 1956, 32 pp.

(3) Carpenter, Finley, "Wanted: More Descriptive Research in Education,"

Educational Research Bulletin 33: 149–154, September 15, 1954.

(4) Cox, C. Benjamin, *A Description and Appraisal of a Reflective Method of Teaching United States History*, Unpublished doctor's thesis, Indiana University, Bloomington, 1961, 267 pp.

(5) Downey, Lawrence W., "Direction Amid Change," *Phi Delta Kappan* 42:186–191, February, 1961.

(6) Glaser, Edward M., *An Experiment in the Development of Critical Thinking*,

Contributions to Education, no. 843, Bureau of Publications, Teachers College, Columbia University, New York, 1941, 212 pp.

(7) Harris, Ben M., *The Recording Operation*, A Demonstration Research Project by the staff of the University of Texas' Mental Health in Teacher Education Program, The University of Texas, Austin, 1960, n.p. mim.

(8) Henderson, Kenneth B., "The Teaching of Critical Thinking," *Phi Delta Kappan* 39:280–282, March, 1958.

(9) Heyns, Roger W., and Lippitt, Ronald, "Systematic Observational Techniques," in *Handbook of Social Psychology*, vol. 1, pp. 37–404, edited by Gardner Lindzey, Addison-Wesley Publishing Co., Cambridge, Mass., 1954.

(10) Kight, Stanford S., and Mickelson, John M., "Problem vs. Subject," *The Clearing House* 24:3–7, September, 1949.

(11) Massialas, Byron G., *Description and Analysis of a Method of Teaching a High School Course in World History*, Unpublished doctor's thesis, Indiana University, Bloomington, 1961, 239 pp., typed.

(12) Medley, Donald M., and Mitzel, Harold E., "A Technique for Measuring Classroom Behavior," *Journal of Educational Psychology* 49:86–92, April, 1958.

(13) Meier, Arnold R.; Cleary, Florence Damon; and Davis, Alice M., *A Curriculum for Citizenship*, Wayne University Press, Detroit, 1952, 413 pp.

(14) Moustakas, Clark E.; Siegel, Irving E.; and Schalock, Henry D., "Objective Method for the Measurement and Analysis of Child-Adult Interaction," *Child Development* 27:109–134, June, 1956.

(15) Nachman, Marvin, and Opochinsky, Seymour, "The Effects of Different Teaching Methods: A Methodological Study," *Journal of Educational Psychology* 49:245–249, October, 1958.

(16) Oliver, Donald, and Baker, Susan, "The Case Method," *Social Education* 23:25–28, January, 1959.

(17) Peters, Charles C., *Teaching High School History and Social Studies for Citizenship Training*, The Miami Experiment in Democratic, Action-Centered Education, DAC, University of Miami, Coral Gables, Fla., 1948, 192 pp.

(18) Phillips, Burr W., "Investigating in the Field of Methods," in *The Contributions of Research to the Teaching of the Social Studies*, pp. 45–74, edited by Charles C. Barnes, Eighth Yearbook, National Council for the Social Studies, Cambridge, Mass., 1937.

(19) Quillen, I. James, and Hanna, Lavone A., *Education for Social Competence*, Scott, Foresman and Co., Chicago, 1948, 572 pp.

(20) Ryans, David G., *Characteristics of Teachers*, Council on Education, Washington, D.C., 1960, 416 pp.

(21) Smith, B. Othanel, A *Study of the Logic of Teaching; The Logical Structure of Teaching and the Development of Critical Thinking*, Bureau of Educational Research, College of Education, University of Illinois, Urbana, 1959.

PRIORITIES OF NEEDED RESEARCH
ON VALUES IN EDUCATION

Roy A. Price

What are the most needed future emphases or directions for research on social studies? This report comes from the director of a recent conference that brought together social scientists and social studies educators to consider the question. This selection gives his report of three varying outlooks, presented at the conference, on the role of values in education generally and in social studies particularly.

VALUES IN EDUCATION

THE THREE positions quoted below are indicative of a significant difference of opinion among conference personnel on the role of the social studies in relation to the development of attitudes, beliefs, and values. Opinions ranged from the indoctrination of beliefs, attitudes, and values, to the position that the one value to which we are (or should be) committed is that of scientific method.

Hanna

We are at a stage in our history where science and technology have forced us to form larger communities of men. We have been forced to invent new social technologies to operate in this larger area. Each time society enters a transition period, social invention is needed to take care of technology in the larger community. We in our time have need for more social invention, more creative effort. We need research to discover the commonality of values, and education to reinforce those values which have been built up in our society over a long period of time, and we need research on which to develop and base new attitudes and loyalties for this generation.

Frankel

As teachers and citizens we have an obligation to meet the legitimate demands of our society that certain general attitudes be generated. As long as there is any element of authority in the classroom, it is disingenuous to say that we merely invite students to make up their own minds. We are not doing *just* that and we ought to face it.

FROM *Needed Research in the Teaching of Social Studies*, Research Bulletin no. 1, Roy A. Price, ed., Washington, D.C.: National Council for the Social Studies, 1964, pp. 4–8. Used by permission. Dr. Price is a professor at the Maxwell Graduate School of Citizenship and Public Affairs, Syracuse University.

Metcalf

Any attempt to inculcate any set of values invariably calls for distortion of knowledge. One is not free to choose freedom unless he is free to compare freedom with its alternative.

A conference highlight was reached in the address of Charles Frankel who raised three basic questions in this area: (1) What is the relationship of social studies to values? Are the social studies dependent upon a value system, committed to a value system, or are they neutral? (2) What is the practical role of the social sciences in the education of the young, particularly with regard to the transmission of certain social values? (3) What is the relationship of the social studies as inquiries into the sore spots of our society, and the other quite legitimate goal of American schools, which is to help students to live together, to learn mutual respect for one another and the like? That is, what is the goal of the American schools as a socializer?

Frankel suggested that preliminary to any rationally devised program of research aimed at improvement of the teaching of the social studies we are required as citizens and as teachers to be clearer than we are now about our own attitudes, beliefs, and values. To deal successfully with these questions it is first necessary to pin down some fundamental principles and to make certain basic moral decisions. This would suggest not only "scientific" inquiry, but self-interrogation, a "disciplined dialogue with oneself and others," an effort to find out just what the principles are to which we, as teachers of the social studies, are willing to commit ourselves. Among the perplexing questions raised were:

1. What is our purpose in conducting new research in social attitudes, beliefs, and values?
2. What sort of information do we want?
3. Should we stress the contrasts between principles men profess and the principles evident in their conduct?
4. Do we wish merely to discover the values, beliefs, and attitudes we hold, or do we have an obligation to make inquiries about values, beliefs, and attitudes as they "ought" to be?
5. Do teachers simply have the obligation of transmitting the values of society?
6. How far do we really wish to go in studying beliefs, attitudes, and values in the context of alternatives?
7. Are we prepared to accept sweetly diluted discussions of difficult social problems, or are we going to insist that the truth, the whole truth, and nothing but the truth be taught?
8. Do not schools have a legitimate mission of promoting a common sense of citizenship among their students?

9. Does not a school have an obligation to pass on a certain attitude to the young?
10. Is it appropriate to induce belief on their part in the strength and rightness of the society to which they belong?

It may be useful to return to Frankel's three basic issues, although it is admittedly hazardous to summarize too briefly his views on these issues. As to whether the social studies are dependent upon a value system, committed to a value system, or neutral, he suggested that if the social studies are not value free they have no claim to being neutral or objective. If, on the other hand, they are value free, are they not irresponsible? Students have simply not been introduced to the concept of social study unless they clearly grasp the idea that nothing is sacred, even their own ideas.

His second basic issue concerned the role of the social studies in the education of the young, in regard to the transmission of certain social values and certain political values. Here Frankel noted that the school system is, of course, committed to the transmission of certain desirable attitudes for the young. Moral and social attitudes are indeed transmitted by the very cultural atmosphere of the school. Social studies cannot be looked to as the sole or even principal transmitters of the values of the community which are thought desirable. The social studies do, however, incorporate certain special values such as the attempt to be objective, to look at oneself in one's own group dispassionately, to recognize how stubborn are diversities between different individuals and different groups, to distrust simple formulas in study of human affairs. He suggested particular attention to the field of constitutional government and particularly the American Bill of Rights.

Frankel's third issue concerned the paradox between the role of the school as committed to the transmission of certain legitimate goals of the school system as a socializer, and the function of the social studies as inquirer into the sore spots of our society. There is a certain antagonism between the goals of the social studies and the goals of the school in the formation of a single national community in which people have learned tolerance, mutual respect, and fidelity to democratic process. The more vigorous and candid the teaching of social studies becomes, the more likely we are to deal with subjects which are diverse and explosive when presented in a classroom. There is an obvious difference between teaching students what is so, and inviting them to discover what is so by examination of evidence. There is an equally obvious difference in atmosphere in schools in which it is permissible to say that the teacher is wrong or at any rate unconvincing, and schools in which it is not.

The consensus on this basic issue seemed to be that we are simply not teaching the social studies unless the attitudes, beliefs, and values in a community, including the attitudes, beliefs, and values of the teacher and students are held up to critical examination. Frankel cautioned against the introduction of too-complex controversial issues too early in the school curriculum. He cited visits to sixth-grade classrooms where questions of race relations were being studied. Generally discussion was limited to platitudes, which was doubly wrong because too much was left unsaid and students were led to believe that an exchange of such platitudes is synonymous with social inquiry.

It is probable that had the opportunity arisen to reach consensus among the participants, Frankel's position would have been supported in that: (1) society has a right to expect that certain social attitudes be generated, (2) all science, natural as well as social, involves value questions, and (3) the social scientist has an obligation to point out what the value implications are, and what alternative policies might be, but not to label alternatives as good or bad.

Lawrence Metcalf prepared a summary statement at the conclusion of the conference on this aspect, from which the following is quoted:

Whenever we teach an understanding of society there is a tendency sometimes to omit those facts or understandings which might undermine the values we would like to teach. These omissions often result in social misunderstanding. The teacher therefore feels caught up in a dilemma: shall he teach an understanding of social reality regardless of the effect on values, or shall he tailor his handling of context according to the norms he wishes to inculcate. The first course of action is often rejected on the ground that immature learners will acquire "wrong" values and a cynical outlook on life. The second alternative is often rejected on the ground that it amounts to the kind of distortion and social education in every totalitarian and monolithic society.

One form of knowledge about values has to do with the consequences of acting upon certain values. Is a society that values equality before the law a better society than one which does not? This question cannot be answered without some knowledge of consequences. What would be the consequences for the human condition of building a society in which the law treated individuals differentially depending on the race, religion, nationality, or social class of individuals? Again, a knowledge of such consequences can be garnered from the subject matter of history and social science. Consequences represent one necessary step toward making clear the meaning of free choice. One is not free to choose freedom unless he can compare freedom with its alternatives.

We need in value education the kind of policy that frees the learner for making his own value choices. He will make these choices in some way but a free society cannot survive the chance guesses of confused minds. Freedom to choose means knowledge of what one is choosing, its alternatives, and its consequences. In anthropology this kind of study is called the comparative study of cultures. It involves this and much more—for example, a comparative study of choices within a culture.

In our culture many individuals make choices without an adequate knowledge of what their choices entail. What should be our attitude toward socialized medicine, to mention only one of the alternatives that confront us, and have our social studies educators helped us to make this kind of choice? It would help if individuals knew the meaning of socialized medicine and its consequences as revealed by scholarly studies in England, Wales, Sweden, New Zealand and other places. True, this kind of statement cannot guarantee that students will either oppose or support socialized medicine. But it is the only treatment of value that is consistent with a valuing of knowledge, scientific method, and freedom.

2

Changing the Curriculum

A DISCIPLINE FOR THE SOCIAL STUDIES

Samuel P. McCutchen

What the field of the social studies most needs, contends the writer of this selection, is development as a discipline in its own right. Here he outlines characteristics that the field needs to advance or acquire if it is to attain that status. The suggestions may strike some teachers as proposing an overly rigid, or even authoritarian, approach. Others may react with the feeling that the author proceeds insufficiently in desirable directions. All readers should find the stimulation to consider carefully whether the social studies do need rigorous redefinition and refinement.

HYPOTHESIS AND DEFINITION

FOR NEARLY fifty years after the achievement of American independence, it was grammatically proper to say "The United States are. . . ." After that half-century the separate states had welded themselves into a unity with a sufficient integrity to permit properly the usage, "The United States is. . . ." After a similar period of growing together, we have now reached a point where properly we may say "The social studies *is* a subject taught in schools" instead of "The social studies *are*. . . ."

The analogy between the United States and the social studies is not a strong one; too much traffic on it might wear it out, but at least superficially, there are some elements of comparability. The states maintained their basic sovereignty until living together strengthened a nationalism which built its pattern of values and inculcated them in the American people. The social studies has its components too, and their separateness has been quite discernible even to those whose view of the educational scene is only surface deep.

The hypothesis which I propose to consider is this: the existence of a discipline can weld separate elements of subject matter into a single field which will have its own integrity.

FROM *Social Education*, 28:61–65, February, 1963. Used by permission. Dr. McCutchen is a professor of social studies education at New York University.

The key term here needing definition is "discipline." Let me attempt it. A discipline is a pattern of values which imposes a pattern of behavior on its disciples. This definition seems to me to be accurate when applied to religions, to isms, to social discipline, family discipline, schoolroom discipline, self-discipline. I assume it can properly be applied when we speak of the scholarly disciplines. If this assumption is correct, then each of the scholarly disciplines imposes its unique or peculiar pattern of behavior on those of its disciples who have been properly and thoroughly trained. All historians worthy of the name ought to have common elements in their professional behavior—in research, thought, and pronouncement. The same should be true of all economists, geographers, sociologists, *et cetera*. This seems, soberly and seriously, to be the case.

Associated with each scholarly discipline is a body of content in which the disciples work. It is the material which is most congenial to the values and behavior of the discipline; it is necessary to the discipline, but it is not an integral part of it. The untrained neophyte working in historical material is quite likely to commit errors of both commission and omission which the historian would avoid with ease and certainty.

The trained practitioners in a scholarly discipline are primarily engaged in exploring their area of content, in pushing forward its frontiers, and in organizing the data thus amassed into systematic frameworks. It seems to me important to note that these systems of organization are generally those most useful to the disciples and practitioners, and not those most meaningful to the public.

Actually, the lines of demarcation between the several scholarly disciplines are not as sharp and clean-cut as we are sometimes led to believe. The principles of sound research, of critical thinking, and the tenets of good scholarship are basically similar even when separate terminology may be used to describe them. Neither are the lines demarcating bodies of content clearly drawn. The economist must invade political science, the sociologist makes use of social psychology, the historian deals with any of these fields, and the geographer professes to offer basic grounding for them all.

Whatever the kinship of disciplinary values and the areas of content held in common by the scholarly disciplines, the various organized groups of scholars now are urging the inclusion of their disciplines in the elementary and secondary social studies programs. The professional organizations of anthropology, economics, geography, history, political science, and sociology have each established committees or task forces for this purpose. Each one, independent of the others, has proposed (or hopes to propose) a curriculum comprehensively covering grades K through twelve. Without machinery for coordinating these drives and without plan for selecting content functional to a higher purpose, the end result of these independent efforts can only be a struggle of power politics in which the scholarly discipline with the loudest voice and longest purse will capture the coveted later years of the senior high school, pushing the weaker fields into the elementary grades.

An alternative to this destructive struggle can be advanced in the hypothesis presented here: The existence of a discipline can weld separate elements of subject matter into a single field with its own integrity.

For our part, our failure to bring coherence to the social studies can quickly be demonstrated by a glance at the past. Taught in a sequence prescribed in 1916, the social studies grew out of history and political science, then history plus geography. As economics and sociology have come to be included, the resultant melange has become more complicated and we have attained a goulash in which the meat, potatoes, and onions are in the same pot but are still not truly synthesized, digested, integrated.

This has been largely due to the fact that social studies teachers have been trying to use the various separate organizations of content, each designed by the logic and for the convenience of the various scholarly disciplines. Failing thus far to achieve and accept a discipline of our own, we have tried to use the discipline of history (or occasionally geography) to make the content of economics, political science, and sociology fit into our scheme of teaching, while retaining the multiple frames of content organization. The perplexity will mount as anthropology and sociol psychology move over the horizon and into use.

The beginning of wisdom in discerning, describing, and defining a discipline for the social studies is to establish the basic task, the *raison d'être* of the social studies. Perhaps the most basic reason for our public, tax-supported schools is that the school is the agency set up to induct the young into this society—a society, be it noted, which distinctively aspires to be self-perfecting.

Of the various tools, or areas of study, available to the school, the social studies is the one most heavily relied on to carry out this assignment. English, with its combination of literature, composition, and speech, has a part of this task but its preferred outcome is not civic competence but rather a heightened aesthetic enjoyment and an increase in the effectiveness of communication. Physical education undertakes to provide sound bodies, leaving the training of sound minds to others. Mathematics, on the other hand, would train the mind to logic, but it is the sterile logic of mathematical abstractions. Home economics and other vocational training are satisfied in the main to increase the earning, using, spending poewrs of the new generation. Science may explain the physical world to the neophytes; it has improved health and raised standards of living, and through research pushed into new frontiers of knowledge (even Venus is not safe from science!), but if the scientists are trying to aid a society to perfect itself, the hydrogen bomb is a queer tool!

Having thus stirred up feuds with fellow teachers which were never dormant anyway, I return to my thesis that the social studies' major responsibility is to induct the young into a self-perfecting, though tough, society. Our program, curriculum, and teaching should be functional to this assignment. The word *functional* is important. Keep it in mind.

MAJOR ELEMENTS IN THE DISCIPLINE

Our program must induct young people into today's society, help them to understand it, to find meaningful places in it, and make it more livable; that is, move it closer to its ideals. This task identifies these four elements of the discipline of the social studies:

1. The societal goals of America.
2. The heritage and values of Western civilization.
3. The dimensions and interrelationships of today's world.
4. A specific process of rational inquiry and the tenets of good scholarship.

It may be profitable to look briefly at each of these disciplinary values.

The societal goals of America are those ideals of the nation formulated during past generations and accepted by the society of today. In 1957 the National Council's Committee on Concepts and Values proposed a list of fourteen social goals which it recommended as the bases from which social studies content should be derived. Its report is a National Council publication entitled *A Guide to Content in the Social Studies*. (1) Excerpts from its introduction may clarify this important element of the social studies discipline:

"The most inclusive aim of social studies . . . is to help young people learn to carry on the free society they have inherited, to make whatever changes modern conditions demand or creative imagination suggests that are consistent with its basic principles and values, and to hand it on to their offspring better than they received it. . . . We cannot foresee the specific problems of the next generation or give the answers in advance; it is the right and duty of free men to think for themselves, to find their own answers, to unite in resolute action.

"Hence we cannot indoctrinate, in the sense of teaching children specific answers to specific problems but we can teach them the central principles and values of a free society. For example, the very principle that it is their right and duty to think for themselves is a principle that has to be inculcated. Competence in thinking for themselves is an ability which children can develop only through practice."

The heritage and values of Western civilization are a second ingredient in the pattern of values which make up a discipline for the social studies.

The competition between West and East is a phenomenon too obvious to require belaboring. The challenge of communistic ideology gives depth to the competition between Russian and American power. Emergent nations in Asia and Africa waver between totalitarianism and democracy. If we are to persuade others to our way of life, we need to know—and teach—its essential and distinctive ingredients. Some of those elements, best taught in the historical setting from which they emerged and in which they developed, are:

1. The solutions of ancient Egypt and Persia to "the problem of empire."
2. The emergence of monotheism in Hebrew history.
3. Pure democracy in the Hellenic city-states of Greece.
4. The philosophies of human relations—Epicureanism, Stoicism, early Christianity—in the Hellenistic period.
5. The concept of law in Rome, and the Roman success in building a stable, polyethnic state flourishing in the *Pax Romana.*
6. The unquestioning piety of the high Middle Ages in Western Europe which built the cathedrals, and the stability furnished to that period by the feudal, manorial, and guild systems.
7. The Renaissance, emphasizing the importance of the individual and of the questing mind, alert for new learning.
8. The Industrial Revolution, substituting machines for muscle power.
9. The democratic revolutions in England, America, and France.
10. The swelling burst of nationalism which characterized the nineteenth century in the Western world.

These make up a minimum list of the heritage of Western civilization—an essential part of the discipline of the social studies.

Basic to the induction of the young into the culture is the responsibility of the teacher to know the dimensions, the major components, and the interrelationships of today's world. To this responsibility, pertinent content from the various social sciences must be drawn. This element in the discipline of the social studies has two bearings: The first is the new and significant developments affecting the American scene; the second, the nascent non-Western cultures pressing into contact with our everyday lives.

For the new developments now affecting the American scene, I know of no better analysis than that presented in the 1958 report of the Commission of the Social Studies of the National Council. There some seven basic changes and movements which characterize contemporary American society are listed. *First* is the ongoing and accelerating scientific revolution. . . . *Second* is the contracting world of complex international relations. . . . This immediately calls attention to the *third* factor—the current population explosion. . . . The *fourth* factor is the penetrating influence of public policy in all phases of life. . . . Factor *five* deals with changing economic structures and patterns. . . . The *sixth* factor is the emergence of the behavioral sciences. . . . *Finally,* today's social world is witnessing changes and conflicts in values and ethics.

These seven factors affect the American scene. The new, non-Western nations also call for our attention and study with the same level of depth and thoroughness which we have been devoting, and still should give to representative nations within Western culture.

It is obvious that when the roster of membership in the United Nations has reached more than 100, we cannot study each in depth. This means selection of European, Latin American, Asiatic, and African nations from among the total of possibilities, making sure that geographical range as well as variety of cultural complexity enters into the choice. The geographical areas selected can be specific enough to be identified as nations or broad enough to be the culture areas proposed by the 1959 Yearbook of the National Council.

Perhaps the cultural anthropologists may yet furnish us with the proper outline by which to study culture areas. Until they do, let me suggest this six-point profile: (1) the physical environment; (2) the economic activities; (3) the social institutions; (4) the political machinery; (5) the value system (folkways, mores, morals, ethics, religion); and (6) the history of the development from primitive to complex culture.

The fourth and final major component of the discipline for the social studies deals less with content and more with method—less with WHAT and more with HOW. In my judgment it is the crux of the whole problem of a discipline. Without a specific process of rational inquiry—or critical thinking, or the problems approach (there are many synonyms)—we are only drillmasters of a content which has little function and is quickly forgotten.

Indulge me, please, if I turn slightly autobiographical. I was trained in history as pure and as undefiled by applicability as the University of Chicago in the 1920's could make it. . . . Then the circumstances of my teaching challenged me with a problem of immensely greater magnitude: "How can we teach so that all of our students will habitually behave in ways consistent with our society's ideals?"

It is a question which will, I still believe, yield to research. When it does and we find good answers, we can accurately speak of a science of education. Until we find those answers, we are truly little more than witch doctors, muttering incantations and waving symbols. It is a problem to which a man may devote a professional career, end that career with nothing more than a promising hypothesis, and yet feel no sense of uselessness and failure.

The hypothesis to which I have been committed for thirty years is the problems approach. In 1932 it was radical; in 1962 it is conventional; perhaps by 1967 it will have been replaced by another alternative such as togetherness and group dynamics. On its merits I now insist that the discipline of the social studies requires us to formulate a specific process of rational inquiry, to use that process in our professional work, to teach the process both in its component steps and in its entirety, and to teach it so well and so enthusiastically that our pupils will understand it, become skilled in it, and will use it intelligently on the social problems which confront them as citizens of a free society. . . .

CONCLUSION

A discipline should impose a pattern of behavior on its disciples. The discipline of the social studies should impose itself, then, on the teachers of social studies, directing what they teach and how they teach it; on the pupils in their behavior of learning, making it more purposeful and orderly; and on pupils and teachers alike in their civic behavior.

Unless we can focus sharply and successfully and demonstrate that we can really develop civic competence, our place in the school curriculum—our percentage of student time—is sure to diminish. Mere acquaintance with cultural niceties cannot compete with driver education.

This paper is not an attempt to propose revolutionary educational doctrine or to create a startlingly new point of view. Practically everything said here has been said before by someone who probably said it better. What has been attempted is to pull together these several pieces, to propose a thesis for their synthesis, and to examine their relevance to the thesis. The existence of a discipline can weld the separate elements of subject matter into a single field with its own integrity.

If we become aware of our discipline and of our discipleship, we need not further suffer under such apologies as "history and the social sciences" or "interdisciplinary." Ours are the proud tasks of (1) patriotism, (2) Western culture, (3) the contemporary world, and (4) rational inquiry.

(1) National Council for the Social Studies, Committee on Concepts and Values. *A Guide to Content in the Social* *Studies.* Washington, D.C.: The Council, 1957. $1.00.

SOME GUIDELINES FOR CHANGING
SOCIAL STUDIES EDUCATION

Lawrence E. Metcalf

The author of this selection is at his best in direct and forthright criticism of the social studies. Here he identifies what he considers major weaknesses of the field and suggests some approaches that may help to overcome such deficiencies.

FROM *Social Education*, 27:197–201, April, 1963. Used by permission. Dr. Metcalf is a professor of social studies education at the University of Illinois.

A MAJOR reform of the social studies curriculum is long overdue and, hopefully, may be about to take place. The purpose of this article is to discuss certain deficiencies of the present curriculum, and to offer suggestions for their remedy. Among the many deficiencies space will permit discussion only of the following.

AIMLESSNESS OF INSTRUCTION

Curriculum bulletins and resource units in the social studies always begin with a long list of purposes. Usually there are more purposes than any staff could achieve during a lifetime of instruction. Because these purposes are stated non-operationly without any suggestion as to how they might be achieved, propaganda analysts would call them glittering generalities. This operational vagueness is even true of those objectives which are said to be stated in behavioral terms. Clearly, behavior is broadly and roughly conceived by those who write purposes. But more to the point, the writers of curriculum bulletins and resource units seldom recommend method or content that is consistent with their poetically expressed objectives. Apparently, the practice of writing down purposes has become a kind of ritual that no teacher is to take seriously. By recourse to chant and incantation proper respect is paid to our democratic heritage. After the ceremony is over, everyone settles down to the job at hand which usually has no purpose at all other than to keep youth busy and out of mischief.

Because statements of purpose seem to have had no effect upon what teachers teach, or the way in which they teach, some reformers are now taking the position that purposes are unimportant, and that we ought to roll up our sleeves and seek improvement in courses without very much worry about our purposes. This is a healthy attitude to the extent that certain purposes are granted for the sake of working diligently on construction of the means necessary to their achievement. Unfortunately, our culture is riven with conflict, and if national goals are vague and subject to debate, some clarification of values is essential to all curriculum planning. The current debate over whether we can have both equality and excellence as educational goals is case in point.

In 1955 this writer collaborated with Maurice Hunt in writing a social studies methods textbook in which the radical suggestion was made that the social studies pursue a single purpose. (1) . . . It was suggested that "The foremost aim of instruction in high school social studies is to help students examine reflectively issues in closed areas of American culture." (2) Closed areas were defined as areas of belief and thought which are largely closed to rational thought. These areas abound with prejudice, taboos, inconsistencies, and perplexities. In such areas as sex, economics, religion, race, and social class, people react with their blood and common sense, and without logic and scientific knowledge. Teachers who touch upon the closed areas are expected to justify their temerity by inculcating right answers, right attitudes, right beliefs. The process of teaching in the closed areas is an amalgam of suppression, indoctrination, distortion, manipulation, prescription, and persuasion. When this sort of thing is practiced in the Soviet Union or Red China, we call it brainwashing. Its use in this country is called patriotism.

Many teachers, educators, and social scientists see nothing wrong with this kind of process. The belief that schools exist for the preservation of society, its cultural heritage, is wedded to a reinforcement theory of learning. Doubly armed they can practice the educational totalitarianism of the Soviet Union while loudly proclaiming their opposition to communism. Current attempts to teach students an "understanding" of communism exemplify almost perfectly this totalitarian philosophy. It is a major source of alarm to note that not only educators, who can use ignorance as their excuse, and publishers with the usual eye for patriotically inspired profits, but also respected social scientists have participated in this orgiastic assault upon the innocence of children and youth. (3) In place of charlatantry and incantation we need an honestly reflective study of contrasting ideologies with no suppression of knowledge as its intent or by-product. This kind of teaching would preserve that part of our cultural heritage which merits survival, and would build the only kind of patriotism compatible with democratic values.

The suggestion that the social studies limit its purposes to the fostering of reflective thought in the closed areas will not be popular with those who call themselves eclectics, and who value equally a variety of instructional aims. The trouble with many of our eclectics is that they have not included consistency as one of their philosophical criteria. A careful reading of their stated purposes leaves one with the feeling that they are not really for anything at all, since their lists of impeccable purposes are shot through with contradictory and imcompatible destinations. It is fair to say that a person who wants to ride off in all directions is essentially aimless in his equestrian activity.

The single aim, reflection in the closed areas, may not be consistent with all the aims that social studies education would like to hold, but it is consistent and contributory to many of them, particularly to those that share an abode with the values of a democratic society. The responsibilities of social studies in the realm of values will be discussed more fully later in this article.

THE PROBLEM OF MOTIVATION

It is a matter of everyday observation among teachers that students are not very much interested in the social studies. Low interest is coupled with high forgetting. Attempts to solve this problem in civic apathy have tried to make a standard content interesting, easy, and attractive. Under this approach instructional materials receive a beauty treatment. The modern textbook is replete with the kind of colorful art work that one associates with the cosmetics industry. Charts, graphs, tables, end-of-chapter assists, and even teachers' manuals cope with levels of aspiration. An outstanding example of the beautician treatment of history is the hardback magazine, *American Heritage*. The trouble with this approach is that it misses the target. It is the uselessness of the content against which students have rebelled. Many of our students who dislike the social studies are hard at work on much more difficult content in their science and mathematics courses. Some of this interest in the natural sciences merely reflects the fashions of the day, but much of it expresses a genuine interest in content that, once mastered, has a wealth of meaning. Much of the content in the social studies, if properly understood by the student, has no meaning at all, and our brighter students sense this almost from the beginning of their study.

Some of the content we are now teaching would acquire meaning if its relevance to current problems and issues were perceived by students. Some of the content has no such relevance, and should be replaced by content that does. This principle does not mean that history has no value unless it is modern history. Some of the most relevant content for understanding contemporary society is to be found in the histories of Greece and Rome. A teacher can use the content of history and social science as evidence within a reflective process that tests propositions and clarifies conflicts. A student who wonders whether to believe a proposition or its opposite will be motivated to resolve discrepancy, if we are to believe recent theories of cognitive dissonance. (4) A shift from content that has become standard to one that is needed in the study of cultural disjunctions is essential to successful attempts to solve the problem of student motivation. (5)

Problem-Solving Reconsidered

The problem-solving method has never been dominant in social studies teaching and, when used at all, has seldom been interpreted, psychologically or logically, in terms that would foster intellectual growth in students. We have been wrong most of the time in our conceptions of both problem-solving and problems.

A problem is any unanswered question that can be answered experimentally. It is a perplexity felt by a student. Problems cannot be listed or handed to students on a sheet of ditto paper. It is foolish for teachers to list as thought questions those that are different in wording from questions that are said to be recall in nature. What is a recall question for one student may be a thought question for someone else. It is true that many students have in common certain perplexities that concern them, particularly in the closed areas, and these may be identified in advance as possible problems. But a part of the meaning of any problem is psychological. We create problems for our students when we are successful in questioning their beliefs to the point where they have genuine doubt as to what to believe. Without doubt, there is no problem, and all problems are in a generic sense a problem in what to believe.

Problem-solving is logical and scientific. One cannot rely upon hunches, feelings, intuitions, or even trials and errors for solutions to problems. The intuitions of students may supply them with hypotheses, but all such ideas must be tested with data before students can learn whether any of their ideas merit the status of belief. Problem-solving has been advocated by some of our eclectics as the best method for some purposes. True to their faith in variety for its own sake, they have urged other methods for other purposes without considering whether their methods and their purposes, taken as a whole, constituted a consistent theory of teaching. Research findings on the effectiveness of this method have been inconclusive, partly because its many investigators have never understood the method well enough to put it to experimental test. (6)

Social studies educators have had their greatest difficulty in their attempts to apply problem-solving to the teaching of history. A part of their difficulty has been their view of history as a chronological narrative couched in factual terms, free from an emphasis upon concepts or generalizations. Believing that there are no laws in history, they have viewed any attempt to examine reflectively the generalizations of historians as an attack upon history which would reduce the student's faith in historical knowledge. A second part of their difficulty has been the conception that a problem ceases to be a problem, once anyone has solved it. Problems, so conceived, have to be contemporary, never historical. Problem-solving in their hands is oriented to the future, to values, and to action. Under this conception, problems take the form of how can we beautify the school plant, reduce noise in the cafeteria, forestall inflation, or end the cold war. Personal problems receive more attention than social problems because action is more feasible for one than for the other. Teachers who view problem-solving from this kind of perspective are somewhat confused by the suggestion that students be asked to solve the problem of what is imperialism, and what are its causes and effects. The understanding of imperialism is assigned to the method of assertion and recitation rather than to problem-solving.

The erroneous nature of this conception has been suggested by several uncommon sources. An excellent discussion of problem-solving in the teaching of history is available in an unpublished dissertation by Alan Griffin. (7) Another is to be found in an out-of-print work by Ernest Bayles. (8) More recent studies by Leonard Swift and by John Palmer are suggestive on the same point. (9) . . .

NORMATIVE ASPECTS OF SOCIAL STUDIES

Social studies teachers believe in teaching values as well as facts. Their many objectives always include a few intents to teach students to be good.

How this can be done without indoctrination has never been clear to most of us. We deplore what goes on in Russian schools. But in this country, under the revealing rubric, Know Your Enemy, students are taught to hate communism and to favor free enterprise. The only difference between what we do and what the Russians do is in the specific attitudes that schools attempt to inculcate. Both countries take a polar view on all ideological issues, and engage in emotionalisms, illogical thinking, and suppression of knowledge.

American educators who look upon dissemination of knowledge as a major purpose of public education take alarm when value commitments take precedence over cognitive obligations. Does the teaching of certain values mean that many facts will not be taught, they ask. They occasionally point out that a major difference between a democracy and a totalitarian culture is in the way beliefs are maintained and modified, not alone in the specific beliefs that happen to be dominant at a particular time in a particular country. They desire a kind of value education that would develop in everyone some capacity to do his own valuing. They do not find this concern or emphasis in most attempts to teach anti-communism.

A further complication is that any attempt by teachers to teach values that are not already dominant in the culture is unlikely to succeed, and there seems little point to teaching people to value what they already value, or are certain to value whether the school does anything or not. Moreover, very few teachers feel that they have the right, the freedom, the strength, or the courage to teach values that fly in the face of custom.

Perhaps a return to subject matter, a reinterpretation of problem-solving, and a new emphasis upon logic will help teachers to entertain the hypothesis that teaching people to be good is not their province. Teaching an understanding of how values affect and even distort perception is within their province. Teaching that certain values are inconsistent with other values is within their province as logicians. It is even their job to teach that some values are democratic, and how democracy is different from other systems in its effects upon human development. But no one, least of all our teachers, can tell the American people what their values are to be.

This position does not deny to knowledge a normative role but emphasizes that we teach *valuing*, not values. The role of knowledge within a process of valuing can be illustrated by a discussion of how a teacher, ideally, would handle the topic, socialized medicine. If students are to decide whether they are in favor of socialized medicine, they will find it helpful to learn what socialized medicine is, and what results from it. They will not acquire this knowledge from the free pamphlets of the American Medical Association. Neither can they learn it from any teacher who also has a specific attitude to purvey.

A fair and objective teacher will help his students find or develop a clear and noncircular definition of socialized medicine. He will also help them find data, if it is available, on the achievements and other effects of socialized medicine. He will help them to cope with the logic of those who are opponents or proponents of this institution. He will encourage them to speculate upon what the effects of socialized medicine would be if it were tried in this country. He would even ask them to rate these effects according to their desirability or undesirability. Although his knowledge of effects would give him no right to expect or demand that his students rate effects the way he would rate them, his commitment to logic would require him to expect his students to learn to rate effects according to consistent criteria. For instance, the student who favored socialized medicine, while opposing public education, might be asked to consider whether his valuing was entirely consistent. It is this building of a value structure in everyone that makes it possible for education to help youth discover who they are, and what they might become.

Some educators have expressed alarm at the idea that the concept of structure might achieve preeminence in social studies curriculum planning. They have feared that efforts to teach the structure of a subject would mean that our concern with values and needs would be lost from view. The teaching of structure is undoubtedly a threat to those who desire to teach their own values, for knowledge of the social sciences does not dictate a particular set of values. Students who possess the same knowledge may vary widely in their attitudes. On the other hand, a knowledge of the structure of social sciences has a key role to play in all valuing, and there is no conflict between those who want to teach the basic content of a field, and a process of intelligent valuing. A central assumption in reflective teaching is that attention to valuing is probably the only effective approach to the teaching of values.

(1) Maurice P. Hunt and Lawrence E. Metcalf. *Teaching High School Social Studies*. New York: Harper and Brothers, 1955.

(2) *Ibid.*, p. 223.

(3) Lawrence E. Metcalf. "Anticommunism in the Classroom—Education or Propaganda." *The Nation*. March 10, 1962. P. 215–216; 224.

(4) Leon Festinger. A *Theory of Cognitive Dissonance*. Evanston, Ill.: Row, Peterson and Company, 1957. Also Prescott Lecky. *Self-Consistency, a Theory of Personality*. New York: Island Press, 1945.

(5) Robert Lynd. *Knowledge for What?* Princeton, N.J.: Princeton University Press, 1948.

(6) The writer has summarized some of this research and its inadequacy in a chapter in the recently published *Handbook of Research on Teaching*, edited by N. L. Gage, and published by Rand McNally in 1963.

(7) Alan Griffin. "The Subject Matter Preparation of Teachers of History." Unpublished dissertations. Ohio State University, 1942.

(8) Ernest Bayles. *Theory and Practice of Teaching*. New York: Harper and Brothers, 1950.

(9) Cf. Leonard Swift and John Palmer. Unpublished dissertations. University of Illinois. Also assorted papers and articles.

SOME PROMISING DEVELOPMENTS
IN CURRENT PROJECTS

John U. Michaelis

Probably the most exciting signs of emerging change in the social studies are coming from a substantial number of organized research, experimental, and developmental projects. While these efforts may not yet be so extensive as those that have characterized some other fields of the curriculum, such as mathe- *matics and science, during the past several years, the current projects in social studies are considerably greater than previous attempts to improve this field. One of the most recent analytical reports on the projects to date appears in this selection. Major projects are listed on pages 407–408.*

SUMMARIZED below are promising developments in some twenty-five to thirty curriculum projects dealing with one or more aspects of social sciences education. The developments are drawn from project materials, project reports, and other information received from project directors. Grateful acknowledgment is made to those directors who shared materials with the writer.

OBJECTIVES

Objectives of instruction in materials for teachers and students tend to be focused on the attainment of intellectual outcomes associated with history and the social sciences. Most projects include specific reference to concepts, themes, methods of inquiry, attitudes, and values that are drawn from the disciplines. Less attention is given to global purposes of education or citizenship education, although contributions to broad goals and to citizenship education are outlined in some projects.

CURRICULUM ORGANIZATION

Both logical and psychological aspects of currriculum planning are being employed with increased attention to logical sequencing of instructional materials. And there does not appear to be any debate over logical vs. psychological planning. Logical planning is evident in the arranging of facts, concepts, generalizations, skills, and methods of inquiry in sequences related

---

An address presented at the Annual Meeting of the National Council for the Social Studies, November, 1965. Used by permission. Dr. Michaelis is a professor of education at the University of California, Berkeley.

to the statements of the structure of disciplines. The use of logical processes is apparent in the modes of instruction in many projects—involving such elements as deducing hypotheses, and categorizing and classifying data in terms of criteria, systematic testing of conclusions, and criticizing evidence and proof. Psychological aspects are evident in the attention being given to such cognitive processes as classifying, generalizing, and evaluating, and in using methods that move students to higher levels of thinking in a teaching sequence.

Economics and the behavioral sciences have a prominent place in program planning at all levels. Many projects include considerable material drawn from economics and the behavioral sciences in both separate-subject units and in units that cut across disciplines. At all levels of K-XII instruction in general projects one can find concepts and methods from economics and behavioral sciences. Specific units or courses on economics are available or are being produced for primary grades, grades IV and V, and grades IX and XII in various economics projects. In the behavioral sciences specific units are available or are being prepared for primary grades, middle grades, and secondary grades in anthropology and sociology projects. The time is ripe for a contemporary Beard to write on "The Rise of Economics and the Behavioral Sciences in the Schools."

Relationships within and among disciplines are stressed even when primary emphasis is upon topics and problems in a single discipline. It does not appear that instructional programs will be broken down into discrete segments that isolate relatable ideas in one discipline from those in another. Relationships are evident in separate discipline projects as well as in multi-discipline projects. For example, in economics projects one can find material drawn from geography (resources, population distributions, transportation networks), history (migrations, political events, military events), political science (governmental policies, political issues, decision-making), and behavioral sciences (variations in tastes, social classes, values). Many of the criticisms of separate subject approaches of the past have been eliminated because of interrelationships that are highlighted in current economics, geography, anthropology, and history projects.

The structure of disciplines is being outlined in ways that highlight fundamental concepts, themes, and generalizations to emphasize throughout the program of instruction. Excellent examples are provided in economic projects. One project outlines three groups of ideas (scarcity and economic activity), and two analytical themes (marginal analysis and institutions) as the basic structure (Lovenstein).* Another project includes a spiral development of such concepts as economic systems, scarcity, equilibrium, and growth along with such themes as efficiency of economic systems (Sperling and Wiggins). A third project has a micro-structure that deals with a part of economic

---

* Names of project directors, cited parenthetically throughout this article, are stated fully in the classified list of projects beginning on page 407.

systems—production and consumption of goods and services (Rader). Other projects have defined structure in terms of concepts, themes, main ideas, and generalizations.

Diverse patterns of curriculum organization, quite different from traditional patterns, are being developed. There is earlier introduction of topics at all levels of instruction, ranging from children of other lands and the earth as the home of man in Kindergarten and families around the world in grade I, to college-level history in grade XI and inquiry-centered courses on value conflicts and Asian countries in XII. Ancient, classical and medieval civilizations are introduced in grade V (Greater Cleveland), man and culture—institutions in VII (West), and comparative political and economic systems in IX (Fenton). The old expanding environment sequence has been replaced in most projects by sequences that include other communities and lands in the early grades and area studies as early as grade IV. A combination of separate discipline and multi-discipline approaches are evident in most projects.

NEW EMPHASES AND APPROACHES

Increasing attention is being given to Asian countries and to Africa. In current projects one can find materials on Asia for every grade Kindergarten through XII, with the exception of grade VIII. The offering ranges from children of Japan in Kindergarten and family life in India, Japan, and China in grade I to area studies of China and India in XI and a course on Asia in XII. Materials on Africa are being prepared for grades K, II, IV through VII, and IX through XII. The offering ranges from the Pygmies in Kindergarten and the Hausa family in II to Sub-Sahara Africa in X and research on underdeveloped areas in XII.

Area studies are being designed to give a cohesive view of selected countries and regions. The area-studies approach is used in several projects that are developing units and courses on Changing Japan—middle grades, India—grade IV, the Middle East—grade V, Latin America—grade VI, China and Japan—grade VII, and Europe, USSR, China, and India—grade XI. Geographic, historical, and anthropological approaches to area studies are being used.

American studies are being introduced at different levels and efforts are being made to overcome problems arising from the traditional three cycles of U.S. history. In one project Anglo-America is studied in grade III, a year's study of American history is provided in grade VIII, and American history is included in other courses in other grades (Greater Cleveland). In another project American history is emphasized in grades VI and X (West). New approaches to American studies are being developed in two projects (Lee, Price). American studies are a part of case studies in a project dealing with public controversy (Oliver). Units based on source materials are being prepared in a project focusing on U.S. history in junior and senior high school (Halsey and Brown). An advanced placement course is being developed for use in grade XI (Fenton).

Case studies of communities, areas, values, conflicts, and processes are being developed at both elementary and secondary levels. Among the cases under development are those on selected cities in the United States, Canada, and Latin America for grade V (West), the due process of law materials for grade V (Wilson), governmental processes for grades VII–XI (West, Leppert, Fenton), controversies and conflicts for use in high school (Oliver), microeconomic studies for use in high school (Cawein).

TEACHING STRATEGIES AND INSTRUCTIONAL MEDIA

Unit plans and guidelines for teachers to use in specific lessons are in general directive without being prescriptive. Although most projects are developing detailed guidelines for using instructional materials it is generally recommended that teachers alter them and improve them to meet local needs and conditions. The three-version case studies in one program (West), and the units for less-able students based on source materials are illustrative of attempts to differentiate instruction. A widely used pattern in teaching plans is to open up or clarify the issue or problem, set questions to guide study, provide for analysis of source materials and other media, discuss and compare findings, provide further study, and summarize conclusions in discussions or in writing. Unit plans are set up to highlight relationships among objectives, content, key concepts and generalizations, learning activities, instructional media, and evaluation.

Teaching strategies typically involve inductive approaches in which students are directed in analyzing and synthesizing information. Most projects employ some form of inductive approach in which questions embodying key concepts guide study, issues are analyzed, value-laden situations are considered, independent study is emphasized, and students themselves organize data and formulate generalizations. Models in the form of questions are used to guide study of different areas, periods, and trends in several projects. For example, the study of social change in one project is guided by: What are the main factors in social change? What is it that changes? How does it change? What is the direction of change? The rate of change? Why did the change occur? Or, why was it possible? (Price)

Cognitive processes involved in handling content and values are stressed in most projects. Processes of conceptualizing, hypothesizing, inferring, generalizing, and evaluating are emphasized. The Bloom taxonomy (cognitive domain) has been used in one project to identify process objectives (Fenton), and in a study designed to build questions on varying levels of cognition (Sanders). Value analysis in conflict situations is stressed in several projects, a special report is under development in one center (Morrissett), and one project is focusing on the analysis of conflicts (Oliver).

Models from various disciplines are being made a part of teaching strategies. Predictive, explanatory, and ideal models are differentiated in one project, and a film that introduces students to models has been prepared (Sperling and Wiggins). In several projects use is made of the rational decision-making model from economics—clarifying goals, setting goals in priority, considering alternative ways and ability to meet goals, weighing consequences of alternative ways, deciding on the most efficient way, and assessing the way or ways selected.

A variety of techniques of inquiry from the social sciences may be found in addition to general modes of inquiry. A summary list of 25–30 projects includes such techniques as the interview, questionnaire, polling, census taking, simulation, case study, role playing, participant observation, direct observation, questioning of informants, content analysis, mapping, and photo interpretation. For example, the use of questions to guide interpretation of photographs in the Edmonton geography project is illustrative of techniques employed by cultural geographers (Leeuw). Other examples may be found in most projects because of the emphasis on using techniques of investigation drawn from the disciplines.

Comparative methods as used in the disciplines are employed extensively in project materials. Extensive use is made of cross-cultural comparisons of families and other social institutions, and of economic and political systems. Attention also is given to comparative studies of the growth of civilizations, settlement patterns, value systems, and social change. Some projects are dealing with modes of expressing comparison in ratios, graphs, tables, charts, and maps. Case studies and area studies include comparative material that is useful at varying levels of instruction.

Simulation is being used in several projects to illumine the operation of models. A variety of games are being tried out in various projects. For example, one project is trying out in elementary schools such games as bee language, hunting, and signalling at sea (Morison). At the secondary level are the empire game (Morison), the economics game (Fenton), the civil war game (Lee), the legislative game (Coleman), and downtown redevelopment, park development, and low-cost housing (Leppert). A systematic emphasis may be noted in the use of games in a conceptual framework related to instructional objectives rather than as peripheral activities to stimulate interest, although students do find them to be highly interesting. One project plans to give students an opportunity to devise games (Lee).

Multi-media approaches are evident in most projects with major reliance on reading materials. Although reading materials are dominant in most projects, a variety of related instructional materials are being prepared: transparencies with overlays for overhead projection, single concept films, films, filmstrips, and slides (some with accompanying tapes), kits that include artifacts and models, sets of pictures on selected topics, graphic and tabular materials, charts, and diagrams. There appears to be a strong effort in most projects to bring the instructional media together in a teaching system that is accompanied by detailed teaching plans.

EVALUATION, SPIN-OFFS, SHIFT IN EMPHASIS

Evaluation is being improved by building appraisal devices in instructional materials and by the development of new instruments. A variety of techniques and devices for evaluating outcomes of instruction may be found in project materials: summarizing questions and test items in students' materials, self-checking programmed material, checklists, charts, questions to guide self-evaluation, questions and items to guide teacher evaluation of learning, and end-of-unit tests. Among the formal tests of special interest are the pictorial test of economic concepts for use in grade I (Elkart, Indiana, School System), the tests of economic concepts for grades IV and V (Rader), the essay and objective tests in the Carnegie project (Fenton), the test of cognitive preference and the social science tests in the Illinois project (Leppert), and the tests of anthropological concepts in the Georgia project (Bailey and Rice).

There should be a variety of "spin-offs" of value in improving curriculum development. A key spin-off should be increased research on teaching and learning in the social studies as project materials are tested in different situations. Among the other possibilities are increasing support from the academic community of curriculum development, new knowledge of ways to use structures and modes of inquiry from the disciplines in improving instruction, new insights into concept overlap and other relationships among the disciplines, clearer notions of the value of the separate discipline and multi-discipline approaches, and new conceptions of teaching and learning theories that are grounded in classroom studies.

There is a shift from descriptive social studies to history and the social sciences as they are currently being practiced. This shift is evident in objectives of project materials, in definitions of structure, in methods of inquiry, in instructional materials, and in evaluation of outcomes. It is also evident in the efforts to go beyond description to explanation and prediction, to provide opportunities for hypothesizing and generalizing, to stimulate free and open inquiry, and to employ styles of thought characteristic of historians and social scientists. In short, it can be said that history and the social sciences are truly the foundations of the instructional programs being developed in current projects.

REVISING THE SOCIAL STUDIES

Lewis Paul Todd

The myriad current proposals for changes in social studies threaten to overwhelm teachers and other curriculum-makers. Yet it is probable that every sincere proposal merits consideration, that some warrant experimental tryouts, and that at least a few will prove worthy *of use in the school's social studies program. What are the major criteria by which proposals and results should be appraised? In this article a well-known writer on social studies offers some thoughtful and incisive challenges along these lines.*

As late as the sixteenth century, alchemists were still pursuing the age-old quest for a method of transmuting base metals into gold and silver and for an even more potent agent; namely, the universal cure for all disease. Times and customs change, but myths die hard and as often as not reappear in strange new guises. The search for magical curative agents is no exception. We cling, many of us, to the belief that there is somewhere a universal cure, a quick and easy remedy, for the frailties that plague education in general or, in terms of the present discussion, the social studies in particular. "What we need . . ." And then the proposals come through, proposals that offer relatively simple formulas for breathing life and meaning into the social studies program.

There are no simple formulas. The social studies are concerned with the whole life of man, with the past, the present, and the future that we "now see through a glass darkly." They seek as their ultimate objective the development of individuals equipped with the understanding, the intellectual skills, and the moral courage to come to grips with the formidable problems facing the human race in this critical moment of its history. Man's fate will not be determined by mouthing empty incantations. The crisis confronting mankind is a crisis of intelligence and will. Only by marshaling to the uttermost our collective intelligence and our moral resources can we hope to emerge triumphant from our present travail and begin the task of building a sane and ordered world.

Such is the job for which the social studies must continue to assume a significant share of the responsibility. Our gravest peril is that we will underestimate the difficulties confronting us, not least of which is the ever accelerating rate of change. Every effort to strengthen the social studies

ABRIDGED FROM "Revising the Social Studies" by Lewis Paul Todd, in *The Social Studies and the Social Sciences* by the American Council of Learned Societies and National Council for the Social Studies, © 1962, by Harcourt, Brace & World, Inc. and reprinted with their permission. For biographical note see page 262.

program, if it makes any claim upon realism, must be carried on within the context of Julian Huxley's prediction that "the human species is on the threshold of a new experience as different from ours as ours is from that of the Peking man."

New Dimensions

Although it stretches the imagination to the breaking point, it is not impossible to conjure up a picture of that scene in which a million or so years ago the prehistoric individual we classify as *Sinanthropus pekinensis* crept into the cave near what is now Choukoutien, China, and, his crude stone first hatchet close at hand, lay down to die. The point at which the imagination *does* fail is reached when we try to visualize a world as different from ours as our is from that in which the Peking man lived out his days. And yet, as Huxley warned, it is that literally unimaginable world that we are now entering, or rather are being thrust into, with terrifying speed. And it is in this world of almost limitless complexity and bewildering change that the social studies must play their part.

Rapid and ever accelerating change in every aspect of life is one of the hard facts with which we must contend, and the implications for education are staggering. "How," Margaret Mead asked, "are we who do not know what to do, who do not know how to live in one world, who have no faintest trace of habituated capacity to operate in a world which may actually destroy itself, who do not know . . . how to cope with the spectacle of machines which can do problems which the men who design the machines could not do—how shall we, who are so unfit, prepare a generation which will begin to be fit to face the new problems which confront mankind?"

We desperately needed an answer to the question when Margaret Mead asked it back in 1950. This was before the first hydrogen bomb had been triggered and before anyone dreamed that within a few short years the race for outer space would be on in earnest. We need the answer even more desperately today, not ten years from now, but now, for "things are in the saddle" and driving us hard. . . .

Unanswered, too, either for us or for future generations, is the question of how to deal with the explosion of knowledge now shaking practically every field of human endeavor to its very foundations. It has been estimated that "every minute, 2,000 pages of books, newspapers or reports are published somewhere in the world . . . enough to fill a thousand feet of bookshelves every day." One may grant that the estimate is probably only the roughest of approximations and that, moreover, the rivers of ink flow largely into warmed-over topics, news of merely passing interest, and trivialities. Nevertheless, imbedded in the whole is a hard core of new knowledge sufficiently large to confound even the most devoted scholars. We have reached the point where the most highly specialized specialists are hard put to keep abreast of new developments in their fields, and the continued improvement of computers and other extensions of man's senses and brain only serves to compound the problem.

Let us be completely clear on one point. We are not suggesting that the reader stand back with us and gaze in awe at the new horizons, physical and intellectual, that science is opening before us. We are suggesting and with as much emphasis as we can command that the rapidly expanding dimensions of human life have drastic and far-reaching implications for the social studies. We are thinking, for example, of the startling discoveries that have encouraged biologists to believe that they are on the verge of revealing the chemical code of inheritance. It is generally conceded that the discovery would constitute one of the greatest scientific achievements of all time. It would unlock doors now closed to researchers in many fields of science, and insofar as it provided a key to the basis of thought itself, the discovery would have incalculable consequences for education, and not least of all for the social studies program. . . .

But our vision is blurred, for we enter the new age ridden by anxiety and fearful of the future. The changes have come too swiftly for us to cope with them. We are not prepared for the great adventure upon which, like it or not, mankind is now embarked, and the compelling question Margaret Mead phrased so neatly remains to haunt us: "How shall we, who are so unfit, prepare a generation which will begin to be fit to face the new problems which confront mankind?"

Need for New Emphases

What can the social studies contribute by way of guidance into the new age we are entering? A small boy, as the story goes, had an answer to this question. The boy's father, wishing to read his newspaper but unable to do so because of repeated interruptions from his son, finally handed the youngster a large jigsaw-puzzle map of the world and told him to put it together. Then he settled back with his paper for what he hopefully expected would be a half hour or more of peace. In less than five minutes, however, the boy tugged at his father's sleeve. "I did it," he said. "How did you finish so quickly?" his father asked, looking down at the completed map. "It was easy," the youngster answered. "There was a picture of a man on the other side of the puzzle, and when I put the man together the world was all right."

Unsophisticated though the story may be, it has, we submit, a real point. In Alexander Pope's words, "The proper study of mankind is man." If our commitment to the task of building a decent and ordered world is deep enough to carry us beyond lip service to a serious consideration of way and means, we will be well advised to plunge into "the proper study" with head, heart, and utmost concentration at the earliest possible moment. . . .

Isn't it time we began to take a long, hard, sober look at the urgent problems confronting us? The question is being raised with growing urgency by thoughtful people from every walk of life. Isn't it time we began to try to put the pieces together? Time we began to devote at least as much effort to the search from an enduring peace as we are now devoting to the search for security through armed might and the construction of shelters to protect us on the day of Armageddon? Time we began to devote at least as much time to the study of man himself as we are now devoting to the study of the things man can manipulate with his hands and his ingenious instruments? Time we began to turn increasingly to the social sciences, even as we have already turned to the natural sciences, for help in solving our problems? Time we began to agree that our future depends upon the quality and vitality of a balanced educational program that is as concerned with reaching out for an understanding of man and his relations with his fellows as it is with an understanding of the physical universe?

These are compelling questions. They deserve thoughtful answers from all of us—from the top echelons of government down to the humblest citizen. And if it is obvious that the social sciences have a major role to play in the resolution of the issues the questions raise, it should be equally obvious that an awareness of the issues themselves and the will and courage to tackle the issues must reach the youth of America in large part through the social studies program in the elementary and secondary schools.

APPENDIX

SPECIAL BIBLIOGRAPHIES OF RECENT INSTRUCTIONAL MATERIALS

The advent of federal matching funds for school purchase of instructional materials in social studies has heightened teachers' interest in identifying quality materials for their students. The following bibliographies of selected audiovisuals and printed materials aim to aid in choosing such materials from the tremendous and increasing amount produced. These lists attempt no complete-ness, but they illustrate the variety of worthwhile materials now available. Special emphasis is given materials for civics, geography, and history as NDEA funds may be used for these subjects. Further, the bibliographies complement the considerable citation of selected materials for students in chapters 5, 6, 7, 12, 13, and 15 of Social Studies in Secondary Education.*

RECENT AUDIOVISUAL MATERIAL

This section was prepared by Richard E. Wynn, social studies department head and formerly audiovisual coordinator, London Junior High School, Wheeling, Illinois. Basic information, such as showing time or number of frames, whether the film is in color or black and white, list price, and source, is given for each item. A guide to the names and addresses of producers follows the list of materials.

Motion Pictures

Abraham Lincoln: A Background Study, 15½ mins. b/w $90, color $180 (COR)
The Age of Absolute Monarchs in Europe, 13½ mins. b/w $75, color, $150 (COR)
The Age of Enlightenment in Europe, 13½ mins. b/w $75, color $150 (COR)
American Revolution Series, 11 mins. ea. b/w $60, color $120 ea. (COR)
   The Background Period
   The War Years
   The Postwar Period

* Macmillan, 1965.

Ancient World Inheritance, 11 mins. b/w $60, color $120 (COR)
Andrew Jackson at the Hermitage, 16 mins. b/w $90, color $180 (COR)
Asia: A Continental Overview, 16 mins. b/w $90, color $180 (COR)
The '29 Boom and the '30's Depression, 14 mins. b/w $85 (McG-HT)
Canada: Geography of the Americas, 13½ mins. b/w $75, color $150 (COR)
CBS Reports Series, approx. 30 mins. ea. b/w $150 ea. (McGHT)
China Under Communism, 22 mins. b/w $120, color $240 (EBF)
Citizenship: Whose Responsibility?
  Politics: The High Cost of Convictions, 5 mins. b/w $75
  Censorship: A Question of Judgment, 6 mins. b/w $75
  Vandalism: Crime or Prank? 6 mins. b/w $75 (IFB)
The Civil War: Background Issues, 16 mins. b/w $90, color $180 (COR)
Current Events: Understanding and Evaluating Them, 11 mins. b/w $60, color $120 (COR)
Decline of the Roman Empire, 13½ mins. b/w $75, color $150 (COR)
Dust Bowl, 26 mins. b/w $140 (McG-HT)
The England of Elizabeth, 26 mins. color $225 (IFB)
Films for Curriculum Enrichment, 30 mins. ea. b/w (EBF)
  The Big Parade
  Cimarron
  Northwest Passage
  The Oxbow Incident
Global Concept in Maps, 11 mins. b/w $60, color $120 (COR)
Great Lakes—How They Were Formed, 11 mins. b/w $60, color $120 (EBF)
How We Elect Our Representatives, 11 mins. b/w $60, color $120 (COR)
The Industrial Revolution in England, 25 mins. b/w $135, color $270 (IFB)
Magna Carta, 17 mins. ea. b/w $90, color $180 (EBF)
  Rise of the English Monarchy
  Revolt of the Nobles and the Signing of the Charter
Man in the Middle: The State Legislator, 54 mins. b/w $250 (McG-HT)
Medieval Times: Guilds and Trade, 13½ mins. b/w $75, color $150 (COR)
NBC–TV Documentary Series, approx. 29 mins. ea. b/w $150 ea. (EFB)
The Plantation South, 17 mins. b/w $90, color $180 (EBF)
The Railroad Builders, 14 mins. b/w $75, color $150 (EBF)
The Real West, 54 mins. b/w $275 (McG-HT)
The Rise of Organized Labor, 18 mins. b/w $110 (McG-HT)
Robert E. Lee: A Background Study, 16 mins. b/w $90, color $180 (COR)
The Roman World, 22 mins., color $225 (IFB)
Saga of Western Man Series, 54 mins. ea. b/w $250, color $495 (McG-HT)
  The Piligrim Adventure
  Custer to the Little Big Horn
  1492
  1776
  1898
  1964
Second World War, approx. 27 mins. ea. b/w $150 (EBF)
  Prelude to the Conflict
  Triumph of the Axis
  Allied Victory
The Soviet Challenge: Industrial Revolution in Russia, 26 mins. b/w $150, color $300 (EBF)
Sub-Saharan Africa Series, 22 mins. ea. b/w $120, color $240 (EBF)
  East Africa

West Africa
Continent of Africa
The Republic of South Africa, 17 mins. b/w $90, color $180 (EBF)
They Steamed to Glory: Famous Locomotives and the Pioneer Development of America,
 22 mins. color $195 (IFB)
The True Story of the Civil War, 33 mins. b/w $200 (McG-HT)
The Twisted Cross (Adolf Hitler), 55 mins. b/w $275 (McG-HT)
The White House, Past and Present, 13½ mins. b/w $75, color $150 (COR)
World War I (role of the U.S.), 28 mins. b/w $150 (EBF)
World War II (prologue, U.S.A.), 28 mins. b/w $150 (EBF)

Filmstrips, Charts, Pictures, Recordings, and Transparencies

Africa: Land of Developing Countries, 6 filmstrips, 62 fr. ea., color with 3 12" 33⅓ rpm
 coordinated records, $40.50 set (SVE)
 The Nile Valley
 The Eastern Highlands
 Southern Africa
 The Congo Basin
 The West Central Highlands
 Northwest Africa and the Sahara
The Civil War, 4 filmstrips, approx. 50 fr. ea., color, with 2 12" 33⅓ rpm records, $27.00
 set (SVE)
 Darkest Hours—Then Peace
 A Nation Divided
 High Tide of Valor
 America's Trial and Agony
Communism: What You Should Know About It and Why, 6 filmstrips, 40 fr. ea., color,
 $6.50 ea., $48.00 set (McG-HT)
Democracy: What You Should Know About It and Why, 6 filmstrips, approx. 40 fr. ea.,
 color, $7.50 ea., $39.75 set (McG-HT)
Enrichment Landmark Records, 22 12" 33⅓ rpm discs, $5.95 ea. (ETM)
Enrichment Documentary Records, 2 12" 33⅓ rpm discs, $5.95 ea. (ETM)
The Epic of Man Series, 16 filmstrips, approx. 55 fr. ea., color, $6.00 ea., $80.00 set (Life)
 Stone Age People
 The Growth of Society
 Discovery of Agriculture
 Coming of Civilization: Sumer
 Egypt's Era of Splendor
 The Celts
The Fenton-Wallbank World History Program, transparencies with overlays, $10.00 ea.
 (EBF)
Government in a Free Society, 24 charts in color, mounted, $79.00 set (RM)
History of Our Flag and *The Use and Display of Our Flag*, 2 filmstrips, 36 fr. ea., color,
 with one 12" 33⅓ rpm coordinated record, $15.00 set (SVE)
How The West Was Won, 4 filmstrips, approx. 75 fr. ea., color, $6.00 ea., $20.00 set
 (Life)
 Trail Blazers and Indians
 Covered Wagon Days
 Toward Statehood
 Cowboys, Homesteaders and Outlaws
I Can Hear It Now Series (Edward R. Murrow, narrator), four 12" 33⅓ rpm discs, about
 $5.00 ea. (MFL)

Indian Cultures of the Americas, 6 filmstrips, approx. 48 fr. ea., color, $36.00 set (EBF)
  The Incas, Mayas, and Aztecs
  Indians of the Southeast
  Indians of the Plains
  Indians of the Southwest
  Indians of the Northeast
  Indians and Eskimos of the Northwest
Living in the Iron Curtain Countries Today Series, 7 filmstrips, approx. 55 fr. ea., color, $39.75 set (SVE)
  Yugoslavia
  Romania
  Poland
  Hungary
  East Germany
  Czechoslovakia
  Bulgaria
Living in the Soviet Union Today Series, 7 filmstrips, approx. 55 fr. ea., color, $39.75 set (SVE)
  Natural Resources
  Four Cities
  Transportation and Communication
  Housing and Home Life
  Schools and Pioneer Activities
  Foods, Markets and Stores
Our United States: Its History in Cartovues, Edgar B. Wesley, ed., 2 Flipatran books: 37 map transparencies with notes, atlas, Flipatran holder, $99.50 set abridged (12 map) edition, $45.00 (D-G)
Photo Prints, photographic prints representing people and events in U.S. history, 11 x 14″, mounted, $.60 ea. (DPA)
A Picture History of the Civil War, 8 filmstrips, approx. 50 fr. ea., color, $48.00 set (EBF)
  Federal Armies Invade the South
  Civil War On the Home Fronts
  Armies and Navies of the Civil War
  Grant Takes Command
  The South Fights Back
  The South Declares Its Independence
  Gettysburg and Vicksburg
  The Confederate Armies Surrender
Ranvue World History Series, 32 transparency maps with five student atlases, $97.50 set (RM)
State Geography and Resources Series and *State History Series,* approx. 6 filmstrips per set, color, approx. $40.00 set (AE)
A Stillness at Appomattox, two 12″ 16 rpm discs, 4 hrs, $7.40 set (TBR)
Westward Migration, 4 filmstrips, approx. 50 fr. ea., with 2 12″ 33⅓ rpm coordinated discs, $27.00 set (SVE)
World Landmark Records, 4 12″ 33⅓ rpm discs, $5.95 ea. (ETM)

ADDRESSES OF PRODUCERS

AE   Associated Educators, Box 110, Troy State College, Troy, Ala.
AJN A. J. Nystrom and Company, 3333 Elston Avenue, Chicago, Ill. 60618
C   Coronet Films, Coronet Bldg., Chicago, Ill. 60601
D-G Denoyer-Geppert Company, 5235 Ravenswood Avenue, Chicago, Ill. 60640
DPA Documentary Photo Aids, P.O. Box 2237, Phoenix, Ariz. 85002

EBF Encyclopaedia Britannica Films, 1150 Wilmette Avenue, Wilmette, Ill. 60091
ETM Enrichment Teaching Materials, 246 Fifth Avenue, N.Y., N.Y. 10011
IFB International Film Bureau, 332 So. Michigan Avenue, Chicago, Ill. 60604
Life Life Filmstrips, Time and Life Bldg., N.Y., N.Y. 10020
McG-HT McGraw-Hill Text Films, 330 W. 42nd St., N.Y., N.Y. 10036
MFL Materials for Learning, 1376 Coney Island Avenue, Brooklyn 30, N.Y.
SVE Society for Visual Education, 1345 W. Diversy Parkway, Chicago, Ill. 60614
TBR Talking Book Records, The Listening Library, Long Branch, N.Y.
RM Rand McNally Company, P.O. Box 7600, Chicago, Ill. 60680

RECENT PRINTED MATERIALS

This section was prepared by David E. Meuser, coordinator of special instructional programs, Brevard County, Florida, Schools. The following list includes books that will challenge average and better readers in high schools. Also included are some references intended especially for easy reading. List prices and dates are given for most of the materials but are omitted for series and sets because of the frequent variations among individual items. Paperback (pb) editions are indicated wherever known to be available.

Selected Individual Volumes

ABRAMOWITZ, JACK, *Study Lessons on Documents of Freedom.* Chicago: Follett, 1964. $1.25 pb.

ACHESON, PATRICIA C., *The Supreme Court: America's Judicial Heritage.* New York: Dodd, Mead and Co., 1961. $3.75.

ADRIAN, CHARLES R., *Governing Our Fifty States and Their Communities.* New York: McGraw-Hill, 1963. $3.50

AYLING, S. E., *Portraits of Power: Introduction to Twentieth-Century History Through the Lives of Seventeen Great Political Leaders.* New York: Barnes and Noble, 1963. $2.50 pb.

BONNER, THOMAS N., *Our Recent Past: American Civilization in the Twentieth Century.* Englewood Cliffs, N. J.: Prentice-Hall, 1963. $7.50

BRINTON, CRANE, AND OTHERS, *Civilization in the West.* Englewood Cliffs, N. J.: Prentice-Hall, 1964. $9.25

BRINTON, CRANE, *Ideas and Men: The Story of Western Thought.* Englewood Cliffs, N. J.: Prentice-Hall, 1963. $8.50.

BROWNE, LEWIS, *This Believing World: A Simple Account of the Great Religions of Mankind.* New York: Macmillan, 1944. $1.75 pb.

CADY, JOHN F., *Southeast Asia: Its Historical Development.* New York: McGraw-Hill, 1964. $10.75

CAHN, EDMUND, *The Predicament of Democratic Man.* New York: Delta, 1962. $1.65 pb.

CATER, DOUGLAS, *The Fourth Branch of Government.* New York: Random, 1964. $1.45 pb.

CLAWSON, MARION, *Man and Land in the United States.* Lincoln, Neb.: University of Nebraska Press, 1965. $4.50

COLE, J. P., *Geography of World Affairs.* Baltimore: Penguin, 1963. $1.25 pb.

DEAN, VERA MICHELES, *Builders of Emerging Nations.* New York: Holt, Rinehart and Winston, 1961. $5.00

Eight Courageous Americans. New York: Bantam Books, 1965. $.60 pb.

GOLDMAN, ERIC F., *The Crucial Decade—and After: America, 1945–1960.* New York: Random, 1961. $1.45 pb.

HOFSTADTER, RICHARD, AND OTHERS, *The Structure of American History*. Englewood Cliffs, N. J.: Prentice-Hall, 1964. $4.75 *pb*.

HOYT, EDWIN PALMER, *Jumbos and Jackasses: A Popular History of the Political Wars*. New York: Doubleday and Co., 1960. $5.95

JOB, KENNETH, AND LOIS WEISER, *Study Lessons in Map Reading*. Chicago, Ill.: Follett, 1965. $1.25 *pb*.

KELLY, ALFRED, AND WINFRED A. HARBISON, *The American Constitution: Its Origins and Development*. New York: W. W. Norton and Co., 1963. $8.95

KELLY, FRANK K., *Your Freedoms: The Bill of Rights*. New York: Putnam, 1964. $3.29

KENWORTHY, LEONARD, *Leaders of New Nations*. New York: Doubleday and Co., 1959. $3.95

LEITHAUSER, JOACHIM, *Worlds Beyond the Horizon*. New York: Random, 1955. $6.75

LONG, DAVID F., *The Outward View*. Chicago: Rand McNally, 1964. $6.95

MARTIN, RALPH, *Ballots and Bandwagons*. New York: Signet, 1964. $.75 *pb*.

MORGENTHAU, HANS J., *The Purpose of American Politics*. New York: Random, 1961. $1.95 *pb*.

MORISON, SAMUEL ELIOT, *Vistas of History*. New York: Knopf, 1964. $4.00

OXENFELDT, ALFRED R., *Economic Systems in Action*. New York: Holt, Rinehart and Winston, 1965. $3.95 *pb*.

PARKES, HENRY B., *The American Experience: An Interpretation of the History and Civilization of the American People*. New York: Vintage, 1959. $1.65 *pb*.

ROBISON, SOPHIA M., *Juvenile Delinquency: Its Nature and Control*. New York: Holt, Rinehart and Winston, 1960. $7.25

RODELL, FRED, *Nine Men*. New York: Vintage, 1964. $1.95 *pb*.

ROSSITER, CLINTON, *The American Presidency*. New York: Harcourt, Brace and World, 1960. $1.95

SCHLESINGER, INA, AND JONAH BLUSTAIN, *Communism: What It Is and How It Works*. New York: Macmillan, 1964. $1.75 *pb*.

SCHURZ, WILLIAM L., *This New World: The Civilization of Latin America*. New York: Dutton Everyman, 1964. $1.75 *pb*.

TANNENBAUM, FRANK, *Ten Keys to Latin America*. New York: Knopf, 1962. $4.95

THOMAN, RICHARD S., AND D. J. PATTON, etc., *Focus on Geographic Activity*. New York: McGraw-Hill, 1964. $3.95

WALLBANK, T. WALTER, *Contemporary Africa: Continent in Transition*. Princeton: Anvil, 1964. $1.45 *pb*.

WARD, BARBARA, *The Interplay of East and West: Points of Conflict and Cooperation*. New York: W. W. Norton, 1957. $1.25 *pb*.

WARREN, ROBERT PENN, *The Legacy of the Civil War: Meditation on the Centennial*. New York: Random, 1964. $1.25 *pb*.

WATTENBERG, BEN., *This U.S.A.* New York: Doubleday, 1965. $7.50

WHEELER, JESSE H., AND OTHERS, *Regional Geography of the World*. New York: Holt, Rinehart and Winston, 1961. $8.45

WHITE, THEODORE H., *The Making of the President, 1960*. New York: Atheneum, 1961. $.95 *pb*.

Series and Sets

AMERICAN HERITAGE EDITORS, *American Heritage Junior Library*. New York: Harper and Row

BARNOUW, ADRIAN J., AND OTHERS, *Portraits of the Nations Series*. Philadelphia: Lippincott

BECKER, JAMES M., dir., *Foreign Relations Series*. River Forest, Ill.: Laidlaw

BOHLMAN, H. W. AND E. M., eds., *American Problems Series*. New York: Holt, Rinehart and Winston

CLARK, NADINE I., AND OTHERS, *Studies in Depth Series*. New York: Macmillan

CURRICULUM RESOURCES, INC., *Area Studies in Economic Progress.* Chicago: Scott, Foresman

DEPARTMENT OF STATE (U.S.), *General Foreign Policy Series and Inter-American Series.* Washington, D.C.: Government Printing Office

DAHL, ROBERT A., ed., *Foundations of Modern Political Science.* Englewood Cliffs, N. J.: Prentice-Hall

DEAN, VERA M., *Contemporary Civilization Series.* New York: Holt, Rinehart and Winston

FERSH, SEYMOUR, ed., *Culture Regions of the World.* New York: Macmillan

FIDELER, R. R., AND OTHERS, eds., *Studies in Depth.* Grand Rapids: Fideler Company

GOULD, KENNETH M., AND RICHARD E. GROSS, eds., *World Affairs Multi-Texts.* Englewood Cliffs, N. J.: Scholastic Book Services

HALSEY, VAN R., AND RICHARD H. BROWN, eds., *New Dimensions in American History.* Boston: D.C. Heath

HEATH, MONROE, *Great American Series.* Menlo Park, Calif.: Pacific Coast Publications

Human Relations Area Files. New York: Taplinger

JOHNSON, GERALD, *America: A History for Peter.* New York: William Morrow

Living Democracy Series. Medford, Mass.: Lincoln Filene Center

MANDULEY, LYN S., ed., *American Republics Series.* Washington, D. C.: Pan American Union

NEVINS, ALLAN, AND HOWARD EHRMANN, eds., *The University of Michigan History of the Modern World.* Ann Arbor: University of Michigan Press

New York Times and Encyclopaedia Britannica staffs, eds., *World Affairs Workshop,* Encyclopaedia Britannica, 1966.

ROZWENC, EDWIN C., ed., *Basic Concepts in History and the Social Sciences.* Boston, Mass.: D. C. Heath

SMOKE, STEPHEN D., ed., *Judgment.* Washington, D. C.: Civic Education Service

STAVIANOS, LEFTEN S., AND OTHERS, *Cultural Areas in Perspective.* Boston: Allyn and Bacon

STILES, LINDLEY J., ed., *Today's World in Focus.* Boston: Ginn

TREVOR-ROPER, HUGH R., ed., *Great Histories Series.* New York: Washington Square Press

WILES, KIMBALL, ed., *Global Culture Series.* Wichita, Kansas: McCormick-Maters

WINKS, ROBIN W., ed., *Modern Nations in Historical Perspective.* Englewood Cliffs, N.J.: Prentice-Hall

Atlases, Dictionaries, and Reference Books

Ambassador World Atlas. Maplewood, N.J.: Hammond, 1962. $15.00

Atlas of the World. Washington, D. C.: National Geographic Society, 1963. $18.75

Dictionary of American Government by Sol Holt. New York: Macfadden-Bartell, 1963. $.75 *pb.*

Dictionary of American History by Sol Holt. New York: Macfadden-Bartell, 1963. $.75 *pb.*

Goode's World Atlas, ed. by Edward B. Espenshade, Jr., Chicago: Rand McNally, 1964. $2.95

Illustrated Atlas of Today's World. Chicago: Rand McNally, 1962. 12 vols. $16.00

Sea, Maps and Men: An Atlas of Man's Explorations of the Seas by Geographic Projects, Inc., Garden City, L. I.: Doubleday, 1962. $9.95

The Statesman's Yearbook, 1965–1966, ed. by S. H. Steinberg. St. Martin's Press, annually. $10.00

The U.S. Book of Facts. Pocket Books, annually. $1.95 *pb.*

The World: Its Geography in Maps by Clarence Odell and others. Chicago: Denoyer-Geppert, 1965. $2.00 *pb.*

The World: Its History in Maps, ed. by William McNeil, William H. Buske, and A. Wesley Roehm. Chicago: Denoyer-Geppert, 1965. $2.00 *pb*.

Documents and Readings

BARTEL, ROLAND, ed., *Selected Source Materials for College Research Papers*. Boston: D. C. Heath, 1956. $1.65 *pb*.

BROWN, RICHARD C., *The Human Side of American History*. Boston: Ginn, 1962.

COMMAGER, HENRY, ed., *Living Ideas in America*. New York: Harper, 1964. $7.50

EISEN, SYDNEY, AND M. FILLER, eds., *The Human Adventure: Readings in World History*. 2 vols., Harcourt, Brace and World, 1964. $1.60 ea. *pb*.

FENTON, EDWIN, AND D. FOWLER, eds., *Problems in American History*. Chicago: Scott, Foresman, 1963. $4.20 *pb*.

GOEBEL, DOROTHY B., ed., *American Foreign Policy: A Documentary Survey, 1776–1960*. New York: Holt, Rinehart and Winston, 1961. $7.50

MEYERS, MARVIN, AND OTHERS, *Sources of the American Republic: A Documentary History of Politics, Society, and Thought*. 2 vols. Chicago: Scott, Foresman, 1960. $7.90 *pb*.

MILLER, WILLIAM, ed., *Readings in American Values: Selected and Edited from Public Documents of the American Past*. Englewood Cliffs, N. J.: Prentice-Hall, 1964. $3.75 *pb*.

MORLAN, ROBERT L., ed., *Capital, Courthouse, and City Hall*. New York: Houghton Mifflin, 1960. $3.95 *pb*.

PETERSON, WILLIAM, AND DAVID MATZA, eds., *Social Controversy*. Belmont, Calif.: Wadsworth, 1963. $3.95 *pb*.

REIBER, ALFRED, AND R. C. NELSEN, eds., *The U.S.S.R. and Communism: Source Readings and Interpretations*. Chicago: Scott, Foresman, 1964. $1.95 *pb*.

STAMPP, KENNETH M., AND OTHERS, eds., *Eyewitness Accounts of American History Series*. Englewood Cliffs, N. J.: Prentice-Hall

SYRETT, HAROLD, ed., *American Historical Documents*. New York: Barnes and Noble, 1960. $2.25 *pb*.

TOBIAS, JOHN, AND SAVIN HOFFECKER, *The Adventure of America*. New York: Random House, 1962.

WALLBANK, T. WALTER, ed., *Documents on Modern Africa*. Princeton, N.J.: Van Nostrand, 1964. $1.45 *pb*.

WEST, RALPH O., *The Human Side of World History*. Boston: Ginn, 1963.

SELECTED PROFESSIONAL REFERENCES ON CURRENT CHANGES IN SECONDARY SCHOOL SOCIAL STUDIES

(*See also the bibliographies especially for Chapters 4, 8, and 20 in Jonathon C. McLendon, Social Studies in Secondary Education, Macmillan, 1965.*

For publishers' addresses see Cumulative Book Index or other librarians' aid.)

ALDRICH, JULIAN C., ed., *Social Studies for the Junior High School*. National Council for the Social Studies, 1957.

BERG, HARRY D., ed., *Evaluation in Social Studies*. National Council for the Social Studies, 1965.

CARPENTER, HELEN McCRACKEN, ed., *Skill Development in Social Studies*. National Council for the Social Studies, 1965.

CARTWRIGHT, WILLIAM H., AND RICHARD L. WATSON, JR., eds., *Interpreting and Teaching American History*. National Council for the Social Studies, 1961.

Civic Leader (Civic Education Service), weekly. See also the weekly *Scholastic Teacher* (Scholastic Magazines) and the "Teacher's Edition" of *Our Times* (American Education Press).

ENGLE, SHIRLEY H., ed., *New Perspectives in World History*. National Council for the Social Studies, 1964.

FENTON, EDWIN, *Teaching the New Social Studies in Secondary Schools: An Inductive Approach*. Holt, Rinehart and Winston, 1966.

FRASER, DOROTHY McCLURE, AND SAMUEL P. McCUTCHEN, eds., *Social Studies in Transition: Guidelines for Change*. National Council for the Social Studies, 1965.

GIBSON, JOHN S., *New Frontiers in the Social Studies*. Lincoln Filene Center, 1965.

GROSS, RICHARD E., AND C. V. BADGER, "Social Studies" in the *Encyclopedia of Educational Research*. Macmillan, 1960.

HILL, WILHELMINA, ed., *Curriculum Guide for Geographic Education*. National Council for Geographic Education, 1963.

HUNT, EHRLING M., ed., *High School Social Studies Perspectives*. Houghton Mifflin, 1962.

JAMES, PRESTON E., ed., *New Viewpoints in Geography*. National Council for the Social Studies, 1959.

McLENDON, JONATHON C., *Social Studies in Secondary Education*. Macmillan, 1965.

McPHIE, WALTER E., *Dissertations in Social Studies Education: A Comprehensive Guide*. National Council for the Social Studies, 1964.

MASSIALAS, BYRON G., AND BENJAMIN C. COX, *Inquiry in the Social Studies*. McGraw-Hill, 1966.

MASSIALAS, BYRON G., AND FREDERICK R. SMITH, eds., *New Challenges in the Social Studies*. Wadsworth, 1965.

MEHLINGER, HOWARD D., *The Study of Totalitarianism—An Inductive Approach: A Guide for Teachers*. National Council for the Social Studies, 1965.

METCALF, LAWRENCE, "Research on Teaching the Social Studies" in *Handbook on Research on Teaching*. Rand McNally, 1962.

MICHAELIS, JOHN U., AND A. M. JOHNSTON, eds., *The Social Sciences: Foundations for the Social Studies*. Allyn and Bacon, 1965.

MORELAND, WILLIS D., ed., *Social Studies in the Senior High School*. National Council for the Social Studies, 1965.

MUESSIG, RAYMOND H., ed., *Local Curriculum Improvement in Social Studies*. National Council for the Social Studies, 1965.

OLIVER, DONALD W., AND JAMES P. SHAVER, *Teaching Public Issues in the High School*. Houghton Mifflin, 1966.

OVARD, GLEN F., *Planning Social Studies Facilities for Secondary School*. School Planning Laboratory, Stanford University, 1961.

PATTERSON, FRANKLIN, ed., *Citizenship and a Free Society: Education for the Future*. National Council for the Social Studies, 1960.

PATTERSON, FRANKLIN, *The Junior High School: Curriculum Models for Junior High School Social Studies*. Educational Services, Inc., 1965.

PRICE, ROY A., ed., *Needed Research in the Teaching of the Social Studies*. National Council for the Social Studies, 1964.

PRICE, ROY A., ed., *New Viewpoints in the Social Sciences*. National Council for the Social Studies, 1958.

"Revising the Social Studies" (theme of issue), *Social Education*, April, 1963. See also related articles in other issues of this magazine.

"Social Studies in the Secondary School" (theme of issue), *High School Journal*, October, 1965.

The Social Studies and the Social Sciences. Harcourt, Brace and World, 1962.

SOWARDS, G. WESLEY, ed., *The Social Studies: Curriculum Proposals for the Future.* Scott, Foresman, 1963.

WESLEY, EDGAR B., AND STANLEY P. WRONSKI, *Teaching Social Studies in High Schools.* Heath, 1964.

CURRENT CURRICULUM PROJECTS INVOLVING SECONDARY SOCIAL STUDIES

Sylvia E. Harrison

I. Comprehensive Projects
   A. ACLS-ESI Project
      Educational Services, Incorporated
      44-A Brattle Street
      Cambridge, Massachusetts 02138
   B. Greater Cleveland Social Science Program
      Mrs Ethel K Howard, Administrative Head
      Educational Research Council of Greater Cleveland
      Rockefeller Building, 4th Floor
      Cleveland, Ohio 44113
   C. Project Social Studies
      Cooperative Research Branch
      Office of Education
      U.S. Department of Health, Education, and Welfare
      Washington, D. C. 20202
      1. Dr. Wilfred C. Bailey, Co-Director Social Studies Curriculum Study Center
         Department of Sociology and Anthropology
         University of Georgia
         Athens, Georgia 30601
      2. Dr. Edwin Fenton, Co-Director
         Social Studies Curriculum Study Center
         Carnegie Institute of Technology
         Schenley Park
         Pittsburgh, Pennsylvania 15213
      3. Dr. John R. Lee, Director
         Social Studies Curriculum Center
         1809 Chicago Avenue
         Northwestern University
         Evanston, Illinois 60201
      4. Dr. Ella C. Leppert, Director
         Social Studies Curriculum Study Center
         University High School
         College of Education
         University of Illinois
         Urbana, Illinois 61803
      5. Dr. John U. Michaelis, Director
         Social Studies Curriculum Study Center
         4643 Tolman Hall
         University of California
         Berkeley, California 94720

From A *Summary of Current Social Studies Projects* by Sylvia E. Harrison, Princeton. N. J.: Educational Testing Service, November, 1964, pp. 36–37. For biographical note see page 355. Some zip code numbers have been added by the editor.

6. Dr. Donald Oliver, Director
Social Studies Curriculum Study
Center
School of Education
Harvard University
Cambridge, Massachusetts
02138

7. Dr. Roy A. Price, Director
Social Studies Curriculum Study
Center
Maxwell Graduate School of
Citizenship and Public Affairs
Syracuse University
Syracuse, New York 13210

8. Dr. James P. Shaver, Director
Social Studies Curriculum Study
Center
296 West Lane Avenue, Apartment G
Ohio State University
Columbus, Ohio 43201

9. Dr. Edith West, Director
Social Studies Curriculum Study
Center
University of Minnesota
Minneapolis, Minnesota 55455

D. Providence Social Studies Curriculum Study
Dr. Ridgway F. Shinn, Jr., Director
Rhode Island College
Providence 8, Rhode Island

E. Social Science Education Consortium
Dr. Irving Morrissett, Director
Department of Economics
Purdue University
Lafayette, Indiana 47907

II. Economics

A. Economic Education Committee
of the Southern States Work
Committee
Dr. Marvin Lee, Chairman
College of Education
West Virginia University
Morgantown, West Virginia

B. Economic Literacy Series
Dr. Galen Jones, Director
Council for the Advancement of
Secondary Education
1201 16th Street, N. W.
Washington, D. C.

C. Elkhart Indiana Experiment in
Economic Education
Dr. Lawrence Senesh, Director
Department of Economics
Purdue University
Layafette, Indiana 47907

D. Joint Council on Economic Education
Dr. Martin Essex, Chairman
2 West 46th Street
New York, New York 10036

III. History

A. Committee on the Study of History
Dr. Van B. Hasley, Chairman
Department of History
Amherst College
Amherst, Massachusetts

B. Service Center for Teachers of History
Dr. Walter Rundell, Jr., Director
400 A Street, S. E.
Washington, D. C. 20203

C. World History Project
Dr. L. S. Stavrianos, Director
Department of History
Northwestern University
Evanston, Illinois 60201

IV. Geography

A. Curriculum Guide Committee
Dr. Wilhelmina Hill, Chairman
National Council for Geographic
Education
Office of Education
U.S. Department of Health, Education and Welfare
Washington, D. C. 20202

B. High School Geography Project
Dr. Nicholas Helburn, Director
1785 Massachusetts Avenue
Washington 6, D. C.

V. Behavioral Sciences

A. Authropology Curriculum Study
Project
Dr. Malcolm C. Collier, Director
5632 Kimbark Avenue
Chicago, Illinois 60637

B. Course Content Improvement in
Social Sciences for High School
Dr. Robert A. Feldmesser, Director

Department of Sociology and An-
thropology
Dartmouth College
Hanover, New Hampshire 03755

VI. Civics
   A. Civic Education Project
      Dr. Henry Toy, Director
      American Heritage Foundation
      11 W. 42nd St.
      New York, N. Y. 10036
   B. Lincoln Filene Center for Citizen-

ship and Public Affairs
Dr. Wyman Holmes, Associate
Director
Tufts University
Medford, Massachusetts 02155

VII. Foreign Affairs
    NCA Foreign Relations Project
    Dr. James Becker, Director
    Suite 832
    38 South Dearborn Street
    Chicago, Illinois 60903

79897

DATE DUE

DATE DUE	BORROWER'S NAME
FACULTY	A Evelyn Gearhart
04 16 1	LONG REBECCA J 3
04 30 1	LONG REBECCA J 3

F